# For the Healing of the Nation

# For the Healing of the Nation

## A BIBLICAL VISION

### Russell Pregeant

Foreword by John B. Cobb Jr.

CASCADE *Books* • Eugene, Oregon

FOR THE HEALING OF THE NATION
A Biblical Vision

Copyright © 2016 Russell Pregeant. All rights reserved. Except for brief quotations in critical publications or reviews, no part of this book may be reproduced in any manner without prior written permission from the publisher. Write: Permissions, Wipf and Stock Publishers, 199 W. 8th Ave., Suite 3, Eugene, OR 97401.

Cascade Books
An Imprint of Wipf and Stock Publishers
199 W. 8th Ave., Suite 3
Eugene, OR 97401

www.wipfandstock.com

Scripture quotations are from New Revised Standard Version Bible: Catholic Edition, copyright © 1989, 1993 National Council of the Churches of Christ in the United States of America. Used by permission. All rights reserved worldwide.

PAPERBACK ISBN 13: 978-1-4982-3539-6
HARDCOVER ISBN 13: 978-1-4982-3541-9

*Cataloguing-in-Publication data:*

Pregeant, Russell.

For the healing of the nation : a biblical vision / Russell Pregeant.

xvi + 336 p. ; 23 cm. Includes bibliographical references.

ISBN: 978-1-4982-3539-6 (paperback) | ISBN: 978-1-4982-3541-9 (hardback)

1. Economics—Biblical teaching. 2. Human ecology—Biblical teaching. 3. Violence—Biblical teaching. 4. United States—History. 5. United States—Social conditions—21st century. 6. Christianity and justice—United States. I. Cobb, John B. II. Title.

BR115 J8 P80 2016

Manufactured in the U.S.A. 04/18/2016

To these, in closest company held dear,
Who share the vision and the hope
That's by the common good defined:
Gene, Brad, Lynnea,
and, once again,
Sammie
(my soulmate, sunshine, inspiration)

Who once her hand to plow had put
Has never had a thought of looking back
Nor obstacles allowed to dampen her commitment or her faith
Or ever has the joys of life and love forsworn
But healthy wholeness with a fiery heart relentlessly pursues
To be the change we work to bring about
And heal the nation and the world

And I saw the holy city, the new Jerusalem, coming down out of heaven from God . . . Then the angel showed me the river of the water of life, bright as crystal, flowing from the throne of God, and of the Lamb through the middle of the street of the city. On either side of the river is the tree of life, with its twelve kinds of fruit, producing its fruit each month; *and the leaves of the tree are for the healing of the nations.*

—Revelation 21:2; 22:1–2

# Contents

*Foreword by John B. Cobb Jr.* | ix
*Preface* | xiii

Introduction—Trembling for My Country: A Reflection on Place | 1

## Part 1—"Who Is My Neighbor?" The Tragedy of Dreams Deferred

Prologue to Part 1: A Little Window on a Great Big World | 7

1. A Place Reconfigured: Memories of the Mid-Twentieth-Century South | 10
2. Lessons Learned: Reflecting on the Times | 20
3. Adjusting the Lenses: The Bible, Race, and the Unity of Humankind | 30
4. Ideology against the Bible: A Judgment on the Past | 43
5. Adorning the Tombs of the Prophets: Assessing the Present | 53
6. Reflections on a Sugar House: A Question of Identity | 77

## Part 2—"The Land is Mine": Justice in the Marketplace, Justice for the Earth, Justice in the Forum

Prologue to Part 2: Neither the Margins nor the Middle | 95

7. A Miniprimer on Biblical Economics | 98
8. Applying the Principles: Biblical Economics and Political Philosophies | 116
9. Torah Betrayed: Current Economics in Biblical Perspective | 139
10. "And God Saw That It Was Good": The Bible, Earth, and the "American Way of Life" | 159
11. Vines and Fig Trees in the "Days to Come": Toward Justice, Sustainability, and Democracy | 181
12. But Can We Do It? Overcoming the Impediments | 200

**Part 3—"Not with Swords' Loud Clashing": Violence, Justice, and the Commonwealth of God**

    Prologue to Part 3: A Lifelong Struggle and a Stable Conviction | 219

13  A Complex Heritage: The Bible on War, Peace, and Empire | 223

14  Conquest and Imperialism in U.S. History: The Four Hundred Years' War | 231

15  Conquest and Imperialism Continued: The Path to Perpetual War | 246

16  Justice Untempered, Justice Denied: Courtroom, Prison, Death Row | 273

*Conclusion—Putting Away the Idols* | 299
*Epilogue: Jazz, Gumbo, the Bible, and God* | 303
*Bibliography* | 321

# Foreword

MOST BIBLICAL SCHOLARSHIP IS shaped by university norms. These norms are profoundly unbiblical. The university is organized into academic disciplines, each of which has its limited subject matter. Practitioners of one discipline are not expected to transgress the territory of another. They are all expected to be "value free" even if they are studying the values of others.

The university ethos is shaped by the ideology adopted by science during the Enlightenment. Modern science reacted against the Aristotelian science of the Middle Ages. That science gave special attention to what Aristotle called "final causes." These are the functions of things. One understood the liver, for example, when one learned the role it played in the animal body. The science that won out and became modern science focused on formal, material, and efficient causes. The formal causes became the increasingly complex mathematical formulae, which fill the pages of so many scientific writings. The material causes are the ingredients that make the thing up, as the animal body is composed of cells, a cell, of molecules, a molecule, of atoms, and so forth. The efficient causes are the preceding events or circumstances that necessitate what is now happening. Final causes are shunned.

There is no question but that these choices of modern science stimulated exceedingly fruitful study. This truly wonderful success has led to its emulation in all the academic disciplines. The humanities used to constitute an exception, but this is less and less the case. What once might have been thought of as a decision as to the best research method has now become a worldview. Overwhelmingly, the university socializes people to think that values and purposes, and a fortiori, decisions, play no role in what actually happens. They belong to subjective experience, and everything can be explained without considering subjective experience at all. It is explained by the activities of cells, especially neurons. One may study the values and purposes of others, but the academic study of these subjective states consists in explaining their efficient causes, which are all objective and, therefore, value-free.

Most respected biblical scholarship now fits the academic model. It explains why things happened as they did in terms of efficient causes. One explains where ideas or practices came from and the circumstances that led to their acceptance. As a university scholar one does not consider whether an idea is true or useful or relevant for today.

This method has been extremely fruitful. We understand the Bible today in much greater detail and much more accurately than was possible a century ago. But the understanding we are given is likely to make it seem less relevant to us, and to make whatever relevance it has seem ambivalent. Given the vast influence the Bible has had in Western culture and, indeed, in world history, the information now available to all in university contexts is an important advance over its exclusion from most universities a generation ago.

What does this mean for the Protestant church, which reacted against Rome with the principle of *sola scriptura*? It has intensified a deep divide between "liberal" and "conservative" Protestants. "Liberals" are open to the best scholarship and to all that is now being learned about other communities and traditions; so their instruction of their children about the Bible is now informed by university scholarship. So also is the preaching in liberal churches. Liberals are quite clear that they should understand the Bible as ancient literature, and they are very critical of bibliolatry and of trying to make everything fit into this ancient worldview. Among liberals, the Bible no longer functions much in private or family devotional life. Christianity becomes one tradition among others, and many liberal Protestants are uncomfortable with making any special claims for it.

Those who want to preserve the Bible as the normative Scripture and to live by it are likely to identify themselves as conservatives and to dismiss all this scholarship. They appeal to "faith" against "reason." They intensify tendencies to supernaturalism present in the Bible and in Christian history and often adopt the most extreme views of inspiration. They try to derive even scientific facts from the Bible and treat accepted science simply as one human theory among others.

Both of these trends in Protestantism are distressing. What I understand to be the New Testament meaning of *pistis* is lost. I believe that faithfulness to Jesus is more important today than it has ever been. It provides the possibility of avoiding the worst in the calamities that lie ahead. But it is not encouraged by either liberal or conservative Protestants.

Readers may wonder what my musings here have to do with Pregeant's book. My answer is, a great deal. Pregeant knows well, appreciates, and has contributed to the achievements of university scholarship. But that does not lead him to view reality in general or the Bible in particular from the university's point of view. Instead, he views the scholarly study to which he has long contributed from a perspective shaped by the Bible. When he does so, he finds it in detail profoundly helpful. But he does not adopt its value-free and objectifying point of view. His worldview remains biblical.

To adopt the biblical worldview involves not only the rejection of the university worldview but equally the worldview I have identified with "conservative" Protestantism. The biblical worldview rejects all forms of idolatry, including bibliolatry. Biblical authors learned a great deal from cultures other than their own. Israel's culture assimilated much from the other inhabitants of Palestine and from Egypt, Mesopotamia, and Greece. Self-isolation, defensiveness, and closure are not biblical styles. On the other hand, the biblical authors retain and richly develop their own tradition. They do not view it simply as one possible way of thinking among others. Jesus and Paul are "liberal" Jews, but their liberalism does not weaken their commitment to the Jewish tradition as they understand it in its distinctiveness.

All of this is to say that Pregeant offers us what is now rare—a genuinely biblical perspective on ourselves and our world. Of course, he is not alone in doing so. By no means all Protestants fall into what I have described as the "liberal" and "conservative" camps. Yet the literature that makes clear how to be authentically biblical in our time is limited. Pregeant's contribution to that literature is truly magnificent.

Characteristic of that literature is the telling of stories. Pregeant shares generously his own journey with the Bible and how it led him where it did. This approach allows him to share his convictions in a way that invites others to share theirs. The invitation is to engage in serious discussion.

A truly biblical approach is never defensive. There is no effort to claim perfection for what is reported in the Bible or the biblical way of reporting it. Certainly there is no claim that the Bible is the only possible source of this or that idea or practice. The writings that became Scripture within Israel were often by or about figures who were highly critical of their tradition and who offended their fellows. They were typically minority voices in their own days. Pregeant grew up in a segregated society to which the church had adjusted itself. The Bible was often used to justify slavery and segregation. But like the prophets of old, Pregeant, already as a youth, heard the deeper meaning and message of the Bible, and he has spent a lifetime sharing it even at the cost of opposition to his own father.

This story is far from unique. But its telling in the context of a boy's wrestling with the Bible and its cultural misuse is powerful and convincing. Pregeant's story goes on to show how the nation and its history appear when they also are appraised from an authentically biblical perspective. This threatens the national self-image just as strongly as the southern defense of its racial practices.

Of course, the Bible can be used, and has been used, to support the myth of American exceptionalism. There is plenty of Jewish exceptionalism in the Bible. But again, here, Pregeant shows that being really biblical is to reject all such exceptionalisms and to face the reality of the crimes that have been justified in the name of Christianity.

Pregeant's book probably cannot be studied in universities. It is far from value-free. On the other hand, in my view, if scholarship is in the service of truth, it is more scholarly than what can be taught in value-free research universities. Their worldview precludes discussion of much of the most important truth. If the Protestant churches would become biblical in Pregeant's authentic way, they could lead the world in responding to its terrifying future.

John B. Cobb Jr.

# Preface

JACKS-OF-ALL-TRADES, I KNOW, ARE generally masters of none. Nevertheless, like the proverbial fool who rushes in "where angels fear to tread," in this book I venture far beyond my academic field of biblical studies to engage political, economic, and social issues that face American society today. I *choose* to do this because I believe that the Bible has much to say about these concerns but am distressed with the ways some commentators, influenced by particular political ideologies, make use of it. Even so, to take on so wide a range of matters might seem the height of arrogance to some readers. I am convinced, however, that these issues are so intimately related that none can be fully resolved without attention to all. It has proved disastrous, for example, to ignore the political character of economic policies and their impact on the physical environment. Nor can we deal adequately with the problems we have in race relations without consideration of their economic dimensions. Ultimately, moreover, we cannot really understand the depth of any of the issues we face without examining the values implied by alternative decisions. And this is precisely why religious and philosophical testimonies to the nature of reality and the meaning and purpose of human existence are so important.

I *dare* to make this venture, in part, because I have been blessed with six friends, all possessing expertise I lack, who have been willing to evaluate my work. This is not to say that they agree with me on every point, nor is it to imply that they are in any way responsible for the book's shortcomings. At some points limitations imposed by time and my own abilities prevented me from pursuing all their suggestions. One has to draw the line somewhere, especially in a book of this length. Their help has been indispensable, however, and the book is far better than it would have been without their counsel. I therefore extend my initial thanks to these initial readers: Larry Beeferman, John Hill, Ann Levin, Betty Mandell, Marvin Mandell, and Les Muray. My satisfaction in seeing the book come to press, however, is diminished by the death of Betty Mandell, whose intellect and commitment to social justice remained intact to the end of a long a fruitful life.

I am grateful also that along the way, two friends from my year as a student at Yale Divinity School, Jim Bortell and Ivan Burnett, read selected chapters, as did Emily Norton, a cousin of my wife's who for many years entranced students in political science at Decatur High School in Georgia. John B. Cobb Jr. made room in an unbelievably busy schedule, first to read the chapters devoted primarily to economics and ecology and then to peruse the entire manuscript and write the foreword. I thank him for this but even more for a life, now in its tenth decade, devoted not only to bringing theological insights to an astonishingly wide range of concerns but to relentless action in these areas as well. For me, he represents what is best in the ongoing tradition fostered by biblical faith, and I am honored to have his name associated with my work.

My thanks go out also to the many persons who have contributed to the broader fund of human experiences on which I draw as I try to evaluate my country from a biblical perspective. I mention them as a way of acknowledging the importance of a theme that pervades this book: the interrelatedness of all things. We are who we are only in relation to one another, to the whole of which we are all parts, and ultimately to the One in whom all things cohere. Across the years, there have been friends, colleagues, former teachers, and students who have encouraged me, challenged me, and in innumerable ways deepened my understanding. There are far too many of these to mention here specifically, although a few appear in the chapters that follow. I must, however, acknowledge some, no longer living, whose influence came early in my life. I begin with family. My debt to my parents, Eloise White Pregeant and Victor Eugene Pregeant Jr., is inestimable. Along with the many sacrifices they made for their children, they gave me a sense of personal worth and modeled for me many of the biblical values I discuss in this book. In addition, I have been blessed with a close extended family, distinctive in that two of my father's siblings were married to two of my mother's. I must count also my wife's parents, Samuel T. Maxwell and "Billie" Harvey Maxell, who at a much later stage in life accepted me lovingly into their own fold, as important parts of my life. Beyond this most intimate circle, there were four persons in particular I feel compelled to name: my high school English teacher, Velmarae Dunn, who encouraged me to write, along with three ministers who served the church of my youth and were instrumental in shaping my faith—Ira W. Flowers, Fred S. Flurry, and Edward R. Thomas.

Continuing in the spirit of gratitude, I dedicate this book to four family members without whose love my life would be far less rich than it is.

# PREFACE

Gene Pregeant and Brad Pregeant are the sons of my brother "Buddy" and his wife Norma, both now deceased; Lynnea Godfriaux is Brad's wife. They have given me many gifts, both immaterial and material, including some of the books that have informed this present work. Nor are there any finer companions with whom to share the joys of gumbo, jazz, New Orleans, all things Louisiana, or the Colorado Rockies. Sammie Maxwell, an ordained minister in the United Methodist Church and consummate preacher and storyteller, is my own wife, companion, and the light of my life. Not only did she give the manuscript a meticulous reading, but through the years she has been my confidant and constant discussion partner on all the issues discussed here and my tutor on many subjects. The dedication poem is my inadequate attempt to express my love and appreciation to each of these persons as well as to acknowledge the fundamental values that we all share.

R.P.<br>
Clayton, Georgia<br>
December 2015

# Introduction

# Trembling for My Country
## A Reflection on Place

> "I tremble for my country when I reflect that God is just."
> —Thomas Jefferson

I AM AN AMERICAN. The United States is the land of my birth and my residence of choice. It is, and always will be, my home. Because we are all products of place (that is, of the particular times and circumstances in which we experience life), my perspective on life is shaped largely by American history and values. I have also been shaped by a geographical region, racial and ethnic groups, a social class, gender, a religious background, education, and innumerable personal experiences. All these aspects of place also influence the way I understand my country, just as my identity as an American influences how I understand each of these other indicators of place.

The places from which we view the world are precious gifts, for we can understand life only by experiencing the world in concrete ways. These gifts, however, are also limitations. Those who view the world from one perspective see what others cannot, but they miss what others see. If we want to get beyond merely airing our preconceptions, we must be willing to hear the insights gained from different points of view. It is therefore in a spirit of sharing, as a basis for conversation, that I offer my perceptions of the

United States. I write because I love my country but am deeply disturbed by the trends I observe regarding the values and attitudes operative among us, by the level of public discourse through which we address our problems, and by the political climate within which we currently live. I also want to help those who view the United States differently to understand why I view it the way I do, even as I struggle to understand their perspectives. For this reason the book will be partly autobiographical, as I try to explain how I have arrived at my current views. For the place I occupy is not only multi-dimensional but ever changing, as life offers new experiences; and these experiences have frequently involved encounters with persons occupying places quite different from my own.

To be more specific about my place, I am a Christian and an ordained minister in the United Methodist Church who has spent most of his professional life teaching in the field of religion and specializing in biblical studies. Because it is especially as a student of the Bible that I approach the present task, the various biblical perspectives on life are the lenses through which I approach the issues. At the same time, I recognize that my reading of the Bible is influenced by my experiences so that my particular biblical lenses differ in some ways from those of persons who understand the Bible differently. Thus, just as I will try to explain why I view America as I do, I must also explain why I read the Bible as I do.

Although I will pay attention to political philosophies and the parties and movements that translate them into public policy, my primary loyalty is to the biblical witness, not to some preconceived political stance or organization. My judgments will sometimes parallel those of a particular political theory, but it is my biblically based faith that justifies the theory, and not vice versa. I therefore plead with my readers not to force my views into the categories provided by the current spectrum of social and political options. For my conviction is that this spectrum is shamefully inadequate in the light of the biblical writings. I will thus feel free to criticize both major parties and the perspectives we typically term Left and Right. But I also caution readers not to make the all too common assumption that the best options always lie at a midpoint between two current poles of thought. For I believe that the biblical vision of a just society calls all points on the current spectrum—even that middle, which many Americans hold so sacred!—into question.

There was a sentiment often voiced in the 1960s that I still find relevant. The great divide between people in our society is not really between liberals and conservatives but between those who are closed and those who are open. The divide, in other words, is between people who are willing to reexamine their own presuppositions and those who are so locked into specific ways of thinking that they are unable to converse with those who think differently or to respond to new developments. My hope is thus to encourage persons of various persuasions to expand the places from which they view the country by interactions with the biblical writings and with the places occupied by those who think differently.

The issues that concern me fall into three broad categories. In part 1, I address the attitudes and policies toward "otherness" in our society—that is, matters pertaining to race, ethnicity, and other aspects of human difference. In part 2, I turn to economic policies and political philosophies, their impact on our physical environment, and the implications of current policies for the health of our democratic institutions. Finally, in part 3, I discuss war, foreign policy, capital punishment, and our criminal justice system under the broad heading of institutional violence. The biblical vision, I am convinced, calls us to think more rigorously than we have often thought about all these areas of concern. Because I propose the Bible as a point of reference, I address this book primarily, but not exclusively, to persons who are related to biblically based faith communities. My hope is that those who approach the issues from different perspectives will find enough here that is worth consideration to make conversation worthwhile.

As should now be evident, I write with a troubled heart. Thomas Jefferson, when reflecting on the institution of slavery, said that he trembled for his country when he reflected that God is just; and he ended his statement with the foreboding prophecy that God's "justice cannot sleep forever." I, too, tremble, for similar reasons; but I also write with hope. For I believe that God is not only just but also active in the world, always offering new futures out of our muddled pasts. And my hope and prayer for my country is that this just and merciful God will, in the words of Katherine Lee Bates's "America the Beautiful," *"mend thine every flaw."* The hope for ultimate mending, or healing, is beautifully expressed in Rev 22:2, which describes in visionary terms the biblical hope for the restoration of God's creation. The tree of life, which once stood in the garden of Eden, now flourishes beside "the river of the water of life," putting forth leaves that are "for the healing of the nations." In the title of this book, I have changed the plural "nations" to the singular "nation," not because my concern is limited to the United States, but rather because it is *my* country, the place in the world where I have the greatest opportunity, and thus responsibility, to make my voice heard.

I want to emphasize that my intention is in fact healing, which means not only the mending of our national flaws but reconciliation among the various social and political factions today. Such reconciliation does not mean doing away with differences in perspective. The insights derived from various places remain important, and honest discussion of competing philosophies and opinions is not a weakness but rather a strength of a nation. It does mean, however, reaching a point at which we can speak honestly with one another, offering constructive criticisms rather than mean-spirited attacks. But what we hear far too often in our current debates are caricatures of the opinions of others rather than sincere attempts to understand and evaluate them. My goal is to give fair descriptions of different perspectives and reasoned criticisms of their shortcomings as I perceive them. Some of what I have to say will be difficult for some readers to hear. Indeed, much of it is difficult for me to say; for my own life-journey has involved some agonizing breaks with inherited values and commitments. But I am convinced that the path to true reconciliation, true healing, necessarily leads us through a process of serious soul-searching.

My model for such a process is the Truth and Reconciliation Commission established in the Republic of South Africa as the notorious regime of apartheid came to an end. Its remarkable achievement was to move beyond the desire for revenge against those who had participated in a brutal system in which a privileged minority dehumanized and exploited a majority. What made it work, in my opinion, was this: those guilty of heinous political crimes were offered a chance for clemency in a new society if they would tell the truth about their roles in the maintenance of the racist regime.[1] The price of reconciliation, in other words, was truth. I write this book as a way of asking of all who love this country that we look deeply and honestly into ourselves, listen carefully to one another, and be willing to ask hard questions about the philosophies we embrace and the policies we support. By proposing biblical values as a standard of judgment, I do not mean to be divisive, setting those of biblical faith above others—quite the opposite. For as Rev 21 and 22 proclaim, the ultimate goal of the biblical witness is in fact reconciliation. After condemning in unflinching fashion the sins of the Roman Empire and those who cooperated with it, as well oppressive regimes in principle, the author offers the vision of a new world in which all the wounds that people have inflicted upon one another are healed. And it is precisely such healing for which I hope and pray, within this country that I call my own.

---

1. Tutu, *Dream*, 10.

# Part 1

# "Who Is My Neighbor?"
## The Tragedy of Dreams Deferred

> Just then a lawyer stood up to test Jesus. "Teacher," he said, "what must I do to inherit eternal life?" He said to him, "What is written in the law? What do you read there?" He answered, "You shall love the Lord your God with all your heart, and with all your soul, and with all your strength, and with all your mind; and your neighbor as yourself." And he said to him, "You have given the right answer; do this, and you will live." But wanting to justify himself, he asked Jesus, "And who is my neighbor?"
>
> —Luke 10:25–29

# Prologue to Part 1
## A Little Window on a Great Big World

> The problem of the twentieth century is the problem of the color line—the relation of the darker to the lighter races . . . in Asia and Africa, in America and the islands of the sea.
>
> —W. E. B. Du Bois, 1903[1]

> I had learned that white southerners are a hospitable, courteous, tactful people who treat those of their own group with consideration and who as carefully segregate from all the richness of life "for their own good and welfare" thirteen million people whose skin is colored a little differently from my own.
>
> —Lillian Smith, 1949[2]

THE STREETS IN THE central part of my hometown in southeast Louisiana are lined with beautiful, shade-giving trees. In many yards, broad-trunked live oaks draped in Spanish moss exude an almost mystical quality. The lower limbs of the older ones often droop to the ground, and the higher ones form enormous canopies. On the outskirts of town, the old giant in what was once my Grandpa White's field, torn apart by many a hurricane over the years but still somehow living and putting forth new

---

1. Du Bois, *Souls*, 15.
2. Smith, *Killers*, 18.

growth, reminds me of my roots in a particular environment. But something about it also gives me a sense of belonging that transcends both time and space. The main line of the Illinois Central Railroad (now part of the Canadian National Railroad) runs through the middle of town, crossing the main street and splitting the small city of Hammond into quadrants. It is a quick ride south to New Orleans, and the northern end of the line reaches to Chicago, with connections to Canada. A highway to New Orleans runs through a cypress swamp and then between Lake Pontchartrain and Lake Maurepas, and the channel between the lakes is home to a legendary seafood restaurant that was a frequent destination of my family during my childhood. This town and its surroundings were my first window on the world, where I formed my most basic values and commitments. But it is also where I began to find some of my inherited views challenged as the outside world broke into my safe little sanctuary; and aspects of the town itself betray why that sanctuary faced inevitable shattering.

In the 1950s the center of town was virtually all white, while the vast majority of African Americans lived on the edges of three of the quadrants. The discrepancy in the quality of housing was stunning. Mostly modest, but well-constructed homes adorned most of the streets I have described. Many of the streets in the black neighborhoods, however, were unpaved, and many of the homes were shotgun cottages or unpainted, ramshackle structures. In a few areas, the white and black neighborhoods overlapped, so that one could occasionally find white and black families living side by side. No one was much bothered by this, since the invisible wall of social distance kept the families apart, even if in their earliest years the children might play together across the racial barrier. Invisible as it was, that wall of separation was real and rigid. Behind it was a world we whites simply did not see—a vital community with its own social networks and institutions, but a world circumscribed by the white power structure. There was a small black middle class, but the vast majority of African Americans were locked into severe poverty. The women often worked as maids in white homes and took care of white children for exploitative wages; most of the men held low-paying jobs involving physical labor, without benefits. Blacks did essential work without which the town could not have functioned, but they remained largely invisible to the rest of us. We saw them in the subservient roles that they played for us, but we knew very little of their private lives or of the forms of community that held them together.

Simply said, Hammond was in many ways like most other towns of similar size in the Deep South. The northwest quadrant, however, was home to a small state college, which is today Southeastern Louisiana University. Some of the faculty had come from the North, others had been educated there; and over the years the school, particularly the music department, attracted a respectable number of students from around the country, among them the great jazz pianist Bill Evans. The presence of the college, together with the major highways (now paralleled by interstates) that ran north/south and east/west, as well as the railroad, created a sense of connection to that wider world that eventually broke in and changed things forever. Nevertheless, one had only to drive a few miles into the northern part of the parish to enter an area where the Ku Klux Klan was an ever-present reminder of the threat of racial violence.

In chapter 1, I begin my reflections on the issue of otherness in America with memories from my early years in the environment I have just described, followed by some broader accounts of events that defined the times for me and for many others. With this background in place, I share in chapter 2 some of what I learned from my experiences during those years. In chapter 3, I turn to the Bible as a resource for speaking to the question of inclusiveness, offering my interpretation of relevant biblical texts and my understanding of how the Bible can speak to human beings in our time. Then, in chapters 4 and 5, I venture assessments of my country, past and present, from a biblical perspective; and chapter 6 concludes part 1 with reflections on the meaning of both southern and American identity.

1

# A Place Reconfigured
## Memories of the Mid-Twentieth-Century South

> We accept insult and contumely and the risk of violence because we will not sit quietly by and see our native land, the South[,] . . . wreck and ruin itself twice in less than a hundred years over the Negro question. We speak now against the day when our Southern people who will resist to the last inevitable changes in social relations, will, when they have been forced to accept what at one time they could have accepted with dignity and goodwill will say, "Why didn't someone tell us this before? Tell us this in time?"
>
> —William Faulkner, 1955[1]

For hundreds of years the quiet sobbing of an oppressed people had been unheard by millions of white Americans—the bitterness of the Negroes' lives remote and unfelt except by a sensitive few. Suddenly last summer the silence was broken . . . White America was forced to face the ugly facts of life as the Negro[es] thrust [themselves] into the consciousness of the

---

1. Remarks at the annual meeting of the Southern Historical Association, Memphis, Tennessee, November, 1955; quoted in Egerton, *Speak Now,* 619.

country, and dramatized [their] grievances on a thousand brightly lighted stages. No period in American history, save the Civil War and the Reconstruction, records such breadth and depth to the [Negroes'] drive to alter [their lives]. No period records so many thaws in the frozen patterns of segregation.

—Martin Luther King Jr, 1963[2]

## LEARNING TO SEE WHAT IS IN PLAIN VIEW

My life has been defined largely by two events in my early years. The first was a flash of insight that came in church one Sunday. The minister, Ira Flowers, said something in his sermon that jolted my consciousness with this thought: What we talk about in church is either the most important thing in life or of no importance at all. Deeply moved by this realization, I decided in that moment that my Christian faith was the center of my life and that I would live out my days on that basis. I was, of course, simply echoing the first commandment: "you shall have no other gods before me" (Exod 20:3). And one of the themes of this book is my perception of violations of that commandment—which is to say, idolatries—that have infected my home state, my country, and even the church.

The second event was social rather than personal, but its impact upon me was enormous. In 1954 the United States Supreme Court handed down its decision on school desegregation, *Brown v. Board of Education*, and within a few months much of the white population in the South went into shock. State legislatures and local boards of education frantically devised strategies for circumventing the court order; politicians at all levels ranted and raved; and what had remained largely unquestioned among whites for generations, the so-called southern way of life, became the focal point for bitter conflict. I was a sophomore in a segregated, all-white public high school attached to the college, and I found myself pulled apart by conflicting values grounded in my church, my family, my regional loyalties, and my understanding of the meaning of America. This was a tumultuous time in the South, but I am grateful for having grown up in that place and that time;

2. King, *Can't Wait*, 112.

for the circumstances in which I lived forced me to make value decisions that have guided my life ever since.

No one is "typical." In my earlier years I unconsciously accepted the "Southern Way of Life"—the standard euphemism for a degrading system of segregation disguised by sentimental but fundamentally dishonest paternalism. Indeed, racist attitudes infected my mind and speech habits. I had, however, a dim consciousness that something was flawed in the prevailing social arrangement. For reasons I cannot fully explain, I sometimes addressed the warmhearted African American woman named Isadora who worked for my aunt as "ma'am"; and I recall eminently friendly relationships with other African American adults who were in some way connected to my family. (I was, however, aware of the social distance that qualified those relationships as well as the fact that my ease of conversation with these people had to do in part with our shared subordinate statuses—mine as a child, and theirs because of race.) Also, there was apparently something lacking in my education into supposedly southern values: I was not taught to hate or given explicit instruction in the doctrine of white supremacy. When race became a topic in my home, my parents defended the standard southern doctrine, but they never made an issue of the matter. Many people in the South were taught to hate, however; and it is perhaps partly because I was not that I was able to find my way out of the imprisoning views I inherited.

But other liberating influences were also at work in my life. Some of these came from my parents themselves. Not only did they fail to indoctrinate me adequately in racism, but they were loving people who taught me respect for all persons and empathy for the poor, a category to which almost all the African Americans I knew clearly belonged. In addition, I encountered from time to time people who in varying degrees departed from southern white orthodoxy.

Another important influence was school, where I found aspects of American history both interesting and illuminating. I was particularly inspired by the Declaration of Independence because of its affirmation of the equality of all persons as well as its condemnation of despotism. I also came to admire Abraham Lincoln as the great emancipator, although I was ignorant of the long evolutionary path of his thinking that led eventually to the Emancipation Proclamation, as well as of the initially limited goals of the Civil War. When my teacher stated that many people hated Lincoln when he was alive, I was puzzled. I believed that slavery was wrong and felt embarrassed that my beloved South had ever been involved in it, despite the fact that not long before I had playfully sported a Confederate cap and waved a Confederate flag.

The most important liberating factor was the church. Nearly all of our members accepted the "Southern way of life," but I recall a Sunday school lesson when I was in the sixth grade or so that challenged racial prejudice and debunked popular notions about blood differences. More broadly, the biblical teachings on love of neighbor laid a foundation that I eventually found impossible to reconcile with segregation. Also, our minister during my high school and college years, Ed Thomas, took a progressive stance on the race issue. I suppose that he was responsible for my signing up for a tour of Methodist mission sites throughout the state, and it was on this trip that I had my first encounter with an African American of my own age on an equal basis. By this time I had reached my decision to enter the ministry, and I was delighted to meet another young man with the same goal. As we stood next to each other in a small group around a church piano singing hymns, he placed his arm around my shoulder; and I was struck with two startling insights. First, contrary to all the indoctrination I had received, he and I were united by a common humanity as well as a common faith. Second, we were, however, separated by an evil social convention. Had we lived in the same town, we would probably never have spoken to one another, certainly not as peers. And for the first time in my life I was aware that the social system that granted me privilege on the basis of my skin color also deprived me of relationships with other persons who could have enriched my life.

That system, of course, deprived others of much more. The doctrine of "separate but equal" was an outright lie. I well remember handing in old, battered textbooks during class to be given to the "colored" school, which was housed in a shabby frame building. I also remember the segregated drinking fountains, movie theaters, and waiting rooms. The "colored" section in the theater was the second balcony, with the entrance in an alley; and in every instance of separate facilities the stark discrepancy in quality testified to the reality of white privilege. In some cases, such as soda fountains and hotels or motels, there were no facilities at all for African Americans. I saw all this, but didn't really *see* it until I began to "see" everything differently. When that happened, I also learned something about hypocrisy, as school boards throughout the South began to construct new schools for black students that they could use to show that things were equal after all!

To observe the discrepancies in public facilities was one thing; to see up close how the "Southern Way of Life" affected individuals was something else. Social distance shielded me from much, but on occasion I got a glimpse of the grim reality of the system. One day in a college history class shortly after the school was integrated, the professor subjected us to her views on equality. "People are simply not equal," she said (or something to that effect).

She gave lip service to the distinction between equality before the law and equality in abilities (assuming, of course, white superiority) but then undermined the point. "It doesn't mean that people can go where they couldn't go before," she proclaimed firmly, in an obvious reference to desegregation. Then, stepping forward and glaring at the young African American woman in the front row, the only nonwhite in the class, she spit out a question:

"Do you think people are equal?"

The class was silent as the student softly replied, "Yes"; and I think she added "ma'am."

In a huff, the teacher turned and resumed her lecture. On another occasion she attributed the fall of the Roman Empire to the policy of allowing a measure of home rule among the subject nations. Doing so, she proclaimed, was equivalent to our giving a public office "to a Negro or some other group that filtered in here"—a singularly ironic way of describing the transportation of human beings across an ocean in chains to live in slavery! (Need I mention how the remark showed her uncritical attitude toward Roman imperialism?)

Years later, when I was associate pastor at a church in New Orleans, I was assigned to watch over a piano we had transported to Jackson Square for a districtwide event. I drove there in my car together with a young black man who had just returned from serving in Vietnam, and whose father owned the truck the church had rented to transport the piano. Because it was a cold winter day, we obtained permission from a police officer to park in the mall between the square and St. Louis Cathedral in order to keep warm. We would sit in the car for a while, then get out and walk around to stretch our legs.

As we sat talking, I was startled to see two police cars speeding toward us and coming to an abrupt stop. As officers swarmed around us, I jumped out and approached one of them to explain what we were doing. He listened patiently, but then I realized that on the other side of the car, two others were searching the young man as he leaned against the car with his arms and legs spread. I hurried over and, with trembling voice, asked what the problem was. It seems that someone in the Pontalba Apartments, the historic buildings that face the square, had reported that a black man was milling about the area.

When I repeated my explanation, one officer snapped a reply: "In other words, what he said is right?"

"Yes," I said (as calmly as I could manage), "but you could have asked me that before you pulled him out of the car."

I remain ashamed that my statement reflected the white-black hierarchy I had come to despise, but it accomplished one thing. For a brief moment, I saw in the eyes of the officer a small reflection of the rage and hatred that virulent racism can produce *directed at me*. White privilege was nevertheless at work. Although I had been sitting alongside the "suspect," and was thus an obvious "accomplice" to whatever offense the officers and caller imagined, it was only the black man they questioned and searched. It was only I, moreover, to whom they offered a modicum of respect, I whose word they accepted with no other support than my white skin.

An earlier revelatory event was a long conversation with a fellow seminary student at Southern Methodist University in Dallas. I had accidentally locked myself out of my dormitory room on a weekend during which my roommate was away. So a friend named Dick Stewart, the one African American in the building, let me sleep in his extra bed; and we talked through most of the night. The first thing I learned was why he had no roommate. He had shared the room with a white student, but a member of the seminary's board of trustees had passed by their open door, seen them together, and complained to the administration. The white student was moved to another room. But this story was only the beginning. For the first time, an African American shared with me what it felt like to be a black person in the South. Things that I had known mostly on an intellectual level took on a deeper emotional tone. Even as I began to feel something of his experiences, however, I also realized more fully that I could never really know what his life and the lives of his people were like.

What I could do was try to listen as attentively as I could to what black people themselves had to say. And over the years I did so, through personal conversations, interracial dialogue groups, and such books as Richard Wright's *Black Boy*, Claude Brown's *Manchild in the Promised Land*, and *The Autobiography of Malcolm X*, each of which expanded upon the insight I gained that night in the seminary dormitory. *Every aspect of a black person's life in the environment in which I grew up was affected by white prejudice and white privilege; and what I observed and experienced indirectly at Jackson Square and in my college history class was only the tip of an enormous iceberg. To be black in the South, and to a large extent in the United States in general, was to be constantly confronted with the fact of difference in a way that implied inferiority and consignment to a subordinate position in society.*

## "NIGGERS AIN'T NOTHIN' HERE": A HISTORY OF VIOLENCE, OPEN AND COVERT

My "safe little sanctuary" was an illusion. The placid lives of the white population masked the violent nature of an exploitative social system, concealing as well the inevitability of an explosion born of dreams deferred. The Africans were enslaved by violence, and conditions on the slave ships were so horrific that many of the shackled prisoners died in transport. Masters punished slaves by beatings, and the women were subject to sexual exploitation, whether through concubinage or rape, by both masters and overseers. Although treatment of slaves varied greatly, the system could exist only because of the threat of force. The frequent escapes and attempted escapes, as well as occasional slave revolts and the brutality with which most of them were suppressed, are clear testimony to that fact.

Emancipation, moreover, brought only the semblance of freedom in the South. Following the passage of the Civil Rights Act of 1866,[3] which granted citizenship to African Americans, riots broke out in many southern states, where whites rallied to maintain control of political power. Various terrorist organizations arose, among them the Ku Klux Klan and the Knights of the White Camellia, to intimidate both blacks and the "carpetbaggers" who had come south during Reconstruction. The eventual institution of numerous Jim Crow laws created the system of segregation that ensured white domination. And lest anyone doubt the violence inherent in that system, it is estimated that from 1880 to 1930, "there were 2,018 separate incidents of lynching in which at least 2,462 African-American men, women, and children met their deaths in the grasp of southern mobs, comprised mostly of whites."[4]

The stated reasons for these extrajudicial executions, often accompanied by torture, included white suspicion of murder and rape by blacks. Other reasons included blacks' attempting to vote, arguing with or testifying against a white person, cohabiting with a white woman, and using unacceptable language.[5] The common perception among southern whites was that the majority of lynchings were responses to the rape of white women by black men. As John Egerton notes, however, "fewer than one-third of all lynchings involved even a claim of rape, and the number in which a black assailant was positively identified came to only a minor fraction of the total."[6] The irony, moreover, is that "whether by terror, force, coercion, enticement, persuasion, or mutual consent, *white men were the primary instigators of*

---

3. The act was passed over the veto of President Andrew Johnson. In 1868, the adoption of the Fourteenth Amendment to the Constitution strengthened the act in one sense by asserting that "All persons born or naturalized in the United States, and subject to the jurisdiction thereof, are citizens of the United States wherein they reside." The phrase "and subject to the jurisdiction thereof," however, excluded Native Americans.

4. Tolnay and Beck, *Festival*, 17; cited by Braziel. "Lynching."

5. Tolnay and Beck, *Festival*, 17, Table 2–5; cited by Braziel, "Lynching."

6. Egerton, *Speak Now*, 51.

*physical union between the races in the generations after the Civil War, just as they had been in the generations before.*"[7]

The more visible forms of violence of whites against blacks subsided somewhat in the late 1920s, but they reemerged during the civil rights movement of the 1950s and 1960s. The best-remembered act of violence during this period was the assassination of Martin Luther King Jr. in Memphis in 1968, but it was preceded by a string of brutal incidents that received national attention—

- 1955: in Mississippi, the murder of Emmett Till, fourteen-year-old Chicago boy visiting relatives, after he allegedly said "Bye, baby" to a white woman[8]
- 1961: in Alabama, the burning of a Freedom Ride bus, from which the passengers narrowly escaped; the brutal beating, in some cases near to the point of death, of passengers on other Freedom Ride buses[9]
- 1963: in Mississippi, the murder of Medgar Evers, a field secretary of the National Associated for the Advancement of Colored People and combat veteran of World War II[10]
- 1963: in Alabama, the bombing of Birmingham's Sixteenth Street Baptist church, killing Denise McNair, 11; Carol Robertson, 14; Cynthia Wesley, 14; and Addie Mae Collins, 10[11]
- 1964: in Mississippi, during the "Freedom Summer" declared by civil rights groups, the abduction and murder of three young volunteers, one black and two white—James Chaney, Andrew Goodman, and Michael Schwerner; the arrests and beatings of many other volunteers as well as the burning of numerous black churches, businesses, and homes[12]
- 1965: "Bloody Sunday," Selma, Alabama—the brutal beating of civil rights marchers led by John Lewis and Hosea Williams (headed to Montgomery to demonstrate for voting rights) by state police and local law enforcement personnel; called "the political and emotional peak of the modern civil rights movement,"[13] the march was, as John Lewis

7. Ibid.; italics added.
8. Lewis, *Walking*, 46.
9. Ibid., 140–58.
10. Ibid., 199.
11. United Press International, "Six Dead after Church Bombing."
12. Congress on Racial Equality, "Freedom Summer."
13. Blackpast.org/, "Selma, Alabama."

described it, composed of "an army of teenagers, teachers, undertakers, beauticians—many of the same Selma people who had stood for weeks, months, years, in front of that courthouse."[14]

As important as it is to remember high-profile events such as these, to focus exclusively on them is to miss the larger picture of violence that defined southern society. Among the many less publicized events were the 1955 murders of black activists Reverend George Lee and Lamar Smith in Mississippi, along with the beating of a black girl for "crowding" a white woman in a store;[15] the fatal police shootings of two teenage black males following the bombing of the Sixteenth Street Church in Alabama—one for refusing to halt after stoning cars, the other while riding a bicycle in a suburb of Birmingham;[16] the discovery of the brutalized remains of two black men missing from Meadeville, Mississippi, during the search for the bodies of Cheney, Schwerner, and Goodman.[17]

Violence like this often received implicit sanction from public opinion as well as from local and state law enforcement and judiciary. The men who killed Emmett Till were positively identified by a black witness but acquitted by a white jury anyway;[18] and before Medgar Evers's killer was finally convicted after thirty years, two trials ended in hung juries largely because of an alibi provided by two police officers whose testimony was contradicted by other witnesses. It was forty years before a federal court was able to bring justice in the case of the men from Meadeville,[19] and many similar cases remain unsolved, among them the arson-murder of Frank Morris of Ferriday, Louisiana[20] and the truck bombing in Mississippi that left Wharlest Jackson dead after his promotion to a position previously held only by whites.[21]

Such overt violence, moreover, was accompanied by the subtler violence done to the consciousness of black people on a daily basis. For example, when Dr. King was six years old the father of a white friend told him that "they could no longer play together because he was 'colored'";[22] and John Lewis, one of the freedom riders, who was beaten nearly to death and is now a U.S. congressional representative from Georgia, remembers

14. Lewis, *Walking*, 337.
15. Ebersole, "Mississippi."
16. United Press International, "Six Dead after Church Bombing."
17. Civil Rights Cold Case Project, "Dee and Moore."
18. Lewis, *Walking*, 46–47.
19. Civil Rights Cold Case Project, "Dee and Moore."
20. Civil Rights Cold Case Project, "Silver Dollar Group."
21. Civil Rights Cold Case Project, "Wharlest Jackson."
22. Cone, *Martin*, 23.

being denied use of the public library as a child because it was only for whites.²³ My point is that such incidents were part and parcel of black life in the South, life in many ways defined by the angry statement of a Klansman involved in the beating of the freedom riders: "Niggers get back. You ain't up north. You're in Alabama, and niggers ain't nothin' here."²⁴

W. E. B. Du Bois described the cumulative effect of the system of white privilege as the development of a "double-consciousness." Because whites write the laws and define the values on which society is based, blacks are trained to see themselves through the eyes of the white majority; and although they know themselves to be American, they also experience themselves as "other."

> It is a peculiar sensation, this double-consciousness, this sense of always looking at one's self through the eyes of others, of measuring one's soul by the tape of the world that looks on in amused contempt and pity. One ever feels [one's] two-ness, an American, a Negro; two souls, two thoughts, two unreconciled strivings; two warring ideals in one dark body, whose dogged strength alone keeps it from being torn asunder.²⁵

Testimony such as this is still painful for me to hear, partly because of my complicity in the system I came to despise. One particular memory still haunts me. Waiting in line behind a young black man one afternoon at an ice cream stand, I was startled when the woman at the window strained her neck to look around him and take my order first. The young man was obviously devastated. Haltingly, I gave my order, wondering whether if I objected it would be worse for him, but knowing that my inaction was in part out of fear of challenging "the system." As uncomfortable as this memory is, it reminds me that inward dissent from injustice is inadequate in the face of evil that is systemic, which is to say, embedded in social and sometimes legal structures. To stand idly by as an oppressive system crushes human dignity and hopes and dreams, as I did that day at the ice cream stand, is to give that system implicit support.

---

23. John Lewis for Congress, "Getting into Good Trouble," 1.
24. Arsenault, *Freedom Riders*, cited in Gross, "Get on the Bus."
25. Du Bois, *Souls*, 5.

# 2

# Lessons Learned
## Reflecting on the Times

> The history of the American Negro is the history of this strife—this longing to maintain self-conscious manhood [or womanhood], to merge this double self [American/Negro] into a better and truer self. In this merging [she or] he wishes neither of the older selves to be lost. He [or she] would not Africanize America, for America has too much to teach the world and Africa. He [or she] would not bleach his [or her] Negro soul in a flood of white Americanism, for [she or] he knows that Negro blood has a message for the world. [She or he] simply wishes to make it possible for a [person] to be both a Negro and an American, without being spit upon by his [or her] fellows, without having the doors of Opportunity closed to [her or] him.
>
> —W. E. B. DuBois, 1925[1]

---

1. Du Bois, *Souls*, 3.

## A PARADOXICAL LESSON IN LOVE

My roots in the South and its culture are deep. My father was descended from Cajun ancestors, the French Acadians deported from Nova Scotia during the French and Indian War. Six generations before me, four brothers with the surname Prejean found their way to Louisiana and made it their new home. My great-grandfather founded our little subclan when he changed the spelling to Pregeant, one of several variations. My grandfather, Papa Pregeant, once owned a sugar plantation, but lost everything when hurricane winds blew in salt water and ruined the land; and at least two of my earlier Prejean ancestors owned small numbers of slaves. Mama Pregeant was born in Alabama to southern parents. Grandma White was born in the northern part of my home parish and married a Methodist minister who had migrated from Mississippi, where his forebears had lived for generations. I remember Grandpa White giving a biblical justification for segregation.

Although I could hardly have been more southern, in the eyes of many I became something else. A good friend in high school had an older cousin, a college professor, who was related by marriage to a famous southern journalist who stood courageously against the so-called Southern way of life. The professor, with whom I took classes, was a delightful, eccentric woman, and I wondered what she thought of her noted in-law. So I asked my friend. He said that he had put that very question to her and received this blunt answer: "He's a traitor to the South." So too were both my friend and I, if judged by the prevailing standard. We both had learned by this time, however, that is possible to love something but still admit its flaws, to value something mightily but hold it up for judgment in light of higher ideals. I had thus come to see the social structure of the world in which I grew up as cruel and oppressive—and yet I could somehow still love that world.

## A LESSON IN HYPOCRISY

To some extent, I could identify racism as peculiarly southern. It was only here that white domination was institutionalized by law. However, I became increasingly aware over the years of what southerners called "northern hypocrisy." That northerners were equally capable of racial prejudice became apparent to the entire country when Martin Luther King Jr went north with a campaign for open housing and encountered virulent protests from white neighborhoods. And when I moved to Massachusetts to take a teaching job, I was stunned by the racism rampant in parts of Boston, graphically illustrated by three scenes caught on television: white adults in one neighborhood throwing rocks at school buses carrying black children; the councilwoman from another neighborhood pounding her shoe on her desk in opposition to federally ordered busing; and a white mob carrying an American flag, chasing a black man at Government Center. Along with all this, moreover, my southern upbringing had trained me to decode the implicitly racist comments that I heard far too often.

Individual prejudice, however, was hardly the whole story. The southern segregation laws existed within the framework of a federal judicial system that allowed them to stand and a Congress that failed to legislate against them. The doctrine of "separate but equal" had official standing in U.S. constitutional law beginning with the case of *Plessy v. Ferguson* in 1896, in which the U.S. Supreme Court ruled that segregated public accommodations were legal as long as they were equal; and this ruling remained in force until it was overturned in *Brown v. Board of Education*. Although slavery officially ended in all northern states by 1804, it actually continued much longer. New Jersey did not permanently abolish it until 1846, and even then there remained a few "apprentices for life," who were rightly listed in a federal census as slaves![2] Some framers of the Constitution wanted to abolish slavery, but they relented in order to bring the southern states into the union. Article IV provided that slaves who escaped to the north should be returned to those who held them in bondage, and it was strengthened by the Fugitive Slave Act of 1850. In the *Dred Scott* decision of 1857, moreover, the Supreme Court denied Scott's contention that since he had lived with his master in a free state for a time, he had a claim to freedom. Nor were segregation laws a southern invention. As Egerton reports, "the practice of racial separation that came to bear the Jim Crow tag was modeled after procedures widely used in Northern cities before the Civil War."[3]

If Thomas Jefferson had reason to tremble for his country, so did I, as a young person growing up two centuries later in that same country, when it had long since freed the slaves but seemed determined to condemn their descendants to perpetual servitude of another type. I could celebrate the guarantees of liberty in the Bill of Rights, but I was learning just how seriously we as a nation had failed to live up to the ideals we professed.

---

2. Harper, "Slavery."
3. Egerton, *Speak Now*, 30.

## THE POWER OF SOCIAL SYSTEMS
## AND THE AGONY OF CONFLICTING VALUES

The violence against blacks in the South during the periods I have described could easily give the impression that the vast majority of white southerners over the course of this history were evil people. Even if only a fairly small percentage of the white population participated in actual murders and beatings, most whites supported the oppressive social system that enabled such overt violence. Although I have clear memories of the years when I accepted "the Southern way of life," I look back on those days with incredulity. How could such a system have continued into mid-twentieth-century America? Many of the people I grew up with were kind and loving, and many had a strong sense of the dignity of all human beings. Nevertheless, the vast majority held together a set of admirable values on the one hand and loyalty to a dehumanizing social arrangement on the other. To explain this contradiction, one has to take account of the power of social systems and the roles within those systems of worldview and ideology on the one hand and of wealth, power, and privilege on the other.

The world does not interpret itself to us. Because the places we occupy shape how we see the world, what we accept as truth is a matter of social construction. Each society sets its own moral codes, creates a body of what it considers knowledge, and fosters a particular understanding of reality. Each society also legitimates its moral codes and claims to knowledge by constructing a worldview or "symbolic universe," a comprehensive way of understanding the nature of reality itself.[4] A symbolic universe or worldview is a human construct, but it presents itself as objectively true—as a representation of *the way things really are*. And this representation carries with it an understanding of what it means to be a human being, a member of society, and a part of smaller groups such as clans and families. It defines roles based on gender, age, and the like. In short, it gives each person a specific identity. Thus, to reject the prevailing worldview is to face a loss of identity. Conversely, to break the moral code or to deviate from one's assigned social role is to implicitly reject the worldview. In short, social systems have enormous power over people, because we tend to internalize them and accept them as unchallengeable truth.

The terms *worldview* and *ideology* are often used interchangeably. Audrey Smedley, however, *defines the former as a "systematic and comprehensive" perspective and treats ideologies as the more specific "beliefs, values, and assumptions"* that compose the broader worldview. What is most important

---

4. Berger and Luckmann, *Social Construction*, 92–108.

in her definition is that ideologies "are held on faith alone and generally unrelated to empirical facts."[5] We can thus understand how highly educated persons in various Western societies once invoked supposedly scientific studies, now thoroughly discredited, to support theories of race involving elaborate schemes of superiority and inferiority.[6] Both those who conducted the studies and those who accepted their results believed what they did, not because of actual evidence, but because of prior ideological commitments they would not allow themselves to doubt.

Appreciation of the nature of ideology can also explain how intelligent people can embrace conflicting sets of values, and on this point I am ironically indebted to my racist history professor. In one of her tirades, she railed out against Gunnar Myrdal, author of *An American Dilemma*, a book that the U.S. Supreme Court cited in its decision on *Brown v. Board of Education*. She said sarcastically that Myrdal thought that the average white American went to bed every night conflicted over the race issue. His point was in fact that the treatment of blacks in this country stood in irreconcilable conflict with American ideals rooted partly in Christianity, and that this conflict wore heavily on the American conscience.[7] This was the first time I had heard of the book, and when I later found it on the list of subjects for a book report in a seminary class in Christian social ethics, I chose it and learned enormously from it. I refer to it now because I believe that there was much truth in what Myrdal said. Societies are made up of many subgroups and involve competing strains of teaching about what is true and what is good; and these competing strains can easily come into conflict.

This was certainly the case in the social world in which I grew up. Commitment to democratic ideals and biblical teachings was often sincere. However, a symbolic universe that co-opted God as the enforcer of a hierarchical order based on white privilege was in some cases even more deeply entrenched. To dissent from this view was to undermine the very fabric of white society and the identity of every white individual. It was to violate the natural order of things, usually understood as the will of God; and so it was that many people who were humane and just in most aspects of their lives supported a blatantly unjust system. So it was also that some of these people internalized an ideology so thoroughly and were so overcome with fear when it was threatened that they turned to unspeakable violence against their fellow human beings. We cannot fully understand the power of

---

5. Smedley and Smedley, *Race*, 16.
6. Ibid., 213–27.
7. Myrdal, *Dilemma*, 3–25.

the social system that supported slavery and segregation, however, without taking account of how three other factors interact with race and ideology.

## NAMING THE OBJECTS OF IDOLATRY: WEALTH, POWER, PRIVILEGE, AND RACE

In the mid-1960s, when I was a graduate student at Vanderbilt University in Nashville, I went to hear a talk on the Ku Klux Klan by Will D. Campbell, a Baptist minister and director of the Committee of Southern Churchmen. Knowing that Campbell was a civil rights activist, I expected a righteous condemnation of all that the Klan stands for. Instead of bashing the Klan, however, he spoke of the "redneck" Klansmen as victims of the same social system that oppressed blacks. Alongside his solid commitment to racial justice, he had a deep empathy for the suffering of poor whites and believed that political liberalism, with its reliance upon governmental solutions, was an inadequate solution to the ills of the South. The title of the committee's journal, edited by James Y. Holloway, another Baptist minister, was suggestive of their point: *Katallagete: Be Reconciled*. The subtitle translates the Greek word in the main title, which is taken from the apostle Paul.[8] As Steven P. Miller summarizes the committee's perspective,

> the liberal faith in legislative and political solutions . . . furthered a suspect reliance on state power and contributed little toward achieving an authentically biracial society. Their proposed alternative . . . was an explicitly Biblical model of reconciliation— first, between God and humans, and secondly, among humans themselves. Too many Christians, Campbell and Holloway argued, had relied on political solutions to social problems at the expense of the Biblical promise of human reconciliation by means of divine grace.[9]

I was pretty sure that both Campbell and Holloway engaged in political actions themselves, and I was not about to abandon this route. But I had to agree with them that it presents only a surface solution unless it is accompanied by a deeper level of transformation. It is hypocritical, moreover, to emphasize the oppression of blacks without addressing the deprivation suffered by poor whites, those known disparagingly as "rednecks" or "poor white trash." This is a point expressed powerfully in an allegory Lillian Smith proposed in *Killers of the Dream*, an account of her experiences as

---

8. 2 Cor 5:18–20; also Rom 5:10–11.
9. Miller, "Reconciliation," 1.

a white woman growing up in the South in the generation before my own. I learned of Smith during my first year in seminary when I read her novel, *Strange Fruit*, the story of an interracial love affair and a lynching in a small southern town. Years later, my wife, Sammie (who grew up a few miles from where Smith lived for many years and knew some of her friends), introduced me to *Killers of the Dream*. The first part of the allegory goes like this. "Once upon a time, down South," Mr. Rich White proposed a bargain to Mr. Poor White, and Mr. Poor White accepted it. Mr. Rich White would "tend to the living"—that is, to matters that he knew all about: "things about jobs, credit, prices, hours, wages, votes, and so on." These were the things that Mr. Poor White was "too no-count to learn." But there was one thing Mr. Poor White could learn: how "to tend to the nigger." And this gave Mr. Poor White a great deal of power and responsibility. In fact, Mr. Rich White told him explicitly,

> Anything you want to do to show folks you're boss you're free to do it. You can run the schools and the churches any way you want to. You can make the customs and set the manners and write the laws (long as you don't touch my business). You can throw books out of libraries if you don't like what's in them and you can decide pretty much what kind of learning, if any, you want southern children to have.[10]

Mr. Rich White went on to sanction not only the Jim Crow laws, but also lynching, promising to fix things "with the sheriff and the judge and the court and the newspapers." He added this, however: "*but don't expect me to come to the lynching, for I won't be there.*"[11] And then there was the economic component. Mr. Rich White could maintain and increase his riches, and Mr. Poor White could occupy a position in society superior to that of blacks. This was a subordinate position, and the wages he received in his job would remain low; but, after all, "any job's better than no job at all."[12] And herein lies the tragedy of Mr. Poor White's acceptance of the bargain. Deluded by the promise of power over the black population, he was unable to see how he, too, was a victim of Mr. Rich White's exploitation. Indeed, both men were deluded. For "it never occurred to Mr. Rich White that with a bargain the Negro could help him make money. It never occurred to Mr. Poor White that with a bargain the Negro could help him raise wages."[13]

---

10. Smith, *Killers*, 155.
11. Ibid., 156; italics original.
12. Ibid., 154.
13. Ibid., 157.

This latter point is one that Dr. King also stressed. "As long as labor was cheapened by the involuntary servitude of the black man, the freedom of white labor, particularly in the South, was little more than a myth." For laboring-class whites were "free only to bargain from the depressed base imposed by slavery upon the whole labor market. Nor did this derivative bondage end when formal slavery gave way to the de-facto slavery of discrimination."[14]

Lest anyone doubt the exploitative nature of the economic arrangements engineered by many Mr. Rich Whites, consider Egerton's comments on the institution of sharecropping in 1932. That year has been called the cruelest of the great depression, but the conditions Egerton describes existed in significant measure both before and long afterwards:

> To be a sharecropper or a tenant farmer in the South in 1932 was to be caught up in an existence that often was nothing more than peonage or forced labor—just one step removed from slavery. You rented the land from its owner, and made the crop for him with his furnish of seed and fertilizer and mules and tools; he sold you food and other necessities on credit at high interest in his commissary; he kept the books, handled the sales, and divided with you at harvest time. You were lucky if you broke even; some went in the hole, and not one in ten actually came away with a few dollars profit.[15]

Nor was it sharecroppers alone who suffered under this kind of exploitation:

> The ones with the lowest earned income of all were those who actually did the hardest work. Cotton pickers were paid twenty cents for a hundred pounds—so little that the strongest and swiftest of them had less than a dollar to show for a backbreaking day's work . . . In the textile mills, women and children worked seventy-two hours a week for fifteen to twenty-five cents an hour. And no matter how much or how little the faceless thousands of workers ended up with, the company store quickly relieved them of it.[16]

Poor whites and poor blacks shared these desperate conditions. The old ploy, however, remains remarkably effective in seducing people to act against their own self-interest: divide and conquer. The tactic is effective because of two basic human frailties. The first is our tendency to fear and

---

14. King, *Can't Wait*, 138.
15. Egerton, *Speak Now*, 20–21.
16. Ibid., 21–22.

despise those we perceive as different, whom we name "the other" or "the outsider." The second is our willingness to accept patterns of hierarchy or domination, whatever our specific rung on the ladder of power and privilege. Because those "at the top of the heap" wield the greatest power, they can control systems of education and socialization and thus impose their values, ideology, and worldview on those below them. When that happens, oppressed people can become loyal servants of the system that oppresses them; and persons confined to low-level tasks can become convinced that this is all they are capable of, no matter what their actual abilities might be. (Indeed, the definition of some tasks as "low-level" or "menial" masks the fact that they are indispensable to society and deprives those who perform them of pride in their work.) If we put these two tendencies together, we have the perfect means of maintaining an oppressive social system. As Dr. King wrote, this system weighs heavily upon white workers "because it has confused so many by prejudice that they have supported their own oppressors."[17] As long as the white ruling class can convince the poor whites that blacks are a threat to their jobs, their safety, their status, and their identity, they can stave off the one possibility that might force a change in the arrangement that keeps them wealthy while others are poor. That possibility is that blacks and poor whites would unite in common cause, demanding a just share of the collective wealth for all as well as equal treatment for all in the social sphere.

The fear of this possibility, as well as the "bargain" that served as a defense against it, was present as far back as the colonial period. As Howard Zinn comments, "Only one fear was greater than the fear of black rebellion in the new American colonies. This was the fear that discontented whites would join black slaves to overthrow the existing order."[18] Zinn cites Edmund Morgan, who finds that in the earliest days white servants and black slaves had some sense of "sharing the same predicament," associated with one another in various ways, and occasionally ran away together.[19] To undermine this sense of common cause, in 1705 the Virginia legislature granted to white indentured servants certain benefits when their term of service was up. These included both money and land, so that "once the small planter[s] felt less exploited by taxation and began to prosper a little, [they] became less turbulent, less dangerous, more respectable" and "could begin

---

17 King, *Can't Wait*, 138.
18. Zinn, *History*, 37.
19. Morgan, *Slavery*; cited in Zinn, *History*, 37.

to see [their] big neighbor not as an extortionist but as a powerful protector of their common interests."[20]

There was in the South in which I grew up an irreducible element of sheer racial prejudice that existed in its own right. It interacted, however, in a complex way with economic oppression on the one hand and with a symbolic universe that sanctioned a hierarchical pecking order on the other. These, then, were the idolatries that competed with the biblical faith that so many in the South professed: a naked racism that made a fetish of skin color and named blacks as "the other"; an understanding of the universe that allowed some groups to dominate others and reserve privileges for themselves; and an economic order that distributed wealth so unjustly as to render many people, both black and white, virtually powerless.

Is it really so, however, that the system that I have named idolatrous is incompatible with the biblical faith? One would not think so on the basis of visits to most white Christian congregations in the South during my youth. In fact, in many cases one might conclude that the biblical worldview actually sanctioned "the Southern way of life." This question will be the subject of chapter 3.

---

20. Morgan, *Slavery*; cited by Zinn, *History*, 37.

# 3

# Adjusting the Lenses
## The Bible, Race, and the Unity of Humankind

> Christianity is the white [person's] religion. The Holy Bible in the white [person's] hands and his[/her] interpretations of it have been the greatest single ideological weapon for enslaving millions of non-white human beings. Every country the white [people have] conquered with [their] guns, [they have] always paved the way, and salved [their] conscience[s], by carrying the Bible and interpreting it to call people "heathens" and "pagans"; then [they send] in [their] guns, then [their] missionaries behind the guns to mop up.
>
> —MALCOLM X, 1957[1]

> Despite the fact that the Bible has a favorable attitude about Blacks, post-biblical misconstruals of biblical traditions have created the impression that the Bible is primarily the foundational document of "the white [person's] religion."
>
> —CAIN HOPE FELDER, 1989[2]

---

1. Malcolm X, "Angry Men," quoted in Cone, *Martin*, 166.
2. Felder, *Troubling*, xi.

> It has proved the task and responsibility of marginalized readers today, both female and male, to restore the voices of the oppressed in the kingdom of God. In order to do this, they have had to be able as much as possible to read and hear the text for themselves, with their own eyes and with their own ears. And in the final analysis, they have had to be prepared . . . to resist those elements of the tradition that have sought, even in the name of revelation, to diminish their humanity.
>
> —Renita J. Weems, 1991[3]

One set of lenses through which I viewed my country was the complex of ideals enshrined in its own foundational documents. The other set, through which I read those documents and evaluated them, was the biblical writings. But as the place from which I understood the world was undergoing a process of reconfiguration, so also was my understanding of the Bible, particularly during my college years.

I felt lucky to live in a college town. A private school would have been out of the question, given my parents' limited resources, and even LSU would have presented a severe financial burden. So I was happy to go to Southeastern, whose campus has always been dear to me. An ancient live oak, known as Friendship Oak, stands imposingly at the center; and the original buildings, constructed in the 1930s, are charming examples of the art deco style. For me, however, the most important location was the Wesley Foundation, the Methodist student center, which was linked to the nationwide Methodist Student Movement (MSM). It was through this connection that I attended conferences, heard challenging speakers, and found my world of thought, including my understanding of the Bible, further cracked open and expanded. Here, then, are four Bible lessons that I learned over the years, beginning in college.

---

3. Weems, "Reading Her Way," 77.

## FOUR LESSONS IN READING THE BIBLE

### Bible Lesson 1: On Racism and Bible Abuse

One lesson concerned what I later came to call "Bible abuse,"[4] the distortion of Scripture that turns its liberating message into a tool of oppression. This lesson came in part from a book titled *Segregation and the Bible*, by Everett Tilson, one of the speakers I heard. Tilson wrote when biblical scholarship was still dominated by white males such as himself, and his work has been largely superseded by others, especially by several African American scholars. But his book was important in its time for exposing the absurdities in segregationists' appeals to the Bible. Three examples should suffice to make the point.

The first has to do with Gen 9:25–27, a passage popularly known as the "curse of Ham." These verses conclude an addendum to the story of Noah and the flood, wherein Ham, one of Noah's sons, walks into his father's tent and sees him lying naked in a drunken stupor. Ham reports the incident to his two brothers, who do what he should have done by walking backwards into the tent and covering their father. Since the names of some of Ham's descendants correspond to regions of Africa, most notably Cush, Ham has often been identified as black. And this identification led to the notion that his blackness resulted from the curse Noah issued in verses Gen 9:25–27. As Tilson noted, however, the curse was placed not upon Ham, but upon Ham's son Canaan: "Cursed be Canaan; lowest of slaves shall he be to his brothers" (Gen 9:25). Thus, even on the assumption that the curse fell upon all subsequent generations of Canaan's progeny, because Ham had four sons, "three fourths of Ham's descendants have no reason to regard themselves as the heirs of Canaan's curses."[5] One might add that this includes those clearly located in Africa and that 9:25–27 says nothing about a change in skin color.

The second example concerns Gen 11:1–9, the story of the Tower of Babel. As punishment for their trying to build a tower to reach the heavens, God scatters human beings across the earth and creates different languages to keep the various groups from communicating with one another. Segregationists interpreted this as God's judgment against an attempt to integrate the races, but nothing in the passage suggests that the divisions among

---

4. See Pregeant, *Reading*, 5–6, for a fuller discussion of this term.
5. Tilson, *Segregation*, 25.

human groups were racial or that the building of the tower had anything to do with integration.[6]

A third point of Tilson's should have been enormously embarrassing to segregationists. The genealogy of Jesus in the Gospel of Matthew includes "Rachab, a woman of the Canaanites . . . , a people begotten by Canaan (Gen 10:18–19), one of the four sons of Ham (Gen 6:10)—the one, in fact, on whom the curse fell!"[7] On the assumption that Canaan was black, and on the view among white supremacists that even the tiniest element of black descent renders a person black, Jesus himself would have to be considered black.

While segregationists affirmed the presence of blacks in the Bible precisely as persons placed in subjugation by God, most white biblical scholars believed that they played only a negligible role in the biblical story. African American scholars such as Charles B. Copher and Cain Hope Felder, however, have shown that blacks not only have a significant presence in that story but are viewed in a positive light. In Jer 38–39, for example, a Cushite[8] in the Judean king's house intervenes with the king to rescue Jeremiah from the cistern where he was imprisoned. In Gen 10, Ham's descendants are named Cush, Egypt, Put, and Canaan; and Cush's son Nimrod is called "the first on earth to become a mighty warrior" and "a mighty hunter before the LORD" (10:8–9). Two black queens, moreover, appear in the biblical narratives. One is the queen of Sheba, who visits Solomon in 1 Kgs 10 and 2 Chr 9 and is called the queen of the South in Matt 12:42 and Luke 11:31. The second is "the Candace, queen of the Ethiopians," in Acts 8:27.

Of particular interest is the account in Num 12 of the criticism of Moses by his sister Miriam and his brother Aaron because of his marriage to a Cushite woman. Some scholars have claimed that Cush sometimes names a region in northern Arabia and that the reference is to Zipporah, Moses's Midianite wife who was introduced in Exod 2:21.[9] However, the story probably assumes that Moses took a second wife during his return to Egypt. This is suggested by Num 12:1 ("for he had indeed married a Cushite woman"); and, as Nili S. Fox observes, "Nubia [Cush] was part of the Egyptian empire."[10] More significantly, as Felder notes, the Septuagint

6. Ibid.

7. Ibid., 34

8. Most translations render the Hebrew *Cushite* as "Ethiopian," following the Septuagint, although Cush was probably another African region, south of Egypt.

9. See, however, Bailey, "Beyond Identification" in Felder, *Stony the Road*, 165–68.

10. Fox, "Numbers: Introduction," 308. Fox also notes that "dark-skinned women were considered beautiful, as reflected in the Targum's [Aramaic translation's] rendition of Cushite as 'beautiful.'"

(the ancient Greek translation of the Hebrew Bible) names the woman an Ethiopian[11]; and God's punishment of Miriam—turning her skin "as white as snow"—seems to be "an intentional contrast" to "Moses' Black wife."[12] The story is thus "a rebuke to the racial prejudice characterized by the attitudes of Miriam and Aaron."[13]

Nor is Moses's Cushite wife the only black presence within the Israelite family. According to Exod 6:25, "Aaron's son Eleazar married one of the daughters of Putiel, and she bore him Phinehas." As Copher emphasizes, the name Phinehas "is from the Egyptian Pa-Neshi" and "means the Negro or Nubian, depending on a given translator."[14] Thus biblical archaeologist William F. Albright considered the name "an independent (and absolutely reliable) confirmation of the tradition that there was a Nubian element in the family of Moses (Num. 12:1)."[15] The name Putiel is also probably Egyptian, which is particularly interesting in light of strong evidence that ancient Egypt was, despite the denials of many Western Egyptologists, "intimately (culturally, linguistically, and racially) a part of Black Africa."[16]

It is clear, in short, that "the Bible contains no narratives in which the original intent was to negate the full humanity of black people or view blacks in an unfavorable way."[17] In fact, the whole notion of race is lacking in the Bible. It is actually a modern construct, which has been employed only since the seventeenth century.[18] As Parker Palmer observes, "To the extent that race is even a valid concept . . . it does not come in boxes provided by God or Mother Nature. Race is an undifferentiated continuum of gene frequencies that we break into categories through an act called concept formulation."[19] Not only do human societies place the markers that determine racial groupings, but different cultures place the markers differently; and even within a given culture the markers can shift from time to time. In the United States, for example, around the beginning of the twentieth century neither Irish nor the Italian immigrants were considered white.[20] Smedley and Smedley

---

11. Whether Cush is identified as Ethiopia or another African region is irrelevant to Felder's point; the Septuagint clearly places Cush in Africa.
12. Felder, *Troubling*, 42.
13. Ibid.
14. Copher, "Black Presence," in Felder, ed. *Stony the Road*, 152.
15. Albright, *Stone Age*; cited by Copher, "Black Presence," 155.
16. Felder, *Troubling*, 15.
17. Felder, "Race, Racism," in Felder, ed., *Stony*, 127.
18. West, *Prophetic Fragments*, 100; quoted in Felder, "Race, Racism," 128.
19. Palmer, *Courage*, 130.
20. Gallagher, *Rethinking*, 1.

can thus report that "most geneticists and biological anthropologists agree with the idea that human races, in any kind of biological sense, do not really exist. Human variation . . . is extraordinarily complex, and *there is much greater variation within a population than between populations.*"[21] Because human communities have divided the genetic continuum into distinct categories, however, race is a *social* reality that we ignore only at our peril.

## Bible Lesson 2: On the Nature of the Biblical Writings

My second lesson involved interpreting biblical writings in light of their original historical contexts. On one level, this hardly seems controversial: to understand the Gospel of Matthew, for example, we should try to understand when, why, and perhaps where the author wrote. When we allow historical considerations to enter the picture, however, we encounter evidence that can be disturbing to persons who take everything in the Bible at face value.

Scholars have long been convinced, for example, that the Pentateuch (or Torah, the first five books of the Hebrew Bible, traditionally attributed to Moses) is actually composed of earlier strands of material that appeared at various times in Israel's long history. The evidence is overwhelming: variations in the name of God, competing versions of the same story, different theological perspectives that appear in correlation with different writings styles and vocabulary. Similarly, a comparison of Matthew, Mark, and Luke suggests that some kind of literary dependence was at work in their composition. That is, some writers have copied from and edited others. It thus becomes difficult to hold to the widespread doctrines of verbal inspiration and inerrancy[22] of the Scriptures. If a biblical writer edits earlier material, that writer is undoubtedly more interested in making a theological point than in reporting historical fact; and if the first five books of the Bible are a composite of earlier documents, they cannot have been dictated to Moses by God as a long-standing tradition has claimed.

I do not know how I came to accept the doctrines of verbal inspiration and inerrancy, because I was not taught them in the Methodist Church. The

---

21. Smedley and Smedley, *Race*, 300; italics added.

22. Verbal inspiration means that every word of the Bible is directly inspired (in essence, dictated) by God; inerrancy means that the Bible is totally accurate in all details and free from error. Both doctrines are often qualified by the stipulation that they apply only to the original (autograph) versions of the various writings. Such a qualification is virtually meaningless, however, since we do not have any autograph copies.

literalist or fundamentalist approach was a pervasive aspect of southern culture, however, so I was probably influenced by radio evangelists and peers from more conservative churches. In any case, thinking my way out of this view was more difficult than struggling free from my inherited racist views. Eventually, however, it was as liberating as that other struggle, because it allowed me to approach the Scriptures in a more enlivening way. It freed me from taking such stories as the creation accounts in Genesis or Noah and the flood literally and allowed me to appreciate in a new way the messages such stories convey. It also prepared me to deal with other problematic aspects of the Bible, such as certain views regarding women and slavery and images of God as a vindictive tyrant.

## Bible Lesson 3:
## On Seeing the Bigger Picture; Human Unity in the Biblical Story

If Bible lessons 1 and 2 freed me from unhelpful approaches to Scripture, the third lesson made the positive point that the unity of humankind is central to the biblical faith. Biblical scholars have often wrestled with "the scandal of particularity." Recognizing the Bible's strong emphasis on God's universal love for humankind, they could not ignore a "particularist" strain of teaching that seemed to stand in tension with it. The Hebrew Bible proclaims Israel as God's chosen people and stresses its separateness from other nations, and parts of the New Testament proclaim Jesus Christ as the only means of salvation. Both versions of particularism have raised questions for people of biblical faith. The force of lesson 3, however, is that the Bible's emphasis on God's all-embracing love undercuts all strains of teaching that set one group above another.

The notion that Israel is God's chosen people is central to the Hebrew Bible, and it is related to the concepts of covenant and promise.[23] God chooses Israel for a special relationship, or covenant. God also promises to bless the people, and the people accept the responsibility to obey the divine laws. These laws, both moral and ritual in nature, ensure Israel's holiness—a concept that has to do with apartness from what is ordinary. The Israelites must keep themselves separate from other peoples, who do not have God's law, lest they damage their holiness. Israel's apartness, however, was not absolute. Although one might think that only Israelites could live in the promised land, various passages accept the presence of "aliens" among them; and Lev 17:15–16 applies laws of purity to all persons in the land, whether citizen or alien. Also, some passages "seem to permit something

---

23. See Kaminsky, "Chosen."

akin to conversion (Exod 12:48–49),"[24] and Lev 19:33–34 commands the Israelites not only to treat the aliens as citizens but to love them.

It is also important to understand the role that Israel plays in the biblical drama as a whole. In the story of the garden of Eden, Adam and Eve are presented simply as human beings, not as Israelites; and when in 3:20 Adam names his wife Eve, *"because she was the mother of all living,"* it becomes clear that all humankind issues from this primordial couple. This verse completely negates the "pre-Adamite" theory, according to which God created a race of beings prior to Adam and Eve from which Cain took his wife in 4:17. Racist versions of this theory identified the pre-Adamites as black and sometimes went so far as to "regard the 'Negro' as . . . the tempter of Eve in the Garden of Eden."[25] The plain sense of the creation stories in Genesis, however, is that *all human beings are descended from Adam and Eve, whom God blesses by placing them in an environment designed for their well-being.*

When the sin of Adam and Eve disrupts this well-being, humanity enters a downward spiral described in chapters 4–11. Cain murders his brother Abel in 4:8, and the world eventually becomes so filled with wickedness that God decides to give it a new start by sending a flood to destroy all living beings except the righteous Noah, his family, and the animals they save (chapters 6–9). Again, however, wickedness prevails and God intervenes in two ways—first, through the dispersion of humankind at the Tower of Babel (Gen 11:1–9) and, second, through the call of Abraham (Gen 12:1–3).

The latter two stories are complementary. The dispersion of humankind separates people into distinct groups, and the call of Abraham works within this framework of separateness: God's new strategy is to work primarily with a single group of people. The purpose of the strategy, however, is to bring blessing to all humankind, as we see in God's promise to Abraham in 12:2–3: "I will bless you, and make your name great, so that you will be a blessing. I will bless those who bless you, and the one who curses you I will curse; and *in you all the families of the earth shall be blessed.*" Despite the negative note about the curse, the point is that all human groups will potentially be blessed through Abraham.

Along similar lines, Isa 2:2–4 envisions a future in which all nations will stream to Jerusalem to learn the ways of Israel's God. Even more poignantly, the book of Jonah is a sharp critique of ethnic exclusivism. The prophet flees to avoid God's call to preach to the city of Nineveh, capital of the hated Assyrian Empire. God persists, however, and Jonah carries out the divine command; but when people repent, he grows angry. Presumably

---

24. Ibid., 596.
25. Copher, "Black Presence," 150.

hoping that the repentance is temporary and God will eventually destroy the city, he sits under a bush God has provided and waits. When God makes the bush wither, Jonah grows even angrier; and the book concludes with God's ironic indictment: "You are concerned about the bush, for which you did not labor and which you did not grow; it came into being in a night and perished in a night. And *should I not be concerned about Nineveh, that great city, in which there are more than a hundred and twenty thousand persons who do not know their right hand from their left, and also many animals?"* (Jonah 4:10b–11).

In the New Testament, the risen Jesus commands his apostles to carry his message "to the ends of the earth" (Acts 1:8) and "to make disciples of all nations" (Matt 28:19). In Acts 17:26, the apostle Paul declares that *"from one ancestor[26] [God] made all nations to inhabit the whole earth."* And in the story of Pentecost, when Jesus's followers speak in other languages under the power of the Holy Spirit, people from all over the world hear them "speaking in the native language of each" (Acts 2:6). The symbolism is clear: the language barrier that fragmented humanity at Babel has been broken down. The story of the baptism of the Ethiopian eunuch in Acts 8:26–40, moreover, makes clear that the gospel's inclusiveness extends to all people, regardless of their skin color. As Clarice Martin observes, any reader in the Roman Empire would have known that a native of Ethiopia would be black.[27] In addition, *lest anyone argue for an inclusive but segregated community*, Paul insists that the gospel leaves no room for divisions within the church: *"There is no longer Jew or Greek, there is no longer slave or free, there is no longer male and female; for all of you are one in Christ Jesus"* (Gal 3:28).

That the New Testament presents the gospel as available to all persons is indisputable. Many Christians, however, interpret it as promoting a form of religious exclusivism, the notion that salvation is available only to those who make an explicit profession of faith in Jesus Christ. This view, however, is based largely on two passages. In the first, John 14:6, Jesus says, "I am the way, and the truth, and the life. No one comes to the Father except through me." In the second, Acts 4:12, the apostle Peter says, "There is salvation in no one else, for there is no other name under heaven given among mortals by which we must be saved." To begin with, however, the claim that Jesus is the only source of salvation does not necessarily mean that only those who explicitly name him as their savior have access to the salvation he brings. More important, there are other passages in the New Testament implying

---

26. Some biblical manuscripts read "one blood."
27. Martin, "Chamberlain's Journey," 110–14.

that God might make salvation available on some other basis.[28] In Matt 25:31–46, for example, Jesus offers an imaginative description of the Last Judgment in which acceptance by God seems to rest not upon any profession of faith at all but rather on deeds of mercy. And in Rom 4, Paul seems to treat the faith of Abraham, which is trust directly in God rather than in Christ, as an equivalent of Christian faith.

## Bible Lesson 4: On Scripture, Tradition, Reason, and Experience[29]

Over the years, I became increasingly aware of the variations in perspective in the Bible and to celebrate this phenomenon because it helped me deal with the disturbing elements in the Scriptures. If we recognize these different perspectives, the simplistic proof-texting that proponents of segregation and others often engage in tends to fall apart. The Bible gives no support to race-based discrimination, but there are portions that sanction slavery (e.g., Exod 21:2–11; Lev 25:39–55) and others that demand the subordination of women (e.g., 1 Tim 2:8–15). Other passages, however, call these aspects of Scripture into question. Paul's letter to Philemon, for example, implies that it is unacceptable for a Christian to hold another Christian as a slave[30] (although proponents of slavery interpreted this letter in exactly the opposite way). And both Jesus's interaction with women and Paul's practice of accepting them in leadership positions[31] undermine all gender-based restrictions. In some passages, the Bible presents God as vindictive, commanding the destruction of all inhabitants in the cities of Canaan (Josh 6:17, 21; 8:2), punishing the *descendants* of sinners for three and four generations (Exod 20:5). On the other hand, the Bible defines God's very being in terms of love (1 John 4:7) and stresses divine forbearance and forgiveness (Ps 103:8; 1 John 1:9).

So, what does an interpreter who takes the Bible seriously (but not literally) do with these discrepancies? First, we should look beyond individual passages to identify the most central aspects of the overarching story of redemption. Second, we should test out each of the variant strands of biblical teaching in light of our experience in our contemporary world. Some of

---

28. See Pregeant, *Christology*.

29. This combination of four sources of authority is known in Methodist circles as the Wesleyan Quadrilateral.

30. See Petersen, *Rediscovering*.

31. E.g., Rom 16:1–7; Phil 4:2–3.

these strands cohere with the larger story and some do not; and some make sense in light of what we know in other ways and others do not.

To approach the Bible this way is to understand it not as something static but as part of a process that involves three factors alongside Scripture itself: tradition, reason, and experience. This process begins with human experiences that people interpret, through the use of reason, as encounters with God. Because these experiences have changed their lives, they pass them on to others and thus create tradition. At first, tradition is oral, but in time it takes on written form. Then people collect the various strands of tradition into writings that are eventually accepted as scripture. Religious communities that pass on tradition and maintain scriptures do so because they take them as in some sense authoritative. If, however, we understand that Scripture is part of this ongoing *process*, it makes little sense to cut that process off at the point at which tradition becomes Scripture, since Scripture itself stands in need of interpretation. Thus a new stage of *tradition* begins and evolves as people experience Scripture in new situations. I would thus argue that being faithful to Scripture does not mean taking all aspects of the writings of the Bible as absolute and final but entering into the process that moves from experience through tradition to Scripture and back to tradition through the avenue of experience.

## THE INNER MOTIVATION: GETTING TO THE HEART OF BIBLICAL ETHICS

To read the Bible as I am suggesting is to challenge all the patterns of exclusion and domination that we have inherited from the ancient world. In the parable of the Good Samaritan (Luke 10:25–37), Jesus undermined the Judean prejudice against the Samaritans by making a Samaritan the hero of his story. By having this person, despised because of his ethnicity, act with the compassion that neither of the religious functionaries of Judean society would extend, he forced his listeners to pronounce the Samaritan good.[32] In doing so, Jesus shattered a boundary that divided person from person, and thus defined God's coming realm as something that disrupts all attempts to set one group over another. Similarly, in the parable of the Great Supper (Luke 14:16–24) Jesus dismantled all social hierarchies with a twist in the plot that has the people of the streets replacing those invited guests who have refused the host's invitation. As John Dominic Crossan has argued, the fact that the host's servants invite those encountered at random ensures that persons of different social classes will sit at table with one another. Within

---

32. Crossan, *Parables*, 63–64.

the context of ancient Mediterranean society, this parable was radically disruptive, since table fellowship was a social ritual in which "distinctions among foods and guests mirror[ed] social distinctions, discriminations, and hierarchies."[33] The offense was not the invitation of the poor but rather the mixing of social classes. Jesus's rejection of all social hierarchies, moreover, is clear from passages such as Luke 11:43: "Woe to you Pharisees! For you love to have the seat of honor in the synagogues and to be greeted with respect in the marketplaces."

So far, I have not taken note of what many persons consider the heart of biblical ethics: the commandment to love one's neighbor as oneself. I have delayed discussion of this commandment because of the abstract nature of the concept of love; one can understand it in a variety of ways. It can, for example, take a paternalistic form: the master can love the slave, and the husband the subordinate wife, as a parent loves a child. In fact, the Bible uses the term in this way in some instances (Eph 5:21-33). When the injunction to love the neighbor is qualified by the phrase "as oneself," however, the paternalistic interpretation fails; and both the pervasive biblical emphasis on human unity and Jesus's rejection of social hierarchies make it impossible to interpret his use of the commandment in this way. In Jesus's mouth it is a call to a radical egalitarianism that treats all persons as not only of equal worth but of equal standing in the community and before God.

In the Hebrew Bible, we find the love command in Lev 19:18, and in the New Testament it appears in the Gospels and the Letters. Its centrality is attested particularly by Matthew's version, where Jesus says of the dual injunction to love God and the neighbor that "on these two commandments hang all the law and the prophets" (22:40). This sentiment is paralleled by Paul's declaration that "the whole law is summed up in a single commandment, 'You shall love your neighbor as yourself.'" (Gal 5:14) And 1 John 4:20 goes so far as to say that one cannot love God without loving one's neighbor. Luke's version of the love command, moreover, undermines any attempt to limit the meaning of *neighbor* with ethnic restrictions; for it introduces the parable of the Good Samaritan, which is Jesus's answer to the question, who is my neighbor?

Although the love command does not give concrete instructions on its implementation, it provides the inner motivation for all ethical actions. Rather than an end in itself, it is a beginning point. To love one's neighbors in the fullest sense is not simply to feel a certain way toward them; it is to be motivated to do for them what is right and just. That does not mean to take over their lives as patrons; it means to treat them as persons equal to

---

33. Crossan, *Historical Jesus*, 262.

oneself, to be with them in their joys and sorrows, and to work beside them when they seek freedom from injustice and oppression. As James Cone says, "authentic love is not 'help,' not giving Christmas baskets but working for political, social, and economic justice, which always means a redistribution of power. It is a kind of power which enables the blacks to fight their own battles and thus keep their dignity."[34] During the 1960s, many white Christians argued against civil rights legislation on the grounds that we "cannot legislate love." That contention is true as far as it goes, but it misses the point. We cannot force anyone to love someone else, but we can work to secure the rights of all through legislation and enforcement of the law. We cannot legislate love, but we can legislate justice; and for persons of biblical faith, love is the motivation for doing so.

The biblical vision, however, looks beyond justice as a matter of law to the ideal of a community held together by the bonds of love. Dr. Martin Luther King Jr. spoke of such a society as the "beloved community," and people of biblical faith should hope for no less as our ultimate goal for our country. The question now before us is how this land, which declared its independence with a document endorsing the notion of equality, measures up against the biblical vision that includes both justice and love. This is the question I will pursue in chapters 4 and 5.

---

34. Cone, *Black Theology*, 57.

4

# Ideology against the Bible
## A Judgment on the Past

> I think that the past is all that makes the present coherent, and further, that the past will remain horrible for exactly as long as we refuse to assess it honestly ... I love America more than any other country in this world, and, exactly for this reason, I insist on the right to criticize [it] perpetually.
>
> —James Baldwin, 1955[1]

### WORLDVIEWS IN CONFLICT: "COMES THE MOMENT TO DECIDE"

"We should judge people by the times in which they lived." David McCullough, author of a biography of John Adams, reflected on this sentiment in a speech at the historic Adams House in Quincy, Massachusetts. He expressed agreement with this notion in relation to the issue of slavery. This institution was deeply engrained in the culture of the United States in the eighteenth century, and we should take that into account in evaluating the people of that time who held slaves or supported the

---

1. Baldwin, "Autobiographical Notes," 7, 9.

institution. McCullough urged us, however, to remember that John and Abigail Adams, both of whom were strong abolitionists, were also part of those times. There are always persons who see beyond the conventions of the time and are courageous enough to challenge them, even though there are many more who simply conform to the times. Jefferson had reason indeed to tremble, not only for his country because of slavery, but also for himself as a slaveholder and as one whose own written statements contributed enormously to the ideology of black inferiority![2] Granted that we should avoid the easy self-righteousness of retrospection, we must state unequivocally that the historical treatment of African Americans in this country stands in direct violation of the biblical visions of justice, human unity, and love of neighbor.

We should also remember that place undergoes constant change. There are fateful moments in life in which circumstances give rise to new visions and with them the necessity of decision. James Russell Lowell captured the drama of such moments in powerful verse: "Once to every man [sic] and nation comes the moment to decide, / in the strife of Truth with Falsehood, for the good or evil side." Lowell's "once" is not to be taken literally but rather as a poetic acknowledgement that our choices take place in real time, which is irreversible. Hence the later line: "And the choice goes by forever, 'twixt that darkness and that light."[3] Many of those who were imprisoned in the ideology of the "Southern Way of Life" in my youth may have had limited opportunities to break out of it; but when the race issue burst in full bloom onto the national scene, one could no longer hide from the issue. Confronted with the realities of segregation, we in the South were forced to decide where to stand. The principle is simple: the more knowledge we have, the greater degree of responsibility we have to mend our faults—or, to use the biblical terminology, to *repent of our sins*.

## A GOD WHO TROUBLES THE WATER

It is difficult to admit new knowledge when it challenges our symbolic universe. Rigid attachment to the past, however, is incompatible with biblical faith since the Bible presents God not as the enforcer of a static state of things but as a dynamic actor on the stage of history. In the exodus from Egypt, God upsets the system that depended upon the labor of Hebrew slaves. In Isa 45, a prophet envisions God as empowering the Persian king

---

2. Smedley and Smedley, *Race*, 177–86.
3. Lowell, "Present Crisis."

Cyrus to topple the Babylonian Empire in order to send the Judean exiles home. And the book of Revelation prophesies God's destruction of Rome, naming slavery as one of its evils (chapters 17–18). Nor is it empires alone that we find dismantled in the Bible; the biblical traditions themselves also undergo challenge and change. The book of Job is a critique of the theology of retribution, of the notion that God rewards the good and punishes the evil in this life, which is so central to other parts of the Hebrew Bible. And in the Gospel of Mark, Jesus not only challenges "the traditions of the elders" on the issue of handwashing before meals (15:1–8) but undercuts the dietary regulations in Leviticus when he proclaims that "there is nothing outside a person that by going in can defile" (15:15). In Gal 5:2–6, moreover, Paul denies that the biblical requirement for circumcision applies to Gentile converts.

As the African American spiritual "Wade in the Water" proclaims, "God's gonna trouble the water." That is, God is free to upset any social system or custom that stands in the way of God's vision of the future. These other lines from Lowell's poem are thus quite in keeping with biblical faith: "New occasions teach new duties; Time makes ancient good uncouth."[4] Openness to the new is not apostasy but a sign of healthy faith. It is unwillingness to entertain the possibility that change is necessary that is in fact an act of unfaithfulness, and it is just such unwillingness that characterized the South in which I grew up. In 1963, James W. Silver, a professor at the University of Mississippi, published a book titled *Mississippi: The Closed Society*. The title gets to heart of the issue, and it could apply to the other states of the Deep South as well as to Mississippi. The race issue was simply not up for discussion:

> The all-pervading doctrine . . . has been white supremacy, whether achieved through slavery or segregation, rationalized by a professed belief in state rights and bolstered by religious fundamentalism. In such a society a never-ceasing propagation of the "true faith" must go on relentlessly, with a constantly reiterated demand for loyalty to the united front, requiring that non-conformists and dissenters from the code be silenced, or, in a crisis, driven from the community. Violence and the threat of violence have confirmed and enforced the image of unanimity.[5]

More specifically, this orthodoxy "contended that the Negro, member of an inferior race, unmoved by the ambition and aspiration that motivated the white [person], would labor only under compulsion and was incapable

4. Ibid.
5. Silver, *Mississippi*, 6.

of living without a master."[6] Philosophically, these views depend upon the acceptance of the hierarchically ordered symbolic universe I mentioned in chapter 3, and it is important now to flesh this worldview out in more detail.

## THE BIBLE AND HUMAN HIERARCHIES

This understanding of reality was in full force during medieval times, but its roots reach much further back. Most important for our purposes is the contribution of ancient Greek philosophy, most particularly the thought of Plato and Aristotle. At the heart of Plato's thought was a dualism of mind and matter. According to this perspective, only the world of ideas is truly real; physical phenomena are but a dim reflection of that ethereal realm. A table that we can touch or see, for example, is an imperfect attempt to replicate the *ideal* table—that is, the very idea of "tableness" itself. More important, abstract qualities such as goodness or justice on the human level must be judged by the eternal notions of perfect goodness and perfect justice, which exist only in the realm of ideas.

A positive aspect of this view is that it undermines the notion that ideals such as goodness and justice have no firmer basis than human opinion. For Plato, they are grounded in the nature of the universe itself. A problem arises, however, when we note how Plato applied this view to human society; for he divided humanity into three distinct classes that he placed on a hierarchical scale descending from the ideal, mental world to the merely physical. In his ideal society, or Republic, there were the philosopher-kings, who were qualified to rule because of their wisdom or understanding of the world of ideas. In the middle were those with less capacity, whose job it was to enforce the decisions of the rulers; and at the bottom were those who were qualified only for the more menial tasks. Plato, in other words, had a very low opinion of the intelligence of the great masses of humankind, which resulted in an elitist disdain for democracy and acceptance of a type of dictatorship of the intellectually gifted.

As Western civilization developed through the centuries, it owed much to the Platonic-Aristotelian worldview. The combination of hierarchy with the mind-matter dualism resulted in a vision of the universe that some have termed the Great Chain of Being. According to this scheme, the higher elements in the universe are more spiritual as well as intellectual, and the lower elements more material and thus farther from the divine and of less intellectual capacity. It thus seemed natural that the higher elements should rule over the lower. And in various times and places this vision was invoked

---

6. Ibid., 12.

to justify imperial conquest, the divine right of kings, the subordination of women, the exploitation of the labor of serfs, slavery, and—as in the world of my youth—white supremacy.

Those who supported the notion of the Great Chain of Being pointed not only to Greek thought but also to the Bible to justify their views. After all, the God of the Bible is creator of and sovereign over the universe, and Israel was in some periods governed by kings. However, the major thrust of the biblical understanding of the universe is very different. The physical world is not only real but also "very good," as Gen 1 declares. The apostle Paul makes a distinction between spirit and flesh, but the terms do not refer to a mind-matter dualism. When he indicts those who live "according to the flesh" (Rom 8:1–8), he refers not to material reality but to a way of life that is under the sway of the power of sin and that ignores the spirit. Paul's respect for the physical is evident in the fact that he can use the term "body" in a positive way and understands the afterlife in terms of the *transformation*, not replacement, of fleshly, perishable bodies into spiritual, immortal realities that he still terms *bodies*.[7] Throughout the Bible, moreover, we find references to God's eventual redemption of the physical world. In Rev 21, for example, the "new earth" that appears at the end of the age is clearly material in nature, although united with heaven.

The Bible thus provides only the most superficial support for the disparagement of physical reality. Furthermore, it does not give unambiguous support for notions such as the divine right of kings. The strain of thought in the Hebrew Bible according to which God instituted Israel's monarchy is in tension with another strain according to which the people's request for a king was an act of apostasy. In 1 Sam 8:7, God makes this reply to Samuel after the people ask for a king: "They have not rejected you, but they have rejected me from being king over them." Then, in the following verses (10–14), Samuel issues a blistering indictment of monarchical rule. In the New Testament, when Jesus chooses twelve of his followers to form an inner leadership circle, he looks not to an elite group such as the Sadducees or Pharisees—in fact, he is in constant conflict with the official hierarchy—but rather to the lower classes. To enlist Jesus in support of an ideology of class distinctions is to turn the entire thrust of his teaching upside down.

In sum, *central aspects of biblical teaching stand in judgment not only of slavery and segregation but also of the hierarchical worldview that supported them.* To say this to a white southerner in the mid-twentieth century, however, would have invited the objection that it was actually the South that stood against hierarchical rule by virtue of its dedication to localism. It was

---

7. E.g., Rom 8:11, 23; 1 Cor 6:19–20; 15:42–55.

the South, after all, that advocated states' rights and home rule in matters such as education, with the issue of busing to achieve school integration as the test case. And it was the South that invoked the doctrines of nullification and interposition, which asserted the rights of states to refuse to comply with federal laws they deemed unconstitutional. Such an objection, however, is rank hypocrisy: *before the Civil War, the South rejected these same doctrines when they were invoked in opposition to slavery.*[8]

## POLITICS, THE BIBLE, AND THE CIVIL RIGHTS STRUGGLE

The South was solidly in the camp of the Democratic Party, both in the decades preceding the Civil War and during the Jim Crow era that followed. The civil rights movement, however, caused a deep split between North and South in the party.[9] Symptomatic of this split were the congressional votes on the 1964 Civil Rights Act, which banned discrimination on the basis of race, color, religion, sex or national origin in matters of hiring, firing, and promotion, as well as segregation in schools and public accommodations. Among southern Democrats, the tally on the original House version was 7 yeas and 87 nays, while their northern counterparts registered 145–9 in favor.[10] The Democratic vote on the Senate version, which ultimately prevailed, was 1 for and 20 against the bill among the southerners, and 45 in favor and 1 against by the northerners. Quite clearly, for the southern Democrats the ideology of white supremacy trumped the party's professed dedication to the interests of the common person that dates back to Andrew Jackson[11] and was reinforced by Franklin Roosevelt. In fact, the split in the party exposed an inherent tension in the southern ideology: the doctrine of white supremacy depended upon a hierarchical model of the universe, while commitment to the interests of the common people implied a much more egalitarian understanding.

The Republican Party was extremely weak in the mid-twentieth century South, because of its strong antislavery stance before the Civil War and its role in Reconstruction. The few southern Republicans in the House,

---

8. Silver, *Mississippi*, 7.

9. Here the term "South" refers to the eleven states that seceded from the Union, while "North" refers to all other states without regard to geographical location.

10. Voting totals cited from "Civil Rights Act of 1964."

11. In Jackson's case, however, this dedication was limited by racial considerations. He held slaves and was responsible for some of this country's most inhumane treatment of Native Americans (see ahead, chapter 14).

however, followed suit with their Democratic counterparts on the civil rights bill: 0 yeas and 10 nays on the original House version, and 0 yeas and 1 nay in the Senate. Among the northern Republicans, on the other hand, the original House version prevailed 138–24, and the Senate version prevailed 27–5. Clearly, the bill, although sponsored by a Democratic administration, would not have passed without strong support from northern Republicans. This landmark bill thus stands as an important reminder of a time in which cooperation between the two major parties, in the interests of justice and the common good, was possible.

Although major opposition to the bill came from the South, the number of negative votes from other regions was not insignificant. What ideological commitments could have been at work in these votes? At least one nonsouthern senator, Democrat Robert Byrd of West Virginia (a former member of the Ku Klux Klan who changed his views markedly over time and repeatedly expressed regret over the past) shared the South's commitment to segregation. The broader answer, however, lies in a combination of a commitment to states' rights, a professed belief in individual liberties, and deference toward business interests.

Some of these commitments were already visible in the negotiations prior to the final passage. Senator Dirksen of Illinois, the Republican minority leader, was able to bring many of his party members on board only after getting the northern Democrats to agree (1) to weaken provisions for "federal enforcement against job discrimination and segregation by private businesses" and (2) "to give higher priority to voluntary compliance and greater private legal initiatives (as opposed to Federal intervention)."[12] Apparently, however, the bill was not weakened enough for some opponents outside the South, presumably because it still involved federal power and still curtailed such "rights" as that "to refuse service to anyone." In any case, the controversy surrounding the most famous instance of nonsouthern opposition is perhaps the most instructive: that of Senator Barry Goldwater of Arizona, later the Republican nominee for president. Goldwater himself cited states' rights as his guiding principle, but many of his defenders "claim that his opposition to the Act was a defense of individual liberty—the right of a business owner to choose which customers to serve or reject."[13] As one commentator observes, however, such reasoning

> ignores the fact that southern states and cities mandated segregation by law. If it's a violation of individual freedom for the Federal government to prohibit a business from practicing racial

12. Civil Rights Movement Veterans, "Civil Rights Bill Battle."
13. Ibid., 22.

discrimination, then it must also be a violation of individual liberty for a state government to **require** race discrimination . . . [S]upport for a state's right to mandate segregation by law directly contradicts an individual-liberty stand.[14]

The hypocrisy of the individual-rights argument is well illustrated by a Louisiana law, which was eventually declared unconstitutional, prohibiting racially integrated meetings. This came home to me as a college student at an interracial meeting of the Methodist Student Movement, held in the University Methodist Church near the LSU campus. As we sat in the sanctuary listening to one of the adult leaders give instructions on what to do in case of a bomb threat, we were also aware that those sworn to enforce the law posed a threat of a different sort. Would we be arrested, in a blatant violation of our constitutional right to peaceable assembly, for sitting together, black and white, in a religious gathering?

The argument based on individual liberty also ignores the communal dimension of human society. There is a reason we speak of "public accommodations" even when we are referring to private businesses. Restaurants, for example, are inherently public because their purpose is to serve the general populace. The Bible, moreover, is pervaded by a strong emphasis upon community. Throughout the Hebrew Bible, God shows concern for Israel precisely as a *people*. Lev 26:12 is a typical expression of such a sense of communality: "And I will walk among you, and will be your God, and you shall be my people." In the New Testament, we find a corresponding emphasis on the church as the community of God's people. The apostle Paul, for example, envisions the church as an organic unity, which he terms "the body of Christ." As he writes in 1 Corinthians, "For just as the body is one and has many members, and all the members of the body, though many, are one body, so it is with Christ . . . If one member suffers, all suffer together with it; if one member is honored, all rejoice together with it" (1 Cor 12:12, 26). Paul also expresses concern for the welfare of the group as a whole when he addresses problems in the Corinthian church. Although he agrees with some members that eating food that had been dedicated to idols will not harm them, he asks those members to forgo their prerogative to eat such food if doing so will confuse others and risk shaking their faith. (1 Cor 8:1–13; 10:14–22) Similarly, when dealing with a question about worship practices in 1 Cor 14, Paul lays down a criterion for making a judgment on such issues. The question to ask is whether or not a practice builds up the *church*, not simply whether the individual has the "right" to such practice.

---

14. Ibid.; italics original.

Paul's statement on eating food offered to idols, however, shows that concern for the community means concern for *each individual*; and this is consistent with his declaration that persons in the community are *individually* members of the body.

We can therefore identify the biblical ideal neither as a collectivism that ignores the individual nor as an individualism with no regard for the community. It is rather a respect for individuals precisely as beings who are fundamentally communal in nature. Thus the African American philosopher-theologian Cornel West identifies the Christian ideal for society as the *"principle of self-realization of individuality within community."*[15] And, as we see in the baptismal formula in Gal 3:28, which obliterates distinctions made on the basis of ethnicity, sex, or social status, the biblical vision of community is specifically egalitarian in nature.

The respect for individual liberties that we know today was widely promoted by philosophers and political theorists by the time Thomas Jefferson penned the Declaration of Independence with its assertion of the "inalienable" rights of all persons to "life, liberty, and the pursuit of happiness." Against the background of traditional societies governed by monarchs and characterized by rigid class distinctions ranging from nobility to peasantry, this new emphasis made a positive contribution that remains important in our time. Eventually, however, it gave rise to an extreme form of libertarianism that understands the individual as free from nearly all constraints by society or government. This one-sided view of freedom is a gross distortion of biblical values as well as of the vision of our country's founders. As John E. Hill demonstrates from sources such as the Mayflower Compact and the writings of John Adams, Thomas Jefferson, John Marshall, and others, those who contributed most to the founding of this country understood individual rights within the context of a strong emphasis upon community and a concern for the common good.[16]

Our modern, secular society is neither a theocracy such as ancient Israel nor a community such as a church bound together by a common theological affirmation. However, the biblical hope for the rule or realm of God on earth, expressed in Matt 6:10, authorizes us to work for the realization of the kind of communal society in the secular realm that Paul envisioned for the church. The extreme forms of libertarian thought we have developed in this country thus stand under just as severe a judgment when examined in light of biblical thought as the hierarchical worldview does, discussed above.

15 West, *Prophesy Deliverance*, 16; italics original.
16. Hill, *Democracy*, 83–103.

When the United States declared its independence from Great Britain and formed a government dedicated to justice, the general welfare, and liberty—as explicitly stated in the Preamble to the Constitution—it took a quantum leap on the stage of human history by offering an ideal that in important ways mirrored the biblical ideal of a "beloved community." It has thus inspired many movements in other lands to pursue their own courses toward freedom, democracy, and the respect for human and civil rights. Both the protesters in China's Tiananmen Square in 1989 and those who began challenging autocratic rulers in the Middle East in 2011 reflect values enshrined in our Declaration of Independence. What I have tried to show, however, is something that I take no joy in observing. Despite the many aspects of this country we have every right to celebrate, we have much to answer for when judged by our own stated ideals as well as biblical standards. As a nation, we have worshiped at the altars of idolatrous philosophical perspectives that undermine the biblical ideal of human solidarity. This judgment, however, has to do with our past. Where are we *now*?

# 5

# Adorning the Tombs of the Prophets

## Assessing the Present

"Woe to you, scribes and Pharisees, hypocrites! For you build the tombs of prophets and decorate the graves of the righteous, and you say, 'If we had lived in the days of our ancestors, we would not have taken part with them in shedding the blood of the prophets.' Thus you testify against yourselves that you are descendants of those who murdered the prophets. Fill up, then, the measure of your ancestors."

—MATTHEW 23:29–32

There is an old African proverb: "When you pray, move your feet." As a nation, if we care about the Beloved Community, we must move our feet, our hands, our hearts, our resources to build and not tear down, to reconcile and not to divide, to heal and not to kill. In the final analysis, we are one people, one family, one house—the American house, the American family.

—JOHN LEWIS, 1998[1]

1. Lewis, *Walking*, 503.

AFTER MANY YEARS IN New England, my wife and I have moved back south, to the mountains of northeast Georgia, where she grew up. From my study window, I can see a lovely field at the base of Screamer Mountain, where Lillian Smith lived for many years. From the mid-1920s through most of the 1940s, Smith ran a summer camp for girls there and involved them in racially integrated events—a fact that, along with her provocative novel, *Strange Fruit*, earned her the hatred of many local residents. Today, the structure where she held her camp is maintained as the Lillian E. Smith Center and houses her memorabilia; and her picture is prominently displayed in the county library. Not so many years ago I would have been astonished to know that she was in some measure honored here. And sometimes even today, when I see blacks and whites dining together at restaurants in my hometown in Louisiana, I experience a degree of surprise and reflect on how much the South and the country have changed since my youth. I cannot help but wonder, however, just how deep the changes really are.

Some changes can hardly be denied. African Americans now occupy important posts in local and state governments, and here in Georgia civil rights leaders of the 1950s and '60s have held positions of great responsibility. John Lewis is the U.S. representative from the fifth congressional district, Andrew Young was ambassador to the United Nations, and Julian Bond spent twenty years in the state legislature. On another front, the black middle class has expanded greatly, and African Americans can now be found in the higher echelons of business and various professions. We have, moreover, elected and then reelected our first black president. On one level, then, we can truthfully say that we have made progress in the realization of the " dream" of which Martin Luther King Jr., as well as W. E. B. Du Bois and Langston Hughes before him, spoke and wrote so eloquently. A closer examination, however, suggests that we still have a very long way to go when it comes to both social realities and the underlying philosophies supporting the injustices that African Americans and others have suffered.

## DIVIDING THE PIE

In 1968, Dr. King spoke these words to the striking sanitation workers in Memphis:

> With Selma, Alabama, and the voting rights bill, one era of our struggle came to an end and a new era came into being. Now our struggle is for genuine equality, which means economic equality.

> For we know that it isn't enough to integrate lunch counters. What does it profit a [person] to be able to eat at an integrated lunch counter if [she or] he doesn't earn enough money to buy a cup of coffee and a hamburger?[2]

There are many voices in our society who point to the signs of progress I have noted and argue that further efforts toward achieving equality are unnecessary. However, the following excerpt from a report of United for a Fair Economy, titled "Austerity for Whom?" belies any such claim. The figures come from the U.S. Census Bureau.

> In 1947, Blacks earned 51 cents to each dollar of White median family income. By 1977, Blacks were earning 56 cents to each dollar in White income, a gain of five cents. Most of those gains were made in the 1960s. Then, as the backlash took hold, progress slowed—and stopped. By 2007, Blacks earned slightly over 57 cents (57.4¢) to each White dollar, a gain of just over one penny in thirty years. *Two years later, as the Great Recession set in, Blacks lost a half-cent, ending at 57 cents to each White dollar of median family income.*[3]

The most significant point is not the stark discrepancy between black and white incomes but the fact that we are at present moving toward even greater inequality.

The report's reference to the "backlash" is significant. The attention paid to blacks during the civil rights movement created resentment on the part of many whites, and cynical politicians seized upon this phenomenon, nurturing it with divisive rhetoric. The shift in the public mood, together with the earlier escalation of the Vietnam War under President Johnson that drained the country's resources, resulted in the virtual abandonment of serious efforts to address the issue of black-white disparity or of poverty in general. Since that time, moreover, we have witnessed growing disparity in the total population between the rich on the one hand the middle class and poor on the other. This long-term trend has had a disproportionately negative effect on groups, particularly African Americans and Latina/os, who already suffered from higher-than-average poverty rates. The growth of a black economic elite, however, has obscured the plight of those at the bottom of the economic pyramid. As is the case with the general population,

---

2. Honey, *Jericho Road*, 300; quoted in United for a Fair Economy, "Dream," 8.
3. Ali et al., "Austerity for Whom?" 8; italics added.

"gains in both Black and Latin[a/]o communities have gone disproportionately to those at the very top."[4]

> Over the last 30 years, the overwhelming share of income growth within the Black community went to the top 20 percent of families, with the top five percent receiving particularly large shares . . . The vast majority of Blacks saw minimal gains; some even lost ground . . . *The bottom 20 percent of Blacks, those earning less than $16,114, saw a decrease in their earning power, despite already living under poverty conditions.*[5]

Similarly, "of the scant income growth Latin[a/]os have experienced in the last 30 years, almost all of it went to those at the top. The bottom 40 percent of Latin[a/]os had negative income gains over the last 30 years, while the middle 20 percent barely maintained their income level."[6]

This disturbing trend, moreover, "coupled with increased economic segregation as middle-class families moved out of poor communities, has created areas of concentrated poverty where opportunities are few."[7] Poor people face hardship under any circumstances, but it is multiplied for those in neighborhoods in which almost everyone is poor. For such an environment breeds a sense of hopelessness that creates a vicious circle in which poverty is both the cause and the result of a host of other social ills:

> The concentration of poverty has profound effects on those who live in poor communities . . . It hinders access to employment, and contributes to poor health. It exposes children to high rates of crime and violence, to low quality foods and to some of the worst performing schools. Additionally, living in an impoverished neighborhood increases the likelihood that a child of any race will move down the income ladder.[8]

In *Amazing Grace: The Lives of Children and the Conscience of a Nation*, Jonathan Kozol has recorded the voices of young people living in a pocket of concentrated poverty in the South Bronx. The words of a sixteen-year-old he calls Maria are particularly moving. "Think of it this way," she begins. "If people in New York woke up one day and learned that we were gone, that we had simply died or left for somewhere else, how would they feel?" Kozol asks, "How do you think they'd feel?" Her answer is riveting:

4. Ibid., 11.
5. Ibid.; italics added.
6. Ibid.
7. Ibid.
8. Ibid., 11–12.

> *I think they'd be relieved*... I think the owners of the downtown stores would be ecstatic. They know they'd never need to see us coming in their doors, and taxi-drivers would be happy because they would never need to come here anymore. People in Manhattan could go on and lead their lives and not feel worried about being robbed and not feel guilty and not need to pay for welfare babies.[9]

No less significant are her remarkable insights into the effect of social environments on the lives of individuals:

> If you weave enough bad things into the fibers of a person's life–sickness and filth, old mattresses and other junk thrown in the streets and other ugly ruined things, and ruined people, a prison here, sewage there, drug dealers here, the homeless people over there, then give us the very worst schools anyone could think of, hospitals that keep you waiting for ten hours, police that don't show up when someone's dying, take the train that's underneath the street in the good neighborhoods and put it up above where it shuts out the sun, you can guess that life will not be very nice and children will not have much sense of being glad of who they are. Sometimes it feels like we've been buried six feet under their perceptions. This is what I feel they have accomplished."[10]

I have had enough conversations on matters such as this to anticipate a response to these statements revolving around the need for personal responsibility and positive values, and I have no intention of denying that need. However, in his book *Race Matters*, Cornel West identifies "the major enemy of black survival in America" as "neither oppression nor exploitation" but rather the "loss of hope and absence of meaning."[11] He indicts some political liberals for failing to address the issue of values lest they obscure the role of social circumstances in shaping behavior. But he is also critical of those conservatives who "talk about values and attitudes as if political and economic structures hardly exist."[12] It is easy to say that many of the problems in poverty-stricken neighborhoods could be solved by a change in attitude, but it is insensitive to preach values and responsibility to persons who see no way out of the horrific circumstances in which they feel trapped. As West observes, "How people act and live are shaped—though in no way dictated or determined—by the larger circumstances in which they

---

9. Kozol, *Amazing Grace*, 39; italics added.
10. Ibid., 39–40.
11. West, *Race Matters*, 15.
12. Ibid., 13.

find themselves. These circumstances can be changed, their limits attenuated, by positive actions to elevate conditions."[13] But what is it that creates these circumstances?

## NO CHILD LEFT BEHIND?

Many white Americans, influenced by politicians, talk show hosts, and biased media reports, believe that government programs to deal with our social ills have universally been colossal failures. This is simply untrue, however. As Linda Darling-Hammond reminds us, Lyndon Johnson's war on poverty and Great Society programs "dramatically reduced poverty, increased employment, rebuilt depressed communities, invested in preschool and K-12 education in cities and poor rural areas, desegregated schools, funded financial aid for college and invested in teacher training programs that ended teacher shortage."[14] As a result, *"The black-white reading gap shrank by two-thirds for 17-year-olds, black high school and college graduation rates more than doubled, and, in 1975, rates of college attendance among whites, blacks, and Latin[a/]os reached parity for the first and only time before or since."*[15] If this is the case, however, how do we account for the current rates of poverty and unemployment, the persistence of blighted neighborhoods, and the continued underachievement by minority students? The answer lies to some extent in the dramatic turnaround in public policy. Nearly all the programs that worked so well for a time

> were ended or shrunk in the 80s, targets of the Reagan revolution, which systematically sought to dismantle federal supports for urban and rural development, housing, social services and education. Poverty and homelessness increased sharply. As the federal education budget was cut in half, funding for urban and poor rural schools declined precipitously, desegregation aid was discontinued and teaching supports were reduced, leading to growing shortages when teacher demand increased in the late 1980s. Despite some moderate pushback during the Clinton years, the momentum toward increasing inequality was not reversed.[16]

---

13. Ibid.
14. Darling-Hammond, "Redlining," 11.
15. Ibid., 12; italics added.
16. Ibid.

Lest anyone doubt the devastating effect of poverty on student performance, moreover, Darling-Hammond reports that "in 2009 U.S. schools with fewer than 10 percent of students in poverty ranked first among all nations on the Programme for International Student Achievement tests in reading, while those serving more than 75 percent of students in poverty scored alongside nations like Serbia, ranking about fiftieth."[17] *And lest anyone doubt the relationship between funding and performance*, she adds that "*most* American states spend three times more on their wealthiest schools than they do on their poorest."[18]

To make matter worse, recent efforts to address these problems in education have often been counterproductive. For example, the No Child Left Behind program, passed with bipartisan support under the George W. Bush administration, took what Darling-Hammond terms a "test-and-punish approach" that threatens schools whose students score low on standardized tests with staff firings or even closure. This "has already made it more difficult for schools labeled as failing to attract and retain well-qualified educators—thus, ironically, reducing the quality of education for students even further."[19] The mass firings have in some cases "resulted in a less qualified teaching staff and lower achievement after the reform," and the promise of charter schools has not materialized: "The largest national studies of charters have found that while some are highly successful, *most are more likely to underperform than to outperform district-run schools serving similar students*."[20]

## THE POLICY OF MASS INCARCERATION

There is no more telling result of poverty and the vicious circle of decay to which it gives rise than the discrepancies in incarceration rates among different racial/ethnic groups. As Pamela Oliver of the University of Wisconsin–Madison summarizes, "African Americans are imprisoned at least eight times as often as European Americans, while American Indians and Hispanics are imprisoned at two to three times the European American rate ... About a third of African American men are under the supervision of the criminal justice system, and about 12% of African American men in their 20s and 30s are incarcerated."[21]

17. Ibid.
18. Ibid.
19. Ibid.
20. Ibid., 14; italics added.
21. Oliver, "Racial Disparities," 1.

Oliver also observes that the incarceration rates found among impoverished minorities are a direct result of the *greater use of incarceration for lesser offenses and drug offenses*" since the mid-1970s.[22] The disproportionate imprisonment of African Americans for drug offenses is well known, but as civil rights lawyer and Ohio State University professor Michelle Alexander has found, "*People of all colors use and sell illegal drugs at the same rates.*" Yet the offenses for which blacks are arrested and imprisoned are "*the same kinds of offenses that occur frequently in middle-class white communities and are largely ignored.*"[23] For reasons such as this, Alexander concludes that our prison system functions more as a tool for social control of people of color than as a means of crime prevention. And the irony is that it is our society's claim to "colorblindness" that feeds insensitivity to the experiences of racial groups.[24]

As to why the majority population has supported the increased use of incarceration, it is difficult to avoid the conclusion that an implicit form of racism is at work. Egged on by politicians and segments of the media, many people have come to see imprisonment as the most obvious solution to the problems, both real and imagined, in areas of concentrated poverty, populated largely by racial and ethnic minorities. This approach has proved to be a false solution, however. As Oliver comments, "high incarceration rates ruin people's lives and make the problem worse, by making it harder for young people who have done wrong to be rehabilitated, find jobs, and become productive members of society."[25] Alexander finds even more difficulties: "Ex-offenders are locked out of the legal economy. They are denied access to public housing; they are denied food stamps. And to make matters worse, they are saddled with hundreds of thousands of dollars in fees, fines, and court costs—and often the need to pay back child support." In sum, "we have . . . created a vast new legal system for racial and social control, a penal system unprecedented in world history—a system that locks the majority of black men in urban areas into a permanent underclass status. And yet we claim, as a nation, to be colorblind."[26]

Alexander also demonstrates that the permanent underclass is the result not of a rising crime rate but of consciously chosen governmental policies. "Sociologists have frequently observed that governments use punishment primarily as a tool of social control, and thus the extent of

---

22. Ibid.; italics added.
23. Alexander, "Criminal Injustice," interview by Amy Fryckholm, 22.
24. Alexander, *New Jim Crow*, esp. 1–19, 178–220.
25. Oliver, "Racial Disparities," 1.
26. Quoted in Alexander, "Criminal Injustice," 23.

punishment is often unrelated to actual crime patterns."[27] Unfortunately, this is particularly so in the United States, as we can see when we compare the crime and punishment statistics of the various Western countries:

> Although crime rates in the United States have not been markedly higher than those of other Western countries, the rate of incarceration has soared in the United States while it has remained stable or declined in other countries. Between 1960 and 1990 . . . official crime rates in Finland, Germany, and the United States were close to identical. Yet the U.S. incarceration rate quadrupled, the Finnish rate fell by 60 percent, and the German rate was stable in that period.[28]

What is most disturbing is that although now "U.S. crime rates have dipped below the international norm . . . the United States now boasts an incarceration rate that is six to ten times greater than that of other industrialized nations—a development directly related to the drug war."[29]

Our country, in short, has *chosen* to pursue a policy of mass incarceration and has *chosen* to institute enforcement policies that impact minority, and particularly black and Latina/o populations, disproportionately. If this is difficult for many of us to admit, the problem is that, as West observes, "we confine discussions about race in America to the 'problems' black people pose for whites rather than consider what this way of viewing black people reveals about us as a nation."[30]

## "BLACK LIVES MATTER"—OR DO THEY?

"I don't remember seeing anything like this in the United States of America in a long time." These are the words of a television journalist, as quoted by Kareem Abdul-Jabbar, concerning the 2015 uprising in a black neighborhood of Baltimore following the death of a young man named Freddie Gray while in police custody. In response to the remark, Abdul-Jabbar asks a crucial question: "How could a journalist not remember the recent riots in Ferguson, [Missouri], Los Angeles, and New York?"[31] How, indeed? For months, the national news outlets had been flooded with accounts of protests in black neighborhoods following the deaths of unarmed black males

---

27. Alexander, *New Jim Crow*, 7, citing Tonry, *Thinking about Crime*, 14.
28. Ibid.
29. Ibid., 7–8, citing Tonry, *Thinking about Crime*, 20.
30. West, *Race Matters*, 3.
31. Abdul-Jabbar, "Baltimore," 1.

at the hands of police, eventually followed by outbreaks of violence. And no American, least of all a journalist, should have been surprised by any of this. For a very long time, young black males have complained that they are constantly detained by police for no legitimate reason, and there have been many reports of what Ralph Nader calls "aggressive arresting practices of local police" that created a "climate of fear" among persons of color.[32] Matt Taibbi describes the situation in graphic terms:

> Go to any predominantly minority neighborhood in any major American city and you'll hear the same stories: decades of being sworn at, thrown against walls, kicked, searched without cause, stripped naked on busy streets, threatened with visits from child protective services, chased by dogs, and arrested not merely on false pretenses, but for reasons that don't even rise to the level of being stupid.[33]

All of this goes largely unnoticed by the media and the general public, however, until a particular death or a protest or riot demands our attention. Then a familiar pattern recurs. There is a media frenzy, politicians and pundits weigh in on one "side" or another, and the justice system deals with the immediate issue in one way or another. Things eventually die down, and the media and the public "forget," moving on to other concerns. Then, as Abdul-Jabbar writes, "nothing happens until the next death, which is often tragically close behind. About 70 unarmed blacks have been killed by police between 1999 and 2014."[34]

Is it any wonder, then, that those who protest the deaths of unarmed African Americans at the hands of the police feel the need to proclaim that "Black Lives Matter"? There is substantial evidence that for some persons involved in law enforcement they do not. I do not mean to disparage the many police officers in this country who are committed to the protection of all persons, who risk their lives on a daily basis, and who are often quite heroic in carrying out their duties. Such persons have my respect and admiration, and I mourn for those who are killed or injured in the line of duty. We cannot, however, either ignore the abuses of power that are well substantiated or simply write them off as the actions of "a few bad apples." For investigations of a number of police departments around the country have uncovered some disturbing facts.

Consider, for example, the U.S. Department of Justice report on the Ferguson, Missouri, Police Department, published on March 4, 2015.

---

32. Nader, "Suddenly Baltimore," 1.
33. Taibbi, "Why Baltimore," 3–5.
34. Abdul-Jabbar, "Baltimore," 1.

Because of the constant pressure to increase revenue from municipal fines, the report states, "many officers appear to see some residents, particularly those who live in Ferguson's predominantly African-American neighborhoods, less as constituents to be protected than as potential offenders and sources of revenue." They are also "inclined to interpret the exercise of free-speech rights as unlawful disobedience, innocent movements as physical threats, indications of mental or physical illness as belligerence." In addition, those in supervisory positions "do too little to ensure that police officers act in accordance with law and policy, and rarely respond meaningfully to civilian complaints of officer misconduct." The result is unsurprising: "a pattern of stops without reasonable suspicion and arrests without probable cause in violation of the Fourth Amendment; infringement on free expression, as well as retaliation for protected expression, in violation of the First Amendment; and excessive force in violation of the Fourth Amendment."[35] This pattern, moreover, impacts African Americans disproportionately. They are, for example, "more than twice as likely as white drivers to be searched during vehicle stops, even after controlling for non-race based variables such as the reason the vehicle stop was initiated, but are found in possession of contraband 26% less often than white drivers, suggesting officers are impermissibly considering race as a factor when determining whether to search."[36] The existence of racial bias in the police department and among the court staff is also confirmed by the viciously racist e-mails that circulated among some of these personnel.[37]

The policies at work in cities like Ferguson, Baltimore, Los Angeles, and New York are not the result of mere thoughtlessness. Taibbi traces many of the abusive practices to a particular philosophy of policing known as "Broken Windows," which gained currency in the 1990s. The theory was that any form of disorder (symbolized by a broken window in a building) leads inexorably to crime, which will inevitably spread. The remedy, then, was that police should "stop people in troubled neighborhoods for any infraction, no matter how minor—a broken taillight, a hopped turnstile, an open beer—in hopes of deterring more serious crimes."[38] Out of this mentality grew the "stop and frisk" policy (which was eventually ruled unconstitutional) along with the "zero tolerance" policy; there was increasing pressure from police departments for officers to demonstrate results in the

---

35. United States Department of Justice, "Investigation," 2–3.
36. Ibid., 4.
37. Ibid., 5.
38. Taibbi, "Why Baltimore," 8.

form of arrests.[39] In a real sense, then, the abusive tactics mentioned above are the fruit of conscious political decisions in an effort to curtail crime. Ironically, however, a 2013 study has shown that the "Broken Windows" approach "had little or no effect on the crime rate."[40]

It is understandable that many police officers feel that the entire profession has been unfairly condemned because of the actions of some departments and officers, and that there is often a "rush to judgment" on the part of the public after a police-involved shooting. I am sympathetic to these complaints, because I believe that society as whole has in fact used the police as dispensable pawns to protect the majority from the consequences of our collective political decisions. The protests and riots of 2014–15 have succeeded in initiating a long-needed discussion of policing methods, and it is possible that this will lead to some significant reforms. But there is another dimension to the problem that consideration of policing methods does not address—the underlying causes of the decay of neighborhoods into crime-infested ghettos where policing is admittedly difficult. As Abdul-Jabbar comments, "Baltimore protesters weren't just expressing their anger over the treatment of Freddie Gray; they were expressing their frustration over living in economic circumstances that makes them seem less than human to those in power. Worse, they have little hope that these circumstances will change."[41]

## AN INFINITE SUPPLY OF "OTHERS"

Because of my own particular background as a southerner, I have focused almost entirely on African Americans, but there are other groups who have suffered greatly through marginalization. Native Americans stand out as people who not only lost their land but suffered conscious attempts to destroy their cultural heritages as well as actual genocide. I find it best, however, to address their issues in another context in part 3. Immigrants from many parts of the world, such as Asia, Ireland, Italy, Eastern Europe, and, more recently, the Middle East, have also been targets of discrimination, as have both Jews and Catholics. Indeed, the number of anti-Jewish incidents remains astonishingly high: 887 in 2010, according to FBI statistics, "comprising 67.1% of [hate crimes] linked to religion."[42] Since the attack on the World Trade Center in 2001, Muslims have felt the sting of prejudice and

39. Ibid., 9–13.
40. Ibid., 21.
41. Abdul-Jabbar, "Baltimore," 2.
42. Rusin, "Hate Crimes," 1.

become victims of violence. According to FBI statistics, in 2010 there were 186 anti-Muslim incidents involving 197 victims.[43] Neither are race, ethnicity, and religion the only grounds that some in our country can find for marginalizing people as "other." Despite significant gains over the years in their struggle for equal rights, lesbians, gays, bisexuals, and transgendered still face significant discrimination and frequently suffer from violent attacks and other forms of harassment.[44] In fact, according to a report of the Bureau of Justice Statistics, "hate crimes motivated by sexual orientation were 18% of the total," which means that "gays and lesbians are victimized at six times the overall rate."[45] There are, in addition, still many ways in which women have not achieved full equality.[46] The discrepancy in pay between men and women remains high,[47] and both domestic violence and rape remain significant problems. "In 2005," for example, "1,181 women were murdered by an intimate partner," and, according to the National Center for Injury Prevention and Control, "women experience about 4.8 million intimate partner-related physical assaults and rapes every year."[48]

All these groups and others have stories to tell that call into question our commitment to "justice for all" and to the biblical principles of the unity of humankind and love of neighbor. I cannot begin to give adequate account of all these stories, but at this particular moment in our history the acrimonious debates surrounding immigration make some attention to this issue necessary. The issue of undocumented persons is a difficult one, and one might think that the current reaction against the thousands who have crossed the Mexican border without authorization is justified. They have not "waited in line" as have others—so the argument goes. But this argument ignores four essential factors. First, our own economy depends heavily on the labor of undocumented workers, a fact that many businesspeople, most particularly farmers, will acknowledge. Second, the avenues for legal entry are inadequate in relation to the number of jobs that undocumented workers actually fill. Third, the discrepancy between standards of living between the United States and Mexico, as well as some other countries to

43. Ibid.

44. See Pregeant, *Reading,* 65–68, 77–83; and Pregeant, *Knowing Truth,* 249–59, 339–46 for a contemporary perspective on the Bible's injunctions against same-sex relations.

45. Southern Poverty Law Center, "Hate Crime Statistics," 1.

46. See Pregeant, *Reading,* 68–73 and *Knowing Truth,* 97, 108, 177–79, 239–44, 265–66, 278–79, 280–81, and esp. 333–36 for a contemporary perspective on biblical views regarding the status and role of women.

47. See the website for the National Organization for Women: http://now.org/.

48. National Organization for Women. "Violence against Women," 1.

the south, creates enormous pressure for people in Latin America to seek employment here. Fourth (a point that I will pursue in some detail in part 3), the long history of exploitation of Latin America by forces in our own country has contributed to the poverty that makes crossing our southern border so desirable.

It is easy to preach about legalities and fairness, but it is understandable that in the face of desperate circumstances and inadequate immigration policies, people will resort to unauthorized entry in order to feed their families. There is simply no other way of accounting for the willingness of people to take the significant risks they do in entering the country in this way.

Beyond the specific issue of undocumented workers, we are currently experiencing a significant degree of sentiment against immigrants in general. To some extent, we can attribute this to lingering racism, as recent talk of the "death of white America" attests.[49] But much of this attitude stems from a fundamental misunderstanding of our economy that supports the fear that immigrants are taking jobs away from native-born Americans. The basic misconception is that there are a finite number of jobs available. As Aviva Chomsky notes, however, "the number of jobs is *not* finite, it is elastic and affected by many factors. Population growth creates jobs at the same time it provides more people to fill jobs." It does so "because people consume as well as produce; they buy things, they go to the movies, they send their children to school, they build houses, they go to the dentist, they buy food at stores and restaurants."[50]

At this point I must add that I do not accept either population or economic growth as a solution to unemployment. As I will stress in part 2, the earth simply cannot sustain unlimited growth. So I quote Chomsky on this point only to refute the charge that immigrants "take our jobs." All Americans are aware of the dramatic job losses in recent years, but there are many factors at work in this trend. For one thing, we now live in a globalized economy, so that fluctuation in employment in the United States can be positively or negatively affected by global trends unrelated to immigration. And when U.S. businesses move factories abroad to find cheaper labor, lower taxes, and laxer environmental and safety regulations, this has a ripple effect on employment. Beyond the immediate effect of the loss of factory jobs, many former workers, particularly the young, move elsewhere in search of work, which decreases the local population. Thus "local businesses

---

49. See, for example, Buchanan, *Suicide*.
50. Chomsky, *They Take Our Jobs!*, 8.

also start to close, because the population can't support them anymore."[51] It is convenient to blame the "other" for our problems, especially when ideologies are available to support our prejudices. As Chomsky notes, however, "Immigration rates . . . do not appear to have any direct relationship at all with unemployment rates."[52]

A second factor in the anti-immigrant fervor is the perception that immigration drives wages down by increasing the pool of persons willing to work for substandard pay. Chomsky acknowledges that immigrants compete with low-skilled workers for "low-paying jobs,"[53] but denies that it is immigration per se that creates wage depression. Essential to her argument is the distinction between primary and secondary labor markets. "The *primary labor market* refers to jobs that are regulated. Workers are protected by laws that establish living wages, health and safety standards, and benefits." By contrast, "the *secondary labor market* consists of jobs that are generally not regulated. Wages are low, and working conditions are dangerous and often harmful to workers' health."[54]

This secondary market provides a pool of cheap labor, which serves business interests by lowering labor costs, but it tends to drive wages down across the board. While some might think that the solution to this problem is the curtailment of immigration, Chomsky argues that the problem is not the presence of immigrants per se but a system that creates a class of workers whose rights are not protected by law. In making her case, she documents a long history in the U.S. of legislative creation of a secondary labor market by leaving certain groups outside protections offered others. Even the New Deal, while instituting many important labor reforms, excluded agricultural and domestic workers; and the notorious *bracero* program of 1942 brought in Mexican workers on temporary visas, treating them "essentially as indentured servants of the businesses that hired them."[55]

This program was eventually replaced by other policies. New laws passed in 1965 and 1976 abolished national-origins quotas, in place since 1921, which (as my junior high teacher explained without a hint of indignation) were designed to keep the ethnic composition of the U.S. stable.[56] But the new uniform quota system, which placed a limit on all countries of twenty thousand immigrants each, created new forms of discrimina-

51. Ibid., 9.
52. Ibid., 10.
53. Ibid., 11.
54. Ibid., 14; italics original.
55. Ibid., 17–19; quotation from 19.
56. Ibid., 20–21.

tion even as it abolished other forms. Because large countries had the same quotas as small ones, individuals in the larger countries had less chance of receiving visas. In addition, "the 1965 law ignored the long-standing economic integration, and in particular the labor migration, between Mexico and the United States." The networks of employment that had bound the two countries together did not vanish with the abrupt imposition of quotas, nor did the jobs Mexican immigrants had filled.[57] Thus the limit of twenty thousand immigrants was absurdly inadequate in light of the actual situation, and the result was disastrous: "Because it placed such a low cap on Mexico at the same time that the bracero program ended, the law vastly increased the number of 'illegal' migrants. Abolishing the bracero program without creating any other legal mechanism to allow Mexicans to work in the United States turned people who had formerly worked legally into 'illegal immigrants.'"[58]

Immigration policy thus created a new pool of undocumented workers who, together with those coming after them who continued to use the existing employment network, constituted a convenient secondary labor supply. And if the existence of this pool is a factor in wage depression, the reason is not immigration but the creation, through discriminatory legislation, of a secondary market in which persons are deprived of adequate rights. Therefore, Chomsky concludes, the solution "to the low-wage problem is not to restrict the rights of people at the bottom even more (through deportation, criminalization, and the like) but to challenge the accord between business and government that promotes the low-wage high-profit model."[59]

The failure of the federal government to institute immigration reform has resulted in a variety of state laws that are tinged with racism; cause deep hurt not only to the undocumented but also to documented Latina/o immigrants; and do serious harm to children, students, and families. In some states, police are *required* to detain anyone they have reason to suspect of undocumented status—an incredibly vague provision that invites racial profiling even if a prohibition of that practice is included in the law. In Alabama, authorities can revoke the business licenses of anyone employing undocumented workers, and schools are required to determine and share with authorities the immigration status of students. The Alabama law also voids contracts made with undocumented persons and makes it illegal to give aid to them, a provision that should be particularly troublesome to persons of biblical faith. As Archbishop Thomas J. Rodi of the Roman Catholic

---

57. Ibid., 22–23.
58. Ibid., 23.
59. Ibid., 27.

archdiocese comments, the "law makes it illegal for a Catholic priest to baptize, hear the confession of, celebrate the anointing of the sick with, or preach the word of God to, an undocumented immigrant" as well as for undocumented persons "to come to Alcoholic[s] Anonymous meetings or other recovery groups at our churches."[60]

In light of such laws as these, one has to wonder what has become of the legacy of Ellis Island, the entry point for so many immigrants who came into this country and quite literally helped to build it, in the nineteenth and early twentieth centuries. In fact, honesty requires an admission that this legacy has always been more of an ideal vision than a reality. For alongside the welcoming of many people of diverse origins to our shores stands a counterhistory of exclusion and discrimination. Here are some of the most shameful examples:[61]

- 1882: The Chinese Exclusion Act bans Chinese for ten years; this act is renewed indefinitely in 1902.
- 1903: Epileptics and beggars, among others, are excluded.
- 1917: All immigrants from Asia are banned.
- 1941: Provision is made for interment of "enemy aliens," primarily Japanese.

Although we have moved away from such blatantly racist policies in recent decades, injustices remain; and the new wave of state legislation is taking us backward instead of forward. There are, however, some bright spots in the current situation. One is the creation of a people's movement among Latina/os and others sympathetic to their cause, which is in some ways parallel to the civil rights movement of the 1950s and 1960s as well as the struggle of Chicano farm workers for justice in the 1970s. Other bright spots are the strong responses of some religious bodies in this country in solidarity with immigrants. In Mobile, Alabama, bishops in the Roman Catholic Church, the Episcopal Church, and the United Methodist Church joined together to challenge the new immigration law. In addition, the debate over immigration reform has evoked a number of statements from religious circles. A commission of the United Synagogue of Conservative Judaism, for example, cites the biblical mandate to honor strangers because the Israelites themselves were once strangers in Egypt (Deut 10:19), as well as modern Jews' experiences as immigrants, in an appeal for immigration

---

60  Catholic World News, "Alabama Immigration Law."

61. See the Timeline in Chomsky, *They Take Our Jobs!*, 199–209 for a fuller list.

reform.⁶² Along similar lines, a 2008 resolution passed by the General Conference of the United Methodist Church cites the injunction against oppressing the alien in Lev 19:33–34 in a call for reform.⁶³ Another statement, from the Catholic bishops of Georgia, calls for respect for "the human dignity and human rights of undocumented immigrants."⁶⁴

Having noted these positive signs, however, I must acknowledge the truly ominous statements made by some candidates in the early phases of the 2016 national election, inspired first by the issue of undocumented aliens but then fed by the displacement of thousands of Syrians and the terrorist attacks in Paris and California. We have heard calls to round up and deport all undocumented persons, to exclude all Syrian refugees, and to apply a religious test for those seeking entry. We have even heard a call for a temporary ban on all Muslims seeking entrance into the country. This last suggestion has been met with strong opposition from other candidates and political figures in both parties. A segment of the population has embraced it enthusiastically, however, and more than one candidate is pandering to our baser instincts. I tremble for my country when I consider where the politics of fear, negativity, and demonization of "the other" could lead us.

## TYRANNY AT THE BALLOT BOX

One final issue stands out in my mind. When James Otis gave the American independence movement its rallying cry, "taxation without representation is tyranny," he hit upon a fundamental principle of civil rights. To be subject to *any* laws without a voice in the governmental system that makes them, is tyranny. After Reconstruction, the white South denied its black citizens the right to vote through a variety of means, not only poll taxes and literacy tests, but "white primaries" (a tactic made effective by the dominance of the Democratic Party), which were finally declared unconstitutional in 1944. One would hope that such blatant means of disenfranchisement of U.S. citizens would be a thing of the past. As I write, however, there are Republican-led efforts in a number of states to make voter registration more difficult even though there is no evidence of widespread voter fraud; and in Florida, "groups that help voters register" are being threatened "with stiff fines and possible jail"!⁶⁵ A 2012 analysis by News21, an investigative proj-

---

62. United Synagogue of Conservative Judaism, Commission on Public Policy and Social Action, "Immigrants and Immigration."

63. General Conference of the United Methodist Church, "Call for Reform."

64. Roman Catholic Archdiocese of Atlanta, "Pastoral Statement."

65. Toedtman, "Obstacles," 3.

ect of the Carnegie Knight Initiative,[66] drew this conclusion: "while fraud has occurred, the rate is infinitesimal, and *in-person voter impersonation on Election Day, which prompted 37 state legislatures to enact or consider tough voter ID laws, is virtually non-existent*."[67] So, why, then the hysterical attempt to solve a nonexistent problem? The answer is clear: the law would fall most heavily upon the poor, a group in which African Americans and other minorities are disproportionately represented.

Shortly after Lyndon Johnson signed the Civil Rights Act of 1964, he commented to Bill Moyers that they had "just delivered the South to the Republican Party for a long time to come."[68] Indeed, after more than forty years, the white South remains rather solidly Republican, due largely to the "southern strategy"—an appeal to white voters in the South, adopted by the GOP in Richard Nixon's 1968 presidential campaign. I have already argued that the Democratic Party has much to answer for when it comes to the race issue. Its historical support for slavery and segregation was shameful. The shame of the Republican Party, however, is its current willingness to capitalize on race prejudice. The converse of the movement of southern whites to the Republican side during the civil rights movement was the solidification of the vast majority of black citizens as reliable Democrats. And it is difficult not to see the current proposals regarding voter registration as an attempt to reduce the number of black and other minority voters who tend to vote Democratic.

The same must be said, moreover, of the redistricting that has taken place since the 2010 census. Both parties have been guilty of using the redistricting mechanism to their advantage over the years, but what is happening now seems clearly motivated by racial considerations. As Ari Berman notes, "In virtually every state in the South at the Congressional and state level, Republicans—to protect and expand their gains in 2010—have increased the number of minority voters in majority-minority districts represented overwhelmingly by black Democrats while diluting the minority vote in swing or crossover districts held by white Democrats."[69] The result is the weakening of minority voting power outside areas that would be lost to Republicans under any circumstances. For example, "in the Dallas–Fort Worth area, the Hispanic population increased by 440, 898, the African American population grew by 156,823, and the white population fell by 156,742. Yet

---

66. A joint program of the Carnegie Foundation and the Knight Foundation, designed to foster improvement of journalism schools.

67. Kahn and Carson, "Comprehensive Database," 1; italics added.

68. Germany, "Lyndon B. Johnson," 2. The conversation was not recorded but was reported in Moyers, "Second Thoughts."

69. Berman, "Southern Strategy," 11.

white Republicans managed to pick up two congressional seats in the Dallas and Houston areas. In fact, whites are the minority in the state's five largest counties but control twelve of nineteen congressional districts."[70]

A parallel strategy has been to bring suits challenging section 5 of the Voting Rights Act, which "requires that states covered by the act receive pre-clearance from the Justice Department or a three-judge court in Washington for any election law changes that affect minority voters."[71] Ironically, however, the Republican Party is simultaneously making use of the Voting Rights Act in order to defend their attempts to confine black voters to black-majority districts.[72]

Beyond all this, there have been much more blatant attacks upon minority voting rights. Just after the 2000 election, I had a conversation with a black man who had been in Florida on Election Day. I was horrified as he told me story after story of various ways in which blacks' voting rights had been violated on that day. Eventually, a stunning picture of a deeply flawed election process emerged through the news media, and a subsequent investigation by the U.S. Commission on Civil Rights provided official confirmation that many eligible voters, with African Americans disproportionately represented, were illegitimately denied the right to vote. More specifically,

- "African American voters were nearly 10 times more likely than white voters to have their ballots rejected."

- "Poorer counties, particularly those with large minority populations, were more likely to use voting systems with higher spoilage rates than more affluent counties with significant white populations . . . [and] of the 100 precincts with the highest numbers of disqualified ballots, 83 of them are majority-black districts."

- "Even in counties where the same voting technology was used, blacks were far more likely to have their votes rejected than whites."[73]

We can probably classify some of the factors that contributed to the disenfranchisement of various minority groups as "sins of omission" rather than "sins of commission," to use some apt theological terminology. It is difficult, however, to interpret the state's implementation of a purge list compiled ostensibly in order to prevent fraud as anything other than a deliberate attempt to disenfranchise black voters. The stated purpose of the list was

70. Ibid., 17.
71. Ibid.
72. Ibid.
73. United States Commission on Civil Rights, "Voting Irregularities, 1.

to identify convicted felons whose voting rights had not been restored. In Florida, unlike all but thirteen other states, the rights of convicted felons are not automatically reinstated when their sentences and paroles are completed; former prisoners must petition the Office of Executive Clemency.[74] This in itself has a negative impact upon the African American population, since although "the population of Florida is about 15 percent black, the population of Florida prisons is 54 percent black."[75] But the state's guidelines for compiling the purge list seem clearly designed to increase this impact. As John Lantigua reports, "a person could be included on the list if his or her name, date of birth and/or Social Security number *closely approximated* that of a known felon. In other words, in a state with 16 million people, where many individuals share approximate names and also dates of birth, *exact matches were not necessary*."[76]

Tellingly, in 1999 an official of the database company hired to compile the list sent this e-mail to the Division of Elections: "Unfortunately, programming in this fashion may supply you with false positives," adding that "this seems to be the approach you would prefer to choose, rather than miss any positive true matches." The state official's reply is damning: "Obviously, we want to capture more names that possibly aren't matches and let the supervisors [of elections] make a final determination rather than exclude certain matches altogether."[77] Not surprisingly, numerous errors became evident, and some election supervisors complained. But even though the database company informed the Division of Elections that their loose parameters had caused the errors, the state made no effort to implement the company's recommendations to correct the problem. Astonishingly, moreover, as the 2000 election drew near, the parameters were actually broadened: "Instead of 90 percent of the letters in the name of a person on the purge list having to match with those of someone on the voting rolls, the standard was loosened to 80 percent."[78]

Let me be clear that I am not accusing either the Republican leadership or the Republican populace of the overt racism that once reigned among southern Democrats. What I do assert is that a significant contingent within the Republican leadership seems willing to disenfranchise black, Latina/o, and other minority voters to gain political advantage. Nor do I wish to imply that the sins of the Democratic Party all lie in the past; I will have much to

74. Lantigua, "How the GOP," 6.
75. Ibid.
76. Ibid., 10; italics added.
77. Ibid.
78. Ibid., 11.

say later about the failures of both parties to live up to the biblical ideals of justice. Indeed, I should add this footnote to the earlier discussion of the negative impact on people of color of our policies regarding incarceration: *those policies had strong bipartisan support when they were developed.* To quote Michelle Alexander once again, "Legislators began to compete with each other over who could be tougher on crime. *Democrats and Republicans alike* began supporting harsh new mandatory sentences for minor drug offenses, *sentences even harsher than murderers receive in other Western democracies.*"[79]

What I hope to show in the remainder of this book is that the perception of so many moderates in this country is quite wrong. The Democratic and Republican Parties are in significant measure guilty not of opposite sins but of the same sins in different ways and to different degrees.

## THE STATE OF THE DREAM

What, then, is the state of "the dream"—the dream of African Americans, Latina/os, other ethnic minorities, and all other marginalized persons for full inclusion in this society? What is the state of the dream of a "beloved community" informed by the biblical principles of love of neighbor, human unity, and community solidarity? That dream is still alive for many, although in many serious ways *still deferred.* And what becomes of a dream that is deferred?[80] We have seen it *dried up*, as so many persons remain in hopelessness and despair. We have also seen it *explode*, as it did in the Watts riots in 1965 and other outbursts of anger and frustration. It appears, moreover, that for many others the dream is in fact dead. And if we want to see it awakened and realized, we must recognize that it is hypocritical to celebrate the progress we have made on some levels without taking account of the serious issues that confront us *now*. In the biblical passage cited at the beginning of this section, Jesus condemns those who take pride in claiming that had they lived in the earlier days of Israel's great prophets, they would not have persecuted them as their ancestors did. Jesus, however, rejects the claim, indicting these people for their actions *in the present.* By the same token, it is hypocritical to celebrate the accomplishments of the civil rights movement half a century ago or to honor Dr. King and at the same time oppose efforts to bring the dream of the beloved community to realization in the present.

79. Quoted in Alexander, "Criminal Injustice," 22; italics added.
80. Allusions to Langston Hughes's famous poem "Harlem"; Hughes and Bontemps, ed., *Poetry*, 199.

The dream, in sum, remains a dream, and for this nation the question that the lawyer put to Jesus in Luke 10:29—"Who is my neighbor?"—remains unanswered. I see signs of hope, but I am also aware of the demons with which we must continue to struggle. There are still those in our time to whom the title of Lillian Smith's *Killers of the Dream* applies all too well. Among them are members of the hate groups that still persist and perpetrators of hate crimes. I cannot close this chapter without mentioning the blatantly racist murder of nine persons at Charleston's historic Emanuel African Methodist Episcopal Church in June of 2015. Nor can I, as a Louisiana native, fail to highlight the horrific violence against blacks that took place in New Orleans in the wake of Hurricane Katrina. The media were filled with stories of crimes such as looting perpetrated by blacks during this period, many of which turned out to be false. The most stunning instances of violence, however, were the product of white hysteria. In Algiers Point, for example (an area across the river from the main part of the city), there were incidents that verged on a race war against blacks. Members of a white vigilante group shot innocent African Americans almost randomly, belying the defense that they were merely protecting their families and property. One man actually bragged about his exploits to a Danish video team filming a documentary. "It was great! It was like pheasant season in South Dakota."[81] And a woman told a journalist that her "uncle was very excited that it was a free-for-all—white against black—that he could participate in," adding that "for him, the opportunity to hunt black people was a joy." Even more ominous was an e-mail the woman received from her cousin. As the journalist describes it, "He had attached a photo in which he posed next to an African-American man who'd been fatally shot. The tone of the e-mail, she says, was 'gleeful': her cousin was happy that 'they were shooting niggers.'"[82]

Alongside such violent racists are others whose bigotry is less overt, but who nevertheless hold tightly to illusions of racial or ethnic superiority. Perhaps most important, though, are the vast numbers of white Americans who deny harboring racist attitudes, but who are so absorbed by their own problems, which they are unable to connect to the issues confronting those who are different from them, that they remain passive in the face of gross injustices. In addition to these two groups, moreover, are some who desire the realization of the dream on one level, but whose commitment to a political ideology allows them to subvert it for the sake of other values. We see this with particular clarity in their support for public policies that contribute to

---

81. Quoted in Thompson, "Race War," 16.
82. Ibid.

disparities in wealth, income, and the allocation of educational resources, as well as in the unjust use of incarceration and in the denial of voting rights.

The concrete effects of such ideology on the broader issues of economics, the natural environment, and our democratic institutions will be the subject of part 2. First, however, I want to address one question more explicitly: What does it *mean* to be an American—or a southerner?

# 6

# Reflections on a Sugar House
## A Question of Identity

> If we peel back our fear of conflict, we find a third layer of fear, the fear of losing identity. Many of us are so deeply identified with our ideas that when we have a competitive encounter, we risk losing more than the debate: we risk losing our sense of self.
>
> —Parker Palmer, 1998[1]

## SACRED PLACE, SACRED STORY, AND THE GUISES OF IDOLATRY

On the wall in my study is a copy of an old photograph of the sugar house on the plantation my grandfather Pregeant once owned. I treasure it as a link to my family history and a reminder of the spaces in which that history was lived out. Telling stories and honoring places are two ways in which we make sense of our lives and feel at home in the world. Lives without stories would be no lives at all, because human existence is *historical*—always on the move, pushing toward a future of new

---

1. Palmer, *Courage*, 38.

possibilities, and affected by contingencies. Stories tell where we have come from and present us with choices as to where we might go. There is no story, however, without place. To recognize places as significant is to acknowledge that we are incarnate creatures, flesh-and-blood beings whose experiences necessarily have a physical dimension.

When a religious community uses a story to convey its sense of what is truly ultimate in life, we speak of it as sacred. And when a particular place plays a central role in such a story, it often takes on the aura of the sacred itself. Both sacred stories and sacred places have the power to speak to us of the most important things in life and to ground our most central values. Similarly, what is true in the deepest sense of religious stories and places is true in some degree in our secular lives. Tales of our ancestors and important figures, events, and places in our nation's past can also give us a sense of who we are and what our lives are all about. They are therefore, in a weaker sense, also sacred to us.

Sacred stories and sacred places are fraught with danger, however. The biblical story of the exodus from Egypt culminates in the entrance into the promised land, and without that fulfillment in a tangible space the escape from slavery would remain incomplete. But the very tangibility of the space is a source of danger. As biblical scholar Walter Brueggemann observes, land is something that needs to "be managed, ordered, and administered."[2] But when we manage, order, and administer anything, we tend to think of it as completely under our control and of its value as our own creation. Essential to the story is the fact that the land is God's gift, which is given within the context of a covenant, a relationship between the people and God. With the gift comes an obligation to keep the covenant by remembering God as giver and keeping God's commandments. The gift is therefore contingent, actually more a lease than a transfer of ownership. God's proclamation in Lev 25:23 makes this clear: "*the land is mine; with me you are but aliens and tenants.*" There is, however, a seductiveness about the land; it fosters forgetfulness of God's of actions as liberator from slavery and giver of the gift. So the people begin to think of themselves not as recipients of a gift but as controllers and managers of the land.[3]

It is in the context of this temptation that we must understand the prohibition of the worship of Canaanite deities that pervades the Hebrew Bible. That prohibition, Brueggemann explains, has to do with the *character* of God as liberator and giver as over against the *character* of the Canaanite

---

2. Brueggemann, *Land*, 71.
3. Ibid., 56.

gods and goddesses of the land.[4] In the biblical story, the deities of the land represent the possibility of understanding the land itself as sufficient to meet the people's needs and grant them a secure existence. In addition, the gods and goddesses themselves are viewed as requiring nothing more of the people than ritual and therefore as "subject to manipulation, ready to serve human ends."[5] Whether this is a just evaluation of Canaanite religion is not the point; my interest here is in the values in the story *as story, rather than as literal history,* and thus in "the subtle insight" of the invective against Canaan's deities.[6] This has to do with the difference between the attempt to secure one's own existence and a trust in God's promises. It has to do also with a choice between stagnant stability and openness to the future; for the gods and goddesses of the land represent only the repetitive cycles of nature, whereas the God who acts in history represents new possibilities.

Although our sacred places are central to our religious traditions, then, they have the potential for a kind of self-subversion that ends in idolatry, which can come in many guises. In this instance, the promised land itself tempts people to turn to sources other than God for security. And if we look to postbiblical history, we can see how this potential breeds idolatrous attachments to the land itself, which come at terrible costs. In the Crusades, Christian militants, arrogantly claiming for themselves the inheritance of ancient Israel's sacred place, stormed the Holy Land in brutal attempts to "take it back" from the Muslims. And contemporary Israel has all too often pushed beyond the bounds of a legitimate concern for security to harsh and repressive treatment of Palestinians as well as occupation of their lands.

What is true of sacred places is also true of sacred stories. As I noted in chapter 3, the Bible contains various strands of meaning that sometimes conflict with one another. I therefore urged that if we want to find meaning in the Scriptures for our contemporary world, we must test out those various strands in light of the Bible's overall message as well as insights from our contemporary experiences. The story of the exodus from Egypt and entrance into the promised land is a story of liberation from slavery, but it is also a story of conquest involving brutality and genocide. In Josh 6:21, for example, the Israelites—*at God's command*—"devoted to destruction by the edge of the sword all in the city [of Jericho], both men and women, young and old, oxen, sheep and donkeys."

From some theological perspectives, we must take passages such as this at face value: that is, as divinely inspired in a direct and literal sense.

---

4. Ibid., 57.
5. Ibid., 58.
6. Ibid., 57.

It is therefore hardly surprising to find triumphalist readings of the story, smug interpretations that exalt biblical religion over all other faiths to the extent that it has the right to triumph over them and exercise domination in the world. Such readings, however, suppress central elements in the story. To receive the land as gift is to accept it in humble gratitude, not in an attitude of superiority and arrogance. Triumphalist readings negate the humane and inclusive elements that lie at the very heart of the biblical faith. But a faithful reading of the Bible in our time, when we have the advantage of close encounters among the various religions and cultures of the world, would reverse the process. It would allow the inclusive and humane strains of meaning to call the triumphalist elements into question.

We can say much the same about the secular stories that ground our secondary loyalties. The photograph of my grandfather's sugar house conjures up a complex set of images, memories, and reflections for me. On the positive side are the distinctive landscape of the Louisiana bayou country that stirs my soul, the unanimous testimony of all in the family to the kindness of the grandfather who died before I was born, and my father's stories of plantation life in his childhood. More broadly, there is the epic of the Cajun people—their journey from the western coast of France to build a new life in Nova Scotia, their deportation by the British during the French and Indian War, and their gradual relocation in south Louisiana. It is a story of tragedy, courage, an indomitable celebration of life in the face of hardship, and the creation of a new and vital culture in a different environment. The picture also calls up painful thoughts, however. Plantations throughout the world have been a key element in the exploitation of colonized peoples, and those in the South depended upon slave labor in the pre–Civil War era. The days of slavery were long past when my grandfather bought the plantation in 1909, but many aspects of those days remained long after emancipation.

The picture of the sugar house is thus, for me, a symbol of the complexity of appropriating our heritages, whether religious or secular; for there are no perfect stories. All, whether in themselves or the ways they have been communicated to us, have the potential to suggest strains of meaning that undermine what is most nourishing and humanizing in them. And we are faced with three basic choices in light of these ambiguities. First, we can give unqualified assent to our stories. To do so, however, risks both incoherence and idolatry—the former because of the competing strains of meaning and the latter because unquestioning allegiance to *any* human formulation grants it the place that biblical faith reserves for God. Second, we can reject the stories altogether. In some instances, this may be the best choice. I can find nothing redeemable, for example, in the worldview of the Nazis or the Ku Klux Klan, although I can look behind their stories to understand the forces that led them in such destructive directions. To lose all our stories, however, is to lose our identities, so that my focus in this book is on a third possibility. We can engage in a reflective process of sorting out what is redeemable and what is not redeemable in the traditions history has given us. Such reflection demands honesty, compassion, insight, and constant self-examination, but it offers great rewards.

## READING STORIES THROUGH DIFFERENT LENSES

Along with the photograph on my wall, Thomas Jefferson could well serve as a symbol of the complexities involved in sorting through our heritages. As Smedley and Smedley comment, "Jefferson's life exemplifies the agonizing ambiguities and contradictory impulses that came to warp American life."[7] Although he wrote passionately against slavery and on behalf of freedom and human rights, he held many slaves on his plantation, whom he never freed. Among them was "the young woman who was to share his bed for more than two decades, who gave up a chance for freedom during more than two years with Jefferson in Paris and returned to slavery at Monticello, probably pregnant with her first child."[8] He also compromised his endorsement of equality with what he wrote about race in the same book in which he penned his famous "I tremble for my country" statement.[9] In fact, "he was among the first to embrace, albeit tentatively, an intellectual argument that was much more devastating than any previous ones: the claim that the Negro was an inherently inferior form of human being." The great proponent of "unalienable rights" thus "found himself one of the foremost spokespersons" of a philosophy that shaped this country's racist views for the next century and a half.[10]

How, then, do we view this icon of American democracy? One approach has been to erase the embarrassing elements from our national story, holding him up as unblemished hero. Another would be to erase Jefferson himself from our story. Neither approach, however, seems honest or fruitful in our quest for ideals to guide us in shaping the destiny of this country. The alternative I suggest is to judge him in part on the basis of ideals he shared with the liberating strains in biblical teaching, *precisely because we embrace those ideals*! We can thus call his racism into account on the basis of his own words, revised in light our own growing consciousness

7. Smedley and Smedley, *Race*, 177.
8. Ibid., 179.
9 Jefferson, *Notes*.
10 Smedley and Smedley, *Race,* 180.

of the humanity of all persons: "that all [human beings] are created equal, that they are endowed by their Creator with certain unalienable rights, that among these are life, liberty, and the pursuit of happiness." If we do this, we do not lose him; we honor him by carrying through his ideals in a way that he could not or would not. Such a reading of Jefferson would parallel the way I have suggested reading the Bible, and I propose it also as a model for how to "read" the stories that ground our families and ethnic groups, the South, and the nation.

I can best explain what I mean by recounting a memory. Many years ago my father decided to try to find the site of an old plantation in the bayou country. I am unsure whether it was the one his father owned or one of the other sites with which Papa Pregeant was associated. In any case, we eventually located the foundation of the "big house," upon which a modest home had been built. As we drove around the area, we searched also for the cabin of the black woman who, as a house servant on the plantation, had been an important part of his childhood. The feelings my father expressed reminded me of my own childhood affection for the woman named Isadora who worked for my aunt and whom we knew as Dora. I earlier acknowledged that my friendly childhood relationships with adult African Americans were qualified by paternalism, and I am sure that my father's relationship with the woman on the plantation was even more so. But that is not all there is to say about such connections. Despite the oppressive and exploitative system in which they existed, and despite their socially driven limitations, relationships such as these often produced mutual affection and respect. Above all, there was *something in them that called into question the very system in which they existed and which limited them so severely.* That "something," I suggest, is worth honoring and cherishing—not in a sentimental way that ignores the limitations but in a painfully gained way that fosters *resistance to the system.* If I let my love for Isadora desensitize me to her suffering and the suffering of her people, or to foster the illusion that I have full understanding of what their lives were really like in my childhood, I am using it as an escape from difficult truth. But if I let it fuel my passion to take up the cause of her people and foster continual self-examination, it becomes a pearl of great price! It is a part of my personal story and also an element in the story of the South *that transcends that story and calls aspects of it into question.*

I thus embrace the story of my southern ancestry and childhood, but with a new set of lenses, which is to say with a critical eye. I will honor the memory of my parents, keep my love for them alive, and treat with respect the larger family stories of which they are a part. But I will also allow what is best in that story, defined by the biblical values I hold, to help me to "read" it in a different way—that is, to find within it new strains of meaning and value even as I must pass judgment on other aspects. To do this, I believe, is to engage in a redemptive process; for it frees me to celebrate the deeply human elements that somehow blossomed in the midst of an inhumane system. It also sensitizes me to the creative transformations that took place on both the social and the personal levels during the tumultuous years of my youth. Not only did I see dehumanizing customs give way, but I watched as members of the older generation in my family, my mother among them, altered their views. One might say that they had a change of heart, but I believe that they allowed what was *already* in their hearts, paternalistic affection, to be transformed into genuine mutuality. I regret that others of that generation, my father included, did not live long enough to experience the new social situation that was emerging so that what was in their hearts also could have gone through similar transformation.

My most painful memory of the period is that my father died on a day on which we had bitter words. We argued because he criticized the Methodist ministers in New Orleans who took their children to school, in the face of angry crowds, as the vast majority of whites boycotted the public school system to protest integration. I would change many things about that day if I could, but I cannot in good conscience repudiate the stand that I took on the issues of that time. What I am thankful for is that despite a number of heated arguments, the bond with my parents and other relatives was never broken. In that regard, I am luckier than many of my generation of white southerners who experienced complete alienation from their families. Resistance against an oppressive social system comes at a price, and those who paid it in the midcentury South could certainly have understood Jesus's words in Matt 10:37–39: "Whoever loves father or mother more than me is not worthy of me; and whoever loves son or daughter more than me is not worthy of me; and whoever does not take up the cross and follow me is not worthy of me. Those who find their life will lose it, and those who lose their life for my sake will find it."

So the truth to which I must now bear witness is this: those in the South who paid this price, whether they were black or white, were no less loyal daughters and sons of the South than those who made them pay it. It is easy to see this, if one reads the story through the right set of lenses.

## THE STORY OF THE SOUTH, THE STORY OF AMERICA: AN EXERCISE IN "REREADING"

From early days, Americans have viewed the South as a distinctive region, defined in stark opposition to the North. In his 1941 classic, *The Mind of the South*, W. J. Cash argued that the region as a whole exhibited a "fairly definite mental pattern, associated with a fairly definite social pattern."[11] He thus identified in both North and South "a profound conviction that the South is another land, sharply differentiated from the rest of the American nation, and exhibiting within itself a remarkable homogeneity."[12] He proceeded, however, to demolish the "Cavalier legend" that once defined southern identity—the belief that the planter class came from the lines of English Cavaliers descended the Norman conquerors.[13] Finding only the tiniest grain of truth in the legend (and that confined to Virginia), he argued that the ruling class in the South was drawn largely from the same stock as other white southerners and developed over an extended period. Cash also challenged the entire mythology of the Old South so familiar to all Americans through popular entertainment.[14] Those who still define their identity as southerners on the basis of stereotyped images of noble gentlemen sipping mint juleps, gracious ladies in hooped skirts, splendiferous balls in white-columned mansions, and contented slaves are therefore constructing the present on a flawed memory of the past.

In fact, as James C. Cobb has observed, the very notion of "the South" as a distinct entity actually took its definitive shape only after the Civil War. Before and even during the war, loyalties to individual states or even smaller regions were stronger than a sense of southern nationalism; and it was precisely the South's defeat, which was transformed by the "lost cause" motif into a heroic sense of moral triumph, that was the unifying factor.[15] By the 1880s, this "lost cause" ideology had merged with that of the "New South," which sought economic prosperity based upon northern-style industrialization. It remained, however, tied to the traditional southern attitudes toward race and thus left the standard mythology in place.[16] Much later, in the mid-twentieth century, the term "New South" reemerged with a different meaning, which involved repudiating the doctrines that once seemed

---

11. Cash, *Mind*, viii.
12. Ibid., vii.
13. Ibid., 128
14. Ibid., x.
15. Cobb, *Away Down South*, 57–63.
16. Ibid., 68–74.

constitutive of white southern self-understanding.[17] Some commentators have thus argued that "the South" as a region culturally distinct from the rest of the nation no longer exists. Not surprisingly, the rejection of ideas that were once considered inviolable created for many southern whites "an identity crisis of sorts," causing them "to search frantically for some tangible and demonstrative reaffirmation of their cultural distinctiveness."[18]

That crisis, however, reveals a flaw in the search for a southern identity. The truth is that the definition of that identity in terms of racial segregation and white superiority "effectively excluded the South's black residents in much the same way that both black and white southerners had been 'othered' out of the construction of American identity."[19] But what if we were to view the South through lenses that allowed us to see it from a biblically informed, inclusive perspective that embraces not only the experiences of black southerners but of those whites who have dissented from the "orthodox" white ideology? Doing so certainly helps me as I ask myself how I can love a region with a history of racism, violence, and fixation on the past. The matter begins to look very different when I remind myself that the South has always been more than brutal sheriffs, hooded bigots, race-baiting governors, and unthinking hordes who accept "the ways things are" without question. It is also courageous African Americans who faced down police dogs and fire hoses in the 1950s and 1960s, as well courageous whites who in various ways stood with them. It is both blacks and whites in an earlier time, many of whom were honored in Egerton's account of the generation *before* the civil rights movement, who refused to comply with the demands of the dominant social system. Some perceived the inhumanity of that system early in life, while others found their way to opposition over time and by degrees. Some stood openly against injustice, while others worked quietly. Some were perceptive enough to challenge the very core of the system, while others could see only the most blatant abuses. They were of various political persuasions, but all lived their lives on the basis of values that in some significant way differed from those of the white majority.

In face of the prevailing white "orthodoxy," dissenting journalists played an indispensable role both before and during the civil rights movement. Black newspapers, such as C. A. Scott's *Atlanta Daily World*, P. B. Young's *Journal and Guide* in Virginia, John H. McCray's *Lighthouse and Informer* in South Carolina, and L. C. and Daisy Bates's *Arkansas State Press* "gave voice to the African-American's unquenchable thirst for the same rights and

---

17. Ibid., 212–35.
18. Ibid., 223.
19. Ibid., 5.

privileges enjoyed by other citizens." In publications such as these, "black writers hammered away repeatedly and insistently on the same theme: We want a role—in combat, in the workplace, in the national scheme of things."[20] Among the white dissenters were Ralph McGill of Atlanta's *Constitution* and Hodding Carter II of Mississippi's *Delta Times-Democrat*.[21] Martin Luther King Jr. mentioned McGill in his famous "Letter from Birmingham Jail" as an enlightened white southerner, and Carter advocated not only for the rights of African Americans but for fair treatment of Japanese American veterans returning from World War II. Both went through long processes of evolution in their views, and both were eventually awarded the Pulitzer Prize. Another important voice of dissent was that of a Jewish immigrant raised in New York who settled in North Carolina—Harry Golden, publisher of the *Carolina Israelite*, whose incisive analyses were made all the more effective by his biting wit.[22] Humor was also the main tool of P. D. East of Petal, Mississippi, of whom Egerton had this to say: "No integrationist himself—at least not when he started the paper—East couldn't resist skewering racist politicians and their political action committees, the Ku Klux Klan and the all-white Citizens Council. Typical of his gallows humor were the 'classified ads' he ran for cross-burning kits and summer-weight sheets of 'Cotton Eyelet Embroidery' for Klansmen."[23]

Creative writers, both in earlier and more recent times, have been no less important than journalists in speaking to the issue of race in the South. William Faulkner's voice was not always as unwavering as when he made his "speak now against the day" speech at the 1955 meeting of the Southern Historical Society, but that statement was priceless. And in an appendix added to *The Sound* and *the Fury* in 1946, in which he gave an account of the fictional Compson family, he ended with a two-word appraisal of the black characters in the story that draws a stark contrast between them and the deeply troubled Compsons: "They endured."[24] Not surprisingly, the remarkable endurance of southern blacks in the face of extreme adversity is depicted more explicitly in the works of black southern authors, such as Alice Walker, awarded the Pulitzer Prize for *The Color Purple*; Maya Angelou, whose autobiographical *I Know Why the Caged Bird Sings* was nominated for the National Book Award; and Margaret Walker, whose *Jubilee* won the Houghton Mifflin Literary Fellowship Award. The list of black poets from

20. Egerton, *Speak Now*, 252–53.
21. Ibid., 252–54, 527–28.
22. Ibid., 546.
23. Ibid., 547.
24. Faulkner, *Sound and the Fury*, 427.

various regions is extensive, including such luminaries as James Weldon Johnson, Langston Hughes, and Countee Cullen. And poet, essayist, and novelist Ishmael Reed, who has been nominated for the Pulitzer Prize and National Book Award, has been particularly effective in puncturing the illusion of our supposedly postracial society. Other white authors have also addressed the race issue in powerful ways, among them Lillian Smith, Flannery O'Connor, Carson McCulllers, and Harper Lee, whose *To Kill a Mockingbird* was another Pulitzer Prize winner.

Alongside these prominent figures, there were always ordinary people, both black and white, who in large or small ways resisted the prevailing social system. I have been privileged to know a few such persons. Among them were three white Methodist ministers I came to count as close friends: John Winn and Willie Poole, who testified to a rabidly hostile Louisiana state legislature against discharging teachers who espoused racial integration, almost causing a riot; and Ivan Burnett, who joined a black ministerial association in Mississippi when the white association refused to integrate. Here in northeast Georgia, Dan Hawkes, a black man whom I knew in his retirement years, was generally careful not to cross the invisible lines of racial convention. But he brought suit against the Georgia Power Company for discriminatory wages, winning the case for himself and other blacks. There were others who affected persons close to me. In Rome, Georgia, Jule Levin and Rose Esserman Levin, parents of a friend and teaching colleague of mine, were among the very few Jews in the town and thus quite vulnerable. Yet they openly supported the integration effort and the student sit-ins at local places of business and, unlike many of their friends and neighbors, refused to send their children to an all-white private school when the public schools were integrated. A former parishioner of my wife's tells how her mother, Layla Nixon Miller, lost her teaching job in Arkansas for helping students, both black and white, adjust when the schools were integrated. Her "offense" was apparently trying to make integration work! And my wife's grandfather, J. E. Harvey, was the only dairyman in northeast Georgia willing to deliver milk to the children at Lillian Smith's camp, stating simply that "Children need milk; I don't care what color they are." Driving his wagon one day, with his pistol in his lap and his preschool-age granddaughter beside him, he came upon a group of hooded Klansmen holding a black man. Calling the hooded men's names, one by one, he ordered them to let the black man go—which they did.

There are others I have learned about in other ways. The black theologian James H. Cone writes proudly of his father, Charlie Cone, who resisted southern social convention all his life and filed a lawsuit in 1950 against the Bearden, Arkansas, Board of Education. Originally challenging the inequality of black and white schools, after the *Brown v. Board of Education* decision the suit "became a case for the integration of the schools." Although threatened with lynching for this, Charlie Cone never backed down.²⁵ In 1958, Richard Loving, a white man, and his black-Cherokee fiancée, Mildred Jeter, traveled from Virginia to Washington DC to be married, because in Virginia interracial marriages were illegal. Upon returning to Virginia, they were arrested, tried, convicted, and sentenced to one year in prison. Given the options of leaving the state, living separately in Virginia, or going to prison, they moved to DC but initiated a lawsuit with the help of the American Civil Liberties Union. In 1967, the U.S. Supreme Court ruled in their favor and ordered all states to repeal their anti-miscegenation laws. The Lovings were not political activists, just two people in love who fought for their rights and in doing so changed the country. What is also significant about their story is that in their isolated community in western Virginia, black-white friendship and cooperation seems actually to have been the norm.²⁶

Every story has heroes who express the values that drive the plot. The standard white telling of the story of the South treats as its primary heroes such figures as Robert E. Lee, Jefferson Davis, and John C. Calhoun, and its central themes revolve around the Confederacy and the Civil War. A different set of lenses, however, adds another dimension to this story. It expresses alternative values and it enshrines other heroes. My southern heroes are persons such as those I have listed above, and my version of the southern story is one of resistance and dissent against a stagnant orthodoxy. It is a tale of human endurance in the face of oppression, of courage in the face of danger, and of solidarity in the face of a system designed to divide human beings on the basis of race. Viewed from below, from a perspective that respects the experiences of blacks and nonconformist whites, the South is a place I can call beloved.

Nor am I alone in doing so. I have conversed with African Americans living in the North who speak warmly of their lives in the mid-twentieth-century South—not of their interaction with whites but of their experiences within the black community. And there are many southern blacks who, despite all the negative aspects of the region, think of it as home. Journalist Charlayne Hunter-Gault, who suffered much as one of the first two black students to enter the University of Georgia, writes tenderly of "the almost overpowering sweet smell of honeysuckle and banana shrub seducing bumblebees" and "clouds of black starlings producing shadows wherever

---

25. Cone, *My Soul*, 21–22.
26. HBO, "Loving Story."

they flew over the dusty red clay haze." Then she adds: "This was the part of the South that I loved, that made me happy to be a Southerner, that left me unaffected by the seamier side, which would deny I could have pride in anything but Aunt Jemima."[27] Academy Award winner Morgan Freeman, a native of the South who has returned there to live, speaks of it with equal warmth, naming it "that safe place, that womb of nativity" and acknowledging, "whatever I am I was nurtured there."[28] Even Myrlie Evers, widow of the murdered Medgar Evers, could say that "regardless of what happened in Medgar's life, this was his state. There is a degree of anger but also a lot of love . . . Mississippi is home. It always will be."[29]

So also will Louisiana, and the South in general, always be home for me. But what of the larger space and the larger story? What of America? It, too, is home; it is, and always will be, *my* country. I am grateful for that larger space because of the values and institutions that have helped to redeem the smaller space and the smaller story of the South. I can be grateful for the promise of equal protection under the law, for the ideal of the equality of all persons, for a legal structure that eventually gave recourse to the dispossessed, however belatedly. I nevertheless tremble for my country when I reflect on the tortured route that led to emancipation, the destruction of Jim Crow, the granting of the vote to all, and the *protection* of the right to vote. Even more, I tremble in the face of present realities I cannot deny—the tendency to find new groups to "other" in some way, the new assault on voting rights, the abusive use of incarceration, and the failure to address the deplorable economic conditions of groups that remain in many ways dispossessed. Thus, as with the South, so with my country, I must find my heroes largely among the dissenters, those who resist the ideologies that breed these injustices; and I must "reread" its story through different lenses. I view those who dissent and resist, however, not as subversive of the principles that have made this country great but as prophetic figures, in the biblical sense, who prod America to live up to its own best ideals. We do not lose either the South or America if we hold them to such a standard; we help them toward realization of their own best potential.

---

27. Hunter-Gault, *In My Place*, 232; cited by Cobb, *Away Down South*, 268.
28. Quoted in Cobb, *Away Down South*, 266.
29. Quoted in ibid., 267

## VOICES, STORIES, AND CONVERSATIONS: A RECIPE FOR TRANSFORMATION

I hear voices. Some, which I heard long ago, are nearly silent now, only the echo of distant memories. They are the voices of the past that told me that I dare not depart from a way of life engrained in culture and sanctioned by both God and nature. But there are other voices, those of the future, which speak more clearly and coherently. Some are the voices of those named "other," who tell me how that "way of life" denied their humanity. I also hear the voices of the biblical writers, who had a vision of the universality of God's love and the unity of humankind. And then there is the voice from within, the voice of conscience.

The voices from the past try to tell me what it means to be a southerner or an American, but they define these identities in ways that increasingly seem narrow and disfigured. The voices of the future, however, invite me to think in broader, deeper terms. They suggest that identities are never stable, that individuals, regions, and nations must all be open to change, or they will wither and die. They tell me that we must embrace new experiences, absorb new ideas, undergo growth, or we will fossilize and lose our vitality. These are the voices that call me to personal transformation and to the kind of dissent and resistance that invites regions and nations also to creative transformation. They are the voices that comfort me with the thought that, in the words of George Tindall, "*to change is not necessarily to lose one's identity, to change is sometimes to find it.*"[30]

In the introduction, I invited my readers to engage in conversation regarding the ideas I am offering. To this end, I have tried to explain how I have come to hold the ideas I do regarding the issue of the "other" in our society. Having had my say on the matter, I conclude part 1 with some questions for reflection as a way of renewing that invitation:

- What does it mean to have an identity defined by a region or a country? Does it necessarily entail difference from others? Is it possible to stress one's difference without implying superiority?

- Daniel Patrick Moynihan, a Democrat serving in the Nixon administration, argued in the late 1960s that race relations in this country could profit from "benign neglect," that we should put the issue of race on the back burner because we have talked too much about it. But do we talk too much or too little about race? Would "benign neglect" close the racial divide, or would it allow us to cover over the injustices

---

30. Tindall, *Ethnic Southerners*, 21; cited by Cobb, *Away Down South*, 338; italics added.

that remain? Is race still an American dilemma? Has Jim Crow been resurrected in our time?

- The United States once celebrated its status as "the melting pot of all nations," but recently various groups coming to our shores have sought to preserve their native cultures and languages. Many Americans thus fear that we will lose our distinctive identity, and some support a movement to make English the official language. But how tightly tied must we remain to British culture? Are persons of Spanish, French, Italian, German, Eastern European, African, Middle Eastern, or Asian descent any less American than those with primarily English ancestry? Must they forfeit their cultural ties to be Americans? If identity is a process, should we be more open to transformation than we have been, exposing ourselves to what other cultures have to offer?

As I emphasized in chapter 2, the idolatry of race is closely related to our idolatries of wealth, power, and privilege. I turn now, in part 2, to a focus on these latter attachments.

# Part 2

# "The Land is Mine"
## Justice in the Marketplace, Justice for the Earth, Justice in the Forum

> The land shall not be sold in perpetuity, for the land is mine; with me you are but aliens and tenants. Throughout the land that you hold, you shall provide for the redemption of the land.
>
> —Leviticus 25:23

> The earth is the Lord's and all that is in it, the world, and those who dwell therein.
>
> —Psalm 24:1 (NEB)

> ... that this nation, under God, shall have a new birth of freedom—and that government of the people, by the people, and for the people shall not perish from the earth.
>
> —Abraham Lincoln, Gettysburg Address, 1863

# Prologue to Part 2
## Neither the Margins nor the Middle

"Christian socialism!" The man with a large camera on his hip spit the words out bitterly. I believe it was in the fall of 1959. In any case, the intended insult was directed at the demonstrators outside the drugstore across from the seminary on the day after a sit-in to protest the segregated lunch counter. The event had been cut short when the owner called in an extermination service to fog the building and the public health department ordered us to leave. The heckler was better informed than the high school student who referred to us as members of the Communist Party when we staged a stand-in at a motion picture theater a few weeks later. For the heckler knew that there have been a number of movements called Christian socialism and did not confuse them with Soviet-style communism. The existence of such movements may seem surprising because of the widespread perception that the Bible tends toward the conservative end of the political spectrum. There is, however, a long tradition among both Jews and Christians of activism on behalf of causes identified with the political Left, ranging from liberal to radical. While many Christians and Jews are dedicated proponents of laissez-faire capitalism, others are ardent socialists, and many are distributed at various points between the two poles. As for the students at the protests, I do not recall anyone naming an explicit affiliation. But where do persons of such faith belong on the political spectrum?

In chapters 7 and 8, I explore these questions first by examining biblical texts relating to economic issues and then by employing those texts to evaluate several political and economic options. Because the biblical writings were composed in social circumstances radically different from our own, we cannot transfer the biblical laws directly to our contemporary world. My hope is rather to develop a set of broad, biblically based principles as a starting point in a search for political and economic options appropriate to our time and place. In chapters 9–11, I consider the economic policies that dominate the global market today, exploring their impact on the physical environment and our democratic institutions in the United States and suggesting an alternative course. Chapter 12 then concludes part 2 with a discussion of how to overcome the impediments that stand in the way of that alternative course. As I stated in the introduction, I find the options generally debated by mainstream politicians and the media inadequate to the issues we face today. My intention is thus to look beyond these options, even as I borrow from them, to perspectives that are seldom taken seriously by the public at large or the political establishment. I do not claim that these ideas are original; in fact, they are gaining significant support in many quarters around the world. For the most part, however, they are either neglected or misrepresented in this country. But I believe that they are our best hope for a future in which justice prevails, democracy flourishes, and healthy life on our planet thrives.

My conviction is that many of the persons who are poles apart on the conventional Left-Right spectrum have values in common, although they work them out in different ways. By way of example, I would point to the ideals of democracy, freedom, and human rights. On a more concrete level, I would hold up a concern for the rights of individuals in the face of external power structures; the belief that governmental authority should emanate from below and locally rather than from above and distantly; interest in the welfare of small, locally owned businesses; a desire for the rebirth of manufacturing in the United States; and a preference for the dispersion, rather than the concentration, of political power. Such a claim might seem strange in light of how unsuccessful we have been of late in finding common ground. I believe, however, that our failure stems from the fact that we have contented ourselves with moving back and forth between two deeply flawed poles of thought, congratulating ourselves whenever we have found a middle point on which to compromise. As a result, we leave too many people dissatisfied and undermine attempts to find better solutions; for the flaws lie not simply in the positions at the far ends of the spectrum but in the spectrum itself. It is my hope, however, that by "reading" our problems through the lenses of biblical teaching, we can envision new possibilities.

To illustrate what it means to move beyond a conventional spectrum of possibilities, rather than settling for a position in the middle, I point to the way a high school settled a dispute between black and white students in the early days of school integration in Louisiana. The issue had to do with the election of cheerleaders in a school that was majority white with a large black minority. Given the long history of discrimination, combined with fact that black and white students had not been together long enough to form many friendships, it was virtually certain that a conventional election would result in an all-white squad. A group of African American students thus proposed that a percentage of positions be reserved for blacks. Many white students objected, charging that such a quota system is undemocratic. Arguably, both groups had points worth considering. Standard wisdom would thus suggest a compromise, but what would that mean in such a situation? Granting a smaller percentage of assured positions than the blacks demanded would be no less undemocratic by the white students' criteria and would still be unfair by the black students' standards.

What seemed an impasse, however, became an opportunity for creative problem solving. My brother, who was assistant principal at the time, called a meeting of representatives of both groups. At first, each contingent insisted upon its position; but then someone suggested an innovative system of voting. Each student would have votes equal to the number of cheerleaders to be elected, with the option of distributing these votes in any way she or he wished—all for one candidate or dispersed in any fashion among several. Once it was clear how the proposal would work, everyone agreed to it and went away satisfied. The system remained thoroughly democratic but made a just distribution of positions likely; and, indeed, the students chose a squad of cheerleaders that reflected the black-white ratio of the school. This creative solution did not come easily, however; not everyone is blessed with an active imagination. The principal at first refused to go along with the plan, relenting only after my brother put his job on the line by stating that he wasn't sure he could stay at a school where such a proposal would be rejected.

There are times when a conventional compromise is the only way to mediate between competing interests, but this is not always the case. What made the proposal about the cheerleader election work was less the spirit of compromise than willingness to think outside the box, to put aside a standard practice and entertain new possibilities. But this was not the only factor; a shared sense of fairness was also at work. The white students could have rejected the proposal because they believed that more whites would have been elected under the old system; the black students could have insisted on the safer route of a specific number. The sad truth is that it is not only a lack of creativity or imagination that stands in the way of new solutions. Vested interests are often the greatest impediment to progress. It will thus be necessary, as I evaluate our current arrangements, to identify the forces that keep unjust structures in place. My more immediate task, however, is to identify a starting point in the Bible's teaching on economics.

7

# A Miniprimer on Biblical Economics

*There will . . . be no one in need among you,* because the Lord is sure to bless you in the land that the Lord your God is giving you to occupy, if only you will obey the Lord your God by diligently observing the entire commandment that I command you today.

—Deuteronomy 15:4–5

The Hebrew Bible is traditionally divided into three parts—the Torah, the Prophets, and the Writings. The New Testament is divided into two—the Gospels and the Letters. In discussing biblical economics, I follow this scheme except for treating some of the letters together with the Gospels. What I hope to show is that despite some diversity of perspective among the biblical writings, there is a notable degree of consistency on the issue of wealth and poverty.

## THE TORAH

In the Jewish faith, the most authoritative portion of the Bible is the Torah, which is composed of the first five books, Genesis through Deuteronomy. These writings are held together by a narrative thread, but interspersed along the way are large blocks of legal materials. Many of the laws have to do with economics, and issues concerning wealth and poverty are prominent. To understand the import of ancient Israel's laws on these matters, we need to take account of the distinctive character of the ancient Israelite society.

Before the Israelites adopted monarchical rule, their economic structure contrasted sharply with other systems in the environment, including that of the Canaanite city-states they were replacing. Leslie J. Hoppe notes that the governments of these city-states "supported themselves by taxing the peasants" through both "payment in kind and conscripted labor."[1] This practice created enormous burdens. When subsistence farmers had to forfeit a portion of their produce, little was left for themselves; and when they "were forced to work on the projects of the state or serve in the military, they were unable to work their land." Quite often, then, peasants had to "sell their children into slavery" or "sell their land to satisfy their creditors." Because landlessness inevitably meant poverty, moreover, the Canaanite governments were actually *"responsible for the creation of poverty among their citizens."* They had been under Egypt's domination, but when Israel took over, the land of Egypt "was experiencing a decline that made continued domination of Canaan impossible." Israelite farmers were thus able "to keep the products of their labor and to work together cooperatively for the benefit of the entire community."[2] The word "cooperatively" is important. As Timothy M. Willis observes, the Israelite clans tended to operate as collectives "in agricultural, legal, and military matters."[3]

This spirit of cooperation, moreover, was supported by law. The Torah contains a remarkable collection of legal provisions to keep people from falling into poverty. We cannot be certain when in Israel's history these laws appeared, nor can we be certain of the extent to which the antipoverty laws were enforced. Since their written forms appeared long after the premonarchical period, some scholars have even speculated that they represent efforts by kings in later times "to curry favor with the masses" without significantly alleviating their desperate conditions.[4] The kings of Israel were theoretically protectors of the poor, but the reality was often quite different. It is clear, however, that from early times the Israelites embraced the ideology of a covenant between God and the people of Israel, mediated through Moses, which involved an obligation to ensure adequate provisions for all members of the community. What is most important for our purposes is

---

1. Hoppe, *No Poor*, 8; italics added.
2. Ibid., 9
3. Willis, "Clan," 679.
4. Knight, *Law*, 220.

that the Torah holds up as *ideals* both community solidarity and a commitment to the welfare of the vulnerable masses.

The theological basis for the antipoverty laws is stated most powerfully in Lev 25:23–24: "The land shall not be sold in perpetuity, *for the land is mine*; with me, you are but aliens and tenants. Throughout the land that you hold, you shall provide for the redemption of the land." By proclaiming that the land is God's, this text undermines any human claim to absolute ownership, and the point is underscored by the declaration that the people are "but aliens and tenants" in the land. They cannot do whatever they want to with it, because they remain responsible to God. More specifically, they cannot sell it "in perpetuity," that is, in such a way that the original owner loses all claim to it. Behind this provision is the notion that God distributed the land among the clans as a way of ensuring adequate means of support for all. Difficult circumstances, however, sometimes force a landowner to sell. Thus, if families are to retain their ancestral lands, "redemption" of the land becomes necessary; and the terms of such redemption appear in Lev 25:25–28. Either the original owner or a relative has the right to buy the land back when circumstances permit; and if such redemption is impossible, the land reverts to the family in the Jubilee, which occurs every fiftieth year.

The importance of ancestral land is reflected in the tenth commandment, the proscription against coveting one's neighbors possessions. As Richard Horsley comments, however, traditional translations of two Hebrew words in Exod 20:17 obscure this point. The term usually rendered as "covet" also embraces the meanings of "steal" and "seize," and the one that we translate as "house" actually means "the whole household,"[5] including land, personnel, and animals. The commandment thus covers more than inner attitude. "Coveting" is not merely desire but, as Walter Brueggemann writes, "desire acted upon publicly, whereby one reaches for that which is not properly one's own."[6] And if we read the prohibition of "coveting" one's neighbor's house in relation to Mic 2:1–5, which condemns the seizure of a neighbor's land, we see that "the command concerns primarily land and the development of large estates at the expense of vulnerable neighbors."[7] The "crime" here is not necessarily an actual theft; the point is that "increasing one's holdings always came at the expense of another."[8]

To take advantage of a neighbor's misfortune upsets the God-intended social equilibrium supported by ancestral inheritances. Closely akin to the

---

5. Horsley, *Covenant*, 27.
6. Brueggemann, *Exodus*, 849.
7. Ibid., 852.
8. Hoppe, *No Poor*, 39.

Jubilee is the sabbatical year, every seventh year, in which all debts owed by Israelites to other Israelites must be canceled (Deut 15:1–3). This provision is accompanied by injunctions to lend freely to those in need, not even withholding a loan if the sabbatical year is near (Deut 15:7–12). Exod 22:25–27, moreover, shows that the purpose of lending is to help the poor rather than to make a profit: "If you lend money to my people, to the poor among you, you shall not deal with them as a creditor; you shall not exact interest from them." The sabbatical year also entails rest for the land, parallel to the Sabbath rest for persons and domesticated animals; and Exod 23:10–11 specifies that the poor are entitled to reap what grows up spontaneously on the land during that year. Nor are the rights of the poor to a share of the produce of the lands of the more fortunate limited to the seventh year. Lev 19:9–10 gives both the poor and aliens the right to glean the edges of any landowner's field.

The conclusion of this passage echoes a formula introducing the Ten Commandments in Exod 20:2 and Deut 5:6: "I am the LORD your God, who brought you out of the land of Egypt, out of the house of slavery." The reference to God's deliverance reflects the grounding of the entire law in the Mosaic covenant and establishes the Israelites' God as the champion of the oppressed. The legislation in the Torah is thus linked to the story of God's actions, which holds the five books together. It is therefore not surprising that the emphasis on justice for the poor is represented in the narrative sections as well as the legal materials. In Gen 29–31, for example, we have a story of how Abraham's grandson, Jacob, outwits his father-in-law Laban, who has used deceit to exploit him economically. The story "illustrates how people of means like Laban had to be compelled to give what was justly due to those who were economically dependent on them." The father-in-law thus "represents the people whose wealth is created for them by their servants and their tenants, who enjoy nothing of the wealth that their work produced."[9]

The most notable instance of God's siding with the oppressed is Exod 3–15, the story of the deliverance of the Hebrew people from slavery. When the slaves cry out for deliverance, God sends Moses and Aaron to accomplish the task. In the dramatic conclusion, God parts the waters of the sea to allow the Hebrews to cross over on dry ground but drowns Pharaoh's army as the waters return. God's way of alleviating the people's suffering is therefore radical. In Hoppe's words, "there is no attempt to 'reform the system.' *A political and economic system that so impoverishes people is beyond reform.*"[10]

---

9. Ibid., 20.
10. Ibid., 22; italics added.

The story thus illustrates a theme that runs throughout the patriarchal narratives: "*Poverty . . . does not just happen. It is a creation of the wealthy who, for a variety of reasons, choose to oppress those in their power.*"[11]

It is ironic, however, that the same Torah that takes such a bold stance against oppression fails to indict the institution of slavery itself. Not only do Abraham and Sarah and other key characters in Israel's story hold slaves, but the Torah makes provisions for slaveholding. We are thus reminded that the Bible contains conflicting perspectives on many issues. What is remarkable about the Torah, however, is not that it retains aspects of the oppressive social structures of antiquity but that it contains elements that undermine those structures.

## THE PROPHETS

The second division of the Hebrew Bible contains two types of writings: the historical books, or the Former Prophets, which tell ancient Israel's story from a theological perspective, and the writings bearing the prophets' names, or the Latter Prophets. In the background of all these writings is the establishment of monarchical government in the mid-tenth century BCE, at which point the socioeconomic system began to undergo fundamental changes.

I begin with a passage from the historical narratives, 1 Sam 8:11–17, which gives a glimpse into the nature of these changes. Samuel, a charismatic leader of Israel, indicts the people for their decision to choose a king to rule over them and gives an ominous description of what a king will do:

> These will be the ways of the king who will rule over you: he will take your sons and appoint them to his chariots and to be his horsemen, and to run before his chariots; and he will appoint for himself commanders of thousands and commanders of fifties, and some to plow his ground and to reap his harvest, and to make his implements of war and the equipment of his chariots. He will take your daughters to be perfumers and cooks and bakers . . . He will take one-tenth of your grain and your vineyards and give it to his officers and his courtiers . . . He will take one-tenth of your flocks, *and you shall be his slaves*. And in that day you will cry out because of your king, whom you have chosen for yourselves; but the Lord will not answer you in that day.

---

11. Ibid., 21; italics added.

The irony of this description is that it reflects the exploitative economics that the Israelites rejected when they withdrew from the monarchical systems of the ancient Near East. It is, however, an accurate portrayal of the policies of Israel's third king, Solomon, son of David; and it signals a transformation of Israelite society that monarchical rule brought.

In sociological terms, monarchical rule led to extreme social stratification. In political terms, it brought a concentration of power that undermined the cooperative character of the earlier clan/tribal system of self-governance. As Norman K. Gottwald observes, the state now assumed "a monopoly of force over and above its people," so that armies and bureaucrats could reach "into the fields and villages to take crops and to conscript peasants for social purposes decided by a small minority in the royal court rather than by tribal elders sifting the mind of the people for a consensus."[12] In economic terms, the monarchy enabled a new entrepreneurial class whose practices, such as charging interest on loans to peasants unable to pay, had a devastating effect on families' ancestral land holdings. Many former landholders "ended up as tenant farmers, debt servants, or landless wage laborers." As a result, "tribal economic security and tribal religious identity were undermined, and the social and political trust of the people in their leaders put in radical doubt."[13]

Under David, a new ideology emerged, with the capital city of Jerusalem and the Davidic line at its center. Whereas the Mosaic covenant entailed God's promise to be with the Israelite people, it contained a note of contingency: God's protection and the people's prosperity depended upon their obedience to God's commands. The Davidic ideology, however, stressed God's unconditional commitment to the house of David and the inviolability of Jerusalem (2 Sam 7:8–16, 23:1–7; Ps 2:6–8). Horsley thus claims that "the monarchy stood in opposition to the Mosaic Covenant, in which Israel declared exclusive loyalty to God as their king precisely as a way of avoiding falling back into bondage to a human king."[14]

Aside from the passage from 1 Samuel cited above, the most biting criticisms of the oppressive policies of the monarchies and ruling classes come from the books bearing the prophets' names. The popular misunderstanding about the Hebrew prophets is that they "predicted" future events. They understood themselves, rather, as messengers from God who announced God's attitude and will. This sometimes meant relating God's intentions, but this is different from predicting the future, which assumes that the whole course of history is already set. By contrast, the prophets

---

12. Gottwald, *Hebrew Bible*, 323.
13. Ibid., 324.
14. Horsley, *Covenant*, 57.

often suggested that God's intentions could change if the people changed their ways. What is truly distinctive about the Hebrew prophets is that they typically condemned the sins of the people and their leaders, and the two sins they generally attacked were idolatry and economic injustice. They often spoke of God's coming judgment because of these sins, but sometimes they also looked beyond that judgment to a future in which the relationship between God and the people would be restored. What is most important for our purposes is that economic oppression stood front and center among the reasons for God's judgment.

The most caustic of the prophets was Amos. Drawing upon the story of the exodus, he accuses Israel of forsaking the God who led them out of Egypt (6:1–16); and central to his complaints are his indictments of economic injustice and ridicule of the lavish lifestyles of the rich:

> Hear this word, you cows of Bashan
>   who are on Mount Samaria,
> who oppress the poor, who crush the needy,
>   who say to their husbands, "Bring something to drink!"
> (4:1–2)

Amos accuses the wealthy of using false scales (8:6) and other unjust business dealings (2:6, 8:6) and points also to their corruption of the legal system. In 5:12, for example, he accuses them of bribery and "pushing aside the needy in the gate"—that is, denying justice to the poor at the city gate, where judicial processes took place. In addition, he lampoons their worship practices as hypocrisy (4:4–5): "I hate, I despise your feasts, and I take no delight in your solemn assemblies . . . But let justice roll down like waters, and righteousness like an ever-flowing stream" (5:21).

The message is clear: religious devotion means nothing apart from doing justice to one's neighbor. We saw above that in 2:1–5, the prophet Micah indicts those "who covet fields and seize them," who "oppress householder and house, people and their inheritance" (v. 2). As the oracle continues, he calls the land grabbers enemies of the common people: "But you rise up against my people as an enemy . . . The women of my people you drive out from their pleasant houses; from their young children you take away my glory forever" (2:8–9). Amos also criticizes the Davidic ideology and its assurance of God's unconditional protection in 3:11: "[Jerusalem's] leaders give judgments for a bribe, its priests teach for a price, its prophets give oracles for money; they lean upon the LORD and say, 'Surely the LORD is with us!'"

The theme of justice emerges in a different way in Micah 6:6–8. Verses 6–7 ask what God requires of human beings, criticizing ritual sacrifices as inadequate. Verse 7 then gives the answer:

> He has told you, O mortal, what is good;
>   and what does the LORD require of you
> But to do justice, and to love kindness,
>   and to walk humbly with your God?

Unlike Amos and Micah, Isaiah, a resident of Jerusalem, draws his inspiration from the Davidic ideology. It is thus all the more striking that he, too, condemned the rich and powerful who seized the ancestral lands of peasants. In a passage parallel to Micah 2:1–5, he issues this bitter indictment:

> Ah, you who join house to house,
>   who add field to field,
> until there is room for no one but you,
>   and you are left to live alone in the midst of the land! (Isa 5:8)

In the two verses that follow, Isaiah refers to God's coming judgment in the form of a disaster in which houses of the wealthy will be uninhabited and the land unproductive. As Gene M. Tucker[15] notes, moreover, there is a "genuinely ironic" prior punishment pronounced in verse 8: "the isolation of the greedy." By seizing land in disruption of God's "equitable distribution of it among the tribes and clans," the land grabbers cut themselves off from the community of God's people.

In Isa 10:1–2, the prophet recognizes how the powerful can use the law in their oppression of the weak. Not only can the law itself be misused, but the very process of law making loses its moral weight when vested interests wield undue power.

> Ah, you who make iniquitous decrees,
>   who write oppressive statutes,
> to turn aside the needy from justice
>   and to rob the poor of my people of their right,
> that widows may be your spoil,
>   and that you may make the orphans your prey.

Jeremiah, too, condemns the oppressive policies of the wealthy, as we see in 2:34: "Also on your skirts is found the lifeblood of the innocent poor, though you did not catch them breaking in." In addition, Jeremiah's rejection of the David-Jerusalem ideology comes out in such passages as 7:1–4, where

---

15. Tucker, "Isaiah 1–39," 93.

he ridicules those who think God's protection of the Jerusalem temple is unconditional: "Do not trust in these deceptive words: 'This is the temple of the LORD, the temple of the LORD, the temple of the LORD.'" Calling the temple a "den of robbers" (7:11), Jeremiah even denies that God issued the demands (in the Torah!) concerning the sacrificial cult: "For in the day that I brought your ancestors out of the land of Egypt, I did not speak to them or command them concerning burnt offerings and sacrifices" (7:22). Horsley thus considers Jeremiah's the most radical of all the prophetic critiques in that he condemns the system of centralized power "as hopelessly contrary to the principles of the Covenant."[16]

## THE WRITINGS

The third division of the Hebrew Bible is diverse in terms of genres, themes, and perspectives. Some of the writings are classified as wisdom literature, which can be broadly categorized as an attempt to discern the patterns that govern the world and human life and to give advice on how to live one's life in accordance with them. One of these is the book of Proverbs, a collection of poems and proverbs reflecting the worldview of Israel's ruling classes. Not surprisingly, it contains strains of teaching that view wealth as a blessing from God and the product of virtue, while poverty is the result of laziness. A good example is 10:4: "A slack hand causes poverty, but the hand of the diligent makes rich." David Jobling points out, however, that "the passages in Proverbs that undermine this view are almost as numerous as those that establish it."[17] He cites verses such as 23:4 and 28:6, which warn against striving after wealth; but even more important is the perspective of 13:24, which acknowledges the role of unjust business practices in the creation of poverty. In addition, as Hoppe comments, "Proverbs is not engaging in a sociological analysis of poverty or even in theological reflection on its significance for the community of believers." It is giving advice to "the sons of the wealthy, who must realize that poverty is a threat to their social and economic standing if they are lazy . . . or waste their resources foolishly (Prov 21:17)."[18]

Two other wisdom writings go much further in undermining the tendency to blame the poor for their plight, challenging the widespread notion that one's lot in life is determined by the righteousness or unrighteousness of one's deeds. Ecclesiastes takes a cynical view of life, viewing the attempt

---

16. Horsley, *Covenant*, 74–75.
17. Jobling, "Wealth," 825.
18. Hoppe, *No Poor*, 106.

to make sense or meaning out of it as "chasing after wind" (1:17). It acknowledges oppression and injustice (3:16; 5:8–9) but fails to protest against them. Its denial of "any connection between an act and its consequences," however, "undermines the belief of the wealthy that they have 'worked' for their prosperity while the poor have only themselves to blame for their condition."[19]

The book of Job undermines this view in a more powerful way. The friends who try to comfort Job in face of his misfortunes represent traditional views, particularly that suffering is God's punishment for sin. Job, however, refuses to repent unless he can be convinced of specific sins he has committed. At the end of the story, God overwhelms Job with the divine majesty but also undercuts the connection between suffering and sin with this rebuke of Job's friends: "for you have not spoken of me rightly, *as my servant Job has.*" Hoppe, moreover, points to Job 24:1–4 as "a powerful indictment of the way people of means treated the peasants, reducing them to poverty."[20] Verse 3 is sufficient to make the point: "They drive away the donkey of the orphan; they take the widow's ox for a pledge."

Hoppe also finds that "the oppression of the poor is a frequent subject of ancient Israel's prayers, which are preserved in the book of Psalms."[21] In Ps 72:4, for example, the psalmist petitions God to motivate the king to do justice for the poor: "May he defend the cause of the poor of the people, give deliverance to the needy, and crush the oppressor." Similarly, in Ps 10:1–4 we read of a plea for God's justice when "in arrogance the wicked pursue the poor" and "those greedy for gain curse and renounce the Lord."

## THE GOSPELS (AND RELATED WRITINGS)

The theme of poverty and riches is central to the Gospel of Luke and the companion volume, the book of Acts.[22] This is particularly evident in Jesus's inaugural sermon in 4:16–21, which echoes passages from Isaiah: "[God] has appointed me to preach good news to the poor." The motif emerges even earlier, however. Mary's song in celebration of her role as the one chosen to bear the Son of God includes this powerful testimony to God's actions on behalf of the downtrodden, echoing the frequent biblical motif of the divine reversal of human fortunes:

---

19. Ibid., 110.
20. Ibid., 109.
21. Ibid., 123.
22. See Pregeant, *Knowing Truth*, 170–71.

> [God] has shown strength with [God's] arm;
>   [God] has scattered the proud in the thoughts of their hearts.
> [God] has brought down the powerful from their thrones,
>   and lifted up the lowly;
> [God] has filled the hungry with good things,
>   and sent the rich empty away. (Luke 1:51–53)

This motif also appears in Luke 6:20–26, which includes a version of the Beatitudes, followed by a series of woes. The first beatitude sets the stage for both series by placing them in the context of God's coming kingdom, or rule in the world: "Blessed are you who are poor, for yours is the kingdom of God." The point is not that poverty is a blessing, but that God's rule or realm will lift the poor out of their distress. This is evident from the two blessings that follow:

> Blessed are you who are hungry *now*,
>   for you *will be* filled.
> Blessed are you who weep *now*,
>   For you *will* laugh.

The three woes that follow correspond to the three beatitudes. The blessing of the poor in 6:20 is matched by a woe upon the rich in 6:24, which now makes the present/future contrast explicit. The rich have already received their consolation, while the poor will receive their blessing as God's rule breaks in.

Other passages that side with the poor against the rich are the parable of the Rich Man and Lazarus (16:19–31) and Jesus's contrast between the widow's meager contribution to the temple and the offerings of the rich in 21:1–3. As Frank Matera notes, moreover, Luke makes wealth and poverty central to the conflict between Jesus and the Pharisees by characterizing the latter as "lovers of money" (16:14).[23] On another note, in Luke Jesus challenges those who oppress the poor to change their ways and expects repentance in the form of "concrete acts of benevolence toward the poor."[24] The story of Zacchaeus (19:1–20) illustrates such repentance as this chief tax collector decides to give half of his wealth to the poor and return fourfold to all he has defrauded. His action, moreover, is an implicit indictment of the system of taxation that bred abuse and fell heavily on the poor. The theme of poverty and riches takes a different turn in Acts, which twice describes the community of Jesus's followers as an economic commune in

---

23. Matera, *New Testament Ethics*, 83.
24. Hoppe, *No Poor*, 154.

which no one goes needy (Acts 2:43–47, 4:32–37). Here we see the nascent church modeling itself in anticipation of the economic justice expected with the fullness of God's realm.

Many commentators interpret Matthew's version of the first beatitude (5:3), which has "poor in spirit" in place of "poor," as a spiritualization of Jesus's emphasis on the economically distressed. On this view, Matthew's phrase would mean something like "those who are humble, acknowledging their need of God." Recent scholars have shown, however, that it means those whose spirits have been crushed by oppression.[25] Similarly, the term generally translated as "meek" in the third beatitude (5:6) is better rendered as "the oppressed." It has always been unclear why the reward of the "meek" should be to "inherit the *earth*," but this makes sense as a cry of people who have lost their land through economic oppression. Those who "hunger and thirst" in the fourth (5:7), moreover, are in quest of "justice," not "righteousness" (as the Greek *dikaiosyne* is usually translated here). On this reading, Mark Alan Powell argues, the first four beatitudes refer to people whom social forces have driven into despair, whereas the second four pronounce blessings on "those who help to bring to reality the blessings promised to others in 5:3–6"[26]—that is, those who minister to the needs created by the injustices described in the first three.

Matthew's interest in economic justice is not confined to the Beatitudes. In 11:5 (a passage paralleled in Luke 7:22), Jesus describes his mission as giving sight to the blind, enabling the lame to walk, cleansing lepers, raising the dead, and preaching good news to the poor. Matthew also includes the story of the rich man Jesus counsels to sell his possessions and "give the money to the poor" (19:21), and in Jesus's biting indictment of the Pharisees in chapter 23 he charges that they "have neglected the weightier matters of the law: *justice* and mercy and faith" (23:23).

The Gospel of Mark includes the story of the rich man who refuses Jesus's demand to sell all his goods and give the proceeds to the poor (10:17–22//Matt 19:16–22//Luke 18:18–23) and the charge that the scribes "devour widows' houses" (12:40//Luke 20:47). Mark's version of the story of the rich man, moreover, reinforces the condemnation of unjust economic practices by including, "You shall not defraud" in the commandments Jesus cites. In addition, as in Matthew and Luke, this story is followed by Jesus's saying on "the eye of a needle," which is a hyperbolic portrayal of how riches constitute a major impediment to entering God's realm (10:23–25). In 10:29–30 (another passage paralleled in Matthew and Luke), Jesus declares that those

---

25. Powell, *God with Us*, 119–40; Hagner, *Matthew 1–13*, 89–96.
26. Powell, *God with Us*, 130.

who have left their houses, families, and fields behind in order to follow him will "receive a hundredfold now in this age—houses, brothers and sisters, mothers and children and fields, with persecution—and in the age to come eternal life." We have here a glimpse of the postresurrection community, which is envisioned as a fellowship of shared goods, much as we see in Acts.

This latter motif appears also in the Gospel and Letters of John, which all have a common theological and ethical perspective, despite some variation among them. In the gospel, the account of Judas's betrayal refers to the "common purse" of Jesus and the Twelve (13:29), and the story of the feeding of the five thousand presupposes a similar arrangement (6:5-8). The First Letter of John hints in the same direction regarding an early postresurrection community. In 3:17, the author condemns those who ignore the needs of others: "How does God's love abide in anyone who has the world's goods and sees a brother or sister in need and yet refuses help?" And 4:1-6 shows that the criticism is directed to a faction that has split off from the author's community. It is presumably the same group mentioned in 2:19: "They went out from us, but they did not belong to us." Allan Callahan believes that the dissident group withdrew from a system of common goods.[27] His case rests partly on the use of the Greek term *koinonia*, which appears four times in 1:1-7. Generally translated here as "fellowship," it belongs to a family of words that includes the notion having things in common. If we read it in light of this broader usage and in consideration of 3:17, it would indeed appear that part of the author's complaint against the schismatic faction is that they refused to participate in the communal economy.

## THE LETTERS

The most powerful statements on economic issues in the second division of the New Testament occur in the Letter of James.[28] In 1:27, we find a passage that recalls Micah's definition of God's requirements (Mic 6:6-7): "Religion that is pure and undefiled before God, the Father, is this: to care for orphans and widows in their distress, and to keep oneself undefiled before the world." This statement is followed, moreover, by a warning against partiality toward the rich in 2:1-8 that closes with this biting indictment of the rich and those who cater to them: "But you have dishonored the poor. Is it not the rich who oppress you? Is it not they who drag you into court? Is it not they who blaspheme the excellent name that was invoked over you?" (vv. 7-8) A few verses later, the author proclaims that "faith without works is dead" and

27. Callahan, *Love Supreme*, 17-21; Pregeant, *Knowing Truth*, 204-7.
28. See, further, Pregeant, *Knowing Truth*, 292-96.

A MINIPRIMER ON BIBLICAL ECONOMICS                    111

defines works as deeds of mercy toward the needy. (2:14–17) Then in 5:1–5 comes this invective against the rich who exploit the poor: "Come now, you rich people, weep and wail for the miseries that are coming upon you . . . Listen! The wages of the laborers who mowed your fields, which you kept back by fraud, cry out, and the cries of the harvesters have reached the ears of the Lord of hosts. You have lived on the earth in luxury and pleasure, you have fattened your hearts in a day of slaughter."

In Jas 4:5, we read that God has "chosen the poor to be rich in faith and to be heirs of the kingdom that he has promised to those who love him." We must beware, however, of sentimentalizing this statement, as if God had chosen people *to be* poor rather than choosing them, that is, taking their side, *because* they are poor. The passages quoted above show that poverty does not result from divine decree. It is, as Elsa Tamez writes, "the result of a scandalous act of oppression."[29] We should understand the declaration that the poor are "heirs of the kingdom," moreover, in light of the theme of reversal: it is the oppressed poor, *not* the oppressive rich, who will inherit God's rule.

Economic issues also figure in the letters of Paul. The apostle constantly encourages his communities to contribute to a collection for the impoverished church in Jerusalem (Rom 15:26; 2 Cor 8:1–9:15; Gal 2:10). And on issues pertaining to economics and social status, he consistently sides with the poor and marginalized. In 1 Cor 1:27–29, for example, he proclaims God's own identification with those who are "least": "But God chose what is foolish in the world to shame the wise; God chose what is weak in the world to shame the strong; God chose what is low and despised in the world . . . so that no one might boast in the presence of God." Later in the same letter, as Neil Elliott comments, Paul "criticizes the wealthier Corinthians for distorting the life of the community by celebrating their own material advantage as God given (4:6–11) and showing contempt for the poor in their ritual life (11:21–22)."[30]

On a broader level, as Victor Furnish shows, Paul's letters reveal a concern for the common good in society at large. In 1 Thess 3:12, he counsels his faith communities to "abound in love for one another *and for all*," and in Gal 6:10 he asks them to "work *for the good of all*, and especially for the family of faith." In addition, when Paul asks his readers to "*live your life* in a manner worthy of the gospel of Christ," he uses a verb that has the root meaning of "to live as a citizen." Paul is thus "pointing specifically to the civic, political context in which believers are called to live in a way that is

29. Tamez, *Scandalous Message*, 28.
30. Elliott, *Liberating*, 87–88.

appropriate to the gospel they have embraced."[31] We thus have every right, in a time and place in which ordinary people have some say in governance, to enlist Paul in advocating for economic justice in the secular realm as well as within religious bodies.

The book of Revelation is a prophetic critique of the Roman Empire in anticipation of a new age that the author (like Paul) expected in his own lifetime. Foreseeing the empire's destruction as God's act of judgment, the author condemns not only its persecution of Christians but also its brutality in general and its exploitation of human beings. The self-indulgent lifestyle of its ruling class is the target in 18:7: "As she glorified herself and lived luxuriously, so give her a like measure of torment and grief." In the verses that follow, the exploitative character of Rome's expansive trade network emerges. Noting that the world's merchants "weep and mourn" at the loss of the empire as a market for their goods (18:11), the author lists an astonishing array of expensive cargo that flowed into Rome's ports: "gold, silver, jewels and pearls, fine linen, silk and scarlet . . . all articles of costly wood . . . myrrh, frankincense." And the final "commodity" transforms the list into an indictment: "slaves—and human lives" (18:12–13). The point is that Rome's economy, dependent as it was upon slavery, was a major manifestation of its sin.

## THE INEVITABLE QUESTION: "BUT DIDN'T JESUS SAY . . . ?"

As the evangelical social justice advocate Jim Wallis points out to his consternation, the one thing everyone seems to know about biblical economics is that Jesus said that the poor will always be with us.[32] It is true that at three points in the New Testament, Jesus says, "you always have the poor with you"—in Matt 26:11, Mark 14:7, and John 12:8. But what did he mean by this? In each instance, a woman anoints Jesus with expensive ointment, and someone objects that she could have sold it and given the money to the poor. Jesus replies with the statement quoted above, adding, "but you do not always have me," in reference to his imminent death. And Mark's version makes clear what is implicit in Matthew and John by adding this: "*and you can show kindness to [the poor] whenever you wish.*" The point of telling those around Jesus that they "always" have the poor with them is thus not to pronounce that poverty is ineradicable. It is to say that *one can minister*

---

31 Furnish, "Uncommon Love," 67, 73–74.

32. Wallis, *God's Politics*, 209.

*to the poor on other occasions*, whereas Jesus will not always be available to receive the good deed the woman has performed.

But even if the main point of the passage is not that poverty is ineradicable, doesn't Jesus after all say that it is? Not really. The word (*pantote*) translated as "always" does not mean "forever." There are ways of saying "forever" or "through all eternity" in Greek, but the force of *pantote* is more like "all the time." In addition, the verb translated as "have" is in the present tense, not the future. To say "you *will* always have the poor with you" (as in some translations) might give the impression of "forever," but this meaning is unjustified by the Greek. The addition of "will" to "have" in the second clause is more legitimate, since it refers to a specific event in the future—Jesus's death. *Of course* the other occasions for helping the poor will be in the future of those who are present as Jesus speaks; but neither clause is a statement about the *distant* future. Jesus is telling people *in his own time* that they can minister to the poor whenever the opportunity arises, not predicting the economic realities of centuries to come!

In addition, Jesus's saying is an allusion to Deut 15:11: "since there will never cease to be some in need on earth, I therefore command you, 'Open your hand to the poor and needy in your land.'" *Taken by itself*, the opening phrase might seem to indicate that poverty is ineradicable. The emphasis, however, is clearly on *helping* the poor. Earlier in the same chapter, we find a declaration I emphasized in discussing the Torah: "There will, however, be no one in need among you . . . if only you will obey the LORD your God by diligently observing this entire commandment that I command you today" (Deut 15:4). *Taken together*, the two passages (15:11 and 14:4) suggest that although unforeseen circumstances will always create *need*, the need can be met and *systemic* poverty can be overcome if people will obey God's commandments. And these include the provision for the remission of debts in the beginning of the chapter as well as the commandments to lend and give, such as we find in 15:11. It is not legitimate to claim that these passages endorse individual charity but not efforts to deal with the structural causes of poverty. For legal requirements such as the remission of debts in the sabbatical year are *measures to eliminate the causes of poverty*. To use either Deut 15:11 or Jesus's statements on the poor "always" being available *for help* in order to oppose antipoverty measures is to contradict the main emphases of biblical economics. It is Bible abuse of the first order.

## BIBLICAL ECONOMICS AND BIBLICAL THEOLOGY

In conclusion, this point seems indisputable. *The issue of wealth and poverty pervades the biblical writings, from the beginning to the end; and, despite a few minor departures, these writings side with the poor against the oppressive practices of the rich. Nor is the Bible's counsel regarding the poor limited to calls for charity. There is a clear recognition that poverty is not generally a mere accident of circumstance, and certainly is not decreed by God or nature; it is something often caused by the unjust actions of powerful people.*

Economic injustice, moreover, is the most frequently mentioned *moral* issue in the Scriptures. A central criterion for our evaluation of any political theory or economic system must therefore be the extent to which it offers a remedy for such injustice. It is not the only criterion, however: the centrality of the exodus motif in the Hebrew Bible places human freedom high on the list, and in chapter 3 we saw that a balance between individual rights and community responsibility is central to biblical thought. Our review of biblical economics also reveals a respect for private property, understood primarily in terms of the ancestral lands of families; and a respect for the dignity of all persons is everywhere presupposed.

Fundamental to the entire biblical witness, moreover, are three *theological* affirmations that provide the context for the Bible's moral teachings. The first is the sovereignty of God. By grounding these teachings in the will of God, the Scriptures testify to the objectivity of the values that inform those teachings and thus distinguish them from arbitrary human preference. The second affirmation is that human beings are created in God's image (Gen 1:26–27),[33] which, as Terence Fretheim shows, implies the capacity to act on God's behalf.[34] This confidence in human judgment is qualified by a third affirmation—a recognition of human imperfection or sin. However, the notion of an "inherited" sin rests upon a misreading of Gen 3 and Rom 5:12–13. Gen 3, the story of Adam and Eve, says nothing about their sin being passed on to later generations. And although the Romans passage declares all humanity sinful, Adam's sin spreads throughout humanity not through the process of procreation, as was later claimed, but simply "*because* all sinned."[35] That is to say, Adam and Eve start a *process* of sin, but the sin is *not inherited*. And, in any case, none of these passages denies that human beings are incapable of moral or rational action. They do, however, recognize human sin as a problem to be reckoned with.

---

33. Mott, *Christian Perspective*, 154–59.

34. Fretheim, *Genesis*, 345.

35. Johnson, *Reading Romans*, 88–89. Another possible translation is "with the result that all sinned" (Common English Bible).

To invoke these affirmations as criteria for evaluating political theories does not mean that such theories must acknowledge them in explicitly theological terms, only that they must take account of the issues to which those affirmations speak. In the first instance, every political philosophy reflects specific values and logically implies views of human nature and the character of the universe. It is thus the task of a biblically based analysis to evaluate those implied views. In the second instance, we must ask whether a theory takes sufficient account of the human capacity for moral and rational action. The third affirmation, however, means that we must also ask whether the philosophy is sufficiently realistic in the face of a long history of human injustice and other aspects of human failing.

All these criteria will be important as we turn now to an evaluation of political philosophies and their implications regarding economics. The Bible's pervasive solidarity with the poor, however, remains central for our assessment.

# 8

# Applying the Principles
## Biblical Economics and Political Philosophies

> The ideas of economists and political philosophers, both when they are right and when they are wrong, are more powerful than is commonly understood. Indeed, the world is ruled by little else. *Practical [people], who believe themselves quite exempt from any intellectual influences, are usually the slaves of some defunct economist.*
>
> —John Maynard Keynes[1]

## ON POLITICS AND ECONOMICS

Politics, according to Harold D. Lasswell, is the determination of "who gets what, when, and how." Although too narrow, this definition suggests that politics cannot be separated from economics. While some aspects of politics do not deal directly with the economy, the two overlap significantly. All economic theories have political *implications*, and all economic decisions of society depend upon a political process and have political consequences. Therefore, although economics will be my central

---

1 Quoted in Heilbroner, *Philosophers*, 12; italics added.

concern, I will frame this chapter in terms of four political philosophies: (1) traditional conservatism, (2) classical liberalism / contemporary conservatism, (3) contemporary liberalism, (4) and democratic socialism. Only the second and third of these receive serious consideration in mainstream thought in this country today. The first is generally seen as a relic of the past and the fourth as either pure fantasy or the incarnation of everything un-American. We cannot, however, understand the issues at stake without considering all four; and I begin with an issue that lies at the heart of all these perspectives.

## A FUNDAMENTAL DIVIDE: THE DISTRIBUTION OF AUTHORITY

A critical question in political philosophy is whether authority should be concentrated or dispersed. Democracy, the "rule of the people," is a form of dispersed authority, although it is not as extreme in this regard as anarchism, which opposes the existence of a state and often proposes voluntary, nonhierarchical associations as an alternative. The world has known various forms of governance through dispersed authority. Tribal societies have often governed themselves through consensus, and the ancient city-state of Athens boasted a form of direct democracy, in which an assembly of citizens voted on all matters. Athenian democracy was limited, however, since it excluded women and slaves from the political process. Modern examples are more inclusive but are representative, rather than direct, democracies: the individual's voice speaks through elected representatives. Ideally, in such a system, power ultimately rests with the people as a whole, but the decision-making process tends to concentrate in the elected representatives themselves or powerful persons or groups to whom they are beholden.

Examples of concentrated power are absolute monarchy, dictatorship, oligarchy (the rule of a few) and plutocracy (the rule of the wealthy). Dictatorships have taken various forms, among them Italian Fascism, under Mussolini, and Nazism, or National Socialism, under Hitler. In both cases, power was concentrated in a dictator supported by a party exercising exclusive rule. In both cases also, the state was exalted over individuals and controlled virtually every aspect of life—an arrangement characterized by the terms *totalitarianism* and *statism*. A different form of totalitarian statism appeared in the Soviet Union under Stalin, which involved a perversion of Marxist ideology just as Mussolini's Fascism and Hitler's Nazism adopted perverted versions of capitalism and socialism.[2] Karl Marx envisioned an eventual "withering away of the state," so that the eventual outcome of the historical process would be a stateless society in which authoritarian government was unnecessary. That is what he meant by *communism*, not a statist government such as developed in the Soviet Union. Although these totalitarian movements claimed to act on behalf of the people, they were fundamentally antidemocratic, and they maintained power through the use of terror.

There is strong biblical precedent for the rejection of concentrated power. The Hebrew Bible's emphasis on families' rights to their ancestral lands opposes the power of an elite class to upset God's just distribution of territory. A more direct protest is the antimonarchical strain of teaching that views royal power as a violation of the earlier, more participatory governance and a rejection of God's sovereign rule. In Mark 10:42–44, Jesus sets the ideological tone for policies that are visible at other points in the New Testament: "You know that among the Gentiles those whom they recognize as their rulers lord it over them, and their great ones are tyrants over them. But it is not so among you; but whoever wishes to be great among you must be your servant, and whoever wishes to be first among you must be slave of all." We thus find in Matt 18:15–19 a community-consensus model for settling disputes, and in Acts 6:1–7 the whole Jerusalem church participates in the selection of seven deacons.

There are, admittedly, competing currents in the Scriptures on the issue of authority. Israel eventually institutes a monarchy, and the later writings of the New Testament contain seeds of the emerging hierarchical church, particularly evident in the office of bishop (e.g., 1 Tim 3:1–7). But the antihierarchical strains in the Scriptures are the most distinctive in the context of the ancient world; and Jesus, like many prophets before him, stood squarely against the power structure of his day. I thus conclude that *the biblical tradition serves us best when we allow the antihierarchical elements to override the holdover from ancient despotism found in those portions that favor concentrated authority.*

The biblical rejection of despotism implies a respect for human dignity and a view of human beings as individuals-within-community. Although it is theoretically possible to have a benevolent dictator or oligarchy, even the benevolent rule of one or a few disempowers the many, leaving them in a state of dependency. Nor is there any guarantee that a benevolent dictator will not be succeeded by a tyrant. On the other hand, both democracy and certain forms of anarchism honor the rights and dignity of the individual

---

2. Mott, *Christian Perspective*, 199, 220–24.

while valuing community. No form of anarchism seems workable in our modern mass societies, however; and even democracy is not without problems. Proponents of the consensus model of decision making argue that the process of voting always leaves a minority unsatisfied. Nor will the majority necessarily be wise or just. The problem of a "tyranny of the majority" looms large in light of the human propensity toward sin. Constitutions establishing fundamental rights for all are hedges against such tyranny, but in a true democracy a constitution must be subject to amendment or even abolition. The threat of descent into despotism always remains.

We must therefore recognize that democracy will work only under certain conditions. Persons of biblical faith should be particularly sensitive to the need for a common set of basic values, such as the respect for the rights of all persons, to bind society together. Beyond this, wise decisions are unlikely apart from a well-informed populace, which necessitates free and independent sources of information as well as good, universally available education. I therefore agree with the Christian ethicist Stephen Mott: "Democracy is a process that more effectively reflects the values of its people than do the alternatives," but "it is at the mercy of the culture's state of health."[3] Fragile though democracy is, it remains our one best hope on the political level. As the theologian Reinhold Niebuhr has argued, the human "capacity for justice makes democracy possible; but [the human] inclination to injustice makes democracy necessary."[4] Thus, as I turn now to political philosophies, another criterion for judgment emerges—the extent to which they are compatible with democracy.

## TRADITIONAL CONSERVATISM

Traditional conservatism is a philosophical perspective that was particularly influential in the eighteenth century, especially in England and continental Europe. Although sharing some characteristics with what we call conservatism today, it differs from the latter in important ways. As Mott explains, it is primarily a commitment "to the preservation of the ancient moral traditions of humanity," with the emphasis "on traditions, not moral values in themselves, for it sees values as embedded in traditional patterns of life."[5] While not rejecting social change, it prefers gradual transformation that retains strong continuity with the past. In this regard, it overlaps with contemporary conservatism. Its interests, however, are those of the

---

3 Ibid., 161.
4. Niebuhr, *Children*, xi; quoted by Mott, *Christian Perspective*, 154.
5. Mott, *Christian Perspective*, 116–17.

landed gentry rather than those of the business class.[6] Indeed, many early conservatives opposed capitalism, viewing it as crassly commercial and disruptive of traditional principles.

Traditional conservatism sanctions a class system, based on a frank notion of inequality among persons, which tolerates large discrepancies in wealth and power. It embraces, however, an organic view of society in which each class has its place and dignity and makes essential contributions to the whole. Although it respects the individual and private property, it has a strong sense of community. George Sabine and Thomas Thorson thus note that Edmund Burke (1729–1797), often called the father of conservatism, criticized self-interest and believed that what holds communities together is a "sense of membership and duty" involving moral obligations related to social position.[7] There is also a romanticist strain in traditional conservatism that idealizes the pastoral life and promotes the conservation of land and resources.

Between the individual and the larger community are groups and institutions that, together with the social classes, place checks "on one another, and with their diverse interests provide limits on the power of the state." These groups, among which religious institutions are prominent, "keep the practice of government from degenerating into the control of selfish interest and wanton practice."[8] This unapologetically hierarchical vision gives particular power and responsibility to the upper class; and it speaks to the problem of poverty through the notion of noblesse oblige, the obligation of the nobility to act generously towards those beneath them, but opposes revolutionary solutions to inequality.

Traditional conservatism coheres partly with biblical values. The emphasis on religion is consistent with the Bible's grounding of values in a transcendent realm; and its respect for the natural realm is reflected in Gen 2:5, which understands humanity's role as "to till the ground," as well as in many psalms expressing wonder at God's creation. Likewise, the sense of continuity with the past has significant biblical support. The exodus motif appears throughout the Scriptures as a moment in the past that defines present values, and the New Testament constantly refers back to the Hebrew Bible. The importance of the past is well expressed in Isa 51:1: "Look to the rock from which you were hewn, and to the quarry from which you were dug." Astonishingly, however, another passage in Isaiah makes the inverse point:

---

6 Ibid.

7 Sabine and Thorson, *History*, 563.

8. Mott, *Christian Perspective*, 117.

> *Do not remember the former things,*
> *or consider the things of old.*
> *I am about to do a new thing;*
>   do you not perceive it? (Isa 51:18–19)

These verses, announcing God's intention to bring the people home from exile in Babylon, stress *God's freedom to break with the past, to do something new and unexpected.*

We must therefore recognize a complex relationship to the past involving both continuity *and discontinuity*. We saw in chapter 3 that God appears in the Bible as a disrupter of established social patterns. Now we must acknowledge that *God can disrupt the religious tradition itself*. Jeremiah announces a "new covenant" which "will *not be like* that covenant" that God instituted following the exodus. This time God will write the law on the people's hearts. (Jer 31:31–34) Jesus, moreover, frequently overturns tradition. In Mark 7, he pits the Bible against the "traditions of the elders," and in Matt 5:31–33 and 19:3–9 he contradicts biblical law by closing off a Mosaic provision for divorce. Interestingly, however, Matt 5:31–33 comes in a series of sayings (5:21–48) preceded by a declaration that the whole law remains valid (5:17–20). It would be hard to imagine a clearer example of a paradox of continuity and discontinuity.

Traditional conservatism's regard for community is partially in keeping with biblical thought, but the role assigned to the aristocracy contradicts the Bible's egalitarian emphasis. Mott values its emphasis on diverse groups but criticizes its hierarchy of rewards and responsibilities.[9] Quite clearly, its supposedly benevolent paternalism robs the lower classes of self-determination. With respect to the human propensity for sin, this philosophy shows "insufficient perception of the self-interest of the aristocracy"[10] and undue confidence in their ability to "set aside their own self-interests to represent those who have no power over them."[11] Although the Bible sanctions a type of private property, traditional conservatism's embrace of this value is fundamentally different. In the Bible, God has distributed land to every family, whereas the conservative emphasis is on a landed *gentry*. The biblical understanding of private property, moreover, is "not strictly private ownership" in the modern, Western sense, which involves "the freedom to sell." The biblical model is that of "the cooperative property of the village community" in which "land could not be permanently sold."[12]

---

9. Mott, *Christian Perspective*, 120–21.
10. Ibid., 120.
11. Ibid., 121.
12. Ibid., 125.

Regarding economic justice, traditional conservatism falls far short of the biblical standard. Noblesse oblige not only leaves in place the structural causes of inequality but sanctions them as grounded in nature. It thus undermines the Torah's institution of mechanisms to prevent poverty, the prophets' condemnation of the concentration of land in too few hands, and Jesus's pronouncements of blessings on the poor and woes upon the rich. Although many persons of biblical faith have embraced traditional conservatism, this is largely because they have focused on those aspects of biblical teaching that reflect the hierarchical ideologies of the ancient world. In doing so, they have compromised what is most distinctive in the biblical teaching on economics and power—its portrayal of God as the liberator from oppression, who brings down the mighty from their thrones and lifts up the lowly from the dust.

## CLASSICAL LIBERALISM/CONTEMPORARY CONSERVATISM

It is conservatives who are the true liberals today—or so declared a pamphlet I ran across years ago in Dallas. There is a grain of truth in this claim. The classical liberalism that developed in the eighteenth century is the parent of two schools of thought that do battle today under the labels "liberal" and "conservative." The two heirs developed in different directions but share some fundamental values.

At its base, classical liberalism was devoted to the ideals of "the civil liberties—freedom of thought, of expression, and of association—the security of property, and the control of political institutions by an informed public opinion."[13] It reached its definitive form in the nineteenth century, but it drew upon ideas that had developed over three centuries and was particularly indebted to two streams of influence. One of these was the Enlightenment, an eighteenth-century intellectual movement in Western Europe that touched the American colonies also. Stressing the importance of reason over tradition and faith, it supported science and challenged authoritarian aspects of both religious and political institutions. The other influence, however, was religion. As Sabine and Thorson comment, the "backbone" of the movement was "the nonconformist religious sects." These dissenters, standing outside the religious and sociopolitical establishment, "had every motive to safeguard and extend their religious liberty."[14] Their emphasis on the equality of all believers before God, together with their form of church

---

13. Sabine and Thorson, *History*, 608.
14. Ibid., 611.

governance, "provided grounds for accepting the concepts of the rights of the individual and democracy in the state."[15] It was they who "provided an element of Christian charity and humanitarianism" lacking in some of the other contributing currents of thought.[16]

Both the philosophical foundation and the political programs of liberalism, however, came from the nonreligious Philosophical Radicals such as the English philosopher Jeremy Bentham (1748–1832). Their political proposals were based on utilitarianism, a view that accepted "the greatest good for the greatest number" as a formula for just government and enshrined the egoistic principle of pleasure versus pain as a means for defining the good.[17]

In addition, they opposed the privilege of the aristocracy, tyranny in government, and all arbitrary authority. Accordingly, one "crucial aspect of liberal thought is that society should be self-regulated as much as possible so as to reduce dependence upon human decisions."[18] A major tenet of early liberalism was thus that the economy is a sphere, *separate from the political realm*, which is governed by laws of human nature and can be studied scientifically.[19]

Classical liberalism embraced capitalism wholeheartedly. Indeed, this new phenomenon "was the economic expression of classical liberalism." Much like liberalism itself, "capitalism originated in the middle-class quest for liberty from tradition and aristocratic control."[20] It emerged in opposition to the mercantilist economy, in which governments exercised numerous controls to produce a balance of foreign trade and granted favored status to those "merchants, manufacturers, country gentry, or working guilds" it deemed most effective.[21]

As liberalism evolved, many of its proponents became concerned about the negative effects of capitalism and sought fundamental reforms in the system. I will address this strand in the next section. The other strand is what I indicate here as "contemporary conservatism." The contemporary conservative movement actually embraces proponents of several different perspectives. Present-day conservatives generally share, however, a fierce support of capitalism accompanied by opposition to most government

---

15. Mott, *Christian Perspective*, 135.
16. Sabine and Thorson, *History*, 608.
17. Ibid., 612–17.
18. Mott, *Christian Perspective*, 132.
19. Sabine and Thorson, *History*, 622–23.
20. Mott, *Christian Perspective*, 163.
21. Ibid., 165.

intervention in the economy, a preference for limited government, a commitment to low and relatively nonprogressive taxation, and conservative fiscal policy. They also advocate a strong military; and although there is some division of thought regarding the use of military power, many are ardent interventionists with respect to foreign policy. Many also embrace conservative religious beliefs and opinions on issues such as abortion and same-sex marriage, although there are significant numbers of libertarian conservatives who think differently on these matters. It is, in any case, belief in limited government, applied primarily to the economy, that seems to be the cohesive factor. The economic doctrine that provides the primary inspiration of contemporary conservatism is laissez-faire, the policy of allowing the market to operate with as little government intervention as possible. Most conservatives would acknowledge that a totally unfettered market is impractical in our complex society, but it remains for many an ideal we should strive to approximate as closely as possible.

Contemporary conservatives base their economic views largely on their interpretation of Adam Smith, the eighteenth-century Scottish philosopher often called "the father of capitalism" as well as "the father of economics." The most influential aspect of Smith's thought is his understanding of the market. A basic assumption is that it is self-interest that motivates people to do the work necessary for society to function. As Robert L. Heilbroner explains, however, in Smith's view "a community activated only by self-interest would be a community of ruthless profiteers" who could hold "society up for an exorbitant ransom." Competition is therefore necessary as a restraint upon self-interest, as it prevents profit seekers from raising prices too high and ensures the production of the type and quantity of goods people desire. Paradoxically, then, people's selfish motives "are transmuted into the most unexpected result: social harmony."[22] The market is thus self-regulating: "If output or prices or certain kinds of remuneration stray away from their socially ordained levels, forces are set in motion to bring them back into the fold."[23]

Many aspects of classical liberalism reflect biblical values. Its commitment to democracy, freedom from tyrannical government, and respect for private property echo the Bible's emphasis on the dignity of all persons. Mott argues, however, that it suffers from a "lack of recognition of the radical and irrational nature of sin."[24] There was a tendency in the eighteenth century to regard the universe as mechanistic in nature, as operating on purely me-

---

22. Heilbroner, *Philosophers*, 50–51.
23. Ibid., 52.
24. Mott, *Christian Perspective*, 172.

chanical principles of cause and effect. As the liberal tradition developed, it applied the mechanistic model to the economy. Regarding economics as a "hard" science that could identify immutable "laws" governing both human behavior and the market,[25] it placed the market, understood as a self-contained mechanism, at the center of the human enterprise. The question, however, is whether an impersonal mechanism can tame egoism enough to maintain a just society.[26]

This is a question we can answer only as we examine the actual record of capitalism, as I will do briefly below and more extensively in chapter 9. For now, I note that it is one thing to acknowledge human selfishness as a fact to be reckoned with but something else to enshrine it as a hard-and-fast aspect of human nature. We need to ask whether different social systems, economic arrangements, or ideological frameworks might affect human behavior more than the classical liberal / contemporary conservative tradition acknowledges. If so, we might find the laissez-faire doctrine guilty on two opposite counts: undue optimism about the power of the market to curb the effects of selfishness, and undue pessimism about other means to do this.

Aside from issues raised by biblical economics, we need to assess how contemporary conservatives make use of Adam Smith. To begin with, Smith wrote at an early stage of capitalism, so ideas that might have been appropriate in his day do not necessarily apply today. In addition, recent scholars have shown that laissez-faire proponents have seriously misinterpreted his thought. John E. Hill, for example, notes not only that Smith never used the term *laissez-faire*,[27] but also that his acknowledgement of self-interest was balanced by an insistence on the necessity of moral considerations. He thus had a strong interest in "the general diffusion of plenty to all socioeconomic classes" and argued for adequate wages for laborers. He also lambasted laws favoring the interests of employers over those of workers, condemned poor working conditions, and criticized excess profits.[28] Contemporary conservatives also overstate Smith's opposition to "big government." Heilbroner notes that his opposition "was not so much to government per se as monopoly—in any form."[29] Nor did he oppose government intervention as completely as is often claimed. He objected to "laws which shelter industry

---

25. See Meeks, *God the Economist*, 47–48, on the nineteenth-century exclusion of God from the economy.
26. Goudzwaard, *Capitalism*, 126; cited by Mott, *Christian Perspective*, 172.
27. Hill, *Democracy*, 140.
28. Ibid., 142–46.
29. Heilbroner, *Philosophers*, 63.

from competition" or favor the merchant class, but he supported many efforts to improve the lot of the working class.[30]

However appropriate Smith's notion of a self-regulating market might have been to his own time, the policies carried out in his name in the late nineteenth and early twentieth centuries were disastrous from a social justice perspective. This era knew enormous discrepancies in wealth and income, abhorrent working conditions for the laboring class, and widespread poverty. In fact, many early supporters of the laissez-faire doctrine acknowledged that it creates extreme social stratification. Ironically, some of these were adherents of biblical faith who struggled with the problem and took refuge in the newly minted doctrine of social Darwinism. Applying Darwin's theory of biological evolution to the social sphere, they enshrined the idea of "the survival of the fittest" as the basis for opposing nearly all government intervention. As Leslie A. Muray describes their doctrine, "[to] establish government programs to help the poor goes against the ways of nature."[31] Social Darwinism also embraced a racist ideology that placed Anglo-Saxons at the top of a hierarchy, and some proponents in this country named Americans as "a 'natural' elite" among them![32]

A major problem with laissez-faire conservatism from a biblical perspective is that it tends toward an extreme form of individualism to the detriment of a concern for the common good. As Mott observes, the religious heritage of early liberalism, represented in this country by the Puritans, "placed the individual within the covenantal context, which provided a transcending moral order that defined individual and corporate responsibilities." A different strand of liberal thought, however, "centered upon the individual," claiming that "social good came through the ultimately positive effects of the individual's pursuit of either one's own economic self-interest . . . or of one's own self-enhancement." Both perspectives survive in laissez-faire conservatism, but "the balance has tilted in favor of the individualistic strands."[33] A crucial question thus arises: *even if selfish action can lead to social good through the market mechanism, does not the ideological enshrinement of egoism undermine the moral grounding that Smith himself found necessary to make capitalism work properly?*

One defense of the laissez-faire approach is that although it breeds discrepancies in wealth and income, it raises the standard of living for all. Contemporary conservatives thus frequently refer to President John

---

30. Ibid., 62–63.
31. Muray, *Liberal Protestantism*, 28.
32. Ibid., 29.
33. Mott, *Christian Perspective*, 164.

F. Kennedy's quotation of the proverb "A rising tide lifts all ships." If this could be shown to be true, then we might argue that a noninterventionist policy meets the biblical standard of economic justice after all. It will thus be important, in chapter 9, to ask how the market actually works in our contemporary world. In the meantime, it is important to recognize that issues other than those narrowly defined as economic are at stake.

The contemporary conservative critique of governmental overreach and preference for decentralized power cohere with the antihierarchical strain of biblical teaching. The Bible, however, also insists upon justice for all. What if on the local level authorities institute unjust policies, as did the governments of the southern states did during the Jim Crow era? I must admit that I have come only slowly to favor decentralized authority precisely because of my experiences in the segregated South. I have to wonder whether without the centralized power of the federal government, the segregation laws might still be in place. How to balance this conflict between two legitimate values is a subject to which I will return in chapter 11.

Both classical liberalism and contemporary conservatism have been strong allies of democratic government, and to this extent they can claim biblical sanction. Uncritical support for laissez-faire economics, however, obscures a point that Christian ethicist J. Philip Wogaman emphasizes: "great concentrations of wealth have always influenced democratic process disproportionately."[34] We may credit classical liberalism with challenging traditional conservatism's social hierarchy based on inherited status, but we must also fault the laissez-faire ideology for replacing it with a new hierarchy based on wealth. Indeed, for many proponents of this view "the free market is the fundamental institution," of which political democracy is a mere corollary! The "market ballot"—that is, one's participation in the free market—takes priority over the political ballot. Those with greater wealth thus have more "votes" than those with less. To defend such an arrangement on the basis that the new aristocracy is "one of merit and not one of birth,"[35] moreover, is to sanction an undemocratic arrangement in the name of democracy. It is also assumes that there is a necessary correlation between meritorious behavior and wealth.

A final issue with laissez-faire conservatism has to do with social costs. A sacred principle of this ideology is the maximization of profit, which lies behind this classic statement of Milton Friedman: "Few trends would so thoroughly undermine the foundations of our free society as the acceptance by corporate officials of a social responsibility other than to make as much

---

34. Wogaman, *Great Economic Debate*, 91.
35. Ibid., 92.

money for their stockholders as they possibly can."[36] But what happens when an industry moves from one locale for lower taxes and labor costs, placing the profit motive above human welfare? The economic devastation is only one dimension of the social disruption. Families are often torn apart, with one member having to leave the others to find work elsewhere, perhaps unsuccessfully. And even if the whole family is able to move, relationships to extended families and friendship networks are likely disrupted. There is also a negative psychological effect upon the community that comes with a loss of community pride and confidence in the future. Depression, substance abuse, and crime will almost always increase.

Another social cost is the impact of unregulated industry on the environment. When a company pollutes the air, water, and ground in an area, the negative effects upon human health and can be enormous. As Wogaman points out, moreover, the issue is not only one of public health but of "accuracy in cost accounting." It is a false system that fails to build the restoration of the environment into a company's cost of operation; yet industries have historically expected the public to pick up the tab for such operations, even while resisting legislation to prevent the destruction in the first place.[37]

Without denying the positive contributions of a market economy, Wogaman argues that "an absolute system of laissez-faire" results in "a terrible blindness to the effects of greed and the anarchy of uncoordinated economic activity." It also erodes "the foundation of political democracy by depriving political institutions of the power to act on behalf of the whole community on the economic problems which may affect the community most." Neither does it take account of "the importance of conservation for future generations" or "the intangible beauties of life which are not reducible to the cash nexus of the marketplace." Wogaman thus concludes that *"the miraculous market may be a good servant, but it is almost certainly a bad master."*[38] He is joined, moreover, by Pope Francis, who goes so far as to criticize contemporary global economics, with its singular focus financial gain, of allowing the interests of a "deified market" to push aside all other concerns, including human dignity and the environment.[39]

---

36. Quoted in ibid., 77.
37. Ibid, 93.
38. Ibid., 96–97; italics added.
39. Francis I, Pope, *Laudato Si*, VI.56 (pdf, 17).

## CONTEMPORARY LIBERALISM

In the mid-nineteenth century, the British philosopher John Stuart Mill (1806–1873) made "an important distinction between private and public activity" when considering the nature of liberty. Arguing that the individual is sovereign in the former realm but not in the latter, he found it "legitimate to use power to prevent harm to others." Also, because society provides protection for a person, that person owes something to society as a whole and can be required to make certain kinds of contributions to the common good.[40] This turn in liberal thought came in response to developments brought on by the industrial revolution, which lasted roughly from the mid- to late eighteenth century to the early to mid-nineteenth century. As a new, business-based middle class arose, those former artisans now working in factories generally experienced a sharp decline in quality of life because of unsafe working conditions and long hours at low pay. On the other hand, a new upper class, to some extent replacing the landed gentry, lived in luxury. Against this background, Mill argued that because mere restraint from legislation cannot make persons free, some governmental activism is necessary in order to enhance liberty by equalizing opportunity and removing conditions that limit human possibilities.[41]

To understand how governmental action can increase freedom, we need to consider what we mean by this term. President Franklin Roosevelt spoke of "four freedoms"—"freedom of speech, freedom of worship, freedom from want, and freedom from fear."[42] The first two are sacred to both contemporary liberals and contemporary conservatives, because all they require of government is restraint. To achieve freedom from want or fear, however, requires positive action. If social conditions force people to live in poverty and work in unsafe environments, they are not free to participate fully in society or fully to realize their human potential. Thus, while health and safety requirements and child labor laws may curtail the freedom of factory owners and corporations, they increase the freedom of workers to live decent lives. What is lost, moreover, is the freedom to *exploit*, which is in fact the freedom of only a few. Contemporary liberalism thus expects government to expand freedom by extending it to those who suffer the exploitation that the laissez-faire doctrine allows. In that way, it recovers a sense of community that was present in the religious heritage of classical

---

40. Mott, *Christian Perspective*, 132.
41. Sabine and Thorson, *History*, 646; italics added.
42. Mott, *Christian Perspective*, 138.

conservatism. But it is more in keeping with biblical economics than is either classical or contemporary (laissez-faire) conservatism.

Another element in contemporary liberalism is its recognition that government is not the only possible locus of illegitimately concentrated power. When large corporations are unrestrained by any countervailing force, they wield enormous power over both the market and the government. In this country, the negative effects of such power on the economy were recognized during the Progressive Era of the late nineteenth and early twentieth centuries, as reformers argued either for breaking up monopolies or subjecting them to strong regulation. Today, policies such as this are largely considered leftist, but a strong case can be made against monopolies from a contemporary conservative position. A market is no longer free once a small number of companies dominate it. This is a point on which liberals and conservatives ought to have something in common. Sadly, however, conservatives have largely been reluctant to stem the tide of endless mergers; and, ignoring the voices of some vocal liberals, the (moderately) liberal establishment has all too often gone along with them also!

Contemporary liberalism remains within the capitalist camp but has promoted reforms to alleviate poverty and other injustices. We must ask, nevertheless, whether the new liberalism has distanced itself sufficiently from the ideological roots that gave rise to the excesses of the laissez-faire economy. Although contemporary liberalism modifies classical liberalism's allegiance to egoism with a strong sense of community, its economic doctrine still depends upon self-interest in the form of the profit motive. Wogaman therefore questions whether "social market capitalism," which combines a free market with explicit efforts toward social justice, improves sufficiently on the laissez-faire philosophy. "Does not social market capitalism also depend primarily upon greed as the principal motivation for economic endeavour and as a major psychological leverage in marketing?"[43]

A realistic appraisal of human nature from the biblical perspective—that is, a consciousness of the human propensity toward sin—suggests that any effective economic system must take self-interest into account. Yet we should not count self-interest as sinful in itself. Although often defined narrowly, it can be understood in a broader sense that includes the self in a concern for the welfare of all. Often, however, defenders of capitalism adopt the narrower definition. In any case, we need to ask whether even social market capitalism can deal adequately with the issues of poverty and inequality. For its theorists tend to accept the argument that "we cannot have

---

43. Wogaman, *Great Economic Debate*, 121.

adequate production without incentives that ultimately entail inequalities."[44] As Wogaman states their view, "more would be lost, in moral terms, by insisting upon equality in poverty rather than tolerating inequality in an economy which provided more for everybody." While acknowledging this point, Wogaman finds that too many proponents of social market capitalism remain complacent in the face of the *degree of inequality* that it accepts.[45]

The contemporary liberal agenda relies largely on the theory of the British economist John Maynard Keynes, which encourages government spending for social programs and accepts deficit financing. According to this theory, "recessions and depressions occur because there is not enough demand (or purchasing power) for the products of industry."[46] Government can remedy such a situation, however, by public expenditures that create jobs and increase consumers' buying power. Liberals acknowledge that their approach increases government debt but point out that increases in jobs and buying power raise tax revenues to offset it. Michael Harrington thus notes that between 1945 and 1975, a period in which this approach was dominant, "advanced capitalism went through a period of economic growth and rising living standards for the mass of people."[47]

Keynesian economics eventually fell largely out of favor as the U.S. economy experienced what economists named stagflation, a combination of inflation and unemployment, that created a frustrating dilemma: "By increasing purchasing power in order to generate more production and employment, it also seemed to create more inflation; and by restricting the supply of money in order to deal with inflation it also seemed to increase unemployment."[48] Whether this situation represented a temporary glitch or exposes a basic flaw in the theory remains uncertain since the resurgence of conservative ideology in the late 1970s brought with it a turn away from governmental activism.

Two remaining issues have to do with social divisions. Conservatives make a partially valid point when they complain that contemporary liberalism has depended too much on centralized governmental authority. It is difficult in some instances (civil rights!) to imagine an alternative, and conservatives have tended either to ignore the problems liberals have sought to solve or to offer solutions liberals consider inadequate. Nevertheless, the effect of some liberal policies has been to alienate many people and feed

44. Ibid., 122.
45. Ibid.
46. Ibid., 2.
47. Harrington, *Socialism*, 102–103.
48. Wogaman, *Great Economic Debate*, 4.

an antigovernment sentiment based on the perception that decisions are made in some distant realm disconnected from the lives of ordinary people. Another type of division results from the conflicting interests of management and labor. Large corporations wield enormous political and economic power, in the face of which their wage earners would be powerless apart from strong unions. A balance of power between the two forces can create an equilibrium that may serve the economy reasonably well in many circumstances, and it is probably impossible to do away with all conflicts of interest in an economy or a society. But we cannot ignore the fact that "there is an institutionalization of antagonism in social market capitalism which detracts from mutual commitment to the common good."[49]

## DEMOCRATIC SOCIALISM

The first definition of *socialism* I learned was "government ownership of the means of production," and it was many years before I realized how misleading it is. To focus solely on the means of production is, as Michael Harrington observes, to reduce "a rich conceptual heritage" to a single fragment.[50] For this heritage embraces much more than economics. Socialists have offered a variety of visions that touch on virtually every aspect of the life of a society, and its early theorists were particularly concerned with "morality, community, and feminism."[51] In addition, although socialists have a preference for *communal* ownership of the means of production, this does not necessarily mean *government* ownership.

In the early nineteenth century, several visionary thinkers proposed alternative social arrangements, founded cooperative communities to put their ideas into practice, and inspired movements that came after them. Karl Marx and Friedrich Engels, who drew critically upon their ideas, named them "utopian socialists." Identifying capitalism as the cause of the social ills they observed, the utopians saw mere reform as inadequate and sought radical changes in the social and economic system. As Heilbroner describes their ideals, "they wanted a new society in which Love thy Neighbor could somehow be made to take priority over the mean gouging of each for himself [or heself]. In the communality of property, in the warmth of common ownership, was to be found the touchstone of human progress."[52]

---

49. Ibid., 121.
50. Harrington, *Socialism*, 28
51. Ibid., 29.
52. Heilbroner, *Philosophers*, 116.

The vision was one of harmonious socialization with some form of communal ownership of the means of production as its keystone. And although utopians such as Robert Owen, Henri de Saint-Simon, and Charles Fourier tried to put their ideas into effect in a "top-down" manner through the sponsorship of philanthropists or governmental implementation, those who carried on their ideas after them looked rather to the masses themselves as the primary agents of change. Thus, "the movements they inspired were profoundly democratic."[53] And, despite the blatantly *un*democratic practices of the statist regimes that arose in the twentieth century claiming socialist credentials, a tradition of democratic socialism has survived. Mott's definition reflects this tradition: "Socialism is the conviction that the best society and the best environment for individual self-fulfillment is one where the means of production are both owned and controlled by the community. Both elements should be present to have socialism. Community refers to a democratic participation of all the members of the particular social unit involved."[54]

Mott goes on to distinguish genuine socialism from mere nationalization of industry. "Nationalization by itself provides workers with insufficient control to change their work life. It is merely a switch in the unseen and distant owner, the contradiction of socialists administering capitalism." In a socialist system, by contrast, "each member participates in the ownership and control of the means of production," which means that "each one shares in its planning, formation, production, and profit." Socialism also "presupposes equality in that each individual has equal status in the total community, including the economic community." And "it presupposes democracy in that each person participates in the significant decisions that affect his or her life and community, including the economic decisions."[55]

The statist regimes posing as socialist have created the impression that socialism is collectivist in a way that denies the rights and value of the individual. Nothing could be further from the truth. And it is important in this context to understand Marx's view of the individual since these regimes have claimed to be his ideological heirs. His concern was actually to emancipate individuals from the negative effects he attributed to capitalism and thus to unleash their creativity.

Since the capitalist class monopolized "access to the means of production" and could exclude anyone unwilling to meet their work requirements, workers had no power to demand more than their "worth as a

---

53. Harrington, *Socialism*, 29.
54. Mott, *Christian Perspective*, 198.
55. Ibid., 199.

commodity"—that is, their worth to the owner as a cog in the machinery of production. Because they were forced to work longer than their self-sustenance demanded, without pay comparable to the value they produced, they created "surplus value," which was taken by the owner as profit.[56] As a result, workers suffered from "alienation," which entailed a range of deprivations, including the loss of one's distinctively human qualities of self-determination and the ability to possess the fruits of one's own labors. Thus "instead of being free and self-directed, labor is compelled only by a physical need, as it is for animals. The work is not one's own. In it one does not belong to oneself but to another person . . . The worker also is alienated from the products of labor, from one's own creation. One's labor is appropriated by the employers as capital, which adds to their power over the worker."[57] In addition, workers are distanced from one another through competition for wages. "A person becomes separated from the community, drawn into oneself, and preoccupied with one's own private interests."[58] But Marx's negative judgment on this kind of self-absorption is not a rejection of individuality. For in his understanding of human nature, individuals find true self-fulfillment precisely in community.

It is important to emphasize Marx's insistence on the right of workers to the fruits of their labors in light of the common distortion of his views on private property. This bald statement in *The Manifesto of the Communist Party* is the root of much confusion: "In this sense, the theory of the Communists may be summed up in the single sentence: Abolition of private property." We need to pay close attention to the phrase, "in this sense," because it refers to the preceding paragraph that begins as follows: "*The distinguishing feature of Communism is not the abolition of property generally, but the abolition of bourgeois property.*"[59] The term "bourgeois" refers to the capitalist class, owners of the means of production. And "bourgeois property" refers not to their personal property but to those means of production. For Marx, production is social in nature, and for that reason private ownership *of the means of production* is inherently exploitative. To abolish "private property" in this sense is to transfer ownership to those who actually do the work. And democratic socialists have been clear on distinguishing "private property" in this sense from *personal property*, to which all workers are entitled *as the fruit of their labors*.

---

56. Heilbroner, *Philosophers*, 142–43.
57. Mott, *Christian Perspective*, 189.
58. Ibid.,190.
59. Marx and Engels, *Manifesto*, chapter 2.

If Marx was not anti-individual, neither was he antidemocratic. He advocated "freedom of assembly, freedom of the press, minimization of executive power, and maximization of the representative system. Pushing democratic reforms to the point of genuine popular control from below would eventually extend into the organization of the whole society, including the economy. The fight for democratization in the state was a leading edge of the socialist effort."[60]

We must not, however, confuse mere "procedural" democracy with what some term "participatory" democracy. Neither voting rights nor the freedoms listed above are effective if vested interests with overwhelming financial resources have undue influence over the choices on the ballot and control of the media. Thus, "Marx also saw that genuine democracy does not exist as long as there are gross inequalities and dominating elitist interests."[61]

But what are we to make of Marx's notion of the "dictatorship of the proletariat," which he saw as a stage on the path to true communism? The term "dictatorship" did not have the negative connotations it has today. Marx used it to indicate "the direction of society by the proletariat, who were the majority," in place of the bourgeois class, who had in fact exercised that power previously.[62] Also, he meant the "dictatorship" to be a temporary measure, leading to the eventual "withering away of the state." This phrase has anarchistic overtones, but it is unlikely that it means the absence of the need for any administrative tasks at all, although Marx did seem to look forward to a society in which coercion is no longer necessary.[63] In any case, it is not Marx's theory per se that I hold up for evaluation, but the broad vision of a democratic socialism to which Marx was an important, but not the only, contributor.

We have seen both laissez-faire capitalism and social market capitalism at work and have concrete evidence of their advantages and disadvantages; but that is not the case with democratic socialism. In this case, we are confined largely to the evaluation of a *theory*. So how might we imagine such a system in our present world? Numerous versions of socialism have been proposed so that there is no one model to which all proponents would subscribe. I can identify three principles, however, that seem to me to express the best of current socialist thought. The first is a commitment to a fully democratic system in which the people as a whole (not just an elite

---

60. Mott, *Christian Perspective*, 185–86.
61. Ibid., 186.
62. Ibid.
63. Wogaman, *Great Economic Debate*, 62.

class) have genuine participation in the decisions that direct the course of society. Harrington makes the point as follows:

> Socialization means the democratization of decision making in the everyday economy, of micro as well as macro choices. It looks primarily to the decentralized, face-to-face participation of the direct producers and their communities in determining matters that shape their social lives. It is not a formula or a specific mode of legal ownership, but a principle of empowering people at the base, which can animate a whole range of measures, some of which we do not even yet imagine.[64]

The last sentence is crucial: for Harrington, the principle of universal empowerment is more important than any specific mode of social ownership. The latter would be a matter of constant experimentation and innovation. We can imagine, however, that worker-owned and community-owned companies would be part of the picture. Some large industries might require nationalization or control by individual states, but only if genuine public participation in decision making could be guaranteed. *Personal* property rights would be respected, and small-scale businesses could remain in private hands.

The second principle is that the common good would be a goal to be pursued directly rather than indirectly as in laissez-faire capitalism. That is, public policy would be designed to promote relative equality in distributing the rewards of labor and to provide quality social services to all persons.

The third principle might seem surprising, given the history of socialist thought: acceptance of a market within the limits set by the first and second principles. Although we tend to think of socialism and markets as antithetical, many socialists have come to the conclusion that a market system is more efficient than central planning and that competition provides a necessary incentive for worker management to function well.[65] Adherence to the first two principles, however, would mean that the market would not rule society but would be used "to implement democratically planned goals in the most effective way."[66] Thus, some aspects of the economy—health care and the power grid, for example—might be removed from the market altogether. But Harrington argues *that within the context of socialism and democratic planning*, markets can be employed "to serve the common good as Adam Smith thought they did under capitalism."[67]

64. Harrington, *Socialism*, 197.
65. Mott, *Christian Perspective*, 207–8; Harrington, *Socialism*, 218–78.
66. Harrington, *Socialism*, 247.
67. Ibid., 219.

If we understand democratic socialism as thus envisioned, to what extent does it cohere with biblical principles? Paul Tillich, a German theologian who came to this country after being dismissed from his position by the Nazis, said that socialism "is the only possible economic system from a Christian point of view."[68] And it is not difficult to find support for this judgment in biblical economics. Socialism makes economic justice a priority, something built into the structure of the economy and social life in general, rather than a possible by-product of impersonal market mechanisms. Democratic socialism, moreover, is committed to respect for individual rights and self-development and at the same time to honor the communal nature of the human self. It also makes a place for personal property. And it not only honors human freedom and self-determination but seeks to expand the avenues in which this freedom can be expressed. In sum, it seems highly compatible with the biblical concern to eradicate poverty and injustice. It coheres as well as with the Bible's understanding of the human person as made in the image of God and designed for life in community.

One question we might raise from a biblical perspective, however, is whether the socialist vision gives sufficient recognition to the human propensity to sin. Does it expect too much in terms of the willingness of human beings to act for the common good? What might happen to productivity in such a system? Acceptance of a role for the market should provide some incentive, but would it be enough? Mott also reminds us that "participation in decision making is time consuming, requiring substantial time given to the group. One of the challenges of workplace self-management is the extensive time that can be wasted in discussion."[69] The question is thus whether human beings can be expected to meet this challenge, to transcend the desire for immediate self-gratification for the sake of the longer-range common good. Nor are productivity and creativity the only issues to consider. When people shirk their responsibility to participate in democratic processes, they leave the way open for vested interests to manipulate decision making and for demagogues to seize power.

In sum, the socialist vision is clearly compatible with the biblical image of a just society, but one must ask whether it would work *in practice*. And what makes this question so difficult is that the socialist vision involves a new social system, not just a new economy. So we also need to ask whether it is possible to get to that new social system from where we are now, and whether we can do so through democratic processes.

---

68. Quoted in Wogaman, *Great Economic Debate*, 133.
69. Mott, *Christian Perspective*, 216.

## PRELUDE TO A CONCLUSION: THE TYRANNY OF "-ISMS"

My friends began the conversation with a blunt challenge: "How can you defend ____?" referring to a governmental policy they assumed I supported. They were taken aback, however, when I said I felt no need to defend the policy because I disagreed with it. Their puzzlement resulted from the fact that they labeled me. That is, they classified my political sympathies in terms of an ideology, an "-ism," and projected from that labeling to what they thought my views on the issue must be. What they did is a common practice and the root of a much misunderstanding in our political discourse. Having examined several political/economic theories and identified some strengths and weaknesses of each, I must add a cautionary note. Not only are these theories more complex than a brief analysis can indicate, but they have undergone changes over time and are capable of further modification. We have a tendency, however, to reduce them to caricatures and then to project from the caricatures and assume that a given ideology, or "-ism," necessarily entails this or that view on a concrete issue. Worse than that, we reverse the process and assume that a specific opinion on an issue necessarily reflects a particular "-ism" and then—still worse!—we think we have refuted a view simply by labeling it!

Thus, as we turn now to an examination of our current economy, I want to step back from the labels we typically assign to concrete policies, separating them from the "-isms" with which we generally associate them, and consider them on their own merits. And by that I mean both their conformity to biblical teaching and their practicability. I will ask, in other words, not whether they are capitalist or socialist, conservative or liberal, but whether they are just from a biblical perspective, and whether they are workable. For now, I close with the words of the late Roman Catholic archbishop Dom Hélder Câmara, whom the Vatican is now considering for sainthood. A courageous activist for human rights in the face of a military dictatorship in Brazil, this "bishop of the slums" constantly called the church to stand in solidarity with the poor. I quote him now to illustrate how labeling can be employed to subvert efforts toward economic justice: "When I give food to the poor, they call me a saint. When I ask why they are poor, they call me a Communist."[70]

---

70. Quoted in McElwee, "Sainthood Process."

# 9

# Torah Betrayed
## Current Economics in Biblical Perspective

### THE RISING TIDE THAT SANK THE SHIPS: HOW THE UNTHINKABLE HAPPENED

There must be a strict supervision of all banking and credit and investments. There must be an end to speculation with other people's money.
—Franklin Delano Roosevelt, Inaugural Address, March 4, 1933

They were careless people, Tom and Daisy—they smashed up things and creatures and then retreated back into their money or their vast carelessness or whatever it was that kept them together, and let other people clean up the mess they had made.
—F. Scott Fitzgerald, *The Great Gatsby*, 1925

I BEGIN MY EVALUATION of current economic practices with the financial crisis of 2007–8 and the ensuing recession, not because it is my main concern but because it provides a window into the way our current economy operates. The story of this crisis is one of astonishing greed, arrogance, and hypocrisy; of reckless disregard for the common good; and of the dogged refusal to learn from past mistakes. It is a tale of the collusion of business and government in pursuing policies that serve the interests of the few at the expense of the many and of the triumph of ideological dogmatism over common sense. It is also a textbook illustration of economic practices completely at odds with biblical principles.

## The How and the Why: A Study in "Vast Carelessness"

Joseph Stiglitz, a recipient of the Nobel Prize in Economics, prefaces his account of the "freefall" of the economy that led to what we now call the Great Recession with this observation: "The only surprise about the economic crisis of 2008 was that it came as a surprise to so many."[1] His point is that a number of analysts predicted the financial collapse but were ignored by those in business and government whose decisions created the mess. Stiglitz starts with the year 2000, when prices in the high tech industry dropped 78 percent. We speak of such a collapse as the bursting of a "bubble." When investors overestimate the potential of tradable assets, assuming that their prices will continue to rise, they keep buying in the hope that they can eventually sell at much higher prices. But because the prices exceed the actual value of the assets, some investors eventually realize the situation and begin to sell. This causes a rapid drop in prices, a "bursting" of the "bubble," which encourages others to pull out and can eventually precipitate a collapse, not only of the particular market in question but of the economy as a whole.

When the high tech (or "dot-com") bubble burst in 2000, the country went into a recession. According to Stiglitz, "the administration of George W. Bush used the short recession following the collapse of the tech bubble as an excuse to push its agenda of tax cuts for the rich, which the president claimed were a cure-all for any economic disease."[2] The standard logic for such cuts in the face of a recession is that they make more money available for investment, which will create new jobs. In this case, however, the cuts had a minimal effect, so that it fell to the Federal Reserve to adjust interest rates to get more money in circulation. Although this latter strategy can

---

1. Stiglitz, *Freefall*, 1.
2. Ibid., 4.

often work, low demand meant that industries were unable to make use of their existing means of production. Thus, rather than fostering "investment in plants and equipment," the money flowed in a different direction and replaced "the tech bubble with a housing bubble, which supported a consumption and real estate boom."[3]

The stage was thus set for the recession of 2007–8. Low interest rates made home ownership possible for many people, but the financial industry failed to provide the kind of mortgages that would have helped them "manage the risk of home ownership, including protection in the event their house loses value or borrowers lose their jobs."[4] Instead, "Wall Street firms, focused on maximizing their returns, came up with mortgages that had high transaction costs and variable interest rates with payments that could suddenly spike, but with no protection against the risk of a loss in home value or the risk of job loss."[5] Lured by initially low payments, millions of persons took out mortgages they could not afford and then defaulted on their loans when the payments increased or their income dropped. The consequences were tragic: "As they lost their homes, many also lost their life savings and their dreams for a future—a college education for their children, a retirement in comfort."[6] Beyond this, the collapse of the housing market eventually undermined the U.S. economy as a whole and created a global crisis.

It is easy to criticize those who lost their homes because they overextended themselves by purchasing "McMansions" beyond their means. However, it was the *lower end of the mortgage market* that "became the epicenter of the crisis."[7] The jargon of the world of finance is difficult for the vast majority of people to understand and much more so for the poorly educated and people constantly struggling to make ends meet. In many cases, they simply did not understand the terms of their contracts. They were lured into enormously risky deals by smooth-talking agents peddling financial arrangements "designed to extract as much money as possible from the borrower." In some cases, moreover, those who brokered the deals submitted false evaluations of the borrower's financial resources.[8] Nor was it only those who overextended themselves who were affected. Another recipient of the Nobel Prize in Economics, Paul Krugman, notes that "it eventually became clear that nothing related to housing was safe . . . not even loans made to

3. Ibid.
4. Ibid., 5.
5. Ibid.
6. Ibid., 2
7. Ibid., 78.
8. Ibid.

borrowers with good credit ratings who made substantial down payments." The reason was that "housing was probably overvalued by 50 percent by the summer of 2006," which "meant that practically anyone who brought a house during the peak bubble years, even if he or she put 20 percent down, was going to end up with negative equity—with a mortgage worth more than the house."[9]

Of course, the banks and mortgage companies did not create the crisis alone. There were other culprits, including two major rating agencies that are supposed to identify shaky institutions as a warning for investors. As Mike Taibbi reported, evidence gathered for lawsuits against these firms exposed "the evolution of the industrywide fraud that led to the implosion of the world economy—how banks, hedge funds, mortgage lenders and rating agencies, working at an extraordinary level of cooperation, teamed up to disguise and then sell near-worthless loans as AAA securities."[10] They key word here is "industrywide": it was not the actions of a few "bad apples" that shook the world's economy but a flaw at the very heart of the current financial system.

This flaw, moreover, is a result of conscious decisions made in the last decades of the twentieth century, reversing long-standing policies designed to stabilize the economy. Much earlier in the century, in an attempt to avoid another Great Depression, the architects of Roosevelt's New Deal instituted a series of safeguards in the financial industry. Prominent among these was the Glass-Steagall Act, enacted as an emergency measure in 1933 and made permanent in 1945. It was a response to the thousands of bank failures caused by bank runs in which depositors withdrew their funds en masse out of the fear that the banks were acting irresponsibly with their investments and would close. The Act established regulations to prevent risky speculation with depositors' money and established "the Federal Deposit Insurance Corporation (FDIC), which insures bank deposits with a pool of money appropriated from banks." It also separated investment banks from commercial banks to avoid a conflict of interest and to assure depositors at commercial banks that their money would not be risked in a casino atmosphere.[11]

By the 1980s, however, a changed political climate led to a flood of deregulatory measures, and in 1999 Congress repealed the parts of the Glass-Steagall Act that separated the commercial and investment functions. But what those who pushed such deregulation ignored was the long history

---

9. Krugman, *Return of Depression Economics*, 168–69.
10. Taibbi, "Last Mystery," 2.
11. "Glass-Steagall."

of housing bubbles that had repeatedly made it necessary to bail banks out. Nor did they take into account that *"the only extended period in which this was not the case was the quarter of a century after World War II when there were strong regulations that were effectively enforced."*[12] Deregulation thus opened the way for the kind of hazardous financial practices that undermined the world economy.

The Great Recession was therefore neither an unforeseeable accident nor the result of normal business cycles. It was the predictable result of arrogance, greed, and hard-headed ideological fundamentalism. The arrogance reached its height in some of the largest banks. Having grown to behemoth proportions in preceding decades, they became, in a now famous phrase, "too big to fail." As Stiglitz comments, "They knew that if they got in trouble, the government would rescue them."[13] And their arrogance was matched by their hypocrisy. For there is something truly dishonest about those who oppose regulation in the name of a free market but put out their hands demanding that the government rescue them from a crisis of their own making.

## On Foxes and Henhouses: How Not to Cure a Recession

As the crisis of 2008 deepened, nearly everyone in power agreed that government needed to do something to stop the bleeding. I have no doubt that the efforts toward repair were made in a sincere attempt to restore the economy to health. However, a serious flaw, exhibited by both the Bush and the Obama administrations, was that they entrusted the task to people who shared many aspects of the economic philosophy of those who created the problem. In fact, many of them had worked for some of the worst offenders among the institutions at the center of the crisis.

One early attempt under the Bush administration was known as the Troubled Asset Relief Program (TARP). It involved government purchase of banks' "toxic" assets—that is, assets that had dropped dramatically in value—in order to restore their financial stability and lending power. The idea was to encourage banks to begin lending again and thus stimulate the economy. Although an initial bill to fund this program failed in the House of Representatives, a revised version passed—a version that included $150 billion in "special tax provisions" for the constituents of "thirty-two

---

12. Stiglitz, *Freefall*, 92; italics added.
13. Ibid., 83.

Democrats and twenty-six Republicans" who changed their votes![14] The program, however, turned out to be unworkable and was soon abandoned. The TARP money was eventually paid back, but precious time was lost in this misguided effort.

The next attempt consisted of equity injections—funds to recapitalize institutions in exchange for government shares. Stiglitz admits supporting this move under the mistaken assumption "that it would be done right, that taxpayers would receive fair value for the equity, and appropriate controls would be placed on the banks." Instead, however, "even as taxpayers became the principal 'owner' of some banks, the Bush (and later Obama) Treasuries refused to exercise any control. The U.S. taxpayer put out hundreds of billions of dollars and didn't even get the right to know what the money was being spent on, let alone have a say in what the banks did with it."[15] And of course the continued payment of enormous bonuses to executives with already huge incomes, many of whom had brought their companies to the brink of destruction, was one of the main contributors to the public outrage that developed.

A particularly disturbing aspect of the government's response to the crisis is the way federal regulators coddled the banks accused of improper practices. In 2013 the government reached a settlement with the banking industry that mandated the hiring of independent consultants to examine the banks' mortgage files to discover how many were corrupt. The number that the analysts came up with, however, was so low that "even the *Wall Street Journal* moved to check it out" and found an astonishing percentage of errors in the samples they reviewed. These consultants were paid over $2 billion, which is more than 20 percent of the total settlement of $9.3 billion. Federal regulators, moreover, refused to "turn over the evidence of impropriety they discovered during these reviews to homeowners" seeking to bring suit against the banks. In addition, it appears that it may have been the banks themselves, rather than the consultants, who had the final say as to which homeowners had been victimized and were entitled to compensation! The wronged homeowners, by the way, received an average of $300 each in the settlement![16]

---

14. Ibid., 123.
15. Ibid., 125
16. Taibbi, "Wronged Homeowners."

## The Great Debate: Austerity versus Stimulus

Now we come to ideological dogmatism—that is, to the way in which rigid adherence to an economic theory can stand in the way of reasonable approaches to a problem. It is of crucial importance, as we evaluate the attempts to restore the economy, to distinguish between the bailouts of major banks on the one hand and the institution of stimulus packages on the other. In 2009, President Obama signed into law the American Recovery and Reinvestment Act. It was designed to stimulate the failing economy through investments in a wide range of areas, including health care, education, infrastructure, and renewable energy, along with tax incentives. The idea was to put buying power directly into the hands of the populace, and the measure has had some positive results. Those results were slow in coming, however, and have had minimal effect on persons lowest on the economic ladder. Opponents have been quick to criticize the pace of the recovery, but some supporters, most notably Paul Krugman, said from the beginning that the problem was that the package was too small.[17] And this claim brings us to the long-standing debate over how best to respond to an economic crisis—through stimulus or austerity. One argument against government spending as a cure for a recession is based on an analogy between the household budget and the federal budget. The analogy, however, is simply false. "An economy," Krugman explains, "is not like a household. A family can decide to spend less and try to earn more. But in the economy as a whole, spending and earning go together; my spending is your income; your spending is my income. If everyone tries to slash spending at the same time, incomes will fall—and unemployment will soar."[18] The logic of stimulus as a remedy to recessions is thus to increase government spending in ways that encourage consumer spending, which creates new jobs and leads to even more consumer spending. Although this increases government debt, it provides for eventually paying the debt down: more employment means more tax revenues.

The alternative approach, austerity, involves cutting government spending to decrease the debt directly. The logic in this case was that a large federal debt undermines confidence in the government's financial stability, thus discouraging investment. As investment slows, the economy stagnates. Theoretically, then, massive spending cuts would lead to increased investment, which would revive the economy. One objection to this solution,

---

17. "Nobel Laureate Paul Krugman."
18. Krugman, "Big Fail."

however, is that the cuts in government spending recommended by those who advocate this approach inevitably fall most heavily on persons of limited means. Another objection is that it is based on a false assumption regarding how much debt a country can safely carry in relation to its GDP (Gross Domestic Product, the value of all goods produced within a given time frame). Those who advocate austerity have often cited a study by two Harvard professors claiming that the growth of the GDP slows significantly when the debt exceeds 90 percent of the GDP. It turns out, however, that the study contained a serious error. "Along with several rows not being averaged in the spreadsheet's final tally of GDP growth, economic data from Canada, Australia, and New Zealand was excluded. Those are countries whose debt exceeded 90% of GDP but still experienced periods of economic growth."[19]

A third objection is that austerity is actually counterproductive. As C. Robert Gibson comments, "firing lots of people doesn't help the economy grow, since more people with fewer jobs means fewer people buying stuff. Income tax revenues go down because people's incomes are down, sales tax revenues go down because people aren't buying stuff, and social safety net spending goes up because people have fewer jobs."[20] This judgment, moreover, is confirmed by the International Monetary Fund, which had once endorsed the austerity approach. A paper coauthored by the Fund's chief economist in 2013 concluded "not just that austerity has a depressing effect on weak economies, but that the adverse effect is much stronger than previously believed."[21]

We can thus see that the small size of the stimulus package of 2009 is not the only reason it has had a limited effect. It has to some extent been undercut by a turn toward austerity. President Obama was able to push through the package because of a Democratic majority in the House. When the Republicans took over the House in 2010, however, everything changed. Rather than instituting another round of stimulus, both Congress and the president began to focus on austerity measures. But the earlier stimulus in 2009 had better results than the disastrous austerity policies of European governments, and recent methods of analysis have convinced many economists that stimulus is generally the better approach to recovery.[22] No one wants to see deficits rise indefinitely, but slashing programs that stand between millions of people and poverty undercuts our ability to pay the debt down. And the whole discussion surrounding the debt ignores one potential

19. Gibson, "Austerity."
20. Ibid.
21. Krugman, "Big Fail," 2.
22. "Stimulus v austerity."

source of revenue that could make an enormous difference: the tax dollars lost to this country. As Gibson observes, "the richest 0.01% have anywhere between $21 trillion and $32 trillion stashed in overseas bank accounts simply to avoid paying their fair share of taxes. It's a number that's beyond comprehension. Even if someone had spent a million dollars a day since Jesus was born, they would have spent only $700 billion by today, just $0.7 trillion."[23] If we are looking for a dramatic example of how stimulus can help create a healthy economy, we need only look to the decades following the Great Depression. This was a time of concerted government involvement in the economy, and the result was stunning. By the mid-1950s, the economy was booming, and a new middle class had emerged that was unparalleled in the history of the world. A number of factors played into this development, but government spending clearly played a role. It is a dogma of New Deal opponents that it was not Roosevelt's programs that finally lifted the country out of the depression but World War II. There is some truth to this claim, but it is odd to invoke it as a refutation of the arguments for stimulus. War spending is, after all, government spending.

I do not want to leave the impression, however, that my evaluation of the relative merits of austerity and stimulus constitutes a simplistic endorsement government spending as a cure-all or of a top-down approach to government in general. Nor do I endorse unlimited economic growth. These are matters I will address in detail in chapter 11. My purpose here was to assess the workability of specific policies as a response to a specific situation. In the sections that follow, I take a broader look at our current economy as a whole and, finally, offer an evaluation from a biblical perspective.

## THE GREAT INSANITY: HOW THE DECK IS STACKED

As I stressed above, the recession of 2007–8 was not an accident. Neither was it merely the result of the actions of individual executives and companies, although there are villains aplenty in this story. It was the inevitable outcome of specific public policies that encouraged the "vast carelessness" that created the disaster. What I hope to show now is that these policies are not isolated instances of bad governmental decisions but components of an entire economic structure in which the vast majority of Americans are playing a game with the deck stacked against them.

---

23. Gibson, "National Debt," 1.

## Adam Smith's Nightmare: Profits without Production

We hear a great deal about Yankee ingenuity, the enormous creativity of the U.S. populace, touted as the source of innovations that are the greatest antidote to economic stagnation. However, as Stiglitz observes, the innovations in financial markets in the years leading up to 2008 were not of the type that could help ordinary people but "were directed at circumventing regulations, accounting standards, and taxation."[24] I am not suggesting that all large industries have pursued irresponsible forms of innovation, but I do believe that the practice is widespread enough to constitute a pattern. Take, for instance, the case of Bain Capital, as described in an exposé by Matt Taibbi. Firms like Bain present themselves as saviors of failing businesses, but here is how they operate:

> A private equity firm like Bain typically seeks out floundering businesses with good cash flows. It then puts down a relatively small amount of its own money and runs to a big bank like Goldman Sachs or Citigroup for the rest of the financing. (Most leveraged buyouts are financed with 60 to 90 percent borrowed cash.) The takeover firm then uses that borrowed money to buy a stake in the target company, either with or without its consent.[25]

The problem is that although it is the equity firm that borrows the huge amounts from the bank, it is "the target company that ends up on the hook for all of the debt."[26] The target company is thus saddled with interest on a new debt, which, as a former accountant in the Securities and Exchange Commission puts it, "just sucks the profit out of the company."[27] In addition, the company has to pay the equity firm an enormous management fee. It is therefore left with two choices. It can "fire workers and slash benefits to pay off all its new obligations," leaving it vulnerable to resale by the "savior" company at an enormous profit. Or it can declare bankruptcy, "leaving behind one or more shuttered factory towns." But the "savior" company profits in either case: "By power-sucking cash value from even the most rapidly dying firms, private equity raiders like Bain almost always get their cash out before a target goes belly up."[28]

24. Stiglitz, *Freefall*, 8.
25. Taibbi, "Greed," 4.
26. Ibid., 5.
27. Quoted in Taibbi, "Greed," 5.
28. Taibbi, "Greed," 5.

The pattern that Bain's practices illustrate is the dissolution of the links between profit on the one hand and the creation of wealth and jobs on the other. As Dean Baker of the Center for Economic Policy and Research comments, "companies like Bain are not primarily about producing wealth. They profit largely by siphoning off wealth created elsewhere in the economy."[29] And there are other ways of increasing profits without adding anything positive to the economy. Securing special favors from government through subsidies and tax breaks is one of these. Another is the use of monopolistic status to charge outrageous prices that "don't represent returns on investment, but instead reflect market dominance."[30] In all these cases of "profit without production,"[31] the public suffers. For when enormous profits are available without the risks involved in investment, the incentives for job-creating ventures dry up; and both tax breaks and subsidies place greater burdens on the public at large. The success of companies in lobbying for tax loopholes is a major reason that, as a study by Public Citizen shows, "corporate profits have soared to all-time highs as a percentage of U.S. gross domestic product, while corporate taxes are near record lows."[32] Several of the newer high tech companies are among the most notorious culprits, but the system that allows such "sweetheart" deals

> was shaped from the start by lobbyists from large multinationals. Companies like General Electric lobbied for, and got, provisions that enabled them to avoid even more taxes. They lobbied for, and got, amnesty provisions that allowed them to bring their money back to the US at a special low rates, on the premise that their money would be invested in the country; and then they figured out how to comply with the letter of the law, while avoiding the spirit and intention.[33]

This, then, is "Adam Smith's Nightmare." Whereas the standard justification for profit seeking and the accumulation of capital is that it benefits society as a whole, current economic practice stacks the deck against the ordinary worker.

29. Baker, "Romney's Success," 1.
30. Krugman, "Profits," 1.
31. See ibid.
32. Gongloff, "U.S. Companies," 1.
33. Stiglitz, "Globalisation," 1.

## The "Working Stiff's" Nightmare: Where Have All the Dollars Gone? Gone to...

Job loss is not the only result of a system stacked against the ordinary worker. Ideally, growth in productivity ("the output of goods and services per hour worked") can raise living standards for all classes. Current practices, however, have created a huge discrepancy between growth in worker productivity and growth in the median wages of *persons in nonsupervisory positions*. In the period from the end of World War II until the mid-1970s, compensation of ordinary workers grew in proportion to productivity. At that point, however, a huge discrepancy appeared. As Lawrence Mishel explains in a report of the Economic Policy Institute (EPI), "many workers were not benefitting from productivity growth—*the economy could afford higher pay but was not providing it.*"[34] Increased productivity, however, undoubtedly brought increased financial intake; so what happened to all the extra money? What the study reveals is "growing inequality of wages and compensation," with most of the increases going to the top tiers. Although the wages of most workers stagnated between 1970 and 2007, "the earnings of the top 1 percent grew 156 percent, while the remainder of the top 10 percent had earnings grow by 45 percent."[35]

Another EPI report draws an even bleaker picture of the ever-growing gap between the rich and the rest of us:

> In the long period before the current recession, from 1979 to 2007, inflation-adjusted average annual incomes of the highest-income 1 percent of households grew by 224 percent... Those even better off, the top 0.1 percent... saw their incomes grow by 390 percent. In contrast, incomes of the bottom 90 percent grew just 5 percent between 1979 and 2007—and all of that growth occurred in the unusually strong income growth that occurred from 1997 to 2000, a period followed by declining income from 2000 to 2007.[36]

When we move from income to wealth (assets minus liabilities), the situation looks even worse: "the richest 5 percent of households obtained roughly 82 percent of *all* the nation's gains in wealth between 1983 and 2009. The bottom 60 percent of households actually had less wealth than in 1983, meaning that they did not participate at all in the growth of wealth

---

34. Mishel, "Wedges," 1.
35. Ibid., 3.
36. Mishel and Bivens, "Occupy," 1.

over this period."[37] In addition, lest anyone think that the recovery from the Great Recession has changed things fundamentally, a study by Pew Research concludes that from 2009 to 2011, "the mean net worth of households in the upper 7% of the wealth distribution rose by an estimated 28%, while *the mean net worth of households in the lower 93% dropped by 4%.*"[38] Already in 2009, moreover, "the top 1% of wealth-owning households owned 35.6% of all net worth and an even larger share—42.4%—of all net financial assets that provide direct financial returns."[39]

This depressing picture of the stark inequalities in wealth and income is accompanied by another set of figures that strikes at the very heart of our national self-image. Americans have been famously proud of our status as "the land of opportunity." Our folklore brims over with "rags to riches" stories, and we can easily cite the testimonies of many who have come to our shores and done far better economically than they could have in their native lands. This self-image holds true as long as we compare ourselves to most developing nations and severely depressed economies, but not if we consider our peer nations. A comparison involving seven other developed countries shows us ranking *last* in terms of social mobility, far behind Norway, Sweden, Denmark, and Finland. It also reveals a negative correlation between social mobility and inequality: lower social mobility tends to accompany higher inequality.[40]

Even more disturbing than inequality and lack of social mobility are the poverty rates. As of 2013, 14.5 percent of the general population, 19.9 percent of all children, 36.9 percent of African American children, and 30.4 percent of Hispanic children were living in poverty. And "6.3 percent of all people, or 19.9 million people, lived in deep poverty (had income below one-half the poverty threshold, or $11,917 for a family of four.)[41]

The "rising tide," it would seem, is capable of sinking some ships while raising others. And this happens because the deck is stacked: the current system funnels income and wealth upwards, not downwards. It happens neither by accident nor by the decree of impersonal "laws" of economics but because of specific public policies that *make* it happen.

37. Ibid., 13.
38. Fry and Taylor, "Rise in Wealth," 1.
39. Allegretto, "State of Working America's Wealth," 4.
40. Wilkinson and Pickett, *Spirit Level*, 159. See also Gould, "U.S. Lags."
41. United States Department of Health and Human Services, "Information on Poverty."

## Policy as Perpetrator: The Generation of Inequality and Poverty

My hope is that I have by now shown that our economic woes result in large measure from the collusion of business and government in pursuing policies detrimental to the public interest. I would hope also, however, that I have helped to put to rest all simplistic characterizations of government, either as villain or as savior. There is no question but that the federal government has contributed to the problems explored above by counterproductive action. The antigovernment rhetoric so rampant in our country today, however, obscures the potential of government to "promote the general welfare," as the Preamble to the Constitution of the United States authorizes it to do. So my intention now is not to indict government in principle but to show in more detail how recent policy decisions have worked against the common good, *although at other times governmental policies have in fact promoted it.*

Historians generally refer to the period beginning in the 1870s as The Gilded Age, a time of extreme inequality with enormous wealth in the hands of a very few while a large segment of society lived in poverty. Although we usually view 1900 as the close of this epoch, Krugman notes that the distribution of wealth remained basically the same through the 1920s, right up to the Great Depression.[42] By the mid-1950s, however, things had changed; and Krugman labels the economic turn during this time "the Great Compression." Despite major injustices that remained, "ordinary workers and their families had good reason to feel that they were sharing the nation's prosperity as never before. And . . . the rich were a lot less rich than they had been a generation earlier." The country witnessed "a dramatic downward redistribution of income and wealth that made America far more equal than before—*and not only wasn't the economy wrecked by this redistribution, the Great Compression set the stage for a generation-long economic boom.*"[43] Although a significant percentage of the populace still lived in poverty, many were lifted out of it to form the most vibrant middle class in the history of the world.

This development, however, did not happen by accident: "The more carefully one looks at that equalization, the less it looks like a gradual response to impersonal market forces, and the more it looks like a sudden change, brought on in large part by a shift in the political balance of power."[44] With that shift came changes in policy, and Krugman names three

---

42. Krugman, *Conscience*, 15–21.
43. Ibid., 38, 39; italics added.
44. Ibid., 46.

as particularly important. The first was in the structure of taxation: income taxes became more progressive, with the wealthy paying higher percentages. In the 1920s, the income tax on *the highest portion* of a person's income (not one's *entire* income), was 24 percent, but it climbed to 79 percent during Roosevelt's first term and then to 91 percent in the 1950s. In addition, taxes on corporate profits also rose, as did estate taxes.[45] A second factor was that the federal government, which had formerly sided consistently with management against labor, now "became, instead, a protector of workers' right to organize."[46] The third change was direct government action, through the National War Labor Board, to raise the wages of low-paid workers.[47]

The Great Compression, however, came to an end as political power shifted again, bringing a new batch of policy decisions. For one thing, the tax code has become increasingly less progressive. "What should shock and outrage us," Stiglitz writes, "is that as the top 1 percent has grown extremely rich, the effective tax rates they pay have markedly decreased."[48] Today, the wealthiest individuals pay 39.6 percent on the top tier of the income, and "the richest 400 individual taxpayers, with an average income of more than $200 million [per year], pay less than 20% of their income in taxes."[49]

Another factor is the decline of unions. Although business leaders tend to attribute this to deindustrialization, Krugman notes that "most of the decline in union membership comes from a collapse within manufacturing, from 39 percent of workers in 1973 to 13 percent in 2005."[50] He also notes an assault on unions that often involved illegal tactics. "During the late seventies and early eighties at least one in every twenty workers who voted for a union was illegally fired; some estimates put the number as high as one in eight."[51] Then, in the 1980s, with President Reagan in office, "the campaign against unions was aided and abetted by political support at the highest levels. In particular, Reagan's suppression of the air traffic controllers' union was the signal for a broad assault throughout the economy."[52] The new political climate also brought the stagnation of the federal minimum wage: in 1966 it was $1.25 an hour, which would have the value of about $9.00 today, whereas the current minimum is stuck at $7.25. This means

45. Ibid., 48–49.
46. Ibid., 50.
47. Ibid., 51–53.
48. Stiglitz, "Tax System," 1.
49. Ibid.
50. Krugman, *Conscience*, 150.
51. Ibid.
52. Ibid., 151.

that workers at this level have lost more than 18 percent of their buying power during this period.

In an article titled "The Crime of Poverty," Betty Reid Mandell, professor emerita of Social Work at Bridgewater State University in Massachusetts, discusses other policy changes contributing to the problem. As instances of "shredding the safety net," a process that began in the 1980s, she notes the following:

> Welfare for the childless unemployed virtually disappeared . . . Public housing and subsidized housing for the poor declined. The middle class received the lion's share of housing assistance in the form of mortgage subsidies. Public subsidies for private development and residential projects for the affluent increased . . . Unemployment insurance declined. However, the Obama administration increased unemployment insurance and food stamps as part of the stimulus package . . . Welfare payments for AFDC [Aid to Families with Dependent Children] declined dramatically. They have continued to decline under TANF [Temporary Assistance for Needy Families]. In Massachusetts, for example, the inflation adjusted value of the maximum TANF grant has declined $448 or 41%, since 1988.[53]

Mandell also indicts so-called welfare reform, enacted by a Republican-dominated Congress and signed into law by President Clinton, as a major step backwards. It was a popular move at the time, given the widespread perception of rampant welfare fraud by recipients. As Mandell points out, however, "a Massachusetts study found that 93 percent of fraud was done by vendors—pharmacies, doctors, dentists, nursing homes, hospitals, and sellers of medical equipment."[54] Clinton justified the bill by claiming that it would ultimately benefit the poor by opening up employment opportunities. "As people were kicked off the welfare rolls," however, "poverty increased."[55] And the situation has worsened since the economic crisis of 2007–8. As Janell Ross observes in the *Huffington Post*, "the social safety net is failing to keep pace with the needs of struggling Americans . . . Millions of single mothers are falling through the cracks, scrambling to support their families with neither paychecks nor government aid."[56]

Should anyone still doubt the role of public policy in the creation of poverty and inequality, consider these comparisons between the United

---

53. Mandell, "Crime of Poverty," 142–43.
54. Ibid., 147.
55. Ibid., 146.
56. Ross, "Welfare Reform," 1.

States and its peer nations—those with comparable GDP per hour worked. An EPI study reveals that *we have the highest poverty rate among the nations in the Organisation for Co-operation and Development (OECD).*[57] And *not only is our child poverty rate nearly five times that of Iceland, which has the lowest,* but "U.S. children living in poverty also face higher relative deprivation than impoverished children in other developed countries."[58] Why is this so? The study finds that we have "*one of the lowest levels of social expenditure—16.2 percent of GDP, well below the vast majority of peer countries, which average 21.3 percent (unweighted).*"[59] Whatever other factors are at work, the public policies mentioned above are major contributors to our failing grade on the distribution of wealth and income. We have high poverty because of policies that perpetrate the *crime* of poverty!

## THE GREAT IDOLATRY: WHEN IDEOLOGY GOES UNEXAMINED

> No one can serve two masters. Either you will hate the one and love the other, or you will be loyal to one and have contempt for the other. You cannot serve God and wealth.
>
> —Matthew 6:24, Common English Bible

> Do not be conformed to this world, but be transformed by the renewal of your minds, so that you may discern what is the will of God—what is good and acceptable and perfect.
>
> —Romans 12:2

I have tried, thus far in this chapter, to confine myself mostly to a discussion of concrete economic policies and to avoid sweeping judgments about competing political philosophies and parties. Policies do not materialize out of thin air, however. They result largely from the ideologies that drive their proponents. It would be easy to pile up biblical passages, such as those I

---

57. Gould and Wething, "U.S. Poverty Rates," 2.
58. Ibid., 3.
59. Ibid., 5.

discussed in the preceding chapter, to document how policies that create poverty and inequality violate biblical principles. It is more important at this point, however, to identify the ideology that gives rise to those policies. For our difficulties stem largely from the fact that a particular economic ideology has come to function in an idolatrous fashion in our society.

An ideology, I maintain, becomes idolatrous to the degree that it is held as *unquestionable* truth, subject to no examination from any other point of view. In such a case, neither reason nor fact is able to penetrate the claims of the "true believer"; and the system of beliefs becomes so all-consuming that anyone who does not adhere to it must be regarded as an enemy, a traitor, or a heretic. The ideology, in effect, becomes a person's dogmatically held religion, which is precisely what I find to be at work in our culture today. On the one hand, there are people for whom money itself, combined with the power that goes with it, is an object of idolatry. They apparently embrace a particular ideology because it fosters policies that line their pockets. It is primarily those on the highest tiers of wealth and income who profit from the current system, however—that is, the top 1–10 percent. So there must be something else at work among those who do not profit from these policies but nevertheless support them, often with evangelical fervor. I believe that there is a widespread idolatrous *tendency* among human beings in general, to which persons in faith communities are by no means immune. It is an inclination to allow competing values, promoted by the cultures in which we live, to undermine the commitments that we profess to hold most sacred—an inclination against which Jesus inveighs in his saying about serving "two masters." It is thus easy to forget that the biblical faith is fundamentally *countercultural*, a point the apostle Paul emphasized in his injunction against *conforming "to this world."* And I believe that tendency is at work in those legions whose support is necessary for the tiny ruling class to maintain its privileged position.

But what is the ideology that holds such powerful sway over our particular culture? According to a 2013 poll, 41 percent of Americans view themselves as "conservative" or "very conservative" on economic issues, with moderates at 37 percent and liberals at 19 percent.[60] Although these figures represent a slight shift from the conservative to the moderate position, the vast majority of Americans are steadfast in their adherence to capitalism. It is not capitalism per se, however, that drives current policy but a narrowly defined version of it that is filled with internal contradictions and hypocrisies. Current policy does not follow a consistently conservative line, and it is certainly not Adam Smith's capitalism. While today's proponents

---

60. Dugan, "Fewer Americans."

seek to make taxes on the rich ever lower, Smith actually favored progressive taxation![61] And while Smith opposed government intervention *on behalf of business*, today's proponents are willing to raid the public treasury to keep some private enterprises basking in enormous profits and paying outrageous salaries and bonuses to executives. So we cannot even identify the operative idolatry *as* laissez-faire capitalism! Smith also opposed monopolies, a view that stands in marked tension with the practices of today's business leaders and politicians, who apparently have never seen a merger they don't like, even if it clearly stifles competition, the sacred bedrock of free enterprise!

I suggest, alternatively, that the operative ideology behind current policy is a vaguely defined, highly distorted understanding of *freedom* that uses the labels "capitalism" and "conservatism" to promote an extreme form of individualism. This ideology draws upon central aspects of these doctrines but distorts them at will to serve the god of unrestrained individual liberty at the expense of community responsibility. But it is not even logically consistent in doing so. Professing protection for the rights of individuals, it persistently favors the privileges of a few over the needs of the many and even accords corporations certain prerogatives at the expense of actual persons! In the name of personal liberty, it nurtures a strain of antigovernment sentiment. It reserves this sentiment, however, largely for instances in which government seeks to balance the power of the mighty with that of the many, while it grants approval to government supervision of highly personal aspects of life. Defining freedom primarily in terms of the marketplace, it emphasizes the rights of the entrepreneur but limits the rights of workers to bargain for just wages. Viewing the economy as a self-contained mechanism governed by impersonal "laws," it regards unions as interference in an otherwise self-regulating system.

Although the ideology that serves the rich at the expense of the middle class and the poor has its base in the Republican Party, the Democrats have in recent decades betrayed their progressive heritage by making so many compromises with the Republicans that for many people they do not seem to offer a genuine alternative. As Jack Gerson points out in an article in *New Politics*, it was actually a Democratic chair of the Federal Reserve, Paul Volcker, appointed by President Carter, who took the initial turn toward austerity measures in 1979; and Presidents Clinton and Obama included on their economic teams advisers who were major players in the waves of "deregulation that eventually blew up the market in 2008."[62] Liberal Democrat Robert Reich thus finds that his own party cannot be trusted to keep Wall

---

61. Hill, *Democracy*, 182–83, citing Smith, *Wealth of Nations*, v.ii.b.3, 825.
62. Gerson, "Obama, Austerity," 23.

Street in check, citing Democratic support in Congress for a bill "allowing more of the very kind of derivative trading (bets on bets) that got the Street into trouble." He also criticizes the failure of the Obama administration "to put tough conditions on banks receiving bailout money," to prosecute "top Wall Street executives for the excesses that led to the near meltdown," or "to support a tiny tax on financial transactions that would bring in tens of billions of dollars."[63] As I have said, the two major parties are guilty of the same sins, not opposite sins; and it is partly for that reason, I believe, that the Democratic Party fails to inspire a public hungering for *substantial* change.

Having said that, I should emphasize that *degree* matters when it comes to economic sin, and there are a fair number of Democrats who have stood steadfastly against the tide of unjust economic policies. The Republican Party, on the other hand, has grown increasingly extreme in its support of policies that funnel wealth and income upwards and has turned its back on nearly all its moderating voices. As a result, it is scarcely recognizable as the party that once included a liberal like Lowell Weicker of Connecticut or even a moderate like President Eisenhower. Nor is it easy to grasp that the fiercely antimonopoly Theodore Roosevelt (the "trust-buster") and the aggressively prolabor Robert M. "Fighting Bob" LaFollette of Wisconsin were ever in its ranks.

In any case, there are two formidable challenges that those who would resist economic injustice must face. One is how to bring about fundamental changes in our economic structure without resorting to the top-down approach that with good reason angers so many people—that is, to do so in a genuinely democratic way. This will be my primary concern in chapters 11 and 12. In chapter 10, however, I must address a very different challenge; and it is a game changer. The vast majority of economists across the political spectrum—*and I mean conservatives, moderates, liberals, and socialists!*—have tended to accept economic growth as at least part of the answer to the problems of inequality and poverty. But what if planet Earth is simply incapable of sustaining unlimited growth? And, assuming a *partial* truth in the "rising tide" argument (the notion that economic growth benefits persons on all rungs of the economic ladder), what will become of the poor and near-poor if growth is halted?

63. Reich, "Why Democrats."

# 10

# "And God Saw That It Was Good"
## The Bible, Earth, and the "American Way of Life"

> The earth is God's and all that is in it;
> the world, and those who dwell in it;
>
> —Psalm 24:1–2, The New Testament and Psalms

> God saw everything that [God] had made, and indeed it was very good.
>
> —Genesis 1:31

> We're hard at work transforming [the earth]—hard at work sabotaging its biology, draining its diversity, affecting every other kind of life that we were born onto this planet with. We're running Genesis backward, de-creating.
>
> —Bill McKibben, 2011[1]

---

1. McKibben, *Eaarth*, 25.

> I would gladly give up medicine tomorrow if by doing so I could have some influence on policy with regard to mud and soil. The world will die from lack of pure water and soil long before it will die from a lack of antibiotics or surgical skill and knowledge. But what can be done if the destroyers of our earth know what they are doing and do it still? What can be done if people really believe that free enterprise has to mean absolute lack of restraint on those who have no care for the future?
>
> —Dr. Paul Brand, 1985[2]

"Earth Overshoot Day" is the point in the year at which, according to the estimate of the Global Footprint Network, the human community "has exhausted nature's budget for the year."[3] The "overshoot" is the discrepancy between the rate of consumption of renewable resources and the amount of land able to replenish these resources and absorb emissions of carbon dioxide. The discrepancy is enormous. In 2015, Overshoot Day came on August 13,[4] which meant that for the rest of the year we were living on borrowed natural "capital," digging ever deeper into a life-giving fund that rightly belongs to the future. And the most disturbing part is that our degree of overuse is increasing, with Overshoot Day coming earlier each year.

The problem will only get worse as world population increases; and as developing nations emulate the lifestyles of industrialized countries, the pattern itself will change. Not only will there be more people using resources, but they will use them at a greater rate. Lest anyone cast the blame on people in poverty-stricken areas seeking materially better lives, however, consider this statement in a 2012 report of the World Wildlife Fund (WWF) in conjunction with the Global Footprint Network and the Zoological Society of London: "If all humanity lived like an average resident of Indonesia, only two-thirds of the planet's biocapacity would be used; if everyone lived like an average Argentinian, humanity would demand more than half an additional planet, and if everyone lived like an average resident of the USA,

---

2. Quoted in Daly, "Medical Missionary's."
3. Global Footprint Network, "August 13th."
4. Ibid.

a total of four Earths would be required to regenerate humanity's annual demand on nature."[5]

As Fred Magdoff, Professor Emeritus of Plant and Soil Science at the University of Vermont observes, "the poorest 40% of people on Earth are estimated to consume less than 5 percent of natural resources," and "the poorest 20 percent, about 1.4 billion people, use less than 2 percent of natural resources."[6] We in the industrialized world, who have contributed most to the problem, cannot fault poor nations, or those who live in poverty in the midst of our affluence, for wanting to escape from disease-ridden hovels and decaying slums. Nor should we ignore their desire to share in the comforts that modern innovations have brought to a fortunate fraction of the world's population. We therefore face a three-pronged challenge: (1) to lift the poor out of their poverty, *which will mean an increase in their consumption*; (2) to reduce the impact of the affluent minority on the biosphere, *which will mean a decrease in our consumption*; and (3) to accomplish these goals democratically.

Such goals might appear preposterous from a political perspective, but I can imagine no alternative if we wish to honor both the demands of economic justice and the limits imposed by the earth itself. And for persons of biblical faith or humanistic commitments, not to make the effort would betray their most deeply held values. Realizing that there are many among us who deny that the problem exists, however, I turn to a closer look at the issue of environmental limitations. After that, I will try to show how current economic theory stands in the way of rational solutions and examine an alternative approach to economics that mainstream theorists have largely ignored.

## FACING THE FACTS: REALITY VERSUS PROPAGANDA

### The Nature of the Limits

In 1798, Thomas Malthus, a professor of political economy and clergyperson in the Church of England, observed that human population increases geometrically, that is, with a doubling effect (2, 4, 8, etc.), whereas food

---

5. Global Footprint Network, *Living Planet Report 2012—Summary*, 6; italics original.
6. Magdoff, "Global Resource."

production increases arithmetically (1, 2, 3, 4, etc.). He therefore believed that without a check on population growth, the world would soon be plagued with mass starvation. Malthus overestimated the rate of population increase and underestimated the ability of agricultural innovations to increase crop yields, and for a long time he seemed to be wrong. Improvements in agricultural methods were successful in increasing the available calories per person from the eighteenth to the mid-twentieth century; and in the decades following World War II, "even as human populations skyrocketed, global grain harvests double-skyrocketed."[7]

As environmental journalist Bill McKibben points out, however, since 1986 the trend has reversed. Despite all the innovations in agriculture, "the amount of food per person has been dropping" and *"the number of people with too little to eat is now rising instead of falling."*[8] The size of the population is not the only problem. Another factor is, in Magdoff's words, *"too many rich people living 'too high on the hog' and consuming too much."*[9] The fact nevertheless remains: unlimited population growth is unsustainable. No matter how efficient we might become in food production, there is some point at which the earth will be unable to feed everyone if population growth continues unabated.

Increased population, moreover, means increased use of other resources as well as food. In 1972, a team of systems analysts at the Massachusetts Institute of Technology published *The Limits to Growth*, a book commissioned by a group of European scientists and industrialists known as the Club of Rome. As McKibben describes their work, "they charted the exponential growth of several kinds of emissions, and they also calculated the depletion of a variety of resources, especially fossil fuel. Plugging these and other variables into their computer, they produced a series of model runs that showed much the same thing: *humanity was very likely to 'overshoot' and then collapse.*"[10] Focusing largely on the growing scarcity of non-renewable resources, they reached this conclusion: "If the present growth trends in world population, industrialization, pollution, food production, and resource depletion continue unchanged, the limits to growth on this planet will be reached sometime within the next 100 years." On the other hand, *"the state of global equilibrium could be designed so that the basic*

---

7. McKibben, *Eaarth*, 152.
8. Ibid., 153.
9. Magdoff, "Global Resource," 12.
10. McKibben, *Eaarth*, 91; italics added.

*material needs of each person on earth are satisfied and each person has an equal opportunity to realize his or her human potential.*"[11]

Although critics on both the Right and the Left have attempted to discredit this book, a study by physicist Graham Turner has shown that trends over the first thirty years after the book's publication largely confirm the authors' predictions.[12] A mitigating factor is that as people in developing nations become more affluent, their rate of population growth generally falls; and in some cases they have even reached negative growth. At present, however, *world* population is continuing to grow at an astonishing rate. Nor can we deny that as the poor reach middle class they consume more or that unlimited growth will at some point exceed the earth's ability to sustain life. The more we damage the earth, moreover, the more difficult we make it to lift the poorer nations out of poverty.

An important measure of our ecological "overshoot" is the WWF's Living Planet Index, which measures the changes in the abundance of vertebrates around the world. Astonishingly, the 2012 index shows an overall decline of 28 percent since 1970![13] Although the decline or loss of a species is significant in its own right, the greater problem is the effect upon life-support systems in general, largely through the disruption of the food chain. And human activity is clearly at fault in the rapid decline. The WWF report lists five major factors contributing to the problem. I will delay discussion of the fifth, which I consider "the elephant in the room," and list now only the first four:

1. "the loss, alteration, or fragmentation of habitat" caused by conversion of land for agriculture, aquaculture, industry, or urbanization, and the damming of rivers
2. "overexploitation of wild species populations—harvesting of animals and plants for food, materials, or medicine" at an unsustainable rate
3. "pollution—mainly from excessive pesticide use in agriculture, aquaculture, urban and industrial effluents, mining waste, and excessive fertilizer use"
4. "invasive species"—the introduction of species from one environment into another, disrupting the ecological balance.[14]

---

11. Ibid., 91–92; italics added.
12. Turner, "Comparison"; cited in McKibben, *Eaarth*, 96–97.
13. Global Footprint Network, *Living Planet Report 2012—Summary*, 4.
14. Ibid., 12.

The full impact of the loss of any species is impossible to trace, but in some cases the effects on human civilization are immediate and serious. Consider the dramatic disappearance of honeybees, first noticed in 2006. Although there are likely numerous causes, current research lays much of the blame on a class of pesticides known as neonicotinoids, which were introduced in the 1990s without much investigation of potential ill effects. Unfortunately, the effects are alarming. In the winter of 2012–13, for example, beekeepers in the U.S. lost 31 percent of their colonies. Much more ominous than the loss of honey, moreover, is the potential effect on crops that depend upon bees for pollination. According to Dennis vanEnglestorp, an entomologist at the University of Maryland, "One in every three bites [of food consumed in the U.S.] is directly or indirectly pollinated by bees."[15] Natural predators may be part of the problem, but the fact that 121 different pesticides have been found in bee colonies is significant.[16] By using non-natural substances to increase agricultural yields with limited understanding of their effects, we are undermining the ecological system that makes the growth of food possible.

Along with the drastic reduction of biodiversity, the WWF report points to deforestation, the disruption of the ecology of our oceans, and the reduction of free-flowing waters, as major factors in the planet's declining health. Forests are essential to planetary life for many reasons, including the sequestering of carbon dioxide. Although we have made significant strides in reforestation in Europe and North America, the global picture is different. We lost 13 million hectares[17] of forest land per year between 2000 and 2010; and the destruction continues, as we release enormous amounts of carbon dioxide and other greenhouse gases into the atmosphere.[18] The world's oceans are a major source of food for billions of people, but overexploitation of these resources is rampant. Between 1950 and 2005, the global catch increased from 19 million tons to 87 million tons, resulting in the significant depletion of many larger species.[19] Free-flowing rivers are also important to life on the planet, as they deliver nutrient-bearing soil to farmers in delta areas; but of the 177 rivers worldwide that are at least one thousand kilometers in length, only about one-third remain dam-free.[20]

15. Keim, "Honeybee Colonies."
16. Ibid.
17. One hectare is equal to ten thousand square meters or 2.472 acres.
18. Global Footprint Network, *Living Planet Report 2012—Summary*, 15.
19. Ibid., 18.
20. Ibid., 16.

As a native of Louisiana, I feel compelled to mention the effects of various human projects on the precious marshland along our Gulf Coast, as well as the Gulf itself. The story of the destruction of this unique region is captured in a book by Mike Tidwell, *Bayou Farewell: The Rich Life and Tragic Death of Louisiana's Cajun Coast*. His description of a macabre scene he witnessed with his Cajun friend Tim is stunning:

> There, shockingly, along the bayou bank, I can now make out a dozen or so tombs, all in different stages of submersion, tumbling brick by brick into the bayou water. The rectangular three-foot tall sarcophagi, each entombing a single human being above the ground in the South Louisiana style, look like slow-motion lemmings dropping over the fateful edge, one after the other . . .
> "Are the bodies still in there?" I ask Tim.
> "You leave de dead where dey rest," he says. "No one's touched dem. Dey're gettin' a second burial at sea. Fifty, sixty, seventy years ago, dose people were buried on high ground."[21]

The cemetery is submerged because the entire coastal region is being consumed by the Gulf. As described by Barry Yeoman in a publication of the Natural Resources Defense Council,

> *the Louisiana coast—with its fresh- and saltwater marshes, cypress-tupelo swamps, bayous, and barrier islands—is losing land at the rate of 25 square miles a year. That's more than a football field every hour disappearing beneath the water.*
> Fertile fisheries are at risk. The nation's oil-and-gas infrastructure is vulnerable. Entire communities could get swallowed by the Gulf of Mexico. And the hurricane protection that these wetlands provide, already severely compromised (as we witnessed during Katrina), will diminish further. The loss of storm protection alone could cost coastal communities from Alabama to Texas $700 billion by 2030, according to an October 2010 study.[22]

Why is the land disappearing? Tidwell's conversation reveals the primary cause:

> "This is happening because the Mississippi river doesn't flood anymore?" I ask Tim. "The levees hold back the river water and all the sediment that once built up this land?"

---

21. Tidwell, *Bayou Farewell*, 29.
22. Yeoman, "Saving Louisiana"; italics added.

"Dat's a big part of it," he says.[23]

The levees have been largely effective in saving the land along the "Father of Waters" and its many tributaries from flooding. In retrospect, however, we have a glaring example of how tinkering with the natural world can bring unintended consequences. But the levees are not the sole cause of this destruction. "It's de big mess left by de oil companies, too, dat's cuttin' ever't'ing to pieces," says Tim.[24] He is referring to "the practice of extensive canal dredging that continued for nearly half a century," with the result that "there are few stretches of Louisiana marsh that are not scissored by at least one or two canals," making "some areas—seen from the air—look like intricate city maps." The problem is that "canals, once dredged through the marsh, trigger disastrous erosion."[25] Add to this the damage to the Gulf waters themselves by oil spills such as the British Petroleum disaster in 2010, and one begins to view the financial benefits the oil industry has brought to the region in a different light.

The destruction of the Louisiana coastland touches me emotionally because it signals the loss of a way of life to which I feel deeply connected. My father grew up around Bayou Lafourche and filled me with stories of his boyhood there. The loss, however, has more material costs. "Coastal Louisiana, by itself, accounts for an astonishing 30 percent of America's annual seafood harvest, measured by weight."[26] By allowing its demise, we are not only damaging the state's economy but depriving the country of an important part of its food supply and adding to the loss of biodiversity. As McKibben mourns, "the total number of birds detected by radar crossing the Gulf of Mexico each year has decreased by *half* within the last twenty years," and if the decline continues we can expect "major losses for scores of migratory species—many of them already rare, threatened, or endangered."[27]

The fifth factor contributing to the decline in biodiversity adds to the problem of the Louisiana marshes through its role in the rising sea level. I have saved it for last because it has, unfortunately, become controversial. That factor is global warming, or climate change.

---

23. Tidwell, *Bayou Farewell*, 30.
24. Ibid., 32.
25. Ibid., 35.
26. Ibid., 33.
27. Ibid., 62.

## "The Elephant in the Room": "The Biggest Thing That's Ever Happened"

The problem is an excess of "greenhouse gases"—primarily "water vapor ($H_2O$), carbon dioxide ($CO_2$), methane ($CH_4$), nitrous oxide ($N_2O$)." These gases allow short-wavelength radiation "to pass through the atmosphere," setting up a vicious circle: "This radiation is converted to heat, which warms the earth's atmosphere, causing it to emit longer-wavelength infrared radiation back into space." Then these same "greenhouse gases absorb some of this infrared radiation heading out into space, which in turn heats up the Earth's atmosphere even more."[28]

Although these substances occur naturally in the atmosphere in small measures, human activities have increased the amounts enormously since the beginning of the industrial revolution. Many factors contribute to the problem, but the burning of fossil fuels such as oil and coal is of prime importance; and emissions from on-road vehicles is the single greatest source of the warming effect. Important also are "burning biomass for cooking foods and raising animals for food."[29] Meat production accounts for 18 percent of greenhouse gases, with the beef industry heading the list. Not only do the cattle emit methane, but their consumption of plants deprives us of an important means of absorbing carbon dioxide.[30]

These and other human activities have caused the earth to warm to such an extent that human life on the planet is already becoming more difficult; and if we do not make enormous changes in our way of life we may render the planet unable to support life of any kind. This, at least, is what many climate scientists are claiming. There are many among us, however, who doubt the scientists' claims. Thus, given what a reduction of the kinds of human endeavors that release these gases into the atmosphere would mean to modern civilization, we must ask whether the evidence is strong enough to justify enormous adjustments in our way of life.

As a preliminary response to this question, I propose an analogy. Suppose that you and your family have rented a private airplane to fly you across the Atlantic Ocean. Suppose also that before you leave, you consult twenty expert mechanics about the safety of the plane, and *nineteen* (!) of them say they are convinced beyond reasonable doubt that the engine will fail about halfway across the sea. *Would you take your family on this trip?* If your answer is yes, I doubt that anything I might say now would make sense to you!

---

28. Pilkey and Pilkey, *Global Climate Change*, 2.
29. Ibid., 11.
30. Ibid., 10.

If it is no, then consider the results of a survey of 3,146 *earth scientists* by Peter T. Doran and Maggie Kendall Zimmerman of the University of Illinois. The two key questions they asked the scientists were whether they thought global temperatures have generally risen since the 1800s and whether they thought human activity has been a significant factor in temperature change. Ninety percent answered yes to the first, and 82 percent answered yes to the second. More significantly, when the base was narrowed to those who *specialized in climate science*, "the proportion of positive responses rose to 96.2% for the first question and 97.4% for the second."[31] The conclusion that Doran and Zimmerman drew was unequivocal: "The debate on the authenticity of global warming and the role played by human activity is largely nonexistent *among those who understand the nuances and scientific basis of long-term climate processes.*"[32]

In other words, *no significant controversy exists among those most deeply involved in actual research on the matter*. So why is there so much denial of the results of climate science among the general public? Here is a clue: "Between 1998 and 2005, Exxon Mobil gave almost $16 million dollars to anti–global warming advocacy organizations," and Koch Industries, a multinational corporation heavily involved in petroleum, controls foundations that "doled out $24.9 million to the climate denial lobby."[33] The controversy is manufactured by propaganda funded by corporations with vested interests, especially those involved in fossil fuels. And that propaganda is disseminated by politicians indebted to those corporations as well as media personalities who have grown rich by stirring up public anger.

The propaganda campaign has been successful in perpetuating a number of claims about the issue, but these claims do not stand up against the evidence. Among the important scientific works on the subject is a book by geoscientist Orrin Pilkey and his son, Keith Pilkey—*Global Climate Change: A Primer*. Their work is a model of objectivity, giving careful attention to the relevant evidence *and granting deniers the occasional valid points they make*. What they demonstrate, however, is that almost all the claims of the deniers are false, that these claims are often based upon a misunderstanding of the nature of science and the scientific method, and that climate change is both real and driven largely by human activity.

I will mention four of the many claims they debunk to give a sampling of the deniers' arguments.

---

31. Ibid., 48.
32. Quoted in Pilkey and Pilkey, *Global Climate Change*, 48.
33. Ibid., 49.

1. One simply false claim is that in the 1970s scientists were worried about global *cooling*. In truth, there was no such trend *among scientists*; rather, "at that time human-caused warming dominated the peer-reviewed literature," while "concern about a cooling Earth seems to have come from the media."[34]
2. A claim based on the misinterpretation of an actual fact is that the drop in global average temperature following a then unprecedented high in 1998 proves that the earth is cooling. In fact, this drop was simply one of many fluctuations in an over-all *warming trend*. A report in 2009 showed that "the previous ten years had been the hottest on record."[35] And according to the National Oceanic and Atmospheric Administration (NOAA), 2013 marked thirty-seven consecutive years in which "the yearly global temperature was above average;" and "9 of the 10 warmest years in the 134-year period of record have occurred in the 21st century."[36] Both the NOAA and the National Aeronautics and Space Administration (NASA), moreover, have concluded that 2014 (which did not begin with an El Niño!) was the hottest year in recorded history. But now we find that 2015 exceeded it by a wide margin.[37]
3. An economist in Copenhagen named Bjørn Lomborg denies the *extent* of climate change by misusing data. He makes much, for example, of the fact that "melting sea ice will not raise sea level." It is not melting *sea ice* that concerns climate scientists, however but melting *sheet ice*. Lomborg thus misleads the public by refuting claims scientists do not actually make and ignoring claims they do make.[38]
4. A claim based on a half-truth is that the warming trend is the result of variations in solar input, not human activity. Although such variations do account for some warming before 1975, since that time solar activity has been low while warming has increased markedly.[39]

As the evidence of human-generated climate change has mounted, many deniers have shifted their argument, now simply claiming that the problem is not very serious. Some are confident that we will develop new technologies to offset disaster, and we need not deny the role technological innovation can play. Al Gore, who played a major role in calling climate

---

34. Ibid., 27.
35. Ibid.
36. National Climatic Data Center, "Global Analysis," 1.
37. Miller, "2015 Is Warmest."
38. Pilkey and Pilkey, *Global Climate Change*, 41.
39. Ibid., 27–28.

change to our attention, finds hope in such developments as the declining costs of wind and solar energy. However, he also bemoans the fact that utilities are "fighting back" by not only disseminating disinformation on climate change but "intimidating political candidates who dare to support renewable energy or the pricing of carbon pollution."[40] My intent is not to deny that technology can help but to make this point as strongly as possible: to use the *possibility* of technological solutions as an excuse for continuing activities that contribute to global warming is nothing short of insane. Granted some movements in the right direction, we are a long way from a total solution; and not only is time running out, but the earth's biocapacity remains as a fixed limitation.

Another way of dismissing the seriousness of the situation is to argue that the climate change will actually be beneficial: a frequent claim is that larger portions of the earth will become habitable. The Pilkeys' response to such contentions is that any presumed positive effects "cannot be seen in a vacuum."[41] That is, we need to weigh any possible benefits against the more certain negative effects; and when we do that, it is clear that the negatives come out ahead by a wide margin. To explain why, I turn first to McKibben's summary of what is *already* happening to the environment:

> The Arctic ice cap is melting, and the great glacier above Greenland is thinning, both with disconcerting and unexpected speed. The oceans . . . are distinctly more acidic and their level is rising; they are also warmer, which means the greatest storms on our planet, hurricanes and cyclones, have become more powerful. The vast inland glaciers in the Andes and Himalayas, and the giant snowpack of the American West, are melting very fast, and within decades the supply of water to the billions of people living downstream may dwindle. The great rain forest of the Amazon is drying on its margins and threatened at its core. The great boreal forest of North America is dying in a matter of years. The great storehouses of oil beneath the earth's crust are now more empty than full. *Every one of these things is completely unprecedented in ten thousand years of human civilization.*[42]

The most obvious effects of all this are the threats to coastal cities by the rising seas and the diminished supply of potable water that will be available when the melting of glaciers is complete. But much more is at stake. As far back as 1956, scientists predicted that increased carbon dioxide would

---

40. Gore, "Turning Point," 3.
41. Pilkey and Pilkey, *Global Climate Change*, 97.
42. McKibben, *Eaarth*, 45; italics added.

result in greater acidity in the oceans, and we have in fact seen a 30 percent increase which, according to a 2005 report by the Royal Society of London, "has the potential for a more important impact on marine life than both global warming and overfishing."[43] Acidification also harms the coral reefs and will deprive shorelines of protective breakwater and cause "the loss of a huge number of reef-dependent species of marine organisms." Beyond that, in a vicious feedback mechanism, the absence of the reefs will entail the loss of "sinks" that trap carbon, which means that even more will be released into the atmosphere, adding to the warming effect. I have already noted how forest death creates the same problem, and McKibben lists other feedback processes as well. Melting arctic ice, for example, replaces a "shiny white mirror that reflects most of the incoming rays of the sun back into space with a dull blue ocean that absorbs most of those rays." Likewise, the melting of frozen tundra unlocks enormous amounts of methane. In 2008, Russian scientists found areas on the surface of the waters off the northern coast of their country "foaming with methane gas" and concentrations "a hundred times normal." And the scariest part of this particular phenomenon is that although we started the process, *"we can't shut it off."*[44]

Indeed, the most ominous aspect of climate change is that have set processes in motion that will continue to have destructive effects, even if we shut down every single source of human-generated greenhouse emission immediately. One way to measure where we stand is to consider the level of carbon dioxide in the atmosphere. For most of the ten thousand years of human civilization, it was about 275 parts per million. The current count is close to 390 per million. But what does this mean? What number is compatible with healthy life, or life at all, on this planet? Early estimates were as high as 550, but recent research has called them into question. In 2007, James Hansen, whom McKibben calls "the planet's leading climatologist," concluded "that the safe number, at most, was 350 parts per million."[45] If Hansen is correct, we are on extremely dangerous ground. The Pilkeys doubt whether we can be certain about any such number,[46] but we have no right to assume that any error is on the pessimistic side: it is possible that the safe level is *lower* than 350! In the past, scientific estimations of the extent of the negative consequences of warming have generally erred by being overly *optimistic* when judged by the actual pace of the warming process.

---

43. Pilkey and Pilkey, *Global Climate Change*, 73.
44. McKibben, *Eaarth*, 20–21; italics added.
45. Ibid., 13–15, quotations from 13 and 15.
46. Pilkey and Pilkey, *Global Climate Change*, 36.

The melting of polar ice and the expansion of the tropics, for example, are proceeding about a half-century ahead of the predicted "schedule"![47]

As dramatic as this might sound, I do not believe that McKibben's declaration is an exaggeration: "This is the biggest thing that's ever happened."[48] Despite the bleak picture McKibben paints, however, he holds out hope: "We can, if we are very lucky and very committed, eventually get the number back down below 350."[49] And that is the goal of an organization he founded under the name of 350.org. To reach this goal, however, we will have to make enormous changes in nearly every aspect of our lives. For starters, those of us in the developed world must reduce our consumption and find alternatives to fossil fuels. We will also have to make radical changes in our agricultural practices and in many other ways learn to live "lightly, carefully, and gracefully"[50] on a planet that has already, and to some extent *irreparably*, been severely damaged.

I closed the preceding chapter by noting the nearly unanimous view among mainstream economists that growth in the economy is central to our economic health and necessary for fighting poverty. What we have seen in this chapter, however, shows that the planet is unable to sustain unlimited growth. For economic growth, fueled in part by population growth, necessarily involves ever-increasing use of resources and ever-increasing contributions to global warming. We thus face the difficult question of how we can prosper, put an end to poverty, and reduce inequality, without continued growth. I will pursue that question in chapter 11. To complete the present chapter, however, two tasks remain, and both will take us back into more explicit discussion of biblical values. In the concluding section, I will take a close look at the ideology of economic growth. More immediately, I turn to the biblical view of nature. In the preceding chapter, I concentrated on the injustices the current economic system entails for the human community. Recent theologians and biblical scholars, however, have expanded their concerns to the issue of justice *for the earth itself*. This, too, is an important biblical theme.

---

47. McKibben, *Eaarth*, 14–15.
48. Ibid., 46.
49. Ibid., 16.
50. Ibid., 151–212.

## TILLING THE GROUND: BIBLICAL PERSPECTIVES ON HUMANITY AND THE EARTH

Had anyone asked me before I entered seminary what the Bible says about the natural world, I would have said simply that it is God's creation, and we can find God in it. I was thus surprised to learn that the dominant view among biblical scholars was different: in contrast to ancient religions that saw God at work primarily in the cycles of nature, the biblical perspective focuses on God's actions in human history. I was never fully convinced by those who stressed this point to the nearly total neglect of God's relationship to the created order, but the Bible does spend much more time telling the human story than celebrating nature. On the other hand, recent scholars have shown greater sensitivity to the latter aspect of biblical faith and presented a more balanced account. What a careful reading of the Bible shows, however, is not a single point of view but a variety of attitudes toward nature. It is thus not surprising that some interpreters find in the Bible an emphasis on the inherent value of nature but others think it actually devalues the created order. It will therefore require more than mere proof-texting—piling up passages representing one perspective or another—to get meaningful help from the Bible in responding to the ecological crisis. We will have to bring these perspectives into conversation with one another as we give close attention to them.

Some biblical passages could give the impression that God created the world solely for the sake of human beings. In Gen 1:28, God grants the man and the woman dominion over all living things on the earth; and in both Gen 1:29 and 2:9, the apparent function of plant life is to provide food for human beings. It is also possible to read some texts in such a way as to put the material world in a negative light. In Gen 3:17, God curses the ground because of Adam's sin, and in the Revised Standard Version, Rev 12:12 seems to have similar import: "But woe to the earth and sea . . ." More strikingly, 2 Pet 3:10–12 declares that God will ultimately destroy the earth by fire!

Passages such as these do not necessarily have the force they might seem to, however. To begin with, "dominion" need not imply arbitrary control—a point on which I will elaborate below. In addition, Gen 1:30 shows that God gives plants to animals as well as to human beings for food; and the curse on the ground in 3:17 makes human toil difficult but does not constitute a devaluation of the whole created order. In Rev 12:12, the Greek word translated as "woe" would be better rendered as "alas," as it is in Rev 18:10. It thus indicates God's agony on behalf of the earth rather than God's ill will toward it.[51] As for 2 Pet 3:10–12, this passage is followed by the promise of "a new earth, where righteousness is at home," which is consistent with Revelation's vision of "a new heaven and a new earth" (21:1).[52]

Both of these latter passages, moreover, reflect an important aspect of the Bible's vision of the "end times." The expectation in at least some writings is that when the fullness of God's realm (or kingdom) comes, this new reality will be *on earth*—an earth that has been integrated with heaven (Rev 21:2), but earth nonetheless. Also, we need to interpret all of the seemingly negative passages in light of the Bible's positive evaluations of the earth as God's good creation. In Gen 1, God repeatedly pronounces the created order "good." There could not be a stronger affirmation of the intrinsic value of material reality than the fact that in the Gospel of John the divine *logos*, God's eternal Word is incarnated—that is, *becomes flesh*—in Jesus. Similarly, there are elements in the Christ-hymn in Col 1:5–20 that suggest a divine element with the created order itself: "for in [Christ] all things in heaven and on earth were created . . . and in him all things hold together."[53]

An even stronger sense of the intrinsic value of the nonhuman elements in creation comes through in God's speech in Job 38–39. This discourse removes humanity from the center of things through lengthy reflections on the natural world. Passage after passage describes the lives of wild creatures, emphasizing their independence from the human community: "Who has let the wild ass go free? . . . *It scorns the tumult of the city* . . . It ranges the mountains as its pasture . . . *Is the wild ox willing to serve you? Will it spend the night in your crib?*" (38:5, 7, 8, 9). The result, as Katharine J. Dell comments, is that we "see God and nature in partnership quite apart from the involvement of human beings."[54] There is also a decentering effect in Gen 2. Adam's prerogative to name the animals in 2:19 signifies the special status of humanity, but the "ground" motif qualifies this status. God creates the first human "from the dust of the ground" (2:7), just as both the trees and animals spring from the earth by God's command (2:9, 19). Both 2:5 and 2:15, moreover, define humanity's role precisely as "*to till the ground.*" The man and the woman are thus not only part of the natural world but are in some sense subservient to it. Tilling the soil serves human needs, but human beings have obligations to the nonhuman realm.

We saw in chapter 8 that God, although granting Israel the land, retains ultimate ownership and regards the people as tenants. And parallel to

---

51. Rossing, "Alas," 181–84.
52. See Adams, "Retrieving the Earth."
53. See Santmire, *Travail*, 205–6; and Pregeant, *Knowing Truth*, 274.
54. Dell, "Significance," 66.

God's declaration in 25:23 that "the land is mine," passages such as Ps 24:1 assert God's ownership of the earth as a whole: "The earth is God's and all that is in it." Although Ps 8:5–8 refers to human dominion over the "works of [God's] hand," the preceding verses (3–4) express astonishment over this fact in light of the majestic nature of the created order:

> When I look at your heavens, the work of your fingers,
>   the moon and the stars that you have established,
> what are human beings that you are mindful of them,
>   mortals that you care for them?

The passage thus reflects the complexity of the Bible's views of humanity and the earth. We have a special status, defined at some points as dominion, but it must be understood in light of a broader sense of God's care for creation itself, a realm of which we are only a part. Dominion exercised *on God's behalf* would therefore mean something quite different from domination or exploitation. Indeed, as Terence Fretheim comments, the Hebrew verb translated as "have dominion" (*rada*) "must be understood in terms of caregiving, even nurturing, not exploitation." And although in the next verse God commands the human beings to "subdue" the earth, the reference is to "cultivation—a difficult task in those days," and, more generally, "development of the created order."[55]

In sum, because the nonhuman aspects of nature have value in themselves, persons of biblical faith are obligated to do justice for the earth itself—that is, for God's created order—as well as for the human community. This means using our special status by caring for the natural realm for its own sake, not just for its value to ourselves. To treat the earth as ours to do with as we will, to turn dominion into exploitation, is an expression of human arrogance. The Bible recognizes such arrogance as a primary form of sin, or rebellion against God; and we can find it in many guises, one of which, as I hope to show in the concluding section, stands as a major barrier to the development of a just and sustainable economics.

## DEBUNKING AN IDOL: TOWARD AN ALTERNATIVE ECONOMICS

### A Study in Human Arrogance

Early one evening in the 1980s, I was in Cambridge, Massachusetts, walking toward the campus then shared by the Episcopal Divinity School and

---

55. Fretheim, *Genesis*, 346.

Weston Jesuit School of Theology. When I stopped at a corner, I realized that I was standing beside Professor John Cobb, who was on his way to a meeting of the Boston Theological Society, as was I. I had studied with Cobb several years earlier at the Claremont School of Theology, while on a semester's leave from my teaching position. As we walked along together, I learned that he was a visiting professor at Harvard for the semester. When we arrived at the campus, I discovered that he was giving the paper we were gathering to discuss.

I had long known of Cobb's interest in ecology: at one point, he had considered naming his perspective "ecological theology." What I did not know was that this interest had led him into a serious study of economics, which was the subject of his paper that night. A few years later, I also learned that he had been collaborating with an economist, Herman E. Daly, formerly of Louisiana State University and later with the World Bank. Together they published a major treatise on economics in 1989: *For the Common Good: Redirecting the Economy toward Community, the Environment, and a Sustainable Future*. The paper we discussed in Cambridge provided a preview of the proposals the book offered and gave me a new perspective on economics.

One of Cobb's points had to do with how inadequately mainstream economists, both liberal and conservative, tend to deal with ecological concerns. Because their approach has no *direct* way of taking these concerns into account, they treat them as "externalities"—matters that lie outside the realm of a strictly economic analysis. This is because the dominant economic theory views the economic order as a closed system, a complex of causes and effects (demand and supply, e.g.) that can be analyzed in isolation from other aspects of reality. The problem, however, is that the economy is in fact affected by many things that are "outside" it *only if it is defined in very narrow terms*; and chief among those supposedly external factors is the environment. Economists often recommend adjustments to the economy to satisfy the demands of "externalities," but Daly finds this revealing: "When increasingly vital facts, including the very capacity of the earth to support life, have to be treated as 'externalities,' then it is past time to change the basic framework of our thinking so we can treat these critical issues internally and centrally."[56]

One result of the narrow definition of the economy is that mainstream economists tend to treat nature as inexhaustible. We see this in their continuing use of the Gross Domestic Product (GDP) as a measure of an economy's health. Consider a factory that is rapidly depleting nonrenewable

---

56. Daly, *Beyond Growth*, 45.

resources and dumping enormous amounts of pollutants and greenhouse gases into the atmosphere. Apart from some kind of intervening governmental policy, the damage that this factory inflicts on the environment is completely hidden from economic analysis; it affects neither the company's profits nor the prices customers pay for the factory's products. A price *is* paid, however—by the environment! And it is a price that will eventually find its way into the narrowly defined economy when we have to make huge expenditures to repair the ecological damage and create alternatives to the depleted resources. But when we finally get around to repairing the damage, *the expenditures involved will be counted as positives in the GDP*, along with goods bought and sold to serve human needs! The system of accounting not only *hides* the ecological cost; it actually *rewards* it! As far as the GDP is concerned, no expenditure is any better than any other. Money spent on health care is no better than money spent on cigarettes, and dollars spent to prevent ecological damage are no better than dollars spent creating or repairing that damage.

This stunning fact reveals a fatal flaw at the heart of current economics. To treat the economy as a self-enclosed complex of causes and effects is to ignore the fact that it exists within the broader system of planetary life! And it is only by bracketing out that broader system that economists can envision limitless economic growth; for growth, at least as usually defined, entails the use of natural resources. This insight is the foundation of Daly's doctrine of a "steady-state" or "no-growth" economy—that is, an economy that neither grows nor shrinks but is sufficient to meet the needs of a stable population.

There is, however, enormous resistance to this suggestion from many quarters, most particularly from large industries and mainstream economists. Daly relates a revealing exchange with Larry Summers, who was at the time the chief economist at the World Bank but later became secretary of the treasury under President Bill Clinton and an adviser to President Obama. Daly was also with the World Bank at the time, although something of an irritant within the system. During a question-and-answer period after a panel discussion in which Summers participated, Daly asked him "whether he felt that the question of the size of the economic subsystem relative to the total ecosystem was an important one, and whether he thought economists should be asking the question, What is the optimal scale of the economy relative to the environment." The reply, Daly reports, "was immediate and definite: 'That's not the right way to look it.'"[57] But what *is* the right way to "look at it?"—to pretend that the economy is not dependent upon

---

57. Ibid., 6.

the environment? One might think so, given another astonishing statement by Summers: "There isn't a risk of an apocalypse due to global warming or anything else. *The idea that we should put limits on growth because of some natural limit is a profound error.*"[58]

Part of the problem is that economists tend to view the economy as a kind of machine. Summers actually claims that "the laws of economics . . . are like the laws of engineering. There's only one set of laws, and they work everywhere."[59] But to speak of "laws" of economics and compare them with the laws of engineering is to ignore two factors that distinguish economics from engineering or the sciences like chemistry and physics. One factor is the measure of free will exercised by human beings. There can be no "laws" of economics, first of all, because turns in the economy ultimately depend upon human choice. It is *generally* true that that higher prices will decrease demand, but we cannot treat this observation as an absolute *law,* because in some circumstances people keep on buying a product even when the price goes up. Such breaches in the so-called laws of economics in fact happen often enough, sending economists scrambling for explanations. The second factor is that human behavior is heavily affected by social settings. There are some aspects of human nature that cut across all cultures in all times, but there are many aspects that vary from culture to culture and over time. Many economists, however, seem to think that economic behavior is somehow an exception on this score. Summers thus pronounces that "whenever anybody says, 'But economics works differently here,' they're about to say something dumb."[60] The truth is that there have been many different economic arrangements in human history. Yet, as Cobb observes, "even when giving advice to leaders of a nation, experts in economics often feel little need to know much about the history of its economy."[61] The term for such an attitude is arrogance.

My intention is not to skewer Summers or anyone else as an individual but to expose the assumptions that many economists and politicians cling to so tightly that they seduce both themselves and the public into accepting disastrous policies. I have quoted Summers at length because his statements are so revealing, but also because he has been so important a figure in Democratic administrations. For I wanted to show, once again, that both major parties share the guilt on ecological issues. I must nevertheless reiterate that

---

58. McKibben, *Eaarth*, 95, citing Douthwaite, *Growth Illusion*, 211; italics original.

59. Quoted in Cobb, *Spiritual Bankruptcy,* 116, citing George and Sabelli, *Faith and Credit*, 196.

60. Cobb, *Spiritual Bankruptcy*, 116.

61. Ibid.

the guilt is not equal. We were making some progress in this area under President Carter, but with the election of Ronald Reagan the tide turned. As a symbolic gesture, Reagan removed Carter's solar panels from the roof of the White House. More important, his administration initiated a decades-long frenzy in which "we pumped the carbon dioxide into the atmosphere and the oil out of the ground."[62] Indicative of the thoughtlessness of the frenzy was President George H. W. Bush's statement at the 1992 Earth Summit in Rio de Janeiro—"The American way of life is not negotiable"—which in context had to mean that Americans are unwilling to adjust their habits of consumption. Democrats participated in the crime, but many Republicans began to exhibit an outright hostility to environmentalism—a fact illustrated by the scene at the 2008 Republican National Convention where delegates endorsed the extraction of oil in environmentally sensitive areas with their chant, "Drill, baby, drill!"

As McKibben observes, with the turn we took in the 1980s we passed up "our last chance to avert disaster."[63] As the effects of climate change become more evident, we are paying the price for decades of inaction. It is a good sign that President Obama has placed environmental concerns back on our national agenda. However, his administration undermines efforts to deal with those concerns by allowing the ideology of growth to determine economic policy. His puzzling decision to allow Royal Dutch Shell to drill in the Arctic, moreover, is disheartening. One can only hope that the company's failure to find enough oil to justify the enormous expenditure will discourage such ventures in the future!

It is important, finally, to take note of the *extent* of the arrogance of the defenders of current economic theory. For the bracketing out of environmental concerns is only one manifestation of a general tendency to circumvent moral questions altogether. Because mainstream economists understand their field as a science, parallel to chemistry and physics, they also think of it as value-free. That is, they believe that their analyses, supported by mathematical calculations, are based upon objective observation of the way the economy works and are completely neutral on ethical issues. They will allow moral considerations *after* analyses, but these considerations appear as intrusions into a supposedly natural order of things. They are thus reluctant not only to "interfere" with that supposed order but even to admit the existence of problems that beg for action. For to do so would expose the flaw in the theory; and that is why market considerations generally trump demands for economic justice and justice for the earth. The fact

62. McKibben, *Eaarth*, 94–95.
63. Ibid., 94.

is that mainstream economists too often fail to recognize the values that are at work in their supposedly objective, value-free analyses. By bracketing out moral considerations in their calculations, they imply that we have no standard for what is good other than what human beings *say* is good by the choices they make in the market. And Carol Johnston, a professor of theology and culture at Christian Theological Seminary in Indianapolis, identifies the consequences of this way of thinking: "Since the only way to judge what is 'good' for human use is individual choice in the market, we have no way to judge what to produce or how much, beyond letting individuals with access to the market decide as individuals what they want, without regard to any social need."[64]

But if economic theory operates on the basis that "the only recognizable good is individual choice,"[65] we cannot claim that it is value-free; for in that case human freedom of choice becomes the ultimate value. And if human choice is the ultimate value for this doctrine, we have every right to name that doctrine as idolatrous from a biblical perspective. For it clearly exalts the human will above the commandments of God.

## The "Heresy" We Need to Heed: Questions We Need to Answer

The conclusion is unavoidable: Economic growth, far from the solution to our problem, is in fact a major part of the problem. Our only chance for salvaging the planet is thus to debunk the arrogant ideology of unlimited growth and move to some version of a steady-state economy. To say this is heresy from the perspective of mainstream economics, and the problems we face in moving to such an economy are formidable. Doesn't the economy need to grow to keep up with the increasing population? Beyond that, doesn't a slowdown in the economy hurt the poor most of all? Can a steady-state economy be a just economy, in biblical terms? And even if we accept such a "heretical" goal, how can we achieve it without resorting to top-down, authoritarian rule? I address each of these concerns in chapter 11, as I try to give a clearer picture of the vision that steady-state advocates hold out. Although that vision will be difficult to bring to realization, it just might offer us a way of life that is healthier, more spiritually fulfilling, and more in keeping with biblical principles than the distorted vision of an "American way of life" that we have made into such an idol.

---

64. Johnson, "Whiteheadian Perspective," 189.
65. Ibid.

## 11

# Vines and Fig Trees in the "Days to Come"
## Toward Justice, Sustainability, and Democracy

> but they shall sit under their own vines
> and under their own fig trees,
> and no one shall make them afraid;
> for the mouth of the Lord of hosts has spoken.
>
> —Micah 4:4

> It's not just economy and ecology that that are under siege. So are peace and democracy, which are also intimately connected to economy and ecology . . . And the absence of real democracy is what really prevents us from implementing the solutions the American people already support . . . Piecemeal solutions aren't going to solve this. We've got to fix them all.
>
> —Jill Stein, 2014[1]

---

1. Stein, "Economic and Ecological Transformation," 7.

> Today we have to recognize that a true ecological approach *always* becomes a social approach; it must integrate questions of social justice in debates on the environment, so as to hear both the cry of the earth and the cry of the poor.
>
> —Pope Francis, 2015[2]

## AN UNLIKELY DISSENTER, AN UNEXPECTED JOURNEY

In my youth, I seldom questioned authority or expressed dissent from prevailing opinions; but I did experience discontent with the economic status quo. Part of the reason, but only part, had to do with my family's experiences. Soon after my father lost his Chevrolet dealership in the wake of the Great Depression, the outbreak of World War II brought the cessation of automobile production. This meant that for a number of years he was stuck in low-paying jobs in other fields, and some of my earliest recollections confirm my mother's description of our status at one point as "poor, poor, poor." I remember living in a dilapidated house in Marksville, Louisiana, where the wind blew in around the doors and windows during an unusual event for the Deep South—a full-blown snowstorm. I also remember our old jalopy, the hood of which fell on my head and cut it open as I peeked in when my father stepped away to get a tool.

Things improved greatly after the war, as my father took a position as salesman and sales manager at a dealership in which two of my mother's brothers were part owners. Two factors eventually conspired against my family's well-being, however. One was my father's sudden decline in health following surgery, which made the fast pace of a salesman's life more difficult and limited his earnings. The second factor was the arrival of a new general manager, forced on the dealership by the General Motors hierarchy, who not only terrorized the entire staff but pursued a policy that horrified my father. The man's philosophy of sell-under-any-circumstances, eerily similar to the practices in the housing industry that led to the Great Recession of 2008, resulted in deals with customers unable to make their payments and inevitable repossessions. His brutal demeanor likely contributed to my uncle's debilitating stroke. It also led my father to leave his long-held

---

2. Francis I, Pope, *Laudato Si*, I.49 (pdf, 14); italics original.

position to work for the much smaller Plymouth dealership, where the atmosphere was pleasant but the sales potential was limited. He was relatively content there, but the break with General Motors was painful: he was a true believer in their products and had been rated "among the professionals" by a GM representative posing as a customer.

In the midst of this turmoil, my mother went back to school to complete her degree in order to qualify for a teaching job. She had taught second grade before my brother and I were born but had finished only two years of college. Although cursed with a serious math phobia and fearful of resuming her studies after so many years, she studied heroically and made it through in good fashion. She seemed to enjoy her return to teaching, and the children loved her. After my father's death, she survived on her small income by careful management of her budget. They once had a life insurance policy on my father but cashed it in during hard times, and when he applied again he was turned down for health reasons.

It was clear to me that my parents worked very hard both at their jobs and at home, were good at what they did, and lived within their incomes. They followed the standard recipe for success in this economy but reaped relatively small rewards for their efforts. More important, I knew that my family's struggles were insignificant compared to those of people who were actually poor, both black and white. And I could sense, in general, a huge discrepancy between labor expended and wealth gained. So I built up an immunity against the widespread dogma that in this country all who work hard can achieve anything they desire. Always prone to fantasy, when in about the sixth grade I concocted my own wildly utopian economic system in which people worked solely for the love of their toil and the general welfare, there was no money, and all took from the fund of goods only what they needed. Even at that age, I doubted that any such system would ever come to pass, but it seemed a worthy ideal. So I was a bit miffed when my friends, the twins across the street, scoffed and called it Communism. I thought it was the logical projection of what I had learned in Sunday school and church.

In high school, our study of Franklin Roosevelt's New Deal combined with my rudimentary knowledge of biblical economics to give me a strong belief in government programs to alleviate poverty. It simply did not occur to me that such programs might be outside government's responsibility. My wrestling with the issue of top-down versus bottom-up governance came much later in my life. I sensed, however, that many people had an antigovernment bias, and I wrote a paper on that subject, for either American History or Civics. Observing that "there is a kind of war between the people and the government," I declared profoundly that "this should not be." In an immature and inelegant way, I was struggling to articulate what Lincoln envisioned in his Gettysburg Address—that government should be "of the people, by the people, and for the people."

Many years later I was reminded of that paper by a video I frequently showed to my classes. Produced in connection with the Catholic Bishops' Letter on the Economy in the 1980s, it recorded a congregation's discussion of the first draft of the document. In one scene, a man complained about the call for the eradication of poverty, angrily objecting to governmental action.

A woman replied, "But *we're* the government."

"No, we're not," the man snapped.

"Yes, we are," the woman countered.

And therein lies the key to the issue I was struggling to define in my paper. The man and the woman both had points. When we think of government as an alien entity, lording it over us (which, of course, it can be), then we will naturally resent it; and even good things that it does will become suspect. But when government is truly of, by, and for the people, its actions are an expression of a collective sense of the common good. And the genius of democracy is that it is in fact the rule of the people themselves—*if,* that is, it is true democracy.

By the time I graduated from high school, I was passionately committed to democracy and believed that the government of my country generally served the common good. I knew there were battles to be fought on the economic front, but I assumed that our problems could be solved without major upheavals. My journey after that point, however, is a story of gradual disillusionment and growing consciousness of the need for changes of a more fundamental nature.

Three major factors provided the initial impetus for the new directions of that journey. The first was my growing consciousness of economic injustice. The second was the civil rights movement, which forced me to recognize just how wrong conventional wisdom can be. The third was my conviction that ultimate authority lies with God, not any human being or institution; and the more deeply I delved into the world of biblical thought, the more aware I became of the contradictions between the dictates of human authorities and biblical values. Alongside the first commandment, Acts 5:29 makes this point with the greatest clarity. Defying a prohibition of preaching in the name of Jesus, the apostle Peter declares, "We must obey God rather than any human authority." I thus found myself over the years, as I went through college, seminary, and graduate school, increasingly open to new ideas and perspectives.

The process of rethinking was not always easy; I can remember some challenging moments in the formation of my current views. One of these was a series of extended conversations with P. M. John, a fellow seminarian at Southern Methodist. He was a native of India, a member of the Mar Thoma Church, and an articulate debater. Although I thought myself rather enlightened on economic issues and resisted his arguments as best I could, he eventually convinced me that I had not gone far enough in questioning the prevailing system. "There has to be a revolution," he stated firmly, eventually clarifying that he meant a *nonviolent* one. Another challenging conversation, this time during a year at Yale Divinity School, exposed a flaw in my understanding of democracy. I was trying to defend literacy tests (if fairly administered!) as a qualification for voting. A fellow student shot back, however, with the charge that this was an elitist position that automatically disenfranchised a whole class of people. Recognizing that he was right, and embarrassed about the position I had taken, I immediately relented.

And so my journey of thought has continued, step by step, as I have encountered other conversation partners and had to process new information. Fellow students, teaching colleagues, current events, books and articles, television documentaries, students in my own classrooms, and my wife have provided challenges and opportunities for reflection. In all of this, the ecological crisis stands right alongside the persistence of economic justice in convincing me that our currently dominant economic theories and practices are in need of drastic revision. By the time I left graduate school—and this was before climate change had become an issue—I was thoroughly convinced that the current system is incompatible with just and sustainable life on the planet. My continuing study of the issues, long conversations with friends such as those I mentioned in the preface, and the mounting evidence of global warming have strengthened that conviction. I have come, moreover, to see more clearly that democracy is not real unless it extends to the economy—until, that is, poverty has been eliminated, inequality has been drastically reduced, and workers have greater power to determine their own lot in life.

The most difficult issues for this unlikely dissenter are how to envision political structures that can support a just and sustainable economy and what it means concretely for a government to be "of, by, and for the people." Also challenging is the question of what our social lives would be like in a vastly different economy. For not only are politics and economics inseparable, but these two spheres are intimately connected to social structures. Fundamental changes in government and the financial order will necessarily transform society itself, affecting numerous dimensions of our lifestyles, such as living arrangements, food production, diet, consumption, occupations, transportation, and the geographical layouts of cities and towns. I do not pretend to know exactly which changes will be necessary, or which would be best, in any of these spheres. Readers should thus understand my suggestions not as the dogmatic endorsement of rigid ideas, the exchange of one set of idolatrous commitments for another, but as reflections born of an open-ended trek. For if my journey has been an unexpected one, it also remains an *unfinished* one. But here, now, is my current vision of a society and an economy that is just by biblical standards, genuinely democratic, and ecologically sustainable.

## A VISION OF THE IDEAL: IMAGINING A NEW SOCIETY

I begin with a reiteration of values, taken from various points on the political spectrum discussed in chapters 8–9, which I believe are conducive to the realization of such a vision:

- a preference for dispersed rather than concentrated authority,
    - ◊ *along with a recognition of the need for stable structures through which decisions are made and of the fact that some issues have to be addressed on national and even global levels;*
- respect for the rights of all individuals,
    - ◊ *within the context of a commitment to community and the common good;*
- respect for personal property,
    - ◊ *along with the acceptance of some forms of social ownership to promote maximum exercise of power by all individuals;*
- acceptance of the market,
    - ◊ *within the context of a concern for the just distribution of wealth and income as well as the recognition of the need for regulation.*

If we now, drawing upon chapter 10, add

- *ecological sustainability and respect for the nonhuman world*

to our standards, we are faced with the formidable task of holding all these values together in the context of a steady-state economy. Before I attempt an explanation of how we might do this, however, it should be helpful to elaborate on the latter term. A steady-state economy is one that neither expands nor shrinks in significant degree. It remains relatively stable at a level sufficient to meet human needs without undermining the global ecological network upon which all life depends. To meet the standard of sustainability, moreover, it must operate within these three rules formulated by Herman Daly and summarized by Rob Dietz:

1. Exploit renewable resources no faster than they can be regenerated.
2. Deplete nonrenewable resources no faster than the rate at which renewable substitutes can be developed.
3. Emit wastes no faster than they can be safely assimilated by ecosystems.[3]

The prospect of moving to such an economy raises a number of serious issues, which I will address as best I can in this limited context by responding to an imaginary conversation partner, whose questions, I hope, will reflect some of the concerns my readers might have. I will not, however, presume to supply my hypothetical partner's responses to my answers; for that prerogative belongs exclusively to readers.

*Isn't economic growth necessary to keep up with the increasing world population?*

Yes, but the fact of the earth's limited biocapacity remains. We therefore have no choice but to limit world population to a level compatible with the earth's ability to sustain life. This will entail careful analysis to determine that level and worldwide efforts to make birth control available to all people as well as massive programs of education. And we will probably need to consider other measures, such as financial incentives of some sort. Because particularly in the developing nations poverty contributes to high birthrates, it will also be necessary to lift the people of those countries to a higher standard of living—something demanded, in any case, by simple justice. On the other hand, increased consumption in the developing nations will have to be offset by even greater decreases in consumption in the developed nations than would otherwise be necessary.

*But wouldn't the curtailment of growth result in an increase in poverty?*
Given our current economic structures it would indeed. Thus, if a steady-state economy is to meet the standard of biblically defined economic justice, and not just that of ecological sustainability, we will have to modify those structures. As Daly comments, "without aggregate growth poverty reduction requires redistribution."[4] We will thus have to put in place mechanisms that facilitate redistribution downward, rather than upward.

*How can we accomplish such redistribution?*
There are many tools available for redistribution, and we will simply need to experiment in order to see which ones work best. One immediate

3. Dietz, "Approaching," 1.
4. Daly, "Top 10 Policies," 1.

measure would be to raise the minimum wage to a respectable level; and we could reinstitute a genuinely graduated income tax, such as we had in the mid-twentieth century. Another option, often associated with the political Left but proposed by the Nixon administration along lines designed by the conservative economist Milton Friedman, would be a negative income tax. Similar ideas are a guaranteed annual income and this even farther-reaching suggestion by Daly, which is accompanied by some stunning comparisons:

> Seek fair limits to the range of inequality. The civil service, the military, and the university manage with a range of inequality of a factor of 15 or 20. Corporate America has a range of 500 or more. Many industrial nations are below 25. Could we not limit the range to, say, 100, and see how it works? This might mean a minimum of 20 thousand dollars and a maximum of two million. Is that not more than enough to give incentive for hard work and compensate for real differences?[5]

I personally find Daly's minimum too low, but it is the principle that is important here. To limit the range of inequality in this way modifies the impact of market forces, but it by no means negates them. And as for that other bedrock of contemporary conservative economics, incentive, I think a maximum significantly lower than Daly's would not stifle it. For incentive is a socially conditioned phenomenon, related to expectations. I believe that if we were to institute policies to reduce inequality and eliminate poverty, people in the upper brackets would eventually cease to expect compensation outrageously greater than that of the vast majority of people. In any case, measures to reduce inequality are necessary on two grounds—first of all, simple economic justice, but also to maintain a sense of community, which is "necessary for democracy" but "hard to maintain across the vast income differences current in the United States. Rich and poor separated by a factor of 500 have few experiences or interests in common, and are increasingly likely to engage in violent conflict."[6] And just to show how extreme the recent trend toward greater inequality is, Bill Moyers comments that *"even J. P. Morgan thought bosses should only get twenty times more than their workers, at most."*[7]

*Even measures such as these, however, would not necessarily speak to the issue of job loss as the economy slows. How could this problem be addressed?*

In a number of ways. Among the policies Daly and Cobb endorse is full employment, which could be facilitated in part by shorter work hours,

---

5. Ibid., 2.
6. Ibid.
7. Moyers, *Moyers on Democracy*, 242; italics added.

job sharing, and longer vacations. In addition, a move away from economic globalization, accompanied by the reindustrialization (along ecologically sound lines) of the United States would help enormously. And we could look to the government as an employer of last resort.[8] We might, for example, establish New Deal–type agencies for repairing our shamefully deteriorated infrastructure and rebuilding our inner cities as desirable and ecologically sound living spaces for persons at all income levels. The movement toward sustainable lifestyles would also create new, "green" jobs of all sorts in abundance. On another front, we could be more judicious in our uses of automation, distinguishing between those that promote the general welfare and those that do not. This raises complicated issues, but I agree with Daly that it would help re-create a sense of community to rehire such persons as bank tellers, service station attendants, and supermarket cashiers, who have been displaced. For their growing disappearance has meant that "ordinary human contacts are diminished and commerce becomes more sterile and impersonally digitized. In particular, daily interaction between people of different socioeconomic classes is reduced."[9]

*But wouldn't shorter work hours mean less pay and thus a lower standard of living?*

In the first place, policies such as minimum or guaranteed annual income would help to offset the reduction. But we also need to consider what we mean by "standard of living." We use this term largely to refer to quantity of consumption—the amount of material goods we accumulate and the energy we use. So a family with four gas-guzzling automobiles and innumerable electronic gadgets, living in a "McMansion" with a swimming pool, is considered well-off. Suppose, however, that the wage earners in this family work long hours in stressful jobs involving long commutes or constant travel. Just how well-off is this family? If we put more emphasis on quality of life than on "standard of living," we would undoubtedly evaluate their situation quite differently.

*Are you trying to tell me "less is more," as some are now saying?*

Yes, I am, if I'm allowed to say what we mean by that. We need to ask ourselves what is truly fulfilling for human life. If shorter work hours means lower pay for some people, it also means more time for leisure activities—for families to be together, for recreation, for hobbies, for continued education, for spiritual development, for volunteering. And if more careful use of resources means saying goodbye to private swimming pools, for example, a greater emphasis on community development would bring an

---

8. Daly and Cobb, *For the Common Good*, 309–14.
9. Daly, "Full Employment," 2.

increase in public recreational facilities—again bringing persons of different socioeconomic levels into more frequent contact. As long as our basic material needs are met, yes, in a sense less is indeed more because it means that we are freed from a never-ending scramble for nonessential forms of "more" that are not ultimately satisfying. And a lifestyle less oriented toward consumption ought to promote "family values" in a major way, which is something persons of biblical faith should certainly celebrate.

*Wouldn't some people say that we would be less happy with fewer material goods?*

I'm sure some would, but there is abundant scientific evidence to the contrary: "Economists and psychologists have spent decades studying the relations between wealth and happiness; they have generally concluded that wealth increases human happiness when it lifts people out of abject poverty and into the middle class but that it does little to increase happiness thereafter."[10] One specific study is particularly telling. As John E. Hill summarizes, "happiness researchers questioned freshmen at elite universities in 1976 and again 20 years later; they determined that those with materialistic aspirations as freshmen were less satisfied with their lives than the less materialistic freshmen."[11] In any case, the biblical witness is replete with warnings against devoting one's life to materialistic pursuits. Consider, for example, Jesus's words in the Sermon on the Mount:

> Do not store up for yourselves treasure on earth, where moth and rust consume and where thieves break in and steal; but store up for yourselves treasure in heaven, where neither moth nor rust consumes and where thieves do not break in and steal. For where your treasure is, there your heart will be also. (Matt 5:19)

*Do you mean, then, that persons of biblical faith should be unconcerned about their own material well-being?*

Of course not. Otherwise, the Torah's provisions for economic justice, the prophets' denunciation of injustice, and Jesus's own solidarity with the poor would make no sense. Micah's vision of individuals sitting under their own vines and fig trees (Mic 4:4) presupposes a concern for material well-being. The problem arises when people want too much, more than their fair share, or want things for themselves at the expense of a decent life for others. The biblical ideal is not the rejection of material goods but the pursuit of spiritual values on the one hand and the *sharing* of material things on the other.

---

10. Gilbert, *Stumbling*, 239. See also Seligman, *Flourish*, 223–26. Sources cited in Hill, *Smith's Equality*.

11. Hill, *Smith's Equality*, citing Lyubomirsky, *How of Happiness*, 43.

*So, what would sharing mean, concretely, for our economy?*

To begin with, it would involve efforts such as I've already mentioned to reduce inequality and eliminate poverty. But it would mean more than that. Senator Bernie Sanders, a 2016 candidate for the Democratic presidential nomination, has pointed to Denmark's "solidarity system" as worthy of emulation; and here we get more deeply into the social aspect of the vision I'm proposing. The Danes have a system of free health care for all citizens. It allows people to choose their own doctors, offers inexpensive prescription drugs, and, astonishingly, consumes only around 11 percent of the country's gross domestic product, whereas the figure for the United States is nearly 18 percent. Mothers are entitled to "four weeks of paid vacation before giving birth" and fourteen weeks after the birth, while the "fathers get two paid weeks off" and both parents "have the right to thirty-two more weeks of leave during the first nine years of a child's life." All workers "are entitled to five weeks of paid vacation plus 11 paid holidays." In addition, "the minimum wage is about twice that of the United States, and people who are totally out of the labor market or unable to care for themselves have a basic income guarantee of about $100 per day." In addition, "unemployment insurance covers up to 90 percent of earnings for as long as two years." In stark contrast to the United States, moreover, "virtually all higher education in Denmark is free . . . not just college but graduate schools as well, including medical school."[12]

Sanders is convinced that, although Denmark is much smaller than the United States, there is much we can learn from these aspects of its "solidarity system." Along similar lines, Dr. Jilll Stein, a physician and Green Party presidential candidate in 2012 and 2016, proposes an Economic Bill of Rights that includes "the right to decent affordable housing, a halt to foreclosures and evictions, an expansion of rental and public housing," along with "the right to accessible and affordable utilities . . . through democratically run, publicly owned utilities that operate at cost, not for profit."[13] I would hope that this would give you a pretty concrete idea of what I mean by "sharing."

*But aren't the taxes in Denmark high, in order to pay for all this?*

Senator Sanders admits they are, which leaves us with the question of whether the quality of life that these benefits bring is worth the price tag. But that, of course, is a matter of values. Most Danes seem to think so, since the system has widespread support that spans the political spectrum. And, according to a survey of over forty countries by the Organization for Economic Cooperation and Development, Danes ranked among the very

---

12. Sanders, "What Can We Learn."
13. Stein, "Economic and Ecological Transformation," 10.

happiest people, while the United States did not make the top ten.[14] On the other hand, programs such as those Sanders and Stein suggest would not be nearly as expensive as opponents suggest.

*How can you say that?*

I can say that because in many cases the new programs would circumvent many of the bureaucracies that are currently in place. Something like a Medicare-for-All system would be much more efficient than approaches that combine government with private industry, and a guaranteed income could be administered with far less cost than the current patchwork of agencies designed to meet specific needs. In the case of utilities, the removal of profit from the equation would lower costs, while democratic administration would help to maintain efficiency. In fact, we have a long history in this country of public utilities, such as the Tennessee Valley Authority and numerous municipally owned electric systems.

*Wouldn't many Americans see a system like this make us all dependent on government?*

Perhaps, but such objections are misdirected. If government is genuinely democratic, and thus a true reflection of the will of the people, benefits such as these are not "handouts" or "giveaways" but mechanisms through which a society provides for the general welfare. It is "we, the people," acting together for the common good. And our participation in these programs, by funding them with our taxes and receiving their benefits, is not *dependency* but *interdependency*.

*What's the difference?*

There's all the difference in the world. When two people share responsibilities on the one hand and benefits on the other, there is reciprocity; each contributes, and each receives. A "solidarity system" in society is similar: all contribute, and all receive; and government is not some alien entity standing over us, but an expression of our collective will. As the woman in the video said, "we *are* the government."

*But doesn't high taxation rob the individual of his or her hard-earned wealth?*

With a truly graduated tax system, some persons would actually pay less than they do now. But the main point is that those who think of taxes as robbery misunderstand how wealth is generated. The truth is that no wealth is ever created by an individual alone. The basic resources of life are given, not created by human beings. The farmer draws upon sunlight, soil, and rain; the industrialist draws upon minerals provided by the earth; the inventor discovers potentials already present in the nature of things. And

---

14. Sanders, "What Can We Learn."

the community is always a partner in any enterprise. Farmers depend upon animals, hired hands, or machinery made by others. Factory owners depend upon the labor of workers on the factory floor, as well as on the contributions of those who transport and sell the goods. They also depend upon *government* for transportation networks and various forms of support for those networks. Technological geniuses draw upon the wisdom of countless generations of predecessors and on the tutelage of teachers and colleagues. So taxation is not robbery; it is a way in which individuals pay their debt to the natural, social, and economic systems that help them create their wealth.

*But still, aren't you advocating a top-down approach?*

The measures I'm thinking of are not top-down if they are really expressions of the collective will—that is, if government is truly democratic and responsive.

*Nevertheless, doesn't much of what you suggest come from the federal level?*

Not all of it has to; much could be done by state and local governments. But there are some things that should be dealt with on as broad a level as possible. The insurance of human and civil rights, for example, should not be a matter of local option. Need I remind anyone of slavery and segregation? Some basic environmental regulations belong in the same category, as does basic health care. When it comes to other matters, such as free education, the question is to what extent we want to think of our country as a union of sovereign states or as a single nation. There are many issues we will have to sort out over time, but I would hate to see young people in Louisiana and Georgia denied the opportunities they might have in Massachusetts, Vermont, or California. And we need to put aside our knee-jerk reactions against federal programs long enough to examine the highly successful national education systems in countries like Denmark, France, and Finland.

In any case, it's important to recognize the hypocrisy in much of the criticism of federal action in the name of "free enterprise." Christian Parenti, a professor at the School for International Training Graduate Institute, points to what he calls the "shadow socialism" at work in the early industrialization of this country as an example of how big businesses have profited mightily from governmental intervention on their behalf. For example, federal subsidies were essential to the building of canals and railroads, and the government even subsidized journalism through the purchase of ads and the provision of low mailing rates.[15] To this we could add the many government bailouts of major companies, both before and during the Great Recession. But of course those who have profited enormously from such government

---

15. Parenti, "Rethinking," 14–15.

subsidies never call such disbursements socialism. They reserve this term as a derogatory designation for programs that funnel wealth and income downward rather than upward.

*Now, let me be clear about the extent of your recommendations. Do the "social insurance" policies you have mentioned cover what you mean when you talk about changes on the social level?*

Only partly. If it is difficult for persons separated in income by a factor of 500 to have any sense of commonality, this is equally true for persons separated by enormous discrepancies in power. When management makes all the decisions and workers have no control whatsoever over their working conditions, no say in company policies that affect the natural environment or the communities in which they live, no voice in whether a plant will move to another location, there is a very limited sense in which these two factions have common cause.

*So, what do you suggest we do about that?*

One remedy for this discrepancy in power is the strengthening of unions. This would still leave labor and management in a largely adversarial relationship, however, and there are other ways of addressing the issues of ownership and power. In *For the Common Good*, Daly and Cobb discuss a range of options, including codetermination and worker ownership. Here is their description of one version of the former:

> In Germany, where codetermination has deep roots in the nineteenth century and has been official national policy since World War II, as many as half of the members of a supervisory board of an enterprise may be chosen by the workers. This supervisory board then elects a management board, which also has worker representation. The effect is to give workers a voice in, and in some cases veto power over, management decisions. It also provides a channel of communication from management to labor, such that workers have management decisions interpreted to them by their own representatives.[16]

Although codetermination has not caught on in the U.S., "since 1974 the government has encouraged worker participation in ownership through the employee stock ownership plan, ESOP."[17] As Daly and Cobb comment, however, "employee ownership without participation in making decisions has not been shown to make a great difference in employee attitudes or productivity." They thus suggest that combining it with "something like

---

16. Daly and Cobb, *For the Common Good*, 300.
17. Ibid., 301.

codetermination."[18] But they also go beyond this to recommend actual worker ownership, noting (in 1989) that

> there are already about a thousand firms with half a million workers in which employees own 50% to 100% of the stock. Some of these companies have been outstandingly successful. Existing federal legislation facilitates the process of workers taking over their companies in some instances. Much further support could be given. Dramatic cases have occurred when workers purchased plants or stores that were otherwise to be closed. In several cases they have restored profitability.[19]

In any case, it's important to expand our thinking about democracy beyond the realm of electoral politics. A formal democracy in that realm is severely hampered if people have no control over the immediate circumstances in which they live and work, just as it is hampered by poverty and inequality. Many theorists have therefore begun to talk about workplace democracy and democracy within a whole range of social contexts, including the family. In this regard, the vision is very much one of bottom-up rather than top-down authority, also of dispersed rather than concentrated power.

*What other aspects of our lives would your vision affect?*

What I have in mind is what many ecologically sensitive futurists have been preaching for some time now. On what McKibben calls "a tough new planet," we will have to pursue much more energy-efficient lifestyles. This will mean technological development on the one hand, but there is only so much that technology can do. We cannot create more resources or energy than the planet provides. Recycling helps, but the process requires the use of energy. So, to begin with transportation, we will have to develop more energy-efficient vehicles as well as find new, ecologically sound fuels. But it will also be necessary to limit the transportation of goods as well as our own travel habits. This will be difficult, but it will also give us the opportunity to develop our towns and cities in ways that promote a greater sense of community. Greatly expanded public transportation, smaller (energy-efficient) dwellings in closer proximity to one another and to shopping areas and workplaces, for example, will encourage us to know one another better and work together on common problems. As we reduce the need for motorized vehicles, moreover, we will also encourage healthier lifestyles as we are able to walk or ride bicycles to a wider range of activities.

In addition, as we reindustrialize the nation, we will need to do so in a way that encourages local, relatively self-sufficient economies. Rather

18. Ibid.
19. Ibid.

than huge factories concentrated in large cities, we will have small, labor-intensive industries spread throughout the country, serving relatively small areas and making use of local resources as much as possible. And this, once again, speaks directly to the issue of top-down, concentrated authority versus bottom-up, dispersed authority. Within the limits necessitated by the environment and basic rights, most of the decisions regarding these local economies could and should be made locally.

Daly and Cobb also point out that the use of local resources would mean relative self-sufficiency of local areas in the production of food. Because food is our most basic material requirement, dependency on outsiders for its production weakens a community. For "a region that is economically dependent on centers of power outside it . . . often takes on the characteristics of a colony. It cannot control its internal economic life, and sometimes it cannot take care of its residents." And the tragedy is that current "economic theory encourages such regions to intensify specialization for export. But even if in this way more profits are earned, the region accentuates its dependence on external centers." By contrast, a relatively self-sufficient region, with its basic needs met, "can trade to its own advantage with other regions."[20]

Local self-sufficiency will be meaningless, however, if agricultural practices are unsustainable; and currently they are disastrously so, largely because of the predominance of industrial farming. On the one hand, it has become largely dependent upon oil and gas—nonrenewable resources—and, on the other, it has led to widespread degradation of the land through the depletion of water, soil erosion, and chemical pollution.[21]

Because the use of animals for food involves a less efficient use of protein, changes in food production should also be accompanied by changes in our diet. Significant reductions in our consumption of meat would not only contribute to sustainability but would help reduce carbon emissions and, not incidentally, result in a healthier lifestyle—another way in which "less is more"!

*You are advocating all these changes within the context of a steady-state economy. But how can we maintain such a steady state without abandoning the market?*

The tools we have traditionally used within a market economy, such as the adjustment of interest rates and the implementation of stimulus methods, would still be available when needed. And some of the measures proposed by steady-state advocates would actually serve the market better

---

20. Daly and Cobb, *For the Common Good*, 268.
21. Gever et al., *Beyond Oil*, 14; cited in Daly and Cobb, *For the Common Good*, 273.

than current practices. One essential move would be to make industries pay the true costs of their use of natural resources and effects upon the environment. When a company pollutes the air or uses resources faster than they can be replaced, it is "borrowing" from the future, because at some point someone will have to pay to repair the damage. But if we taxed the industry commensurate with its effect on the environment, we would bring to light the costs that now remain hidden but are passed on to the ordinary taxpayer, future generations, or both. This would not only place the burden where it rightly belongs but also discourage environmentally unsound practices. As Daly puts the matter, "Why tax what we want more of—employment and income? Why not tax what we want less of—depletion and pollution?" The price of goods would undoubtedly rise, but this could be offset by reducing taxes on income in an amount equal to that charged to industry, so that the shift could be made on a revenue-neutral basis.[22]

In any case, it's important to remember that the steady-state policy is not an end in itself; it is a means toward achieving sustainability. The main point is that we would no longer try to create growth for its own sake. As Daly observes, we once pursued growth as a means to an end—full employment. "Today," however, "that relation has been inverted."[23] Economic growth has become an end in itself; and because of that, we have pursued policies such as automation and offshoring that have actually contributed to unemployment.

*Well, then, after all is said and done, where would you place your vision on the spectrum of traditional theories?*

As I have said from the beginning, I don't think it belongs on that spectrum, neither on the Right nor on the Left nor in the middle; I understand it as a "forward" position that draws upon various aspects of the traditional choices. It involves an acceptance of the market, which is a staple of contemporary conservatism but is also embraced by contemporary liberals and many socialists. But it also relies upon tools to adjust the market's distribution of wealth, which is a staple of contemporary liberalism and socialism; and it joins traditional conservatism, contemporary liberalism, and democratic socialism in its emphasis on community. Its emphasis on social ownership draws primarily upon democratic socialism, but this is something contemporary liberals can certainly support. Contemporary conservatives, moreover, can rest assured that the kinds of social ownership I envision are a far cry from *state* ownership. They should also appreciate that such ownership actually *empowers the individual*. On the other hand,

---

22. Daly, *Beyond Growth*, 15.
23. Daly, "Full Employment," 1.

the vision I propose moves beyond all the options usually debated by rejecting the ideology of growth. And it's important to recognize that it involves the rejection of some aspects of social systems that have operated in the past.

*Which, specifically?*

To begin with, the social hierarchy of traditional conservatism, along with the oppressive top-down authoritarianism of both fascism and the statist perversions of socialism. It also opposes the idolatrous doctrine of laissez-faire, which accepts the market as the sole determiner of value and ignores extreme discrepancies in wealth and income.

*So, what would you call the approach you advocate?*

I have earlier expressed my distrust of labels, so in some ways, I'd like to avoid giving it a name. But in order to avoid letting someone else name it for me, maybe *ecocommunitarian* would be a good adjective to describe it.

*You have said that you want to realize all these changes democratically. Can you say more about that?*

To do so, I think, involves persuasion. And that begins with making people aware of the issues, of what is at stake, and of the far-reaching implications of the decisions we make as a society. That is what I'm trying to do in this book, and it's what I would hope the faith communities might begin to do much more than they have in the past. It is also what I wish our educational system would take more seriously instead of settling for job training and the teaching of technical skills and mere facts, as many institutions are doing. In order to change society, we first need to change the way we think, to reexamine our values and commitments and, indeed, the way we understand the world.

*But you do recognize that you're fighting an uphill battle, don't you? You have admitted from the start that your vision is in many ways at odds with the way many people think.*

Of course I know it's an uphill battle. And although the views I express may represent a minority opinion in this country at present, a growing number of people want many of the results I envision, even if they disagree about how to achieve them. On the other hand, there are significant movements in this direction all over the world. Various Green parties, both in Europe and in the U.S., have a similar vision, for example. And Michael Löwy of the French National Center for Scientific Research points to movements among peasants and indigenous peoples in Latin America who are also working toward an egalitarian world based on ecological principles. Victimized by international agribusinesses that are contaminating land at an alarming rate, they are joining with other groups, notably unions and activist Christian communities influenced by liberation theology, to preserve the environment and promote "an alternative way of life" that makes the earth's resources available to all persons.[24] So, I'm suggesting that persons of biblical faith in our country should make common cause with groups such as these; and as the ecological crisis deepens, I believe that more people will awaken to what is happening and what needs to be done. I also believe that as more people come to understand visions such as I have tried to present they will see that these visions actually embrace many of the same values they do—values such as I have listed above.

*So, are you optimistic about the prospects of bringing about the changes you think are needed and to do so through democratic processes?*

Unfortunately, it is too late to avoid a lasting environmental catastrophe. It's already in progress. But I have hope that we can limit the long-range effects of climate change and create, on this severely damaged planet, a just and sustainable way of life. I know, however, that there are many impediments to this, which are also impediments to democracy. As Löwy comments, "the entrenched ruling elites of the system are incredibly powerful, and the forces of radical opposition are still small."[25] And to understand just how formidable the challenge is, we need to take account of two impediments in particular—the role of big money in the electoral and governing processes, and the failure of mainstream media to fulfill their responsibilities.

---

24. Löwy, "Ecosocialism," 28.
25. Ibid., 29.

## 12

# But Can We Do It?
## Overcoming the Impediments

> We have the best Congress money can buy.
> —Will Rogers

> Democracy in America is a series of narrow escapes, and we may be running out of luck . . . We have fallen under the spell of money, faction, and fear, and the great American experience in creating a different future *together* has been subjugated to individual cunning in the pursuit of wealth and power—and to the claims of empire, with its ravenous demands and stuporous distractions.
> —Bill Moyers, 2008[1]

THE KEY TO EFFECTIVE democracy lies in the power of the populace at large to ensure that government reflects the will of the people and serves the common good; for true democracy is, in fact, the rule of the people. The United States today falls far short of that ideal, however; for

---

1. Moyers, *Moyers on Democracy*, 1; italics original.

the electoral and governing processes are seriously compromised by the undue influence of concentrated wealth. According to the preamble to the Constitution of the United States, it is the purpose of government to "establish Justice, insure domestic Tranquility, provide for the common defense, promote the general Welfare, and secure the Blessings of Liberty to ourselves and our Posterity." As long as candidates for office and government officials are beholden to large corporations and wealthy individuals, however, we have little chance that justice will be done, either in the marketplace or for the earth or in the forum, the arena of public affairs in general. There is little hope for decisions that serve the general welfare, rather than that of the ruling classes and corporate interests, or that the blessings of liberty will extend to all. Nor can we, in light of the unfolding ecological catastrophe, expect that they will extend to our posterity, whether poor or rich! Because genuine democracy also depends upon an informed public, moreover, much of the problem also lies with the media establishment, which is subject to the same influence.

Unless we can remedy this situation, we will lose what remains of a government "of, by, and for" the people. I do not imagine an overt fascism, replete with concentration camps and enforced by brown-shirted thugs with assault weapons and armored tanks in the streets. I rather fear a subtler but still sinister version, in which:

- an uninformed and deluded public is complicit in its own enslavement, because the dissenting voices have been shut out of print media and denied the airwaves by economic manipulation carried out in the name of free enterprise;
- the Internet has been taken over entirely by corporate interests;
- mass incarceration and the prison industry have continued to grow exponentially, while the rights of the accused have steadily shrunk;
- voting rights have been further curtailed, ensuring that those most likely to oppose economic policies favoring the ruling elite have less and less representation;
- surveillance of private communications has increased and the definition of subversive activity has expanded greatly; and
- public education has largely given way to private, and both serve largely as propaganda mills for the reigning ideology.

I am aware of how grim a picture I have painted, but I am not alone in my fears; and to anyone inclined to write all this off as paranoid, doomsday thinking, I issue an invitation to consider how far down this path we have already come. My interest now is in the two factors I have mentioned as undermining democracy: the influence of big money and the failure of mainstream media to fulfill their responsibilities.

## WHEN DOLLARS BECOME VOTES: HOW MAMMON BUYS GOVERNMENT

The old man in the church on St. Charles Avenue in New Orleans was, in the late 1960s, about the age I am now. He was the consummate southern gentlemen, nothing at all like Tennessee Williams's crude and uproarious "Big Daddy." His speech was genteel, his manner dignified, his dress impeccable. And I had to admit that he had a very high degree of integrity, in the sense that he always stuck to his principles with unbending determination. But it was precisely some of his principles that bothered me. One of these was his racism—not that of club-wielding mobs shouting vile slogans but of the refined, paternalistic, and outwardly kind master. I was familiar with the type, which was abundant in the South. Another of his principles, however, surprised me. For he was the only person I had ever met who was honest enough to admit outright what his views on political issues clearly implied. "*I don't believe in democracy,*" he said unapologetically. And then he went on to defend his position. Because persons of wealth and education have accomplished more in life and are better informed, they should have a greater voice in government than those of lesser status. The ruling elite of our day are not so honest; for they claim the mantle of democracy, even as they use their wealth and power to subvert it. And here is how they do it.

I begin with the electoral process. What does it mean for an election to be democratic? I should think it means that the people elected to serve in an office are in fact the choices of *the people*. But what if the slate of candidates *offered* in an election is limited by their willingness and ability to garner enormous contributions from vested interests? Is the right to choose among a *predetermined* set of possibilities true democracy? It is possible for candidates without enormous financial backing to get on a ballot; the problem, in a mass society such as ours, is that it is extremely difficult for such candidates to make themselves and their views known *and understood* well enough to be taken seriously. Consider these figures gathered by John Nichols and Robert W. McChesney, who name our current system a "dollarocracy": "In 1960, the total amount of all political TV and radio ad spending was estimated at $14 million, or $109 million adjusted for inflation—*just under 2% of what was spent in 2012, which was about $6 billion.*" To make matters worse, "when we add the amount spent on fundraising, dark money, PACs [political action committees], state elections, ballot initiatives, judicial races and local elections, the figure balloons up to $10 billion, making it the most expensive election in campaign history."[2]

The fact that the party that won the presidential election of 2012 spent the lesser amount doesn't disprove the point. To begin with, the Democrats' total was only slightly less, percentagewise, than the Republicans'—approximately 1.1 billion as over against roughly 1.2 billion.[3] More important, it has long been the practice of corporate interests to dole out contributions to *both* major parties, undoubtedly to hedge their bets and ensure both access to and influence over whoever wins. The Democrats got a good share from Wall Street in 2012, and one needs to remember this when puzzling over the Obama administration's failure to prosecute persons from that quarter, whom many analysts think guilty of serious crimes. That the moguls would have gotten a better deal from a Republican victory is beside the point. As Nichols and McChesney comment, "in 2012, big money beat big money."[4] So the point is that all too often, even when big money loses, it has stacked the deck to such an extent that it gets at least part of what it wants—and the public interest suffers.

It is important, moreover, to understand that big money can indeed be the deciding factor in an election. A case in point is the way PACs influenced the Republican primaries in 2012. As political strategist Doug Schoen observes, "The pro-Romney super PAC, Restore Our Future, spent $4.5 million . . . attacking Gingrich once he rose in the polls. The PAC helped Romney fend off a last-minute surge by Gingrich." And "the pro-Santorum super PAC, the Red, White, and Blue Fund, spent over $240,000 in the days leading up to the February 7th primaries in Minnesota, Colorado, and Missouri, helping Santorum sweep all three races."[5]

The problem has existed for a very long time—witness Will Rogers's famous quotation—but we are now seeing constant increases of gargantuan proportions, and there is no end in sight. There have been many attempts over the years to limit the role of money in elections, but they have had only minimal effect; and the U.S. Supreme Court's 2010 decision on the *Citizens United* case has rendered them virtually impotent. Although the 5–4 decision left in place the limits on contributions made directly to candidates, it overturned two earlier Supreme Court decisions by loosening "restrictions

2. Nichols and McChesney, "Dollarocracy," 23 (box).
3. Ibid., 23.
4. Ibid.
5. Schoen, "Super PACs' Super Influence," 2.

on corporate and individual spending, especially by organizations not under the control of candidates."[6] As a result, we have witnessed "the proliferation of 'Super PACs,'" which "do not have to abide by the $2,500 limit on donations to actual campaigns, and they can easily avoid rules for reporting sources of contributions. For instance, Super PACs have established nonprofit arms that are permitted to shield contributors' identities as long as they spend no more than 50 percent of their money on electoral politics."[7]

Groups not tied directly to a party's campaign can thus spend as much as they want in efforts to influence an election. And the justification of the majority opinion by Justice Anthony Kennedy is both revealing and ominous. By defining financial contributions as speech and limitations on them as violation of freedom of speech, the majority came very close to endorsing the southern gentleman's argument against democracy, although without his honesty. For if money is in fact equated with speech, then those with more money have more voices with which to speak, and thus more power to influence both elections and the governing process. They have, in a very real sense, more votes (*many* more!) than the ordinary citizen. The decision therefore, as Justice John Paul Stevens stated in his impassioned dissent, threatens "to undermine the integrity of elected institutions across the Nation" and "will undoubtedly cripple the ability of ordinary citizens, Congress, and the States to adopt even limited measures to protect against corporate domination of the electoral process."[8]

If the electoral process is severely corrupted by the influence of big money, the same is true for the governing process. Although one may argue that those who contribute to PACs are simply supporting candidates and policies that agree with them on the important issues, as do most individuals, this is belied by the fact noted above—that corporations often contribute to opposing candidates. The only conceivable reason for doing so is to buy influence on whichever candidate or party wins. And there is irrefutable evidence that money does in fact talk in the political realm—which is to say, those with enormous resources, whether individuals or corporate entities, can "buy" pretty much whatever they want. Bill Moyers cites examples on both sides of the Democratic-Republican divide. In 1995, Angelo K. Tsakopoulos, "a long-time Democratic fund-raiser—$165,000 in one year alone"—persisted with the development of eight hundred acres despite the federal government's refusal of a permit in an effort to save endangered species and wetlands. Yet, after he made his case in the White House (as an

---

6. Nichols and McChesney, "Assault of the Super PACS," 11.
7. Ibid.
8. Quoted in Dunigan, "Citizens United."

overnight guest), "an Environmental Protection Agency official in Washington directed the West Coast office to forgo any major fines or criminal sanctions against the developer."[9] On the other side of the aisle, Richard DeVos of the Amway Corporation, who had contributed over a million dollars to the Republican Party, was rewarded with a tax break of around $280 million for Amway's Asian affiliates when Trent Lott and Newt Gingrich delivered a last-minute addition to a tax bill.[10]

After recounting examples such as these, Moyers adds this ironic comment: "This is the same Newt Gingrich, by the way, who said in 1990: 'Congress is increasingly a system of corruption in which money politics is defeating and driving out citizen politics.'"[11] Of course, many politicians have made this observation, often with equal hypocrisy. The truth is that Moyers's examples are not anomalies but illustrations of what all too often happens in the governing process. So, if we wonder how some of the most outrageous policies came to be and persist, we do not have to look far to find the answer. Why are oil companies allowed to operate in environmentally sensitive areas? Why are so many air-polluting coal plants still in operation? Why can natural gas companies engage in hydraulic fracturing ("fracking") even though the toxic chemicals used in the process can contaminate ground water and the drilling can cause earthquakes and dangerous leaks of methane that contribute to global warming? Why are banks deemed "too big to fail" not broken up or nationalized? Why does the legislation creating the prescription drug benefit under Medicare explicitly prohibit the federal government from negotiating with drug companies for lower prices? Why does a health insurance program designed to widen coverage divert so much money to huge profits for the insurance industry? Why, indeed, do efforts to adopt a more efficient, single-payer system that circumvents insurance companies and their needs for profit get so little support from mainstream politicians? And why on earth would Congress insist on funding major military expenditures that the Pentagon neither asks for nor wants?

The answers may be complex in some cases, but the smell of money is always evident and strong! And if these words seem overly harsh, consider what Moyers told an audience in Sacramento in 1997:

> The coalition fighting the new air standards is reported to have something like $30 million pooled in its war chest. The American Lung Association, by comparison, doesn't even have a political action committee. In the House of Representatives, 192

---

9. Moyers, *Moyers on Democracy*, 182–83.
10. Ibid., 184.
11. Ibid.

members have signed on to legislation to force the EPA [Environmental Protection Agency] to delay the new [air] standards for at least two years. These members of Congress have received nearly three times as much in campaign contributions from big air polluters than members who have not signed on to the bill.[12]

Lest we give in to the cynical notion that politics is inherently corrupt, it is important to state that remedies to this distressing situation are possible. Public financing of elections has in fact made a difference in some places. With respect to the pricing of drugs, for example, consider this: "In Maine, where clean elections have been in place since 2000, there have been advances in providing low-cost pharmaceutical drugs for residents, and in making sure that every state resident has medical coverage."[13]

The electoral process is only part of the picture, however. Much of the money in the corporate war chests goes to lobbying, and efforts to moderate the influence of lobbyists have proved largely ineffective. On paper, the lobbying industry is shrinking, but in reality it is increasing. Because of loopholes in the lobbying registration system and a near-total lack of enforcement, lobbyists are able to get away with simply refusing to register. In contrast to the official figure of 12,281 registered Washington lobbyists in 2013, one analyst places the true number at nearly 100,000; and although the official amount spent on lobbying was $3.2 billion in 2013, the same analyst "estimates that the industry brings in more than $9 billion a year."[14] And surely no one is naïve enough to believe that companies would dole out this kind of money without reaping substantial returns on their "investments"—that is, legislation and policies that deliver significant benefits.

The matter is complicated by the fact that in many cases major industries can enlist considerable public support for their lobbying efforts because jobs are at stake. And let us be honest about this: all too often people who complain about "pork-barrel" legislation change their tune when benefits to their own states or districts are on the table. This does not mean that we are simply stuck with the problem, nor does it mean that either the federal or the state governments have no role to play in job creation. My point is rather that if money-backed lobbying did not wield such overwhelming influence, governing bodies could make their decisions on a different basis. In the case of job-creating legislation, for example, they could reject environmentally destructive projects in favor of those that "promote the general welfare."

---

12. Ibid., 186.
13. Ibid., 217.
14. Fang, "Shadow Lobbying," 14.

## WHEN MESSENGERS FAIL: THE COMPLICITY OF THE MEDIA

It is not as if people were unaware of the abuses I have listed; the favorability ratings of both Congress and lobbyists are astonishingly low. The problem is that public outrage is too often based on such a distorted understanding of the issues that it is directed either indiscriminately or at the wrong targets. In the first instance, we unwittingly contribute to the cynicism that inhibits our search for rational solutions. When in frustration people bellow, "Throw them all out," they lump those who actually work for the common good together with those who serve vested interests. In the second instance, when they misplace the blame, they work against the general welfare and often against their own self-interest. I am continually amazed at the number of people I know who complain about the problems discussed in this book but consistently support policies that perpetuate those problems. Part of what is at work here is the power of ideology to distort fact; part, however, has to do with the failure of mainstream media in its role of informing the public.

Essential to an informed public is access to a variety of voices offering different perspectives on the issues. Moyers makes an important point, however, when he writes that "objectivity is not satisfied by two people offering competing opinions, leaving the viewer to split the difference."[15] That is to say, the media have a responsibility beyond reporting the *claims* made by politicians, experts, corporations, or organizations. The role of *investigative* journalism is to seek truth, to look for facts behind competing claims, and to call to the public's attention issues that are either ignored or distorted by the many voices that speak in the public forum. And if we look back through our national history, we can in many ways be proud of the role played by courageous reporters in exposing governmental corruption, corporate irresponsibility, and various forms of social injustice. The "muckrakers" of the Progressive Era exposed numerous social ills and provided impetus for important reforms over the years; John Lewis honors a number of courageous journalists who risked their lives reporting on the crimes against civil rights workers in the mid-twentieth century;[16] and Moyers points to the documentaries by Edward R. Murrow, Fred Friendly, and Frederick Wiseman as examples of investigative journalism at its best. In more recent times, however, the mainstream media have too often settled for the style that Moyers criticizes—the mere presentation of opposing opinions with

---

15. Moyers, *Moyers on Democracy*, 269.
16. Lewis, *Walking*, 274–76.

very little attempt to dig beneath the surface, either in search of actual truth or in an effort at in-depth analysis.

The problem, it is important to say, is more with the media outlets than with individual journalists themselves. Moyers acknowledges that we do not lack "honest and courageous individuals who would risk their careers to speak truth to power." They are largely hampered, however, by the corporate structures within which they work and are thus "not in control of the instruments they play."[17] And here again we see the corrupting influence of big money.

> As conglomerates swallow up newspapers, magazines, and publishing houses, and networks, and profit rather than product becomes the focus of the corporate effort, news organizations—particularly in television—are folded into entertainment divisions. The "news hole" in the print media shrinks to make room for advertisements, and stories needed by informed citizens working together are pulled in favor of the latest celebrity scandals because the media moguls have decided that uncovering the inner workings of public and private power is boring and will drive viewers and readers away to greener pastures of pabulum.[18]

Over the last few decades we have witnessed the concentration of the media in fewer and fewer hands, the narrowing of the spectrum of opinion offered by the major media, and a plethora of shrill commentators uncritically tied to a specific ideology and willing to make misleading and often false statements to advance it. The concentration is astonishing: Between 1983 and 2008, the number of corporations controlling the majority of American media went *from fifty to six!*[19] There are indications that the Federal Communications Commission may be curbing this trend, but the current situation still makes it difficult to get a broad range of perspectives. Add to this the staffing decreases in many media outlets, which has encouraged increased dependence upon government sources, and it becomes clear why the traditional role of the media as checks on government and other influential institutions has largely been abandoned by the mainstream. There are, to be sure, some reliable alternative sources that publish some courageous reporting, and I have drawn heavily on them in this book. It is difficult for the general public to sort them out from the unreliable, however, and they have a terrible time competing with the corporately funded giants.

17. Moyers, *Moyers on Democracy*, 5.
18. Ibid., 5–6.
19. Moyers, "Bernie Sanders," 1.

To give a specific example of the corrupting effect of big money on the commercial media, Nichols and McChesney caution us not to look to these outlets to shed light on the problems of Super PACs: "The Citizens United ruling and its Super PAC spawn have created a new revenue stream for media companies, and they are not about to turn the spigot off."[20] Why are we the public increasingly inundated with political ads, many of which are sponsored by groups not directly related to campaigns? Because there is more and more money available to pay for them, and the mainstream media are more than happy to collect the loot. And why do we get continual, mind-numbing accounts of how much the Republicans and Democrats have raised but precious few stories about Super PACs, how much revenue their ads produce, and *which ideology they serve*? Could the reason be the same?

"Democracy in America," as Moyers has said, "is a series of narrow escapes. And we may be running out of luck." The truth is that our democracy has never been perfect and has always been a work in progress. Our senators were first chosen by state legislatures rather than by the people directly, and the vote was only gradually (and against great opposition) extended to African Americans and women. The Electoral College system, moreover, remains as a direct impediment to genuine majority rule. The saddest part is that our long history of struggling toward a more genuinely democratic system has in recent times been reversed, as forces are pulling us backward instead of forward. So if we hope to solve the problems discussed earlier in this chapter democratically, we must also be at work to restore and extend the democratic processes we claim to value. To do so will not be easy. It will take people willing to use the ballot, their voices, their resources, and their time and energy to challenge "the powers that be." It will demand the courage, determination, and willingness to take significant risks that have characterized the movements dedicated to women's suffrage, just wages and working conditions, civil rights, environmental responsibility, gay rights, and an end to unjust wars. It will take massive educational efforts, largely outside the current educational establishment, as well as cooperation with similar movements around the globe. It will, in short, take a mass movement unified by an unshakable dedication to the common good in all the various dimensions of our individual and collective lives.

If we can in fact develop such a movement, then we have a real chance of creating a new society—a political, social, and economic way of life that

---

20. Nichols and McChesney, "Assault of the Super PACs," 1.

is genuinely democratic, ecologically sustainable, and just by biblical standards. Religious communities can play an important role in achieving this goal, but only if they can be weaned away from the idolatries that have infected our society and brought back to the best and most fundamental values of their traditions. On behalf of those who are grounded in biblical faith, I therefore offer this prayer, for the sake of my country and of the world:

## A PRAYER:
## "THY WILL BE DONE ON EARTH . . ."

Holy One—Creator, Redeemer, Sustainer, Friend—
Whose Kingdom is one of Equity, Righteousness, and Truth,
In which those who are broken down are raised up,
Whose Commonwealth is one of Justice and of Peace,
And of ultimate Reconciliation
    (Between nation and nation,
        Between tribe and tribe,
            Between humanity and Earth),
In which "nation shall not rise up against nation" (Isa 2:4),
And "the nursing child shall play over the hole of the asp" (Isa 11:8),

Hear this our prayer:
"Thy kingdom come,
Thy will be done on earth" . . . (Matt 6:10, KJV)

    And may the process of its coming begin with us.
    So, open, then, our minds, whenever you find them closed,
        Attached unconsciously to some lesser god;
    And open, too, our hearts, whenever you find them hardened,
        Impervious to the needs of neighbor or of the earth,
        Or to your beckoning voice.

"Thy kingdom come,
Thy will be done on earth . . ."
    Which is to say, let *Justice* come,
    Roll down like mighty torrents on our world,
        That poverty be banished from the realm

And no oppressor's heel should grind another down,
Nor hunger ravage some while others feast in mansions made of gold;
That thrones and palaces and grand estates, where lords and ladies rule, shall fall,
Along with oligarchs in boardrooms wielding power only empires ever knew
(Domination of the soil and water, air, and minerals from the earth;
Domination of all creatures and their habitats;
Domination of their workers, bent and broken in their bodies, minds, and hearts);
And may the power brokers such as these give way to people to your image true,
> Persons free to live and breathe, to choose and work and love,
> To sit beneath their vines and fig trees and take leisure from their toil,
> To contemplate, to rest, to pray, to sing and dance and laugh.

"Thy kingdom come,
Thy will be done on earth..."
Which is to say,
Let Justice now be done not just *upon* the earth
But *to* the earth and *for* the earth,
> The earth that at creation's dawn you named as "very good,"
> The earth you made as home to countless creatures,
> Forms of life that from its store of energy spring forth by your own hand,
> Our siblings in a sacred web of symbiosis in accordance with your plan.

"Thy kingdom come,
Thy will be done on earth..."

> Which is to say,
> May we on earth now learn to hear the prophets' words,
> And choose the true in opposition to the false,
> No longer ridicule or stone the ones who speak of judgment as they hold out hope
> But favor them above the ones who tell us what we'd rather hear—

That "All is well, so just continue in your ways."
And may the institutions we create
Be forums where all voices can be heard,
As we, in humble striving for what's right and just,
Do seek the common good with earnest hearts and minds.

And so we now give thanks:
For those who've challenged systems that oppress the poor,
Who've spoken truth to power and felt its vengeful wrath,
Who've cared for your creation when others eat the earth,
Who've stood with common people as they struggle for their rights.

Among the many, then, we name these few, and gratitude express
    For Isaiah and for Amos, those of old,
        Who called the hands of those who grabbed the land and robbed the poor;
    For Jesus, named by Luke a prophet too,
        Who blessed the poor and dispossessed
        and promised restitution for those who lost their land
        ("for they shall inherit the earth");
    For Henry David Thoreau,
        Who modeled well the courage of dissent
        When Right is on one's side,
        And taught us love of Nature by his life;
    For Mother Jones,
        A fearless fighter for the rights of miners, black and white,
        An anomaly in her time;
    For Martin Luther King,
        The sanitation workers' friend,
        Whose economic doctrines are so easily obscured,
        As politicians of a different stripe pay homage as they bite their tongues;
    For Cesar Chavez,
        Who with poor Chicano migrants cast his lot
        And braved the power of the corporate world;
    For Rachel Carson,

Whose work she named *The Silent Spring* gave voice to voiceless Nature
And awakened millions to impending doom;

For John Lewis,
Freedom rider, bruised and beaten, yet undaunted, yet forgiving,
Standing strong for every justice cause in Congress still today;

For Eugene V. Debs,
Who kinship with all life expressed
And stood for working people with this creed in mind:
"While there is a lower class, I am of it . . . a soul in prison, I am not free."

For Helen Keller,
Whose politics admirers in their adulation miss—
Supporter of the working class and Debs's presidential bids;

For John Muir,
Who God in Nature, right along with Scripture, found,
Became an advocate for wilderness and gave us the Sierra Club;

For Bernard "Buck" Corson,
Faithful guardian of New Hampshire's fish and game,
Who bucked big oil, big money, greed and power
And risked his job to save the coastal waters of the state.

For Dorothy Day,
Who lived her faith among the poor and served their needs,
And stood against the system that would crush their souls;

For Rachel Plattus and Farhad Ebrahami,
From New Economy Coalition's ranks,
Who know that economic justice comes to naught
Unless the climate problem's solved;

For Bayard Rustin,
Excluded often as a gay,
But made his mark in linking labor, civil rights;

For Majora Carter,
Environmental activist, south Bronx,
Creating livable urban space all;

For Sojourner Truth,
A former slave who spoke with power seldom known,
Abolitionist and Suffragette supreme;

For Wendell Berry and Wes Jackson,
> Advocates for many causes, visionaries on the use of land,
> With Nature as the model for a style of farming that's sustainable and pure;

For Fannie Lou Hamer,
> Disenfranchised, ranked among the poor, but Bible-taught,
> She rocked the great convention
> With her lessons in Democracy;

For Winona LaDuke, Anishinaabe tribe,
> Who steadfast stands on Mother Earth's behalf
> And fights the vested interests for her people's sake;

For Linda Hogan,
> Environmental writer, teacher, poet, scholar—
> A Chickasaw who also brings us insights of the Natives of this land,
> (Those who from of old have honored well
> Both creatures and the land itself as Spirit-filled)
> To teach us to how live more lightly on the earth,

Yet not alone for heroes, such as these, within the strife,
> But for the *movements of the many*, nameless often on the earthly plane,
> But written bold in Heaven's book
> As those who claimed, not just for self, but for all living creatures everywhere,
> A vine and fig tree as a gift from God
> As sign of what is promised for "the days to come."

And so, we pray, again,

"Thy kingdom come"—
> Though not as domination by a king, but rather as your *kin*-dom, commonwealth, a fellowship of equals in your sight, who strive together that this might come to pass:

"*Thy will be done on earth.*"

Amen.

This prayer expresses three important aspects of the *shalom*, or ultimate well-being, that God's rule, realm, *kin*-dom, or commonwealth entails: economic justice, oneness with nature, and the relatedness of all beings as parts of the created order. There remains another key aspect, named by the term we most often use to translate the Hebrew word *shalom*—peace. The quotation from Jill Stein presented as an epigraph for this chapter suggests that this, no less than democracy, is threatened by the prevailing economic, social, and political practices. I thus turn to part 3 in an effort to show how deeply the violence that is disruptive to peace is entrenched in our national makeup and to propose alternatives based upon biblical values.

# Part 3

# "Not with Swords' Loud Clashing"
## Violence, Justice, and the Commonwealth of God

For not with swords' loud clashing, nor roll of stirring drums;
With deeds of love and mercy the heavenly kingdom comes.

—Ernest W. Shurtleff, "Lead on, O King Eternal," 1887[21]

> "They shall beat their swords into plowshares,
> and their spears into pruning hooks;
> nation shall not lift up sword against nation,
> neither shall they learn war any more."
>
> —Isaiah 2:4

> "You have heard that it was said, 'An eye for an eye and a tooth for a tooth.' But I say to you, Do not resist an evildoer. But if anyone strikes you on the right cheek, turn the other also."
>
> —Matthew 5:38–40

---

21. Quoted from *The United Methodist Hymnal*, 580.

# Prologue to Part 3
## A Lifelong Struggle and a Stable Conviction

I WAS BORN INTO a world at war. Three months before my birth, Japan invaded China; two years later, in 1939, Hitler's army marched into Poland. When Japan bombed Pearl Harbor on December 7, 1941, I was barely four years old. World War II and the years immediately following it left me with indelible memories. Most of all, I remember my feelings. My half-brother and a double first cousin were decorated army pilots, and I was aware of the danger they faced. Both survived the conflict, but for many years I had nightmares involving my brother's death. I also remember how I felt about our enemies. Germany and Japan were "the bad guys," who tortured and killed prisoners, and we were "the good guys," who did not. One day, while picking strawberries, I asked my grandfather, using the usual terminology, "Which do you think are worse, the Germans or the 'Japs'?" He answered simply, "I think they're both pretty bad." I was sure the Japanese were worse, however, because of their depiction in movies. But I also considered Hitler particularly evil, right along with General Tojo, and I hated them both. I once told an older boy what I would do to them if I had the chance, reciting a litany of assaults ending with pouring gasoline on their hair and lighting it. "No you wouldn't," he replied, "because you wouldn't be allowed to." As he continued, I felt a pang of shame as the horror of what I had said came home to me; and by the time I saw the movie *Sergeant York*, after the war had ended, my views on violence and revenge had modified radically. The influence of Sunday school and church was apparently at work, because my admiration of York, a World War I hero, had more to do with the religious convictions that made him reluctant to take up arms than with his courage in battle. I approved his eventual decision to fight but was particularly moved by his effort to take prisoners rather than to kill.

The progression of my ideas on war has been a zigzag, a lifelong negotiation between competing values. There was no hint of pacifism in my family. My father and two uncles served in the army in World War I, and my father believed in universal military training. My full brother joined the air force during the Korean War, although the conflict ceased soon afterwards. He was always my hero, and I admired him all the more because he enlisted out of a sense of responsibility. Because of this background, and because I believed that my country always stood for what is right, the "Sergeant York solution" served me well for a long time. Eventually, however, I became uneasy with it, and the first step was to question one momentous decision our government made in World War II.

Sometime before I entered high school, the minister of our church, Fred Flurry, preached a sermon criticizing the atomic bombing of Japan. Noting that none of us would cut the throats of hundreds of children living in enemy countries, he asked whether the use of the bomb was in principle any different. Then, in college, a book and a poem, both of which I encountered through the Methodist Student Movement, reinforced his point. The book was *Hiroshima Diary*, by Michihiko Hayiya, a Japanese physician's account of his treatment of patients suffering from radiation sickness following the bombing. The poem was Hermann Hagedorn's "The Bomb that Fell on America." Describing not only the effects of the bomb on the people of Hiroshima but its negative impact upon the American psyche, it is a prophetic call to conscience from a biblical perspective. I was largely convinced by the arguments against the bomb, but at some point I began to wrestle with the claim that this option had saved millions of lives by ending the war. The use of a second bomb on Nagasaki, however, seemed altogether unnecessary and inhumane. I found it impossible, moreover, to justify rejecting the suggestion of Robert Oppenheimer, one of the bomb's creators, to invite Japanese leaders to a demonstration before using it. The excuse offered against providing a demonstration (that the device might not work) seemed weak in light of the enormous destruction my country was about to unleash. Eventually, the minister's point prevailed: I concluded, and continue to believe, that the use of the bomb was wrong.

Another step in my questioning came at a conference of the Methodist Student Movement in the early days of the civil rights movement. Listening to a speech by Glenn Smiley of the Fellowship of Reconciliation, I was challenged by his description of some early sit-ins and the philosophy of nonviolence. I began to absorb that philosophy and came to consider myself a pacifist, but this commitment soon gave way as I pondered the ambiguities involved in moral decisions in a seminary course on Christian social ethics. I was drawn toward a position known as situation ethics, which rejects all moral absolutes except the command to love one's neighbor. On this view, love makes different demands in different circumstances, and one determines what is right in any particular situation by weighing the consequences of alternative actions. A college friend, however, had already raised questions about this view with her caricature: "Don't kill—unless you need to; don't steal—unless you need to." So I have never been fully comfortable with the abandonment of absolutes and still struggle to define my position in a satisfying way. I have reluctantly come to believe that *in some instances* killing, particularly in defense of another or in a "just war," is the *less evil* choice; but I have more sympathy for the pacifist position than I did a few years ago.

Although my questioning of the morality of my country's involvement in warfare began fairly early, it was mainly during the Vietnam War that I started to ask more complicated questions. The line between a morally based defense of another nation and imperialist intervention became blurred, and I began to look more carefully at the historical backgrounds of conflicts that once seemed clear-cut cases of right versus wrong. Later on, as I learned more about our relations with the nations to our south, I came to view our supposed anticolonial heritage in a different light and to doubt our government's professed reasons for meddling in their affairs. And the more I pondered the takeover of the continent from the American Indian tribes, the more skeptical I became of the claim that we are not a nation that pursues conquest. More recent events, moreover, have led me to ask whether war might actually define the American identity for many people and to consider how we might redefine that identity in a way more in keeping with biblical principles.

The broad subject of part 3 is my country's use of violence, viewed from a biblical perspective. In chapter 13, I consider biblical views on war and imperialism, and in chapters 14 and 15 I draw upon these in reviewing important moments in our military history. In chapter 16, I turn to another form of violence still practiced in the United States even though many other nations have abandoned it. It is capital punishment, which I treat as one component in a judicial system that I believe in some ways feeds violence. On this matter my journey has not been a zigzag but the refinement of a stable commitment. As far back as I can remember, I believed that taking a human life, when not absolutely necessary for some greater good, is wrong. To do so, it seemed to me, would preempt a prerogative that belongs to God alone. And the Bible's emphasis on the redemption of sinners appeared to rule out a method of punishment that forecloses that possibility for any individual. We must nevertheless reckon with the fact that the Hebrew Bible endorses capital punishment. Nor is the Bible consistent in condemning all violence or in limiting military action to defensive wars. There is therefore much to discuss on the biblical front as I ask how well this nation lives up to the best in the religious heritage it professes to value.

13

# A Complex Heritage
## The Bible on War, Peace, and Empire

As I hope to have shown by now, the Bible speaks not with one voice but with many and is riddled with tensions and contradictions. This is particularly evident regarding violence. The story of ancient Israel's possession of the promised land is one of violence sanctioned by God, whose gift of the land is appropriated by armed conquest, sometimes involving the extinction of all living beings. It is nonetheless clear that the Hebrew Bible's understanding of God's ultimate desire for the world is peace. The life God intended for Eden is one of harmonious existence, and the second sin identified is a form of violence: Cain's murder of his brother Abel. Gen 5, moreover, names violence twice (vv. 11, 13) as a major sign of the earth's corruption that leads to the great flood. And there are few passages in all literature that equal the power of the images of peace in the book of Isaiah—not only the "swords into plowshares" metaphor in 2:4 but also the description of the "peaceable kingdom" that embraces all life.

> The wolf shall live with the lamb,
>   the leopard shall lie down with the kid,
> the calf and the lion and the fatling together,
>   and a little child shall lead them . . .
> The nursing child shall play over the hole of the asp,
>   and the weaned child shall put its hand on the adder's den.
> They will not hurt or destroy
>   on all my holy mountain;

> for the earth shall be full of the knowledge of the LORD
> as the waters that cover the sea.
> (Isa 11:6, 8–9)

The logic of the image is unmistakable: the absence of violence is attributed specifically to the knowledge of God. *To know God is necessarily to pursue peace.*

Earlier verses in Isa 11, however, suggest that the peace envisioned in verses 6–9 has been established through the use of violence. In verses 3–4, the ideal king in the line of David does justice for the poor by killing the wicked "with the breath of his lips." The oft-cited commandment in Exod 20:13, moreover, is better translated as "you shall not murder," rather than as "you shall not kill." The Hebrew Bible clearly sanctions war under some circumstances and gives various justifications for it.[1] Israel's initial war, in which God fights for the people against Pharaoh and the Egyptians, is one of liberation from oppression (Deut 7:7–8). In other cases, defense is the justification, as in Num 21:21–32, where the Amorites deny the Israelites peaceful passage through their land and attack them. The conquest of the land, however, receives different sanctions. Deut 9:5 combines two themes, punishment of evil people and fulfillment of God's covenant promise: "because of the wickedness of these nations the LORD your God is dispossessing them before you, in order to fulfill the promise that the LORD made on oath to Abraham, to Isaac, and to Jacob." Deut 20:18 adds another sanction: the indigenous nations might lead the Israelites into sin.

For many persons of biblical faith, the justifications for genocidal conquest are simply unacceptable, and those for other forms of war are not fully satisfying. We see this in the ways both Jewish and Christian traditions have wrestled with the issue through the centuries. The process begins within the Hebrew Bible. In Deut 20:10, God requires the Israelites to make an offer of peace before engaging in war, although that offer entails the enemy's surrender and acceptance of forced labor. Other passages challenge the militaristic ideology that led to participation in various conflicts long after the conquest. In the eighth century BCE, Isaiah criticized King Hezekiah for entering into a military alliance with Egypt after Judah declared independence from the Assyrian Empire. "Woe to those who go down to Egypt for help, who rely on horses, who trust in chariots because they are many . . . but do not look to the Holy One of Israel or consult the LORD!" (Isa 31:1). This oracle is particularly significant since Isaiah supported the David-Zion ideology, the belief that God had promised to perpetuate David's line and protect Jerusalem from its foes. The prophet apparently understood this

---

1. Wright, "War," 800–805, esp. 801–2.

promise as conditional upon obedience to God, however. As Robert Jewett comments, Isaiah "sought to expose the myth that the chosen people would always prevail."[2] Then in the sixth century BCE Jeremiah's critique went even further. In the midst of the turmoil that ended in the destruction of Jerusalem and the Babylonian exile, he lashed out sarcastically at the belief in God's unconditional protection of the temple. "Do not trust in these deceptive words, 'The temple of the LORD, the temple of the LORD'" (Jer 7:4). Like Isaiah, he opposed futile military action against an oppressive foe and criticized Judah for numerous sins, including what Jewett terms "a dangerous and arrogant perversion of national mission."[3]

Neither of these prophets denied Judah's mission to the world, and both looked forward to a future when an obedient people would enjoy peace and prosperity. What they opposed, according to Jewett, was Zealous Nationalism, a fanatical patriotism that ignores political realities, locates all evil in national enemies, and seeks to redeem the world through their military defeat. In contrast to this ideology, Isaiah and Jeremiah represented a Prophetic Realism that takes account of political realities, recognizes the evil within one's own group, and fosters peaceful coexistence.[4] Jewett cites Amos and Hosea as other examples of Prophetic Realism,[5] and the book of Jonah provides a comical critique of the ethnocentrism characteristic of Zealous Nationalism. It portrays a prophet so obsessed with hatred of the enemy that he initially refuses God's command to preach to Nineveh, the capital of the Assyrian Empire, out *of fear that they will accept his message* (4:2)! When, astonishingly, the people (and animals!) actually repent (3:8-9), Jonah begins to pout, provoking God's declaration of care for all life in 4:9-11. Both Zealous Nationalism and Prophetic Realism have influenced biblically based religious communities through the centuries, and they remain with us today in both religious and secular forms, contending with one another within faith communities and in society as a whole.

With specific regard to empires, the Hebrew Bible is often condemnatory, which is not surprising, since Israel and Judah are frequently the victims of imperial conquest. Sometimes God appears as the fierce avenger who will punish the enemies of God's people. The prophet Nahum, for example, envisions God as "avenging and wrathful" (Nah 1:1), bent on defeating the Assyrian Empire and pursuing enemies "into darkness" (1:8). The book of Daniel, moreover, proclaims God's final triumph over evil: God's

---

2. Jewett, *Captain America*, 17.
3. Ibid., 19.
4. Ibid. esp. 9-24.
5. Ibid., 16-17.

destroying the Seleucid king Antiochus Epiphanes, oppressor of the Jews, thus demonstrating divine sovereignty over all earthly authorities (Dan 11:20—12:4). On the other hand, God often uses empires to accomplish God's purposes, as when Persia conquers Babylon and allows a band of Judean exiles to return home. And the biblical tradition generally takes a quietist attitude toward Persian rule, which lasts for centuries. God can also use empires to punish Israel for its sins, even if these instruments of God's wrath are eventually subject to condemnation for their excesses.

Two streams of tradition developed in the wake of the Hebrew Bible—rabbinic Judaism, which is the parent of modern Judaism, and Christianity. Both streams moved away from Zealous Nationalism. A passage in the Babylonian Talmud, a sixth-century-CE compilation of Jewish tradition, has King Saul challenge God's command to destroy the Amalekites in 1 Sam 15:3. The story does not overturn the biblical injunction, but Norman Solomon observes that "Saul's moral critique is made to appear correct."[6] Solomon also notes that Jewish tradition has guarded against use of the genocidal commands as a justification for similar actions in later times: "This kind of war is of historical interest only, and does not serve as a model within Judaism."[7] Along similar lines, Reuven Firestone observes that in the Talmud generally, "representations of God and humanity tend to be more consistently quietist, though not pacifist." Although God appears "as one who would eventually avenge the enemies of Israel," the stories in this tradition "are carefully constructed so as not to appear as if Jews themselves can take up arms against their enemies as had the great warrior chiefs known in the Bible as the Judges, or the warrior kings of Israel such as David."[8] This is partly because Jews in the postbiblical period were not in a position to wage war,[9] but we can also see at work an emphasis on humaneness, rooted in biblical tradition. Thus a passage in the Jerusalem Talmud[10] proclaims that "he who saves one life, it is equivalent to saving an entire world."[11] Irving Greenberg also observes that the medieval Jewish tradition tends to suggest that "any use of human force or power is inherently violent and therefore morally inappropriate."[12]

6. Solomon, "Judaism," 297.
7. Ibid., 296.
8. Firestone, "Judaism as a Force," 78–79.
9. Ibid., 78.
10. A compilation of Jewish tradition composed in Israel (although in Galilee rather than Jerusalem) in the fourth and fifth centuries CE, thus earlier than the Babylonian Talmud; it is also known as the Palestinian Talmud.
11. Quoted in Greenberg, "Religion as a Source," 100.
12. Greenberg, "Religion as a Source," 94.

In the New Testament, the biblical tradition takes an even clearer turn toward nonviolence, especially in the life and teachings of Jesus. The theme is particularly prominent in the Sermon on the Mount (Matt 5–7). In 5:38–41, Jesus teaches nonretaliation, explicitly rejecting the doctrine of "an eye for an eye" (Exod 21:24). He also condemns anger against one's fellows (5:21–26), commands love of enemies and prayer on behalf of one's persecutors (5:43–48), and praises those who sow reconciliation: "Blessed are the peacemakers, for they will be called children of God" (5:9). Equally important is the fact that he offers no resistance when he is arrested and put to death by the Roman authorities.

At various points, moreover, Jesus's words and deeds are textbook illustrations of Prophetic Realism confronting Zealous Nationalism. In Jewett's words,

> He reversed the idea of divine preference for the chosen people, suggesting that sinners and foreigners would be the first welcomed into the kingdom (Luke 4:16–30). He worked to alter the stereotypes which made zealous warfare seem necessary, picturing a hated Samaritan as humane . . . [and] he thrust a note of realism into the minds of his disciples when one of them began to use the sword against the authorities in Gethsemane: "Put your sword back into its place; for all who take the sword will perish by the sword" (Matt. 26:52[–53]).[13]

Other New Testament materials follow a similar path. Paul, for example, rules out violent confrontations with Roman power with his counsel to "be subject to the governing authorities" (Rom 13:1), although he was clear that one's ultimate loyalty is to God rather than to any human institution. Similarly, the book of Acts depicts early Christian missionaries as nonviolent with respect to the empire.

Nonviolence does not necessarily mean nonresistance, however. As Richard Hays argues, Acts depicts Paul and his entourage as nonviolent but socially disruptive. They introduce "an explosive new catalyst into the sociopolitical order" by "re-socializing them into a community that lives by very different norms."[14] Thus in Ephesus Paul's mission creates a riot (Acts 19:21–41). Helmut Koester has shown, moreover, that Paul uses politically volatile terminology in 1 Thess when he criticizes those who say "'there is peace and security'" (5:3). For he is pointing to Jesus's eventual return "as an event that will shatter the false peace and security of the Roman Empire."[15]

13. Jewett, *Captain America*, 21.
14. Hays, *Moral Vision*, 128.
15. Koester, "Imperial Ideology," 162.

In a similar way, when early Christians proclaimed Christ as "Lord" (Greek: *kyrios*), they were using a term claimed by the emperor and thus implicitly challenging the whole imperial establishment. In various ways, then, the New Testament depicts first-generation Christians as subtly opposing the power and injustices of an empire that was, out of fear or rebellion, notoriously intolerant of social disruption.

If this subtle anti-imperialism seems contrary to the teachings of Jesus, this is largely because Christian tradition has misinterpreted the saying on paying the Roman poll tax (Mark 12:17//Matt 22:21//Luke 20:25): "Give to the emperor the things that are the emperor's and to God the things that are God's." The statement *does not* endorse a theology of "two realms," religious and political, both sanctioned by God. It is rather a cagey way of speaking, common among oppressed communities, which contains a hidden message of nonviolent resistance. As William Herzog notes, the coin bore the blasphemous claim to the emperor's divinity. It was thus "a piece of political propaganda that staked Rome's claim to rule the cosmos," which "must be paid back because it is blasphemous and idolatrous."[16] One has to pay Roman taxes, but one need not, indeed must not, render it the loyalty that belongs to God alone.

The book of Revelation moves beyond such subtle forms of criticism to explicit condemnation. Depicting Rome as both a monstrous beast and a Great Whore (Rev 13, 17) guilty of persecuting the righteous, economic exploitation, and debauchery, it revels in violent imagery symbolizing God's vengeance. Although it shares with Zealous Nationalism this latter emphasis, like postbiblical Judaism it avoids any hint that members of the faith community should themselves take up arms. And despite the fact that at some points it portrays God's destruction of evildoers, it also contains images of ultimate peace and reconciliation, such as the passage that inspired the title of this book: "the leaves of the tree are for the healing of the nations" (22:2). Eugene Boring therefore states that Revelation holds in paradoxical unity the notions of universal salvation and salvation for the righteous alone.[17] Although lacking the stringent note of self-criticism found in some examples of Prophetic Realism, it avoids "the temptation of the oppressed to believe that they are innocent and only their oppressors are guilty." Boring bases this judgment on passages such as Rev 1:5b–6, which make it clear, through references to Jesus's cleansing sacrifice, that "Christian existence is not innocent existence but forgiven existence."[18] In the end, Revelation leaves an

---

16. Herzog, *Prophet and Teacher*, 185, 189.
17. Boring, *Revelation*, 226–31.
18. Ibid., 77.

ambiguous legacy with respect to violence. Regarding empire, however, it is an uncompromising indictment of the violence and exploitation that are attendant upon imperial conquest and rule.

Although the New Testament clearly favors nonviolence, it is debatable whether it actually demands strict pacifism. Since Jesus's injunctions to nonviolence seem focused on personal relations, it is unclear whether they should apply to the question of participation in warfare. John the Baptist's brief injunctions to soldiers in Luke 3:14 mention nothing about refusing to kill, and in Luke 22:36 Jesus counsels his followers to buy swords if they have none. The reference to the sword may be metaphorical, but it could also signal permission for self-defense for Jesus's emissaries. On the other hand, according to Roland Bainton, pacifism does seem to have been the most common position of Christians in the earliest period of church history. Before the reign of the Emperor Constantine, who gave the church a favored position in the empire in the fourth century CE, "no extant Christian writing countenanced participation in warfare."[19] And we have no evidence of Christians in the military "from the end of the New Testament period to the decade A.D. 170–180."[20]

At that point, however, we begin to find Christians in these ranks;[21] and "the succession of Constantine terminated the pacifist period in church history."[22] Under the new emperor, many Christians came to accept the *Pax Romana*—the peace Rome had imposed upon much of the world through conquest—as a gift from God, which had facilitated the preaching of the gospel throughout the world.[23] Thus, Christian theologians, most notably Saint Augustine, eventually took up Greek and Roman theories of "just war" and adapted them. A just war is one that meets such criteria as these: it is fought for a just cause, is declared by a lawful authority, is conducted justly, and is entered into as a last resort. Christian acceptance of war eventually went further than this, however. By the High Middle Ages, the concept of just war was transmuted into that of crusade, in which the church justified wars against those outside the Christian fold and laid aside the humane restrictions of just war theory.[24]

All these varying views on war have existed side by side within biblically based communities through the centuries, and they are still with us

19. Bainton, *Christian Attitudes*, 53.
20. Ibid., 67–68.
21. Ibid., 68.
22. Ibid., 85.
23. Ibid., 86–87,
24. Ibid., 101–16.

today in both religious and secularized forms. Thus, given the Bible's own ambiguous witness on violence, one might think that it is useless when it comes to the issue of war and peace. It remains indisputable, however, that the biblical understanding of God's intention for the world—which is to say, the hallmark of the realm or commonwealth of God—is in fact a just and lasting peace. And it seems equally indisputable that pursuit of Zealous Nationalism and nurture of the crusade ideology are dead ends when it comes to achieving that goal. For both ultimately deny God's care for the entirety of humankind, and both issue from a self-righteous tendency to locate all evil in the other. The issues between pacifism and just war theory are more difficult to sort out, and I will not attempt to do so in this book. For the purposes of evaluating my country on war and peace, I will adopt the lesser standard of just war, which rejects conflicts waged for unjust reasons or in unjust ways, as one form of biblically based Prophetic Realism.

## 14

# Conquest and Imperialism in U.S. History

## The Four Hundred Years' War

IN HIS HISTORY OF Vietnam, Stanley Karnow distinguishes the doctrine of Manifest Destiny, which spurred the expansion of the United States across the continent, from the imperialism that characterized the powers of Europe. "There was little inclination in America for dominating foreign territories," and "Americans were instinctively repelled by the idea of governing other peoples."[1] In response to sentiments such as this, however, theologian David Griffin makes this observation: "The main rationale for denying the existence of an American empire was the equation of empire with the kind of colonial empire Great Britain had. By making that equation and then overlooking the awkward fact that America did have a few formal colonies, American leaders could deny that they ruled over an ever-growing empire."[2]

This country's founders, moreover, did not shy away from the term *empire* in describing the new nation's destiny. George Washington referred to the United States as a "rising empire," and Thomas Jefferson praised the Constitution as conducive to "extensive empire."[3] The assumption was that

---

1. Karnow, *Vietnam*, 12.
2. Griffin, "Empire," 3.
3. Schiller, "Brief History."

unlike empires of the past, the American version would be benevolent.[4] In time, we came to think of ourselves as anti-imperialist and anticolonial. The building of the nation, however, involved both the brutal subjugation of the Native Americans, or "Indians" as Columbus misnamed them, and the acquisition of land from other countries by force. And although America came into existence in the twilight of the long history of colonization, it has employed means other than direct rule to exploit other nations and control their affairs. As Griffin comments, "American business and political leaders . . . made a conscious decision to create a different kind of empire, a *neocolonial* empire, sometimes called an *informal* empire."[5] Behind our self-righteous denials of imperialist ambitions and the claim that we go to war only reluctantly and only for just causes lies a much more complex, and far less innocent, reality.

## FROM COLUMBUS TO THE TRAIL OF TEARS

"What is *that* doing on your wall?" The young woman, a member of the single-adult group at the church where I was associate pastor, asked this question as she glared at the picture of Andrew Jackson in my apartment. Somewhat befuddled, I explained that I admired Jackson for his solidarity with the common people. The young woman, Sammie, eventually married me, which is somewhat miraculous, given this moment early in our relationship. What saved the day, perhaps, is that when she delivered a lecture on a serious gap in my knowledge of American history—Jackson's role in the infamous Trail of Tears—I listened. Later, I took the picture down. Here is why.

The Cherokees, whose territory once included the mountains of north Georgia where Sammie and I now live, had "resisted the early westward push" of white settlement, but their resistance ended with the death of their chief in 1792.[6] From that point, they began to assimilate with whites and adopted many aspects of their culture. One of their own, a silversmith named Sequoyah, developed a syllabary to make reading and writing in their language possible. A high percentage of the people gained these skills, and many became literate in English. Among their accomplishments was to write their own constitution. Their one "offense" proved fatal, however: their refusal to forfeit their land to the State of Georgia. The state's claim rested on its 1802 agreement with the federal government that Georgia could have the land "as

4. Griffin, "Empire," 3.
5. Ibid.; italics original.
6. Tebbel, *Compact History*, 158–59.

soon as the Indians could be moved peacefully." When Jackson took office, Georgia insisted upon removal, and the president engineered the Indian Removal Act of 1830. Thereupon the Georgia legislature enacted a series of laws, "all of them illegal, first extending state laws to the Cherokee territory, and then dividing it up into lots, after which further laws were passed depriving Cherokees of their civil rights." Even before the laws took effect, Georgians began "burning and killing and stealing in Cherokee territory."[7]

The Cherokees appealed to the Supreme Court, which ruled that Georgia "had no right to extend its laws to the Cherokee nation and were not entitled to seize it as they wished."[8] The president ignored the decision, however, giving Georgia a free hand. As Zinn describes the result, "Georgia now put Cherokee land on sale and moved militia in to crush any signs of Cherokee resistance. The Cherokees followed a policy of nonviolence, though their property was being taken, their homes were being burned, their schools were closed, their women mistreated, and liquor was being sold to render them even more helpless."[9] The federal government then pushed through a treaty with a small percentage of the tribe in 1835, which no elected official of the Cherokees approved, involving the forfeiture of all their holdings for a pitiful price and the promise of land in the West.[10] Sixteen thousand Cherokees then signed a petition pleading for justice. As the following excerpts show, it is based upon doctrines that lay at the heart of American democracy, prior treaties, and central biblical principles:

> We wish to remain on the land of our fathers. We have a perfect and original right to remain without interruption or molestation. The treaties with us, and law the United States made in pursuance of treaties, guarantee our residence and our privileges, and secure us against intruders. Our only request is that these treaties may be fulfilled, and these laws executed . . . We entreat those to whom the foregoing paragraphs are addressed, to remember the great law of love. "Do to others as ye would that others should do to you."[11]

The removal was unstoppable, however. Within two years, two thousand of the people complied with the evacuation order, although the majority remained, hoping vainly for reprieve. In 1838, with President Martin Van Buren now in office, General Winfield Scott was commissioned to carry

7. Ibid., 159–60.
8. Ibid., 160.
9. Zinn, *History*, 140.
10. Tebbel, *Compact History*, 161.
11. Quoted in Zinn, *History*, 138.

out the order forcibly. On the long and miserable journey west, the people suffered numerous hardships and diseases, and four thousand died along the way. On reaching Oklahoma, they named their ordeal "The Trail Where They Cried."[12] Not all made the journey, however; some defied the order and hid in the mountains. In the 1840s and 1850s, their only white chief, William Holland, began purchasing land on their behalf, and in 1876 a 56,000 acre tract in western North Carolina—a tiny fragment of their territory that once spread over several states—was officially "demarcated as Cherokee land, outside of federal and state government jurisdiction."[13]

Land was a central issue; the Cherokees presented no military threat in the 1830s. Jackson, more than any prior president, pursued an expansionist policy, to which all Indian tribes presented impediments. The removal of the Cherokees was in fact only one component of his plan to clear the entire southeast of the native population. He engineered a law setting aside land in the West for resettlement, in which no whites would be allowed to live. Subsequently, the government by various means displaced the vast majority of the Chickasaws, Creeks, and Seminoles, as well as the Cherokees.[14] If we understand imperialism as including the subjugation of peoples and incorporation of their territory, although not ruling them as "foreign nations," Jackson's plan was clearly imperialistic. The natives had land, and bit by bit, the expanding new country took it.

Imperialist policy did not begin with Jackson. The European exploration and colonization of the "New World" were acts of powerful empires vying with one another to extend their spheres of influence and exploit new lands. And despite instances of friendships between the new arrivals and the natives, the latter stood in the way of what eventually developed as the goal of two central players in the drama, England and France: control of the continent. Conflict thus erupted nearly everywhere the encounter of cultures took place. Nor did the imperial impulse die when the English colonies won their independence. The United States quickly began encroaching on the territories of peoples who had lived in the land for centuries and was thus constantly at war. John Tebbel therefore looks upon the many conflicts between the white invaders and the Native Americans as "one great war," lasting "roughly from 1500 to 1900." He adds that "to the hopelessly huddled and often starving survivors in the concentration camps we choose to call reservations, it is a war that has never ended."[15]

12. Tebbel, *Compact History*, 161.
13. Hill, "Qualla Boundary," 1.
14. Brown, *Bury My Heart*, 5–6.
15. Tebbel, *Compact History*, 9.

A more precise beginning point would be 1492. Drawing on Columbus's journal, Zinn describes how the "discoverer" of the New World responded to the friendly welcome by the peaceful Arawaks of the Bahamas by taking prisoners he hoped would lead him to rich deposits of gold. On his second expedition, he sought not only gold but slaves. With a base in Haiti, he captured 1,500 Arawaks and put 500 on ships to Spain, 200 of whom died en route. Gold proved to be scarce, but natives were forced to deliver a specific amount, and those who did not "had their hands cut off and bled to death."[16] Columbus's brutality, moreover, was repeated by later Spanish invaders on the East Coast and northern shore of the Gulf of Mexico, where the Indians came to understand the intentions of the invaders and began to fight back.[17]

As for the English, Sir Richard Greenville, landing in Virginia in 1585, was received with warm hospitality, "which he repaid by burning and plundering a village in revenge for the theft of a single silver cup."[18] By 1607, when the Jamestown colony was founded, the natives along the coast had undoubtedly heard of such incidents and greeted the settlers with initial hostility. Two outstanding leaders, however, John Smith and Chief Powhatan, negotiated a truce that lasted, with minor interruptions, until the latter's death. At that point, Powhatan's brother assumed leadership and, resolving to drive the invaders out, initiated a bloody conflict that ended in his defeat.

In New England, Chief Massasoit of the Wompanoags gave land to the Mayflower Pilgrims as well as help that was essential to their survival. What eventually happened, however, was the story of the conquest of the continent writ small: "as colonization spread, inevitable frictions began to develop." When the invaders pushed into the Connecticut River valley, where the Pequots were being squeezed by the Dutch moving up from Manhattan Island, a conflict broke out that ended with their extermination. Although a forty-year peace ensued, after the death of Massasoit his son Metacomet, or King Philip, allied with other tribes to form a secret army. When violence erupted, the English prevailed, but with great cost to both sides.[19] The pattern was thus set: the invaders' expansionist tendencies continued unabated, and the natives resisted and were defeated.

Ever since the empires of Europe had begun to vie for control of the continent, the Native Americans had been forced to navigate treacherous waters. Some tribes maintained neutrality, while others formed alliances

16. Zinn, *History*, 1–4.
17. Tebbel, *Compact History*, 11.
18. Ibid., 12.
19. Ibid., 16–24.

with one or another of the invaders. In the Revolutionary War, some sided with the Americans, but most joined with the British—an understandable but fateful decision. In 1779, as battles raged in New York's Mohawk valley and western Pennsylvania, General Washington commissioned a campaign against the Six Nations allied with the British. His instructions "were explicit. He wanted 'the total destruction of their settlements and the capture of as many prisoners of every age and sex as possible.' Moreover, he wanted the country of the Iroquois not only '*overrun but destroyed.*'" General Sullivan complied by burning "every Iroquois village to the ground."[20] Washington's views toward the natives moderated after the Revolutionary War, but as president he authorized the governor of the Northwest Territory, where Indians "were engaged in a constant guerilla warfare against the advancing frontier,"[21] to form an army and stop the attacks. That campaign failed, but the Treaty of Greenville brought a temporary peace in 1795, establishing a boundary for white settlements. It ceded to the Americans "a vast territory which included the entire state of Ohio . . . and a good part of Indiana as well."[22] And yet the westward advance continued. "By the time Jefferson became president, in 1800," Zinn writes, "there were 700,000 white settlers west of the mountains," outnumbering the natives about eight to one. In time, this great proponent of equality would issue the initial authorization for the removal of the Cherokees and the Creeks from Georgia, although that atrocity would be long in coming.[23]

There were, all along, some American leaders who hoped for a different way of settling the issues between the new nation and the natives. Some even had a vision akin to that of Tecumseh, who united many tribes in a fight to forge "nothing short of an Indian United States, running between the Americans and the British on the north and the Spanish on the west."[24] Neither the voices of the sympathetic whites nor Tecumseh's forces, however, were able to stop the expansion. Tecumseh's defeat was decisive, but he had inspired a spirit of revolt that caught fire in 1813 among the Seminoles and Creeks. The general commissioned to quell the insurrection was Andrew Jackson. His defeat of the Creeks was sealed with a treaty, "another shameful document in the increasingly long list—which took away most of the Creek territory not only from the hostile Indians but those who had tried to help

---

20. Ibid., 68–70; italics original.
21. Ibid., 79–80.
22. Ibid., 92–93.
23. Zinn, *History*, 125.
24. Tebbel, *Compact History*, 104.

the government as well."²⁵ The Seminoles' defeat did not come until 1841, under General William J. Worth, who succeeded only by "systematically destroying crops, shelter and every source of supply on which they depended." Even then, some of the tribe remained in the Florida swamps, refusing to sign a treaty. In the end, this victory had cost the government twenty million dollars and had employed the services of thirty thousand troops, 1,466 of whom were killed.²⁶ The conflict thus showed "what a high price, both moral and material, the government was willing to pay for total domination of the Indians."²⁷

The extent of the moral price, moreover, had been demonstrated three years earlier when Jackson's authorization for the Trail of Tears was carried out. That is why I took Jackson's picture down and why my wife can scarcely stand to look at a twenty-dollar bill. These events were not anomalies, moreover, but the results of a much broader policy of imperialist expansion that would not stop at genocide—or at the Mississippi River.

## HOW THE WEST WAS WON (OR LOST?)

Popular versions of the westward movement stress the courage and adventurous spirit of pioneers setting out to build new lives in a land filled with danger but brimming over with promise. These versions tell a tale of epic proportions that functions as a "foundation myth," a sacred story that helps our nation define its identity. That story includes American Indians, but it tends to press them into caricatures such as the "noble savage," the unspeakably brutal renegade, or the comical figure. And it too often downplays the depth of the losses these people suffered and lacks an adequate account of how the tale might read from the places they occupied. Only recently has the majority population begun to recover these other perspectives, from which the story is one of how the West was *lost*. There were people in the emerging nation who could see the movement from the perspectives of "the others" early on, asking how Americans would feel about endless hordes invading *their* land and claiming huge portions of it for themselves. Their voices, however, were drowned out by the drumbeat of expansion; and the westward drive was intensified by many forces. The Louisiana Purchase in 1803 doubled the size of U.S. territory, and within the next half century the country's holdings had spread to the Pacific Ocean. The annexation of Texas, the acquisition of California and nearly all of New Mexico and Arizona

25. Ibid., 130.
26. Ibid., 145.
27. Ibid., 144–45.

as the spoils of the Mexican-American War, and the creation of the Oregon Territory through a treaty with Great Britain—these momentous additions completed the "legal" aspect of the advance. In the economic sphere, the discovery of gold, first in California and then in Colorado, added to the frenzy of the movement; and of course that drive to make a better life in a new land was still at work.

Feeding the annexation movement, moreover, was a new articulation of the expansionist ideology that emerged in the 1840s: Manifest Destiny. Imbued with religious overtones, it expressed the belief that the United States was endowed with unique characteristics that gave it a special role to play in human history involving domination of the continent. Although opposed by most Whigs and such notables as Abraham Lincoln and Ulysses S. Grant, it had the support of Democratic President James K. Polk, an heir of Jacksonian democracy, who pursued the war with Mexico. In its explicit form, it faded from American history, but it accomplished its purpose. And although it first surfaced in relation to the Mexican-American War, it gave impetus to that other war—the four hundred years' war against the American Indians. For "legal" title to the land, based on agreements with European empires was one thing; actual settlement was something else. What stood in the way of settlement were the Indians who had possessed the land for centuries, and many were willing to fight to keep it.

And so the war continued, as Jackson's promise of a Permanent Indian Frontier lay forgotten. The settlers and traders pushed relentlessly westward, as did the U.S. Army, and the West was won, or lost, according to one's perspective. Tebbel identifies an incident in the Mexican-American War as the first significant foray in this phase of the conquest. Although tribes in the Southwest were generally under the control of the Americans during the conflict with Mexico, when most of the conquering troops moved on toward California the Pueblo Indians rebelled. The army, equipped with howitzers, won two preliminary skirmishes and then took the main stronghold of two pueblos. After a charge on the church in the first compound, "the Indians were routed out and fled from the fort, where the dragoons cut down most of them before they could reach the hills." Those in the second pueblo pled for mercy, and Colonel Price compromised by executing only the leaders deemed responsible for an initial uprising in which the American governor had been killed. In the end, "at least 150 of the pueblos' defenders lay dead, out of a garrison of 650, and many others were wounded."[28]

In a history of the West from a native perspective, Dee Brown describes the experience of a band of Navajos who tried the way of peace.

28. Ibid., 176–78.

Manuelito, their leader, signed a treaty with the Americans, which he did his best to keep. Because of the actions of a few young renegades, however, "the soldiers came and burned his hogans and killed his livestock." This changed everything: "He and his band had been rich, but the soldiers had made them poor." In desperation, the Navajos began raiding the Mexicans, who had been taking Navajo children for slaves. However, "the Navajos were not citizens because they were Indians, and when they raided the Mexicans, soldiers would come rushing into Navajo country to punish them as outlaws."[29] Then came the spark that ignited all-out war. Fort Defiance was located in a valley in Navajo territory that had long served Manuelito's people as pastureland. The fort's commander, however, wanted it for the army's horses and forbade the Navajos to use it; but because it was not fenced in, the Navajos' livestock sometimes strayed into it. As punishment, "a company of mounted soldiers rode out of the fort and shot and killed all the animals belonging to the Navajos." Thus, "to replace their horses and mules, the Navajos raided the soldiers' herds and supply trains" and "the soldiers in turn began attacking bands of Navajos."[30] There followed a nearly successful Navajo attack on the fort, further fighting, and a period of negotiated peace.

That peace was broken, however, in a dispute over a horse race in which the soldiers cheated and a Navajo was killed trying to force his way into the fort. An Army captain described the aftermath: "The Navajos, squaws, and children ran in all directions and were shot and bayoneted . . . Meanwhile the colonel had given orders to the officer of the day to have the artillery [mountain howitzers] brought and to open upon the Indians."[31] The officer at first ignored the command but eventually complied. Further battles ensued, and the arrival of General Carleton, who was covetous of the rich land and hungry for battle, fanned the flames. Although Carleton's terms for peace involved removal to a reservation on decidedly inferior land, some Navajo leaders accepted it; but Manuelito held out. Eventually faced with starvation, however, he surrendered and brought his people to the reservation at Bosque Redondo; but the land was so poor that many of the people died. Indeed, the conditions were so horrific that the federal government sent investigators and eventually negotiated a new treaty allowing the Navajos to return home. But here is the telling note with which Brown concludes his account: "When the new reservation lines were surveyed, much of their best pastureland was taken away for the white settlers. Life would not be

---

29. Brown, *Bury My Heart*, 14.

30. Ibid., 15.

31. United States Congress. 39th. 2nd session. Senate Report, 156, 314; quoted in Brown, *Bury My Heart*, 18.

easy... *Bad as it was, the Navajos would come to know that they were the least unfortunate of all the western Indians. For others, the ordeal had hardly begun.*"[32]

But it had. Tebbel describes a pattern "of seizure of land and betrayal through treaties and broken agreements" that "spread past the Southwest and the Plains into the Northwest."[33] The story of the war in the West, like that of the war in the East, involves both heroism and brutality on both sides. But we should never forget that from the perspective of the *American Indians*, the entire war was one in which they were defending *their* land and *their* ways against *invading* hordes. Nor should we overlook the fact that it was the advancing new country that continually practiced deception, forced unjust treaties and then broke them, and tried either to impose its ways upon the natives or simply to destroy them. It was the advancing nation, moreover, that treated the physical environment with such lack of care that to the natives the whites seemed actually to *hate nature*. The story of "how the West was won," so central to American self-understanding, is thus, when read from an alternative place, one of tragedy, loss, and environmental destruction. I can give no more than a brief, impressionistic account of the remainder of that story, by sketching these few representative events:

- 1851–52, *California: State government encourages destruction of Indian villages,* spending over a million dollars to reimburse miners and settlers for expenses during raids; by 1865, Wintu reduced from fourteen thousand "to less than a thousand weakened, wholly disoriented survivors"; by the end of 1860s "all that was left of the Synkone was a handful of survivors with ghastly memories of what had happened"—one of them saw white men cut her baby sister's heart out.[34]

- 1856, *Arizona*: Apache chief Cochise welcomes Americans, allows stagecoach station; five years later, Cochise was falsely accused of child stealing; he evades arrest but his relatives are held; a quarter century of war ensues; after the Civil War, *the government institutes policy of extermination of Apaches,* enlisting their enemies, Papagos and Pimas, in the effort; after ten years, the government tries negotiation[35] and brings most Apaches onto reservations, then abrogates agreement,

---

32. Ibid., 20–36; quotation from 36; italics added.
33. Tebbel, *Compact History*, 183.
34. Nabokov, "Long Thread," 312.
35. Brown, *Bury My Heart*, 192–217; Nabokov, "Long Thread," 328–30.

and reservation conditions become unbearable; fifteen years of rebellions under Geronimo, Victorio, and Nana.[36]

- *1864, Sand Creek, Colorado*: Colonel Chivington leads seven hundred troops against peaceful Cheyennes encamped in compliance with government order; chief raises American flag and white banner in vain; two hours of slaughter: "Babies and mothers, warriors and grandparents," over one hundred total, three quarters women and children, lay dead;[37] chiefs who sought peace are dead or disempowered; the Colorado territory of Cheyennes and Arapahos lost.[38]

- *1868, Oklahoma*: Comanches and Kiowas ordered to Fort Cobb under threat of extinction; *leaders come for parlay, arrested by General Custer upon refusing to order people into fort*; they are held hostage under threat of death until people surrender; as tribes come near starvation in 1870, some go on buffalo hunts outside reservation; unsuccessful attack on buffalo hunters; many leave the reservation and live in the old way until U.S. Army brings them in and sends many to prison.[39]

- *1868, Fort Laramie, Wyoming Territory*: Chief Red Cloud, after extended war, signs treaty involving army's withdrawal from Bozeman Trail and abandonment of forts, ensuring land for Sioux; *General Custer violates treaty, bringing mining experts into Black Hills and spreading word of gold deposits*; the government, anticipating white incursions, orders Indian hunting parties to report to agencies; Sitting Bull, Crazy Horse, and others resist; 1876, Custer defeated at Little Big Horn; Sitting Bull's group escapes to Canada; Crazy Horse eventually brings his people into reservation, where he resists attempt to arrest him secretly and is killed; Sioux forfeit Black Hills.

- *1877, Oregon*: President Grant sends General Howard to remove Nez Perce—*who had befriended Lewis and Clark and never killed a white*—from Wallowa Valley, two years after promising it to them forever; Chief Joseph brings a prophet to meet with Howard, who arrests the prophet and orders Joseph to move people to reservation; some of tribe counsel war, but Joseph chooses to evacuate; livestock lost on the way, more talk of war; a small band slips away, kills eleven whites; as soldiers attack, Joseph stays with people and fights; they win a battle, flee toward Canada; attacked by soldiers under orders to take no

36. Brown, *Bury My Heart*, 392–413.
37. Nabokov, "Long Thread," 330.
38. Brown, *Bury My Heart*, 68–102, esp. 92–102.
39. Ibid., 243–71.

prisoners, but escape into Yellowstone; General Sherman sends troops under Bear Coat Miles to intercept them; under desperate conditions, Joseph surrenders; *despite his promise to send the people to a reservation, Miles ships them to swampy land at Fort Leavenworth as prisoners of war*; Joseph is visited by dignitaries and allowed to visit Washington, makes impassioned plea for justice, but in vain; Joseph and 150 others, considered too influential, eventually separated from the people and sent "to Nespelem on the Colville Reservation in Washington, and there they lived out their lives in exile."[40]

There were tragic incidents after this, including the 1890 massacre at Wounded Knee Creek in South Dakota, which Peter Nabokov describes in this way:

> Seventh Cavalry troops, having rounded up a band of Hunkpapa Sioux suspected of potential trouble (fully two thirds of them were women and children), herded the Indians into a tight group surrounded by five hundred soldiers, their normal armament reinforced with four Hotchkiss guns. In the morning, the Sioux men were culled out, lined up, and disarmed. Someone is said to have discharged a weapon. Immediately, the Hotchkiss guns opened fire, and most of the men were killed in the first five minutes . . . Some Indians fought back, with whatever they had, stones or sticks or bare hands (leaving twenty-nine soldiers dead), while others tried to flee. Within an hour some two hundred Indians were dead or dying. A few women got as far as three miles before being caught and killed. The rest, about one hundred souls, fled and later froze to death in the hills.[41]

Nabokov goes on to make two important points. First, popular culture has allowed this tragic event to "to validate the 'myth of the vanishing Indian' by implying that an entire way of life had ended symbolically in this terrible finale." For such a reading of history ignores the revitalization movements that provide "succor and hope to native peoples caught between the often contradictory creeds of two cultural worlds." Second, "it was not so much sensational battles and deplorable inhumanities that, in the long run, cost Indians their autonomy after the Civil War, but rather the devastation wrought by disease and the expropriation of their land through the bloodless process of treaty making and anti-Indian legislation." As an example of the latter, Nabokov points to the General Allotment Act, passed by Congress in 1887, which subdivided the people's land into family-owned plots.

40. Ibid., 315–30; quotations from 329, 330.
41. Nabokov, "Long Thread," 365–66;

Although this was supported by some American Indians, there were warnings that it would make the Indians' holdings more vulnerable to the wiles of land sharks. And that proved to be the case, as these holdings shrank radically in the years following the act. The allotment resulted in government acquisition of "13 million acres by 1890, 23 million acres by 1891, and over 30 million acres by 1892."[42]

This is not the only problematic aspect of the act. One of the major tools of imperial conquest is the destruction of the cultures of subdued peoples, and the division of the once communally held land into family plots was an attempt to replace the values of the natives with those of the white population—that is, a sense of "ours" with a sense of "mine." It thus stands alongside early reservation schools that forbade the use of native language and native dress as a way of making American Indians into Euro-Americans. The conquest of the tribal peoples was by no means bloodless, but neither was it limited to military action. Although sometimes pursuing genocide, the conquerors were often willing to settle for capturing the hearts and minds, along with the lands and resources, of peoples who were quite happy with their traditional ways of life. Alongside the physical violence that the conquest involved, then, we must recognize two other forms of violence at work in the four hundred years' war. One was the assault upon the human consciousness through the attempt to undermine deeply held values; the other was the acquisition of the material means that had sustained traditional ways of life.

Nor have these forms of violence ceased. In the early 1960s, for example, President Kennedy ignored a treaty made during George Washington's administration by building a dam that flooded a Seneca reservation. Later in the decade, a coal company began strip mining on Navajo and Hopi land, endangering the water and destroying grazing land,[43] and in 1971 Michigan violated treaties made with the Chippewa in 1836 and 1855 by refusing to "distinguish between Indians and non-Indians in its enforcement of state game laws."[44] A new phase of Indian activism achieved some successes in the courts in the 1970s, notably a decision denying Michigan's right to regulate Chippewa fishing.[45] As Philip J. Deloria documents, however, the changing political climate brought significant setbacks in the American Indian struggles for justice. After the protest at Wounded Knee in 1973, the FBI infiltrated groups such as the American Indian Movement, provoking them

---

42. Ibid., 366–69; quotations from 366, 369.
43. Zinn, *History*, 515–19.
44. Deloria, "Part Five," 443.
45. Ibid.

"into acting against their own best interests."[46] And the resurgence of laissez-faire economics during the Reagan administration was disastrous for the native population. Although the Indian appropriations had composed only ".04 percent of the federal budget," under Reagan "in 1982, 2.5 percent of *all* federal budget cuts came directly from that .04 percent." These cuts brought job loss and the devastation of tribal economics that made reservations vulnerable to offers of multinational corporations to "solve" the problem by turning the land "into strip mines or toxic waste dumps."[47] Tribes have thus been faced with agonizing dilemmas as they have been forced to choose between short-range economic advantage and traditional values. The push for the KeystoneXL pipeline, designed to bring tar-sands oil from Canada through Indian territory, perpetuated the pattern. Some American Indians were open to the plan, but others were concerned about possible violation of grave sites and ecological damage. Although this specific plan has now been laid to rest, the threat of similarly disastrous operations remains.

Winona LaDuke of the Anishinaabe Nation, cofounder of Honor the Earth and two-time Green Party vice presidential candidate described in graphic terms the "damage to Mother Earth" that such projects bring. "I see water being taken from creeks where water belongs to animals, not to oil companies. I see toxics by the side of the road . . . I see a community where oil has made some very rich and many stayed as poor as they were, where two or three families live in a house." The pipeline, she argued, would be "bad for the climate, bad for the people, and it's all about profits."[48] I quote these words as I conclude this chapter because they remind us of the interconnections among the various forms of idolatry. The violence done to Native Americans as the country expanded was not just about making room for an increasing population; it was also the result of an unquenchable lust for profit. The discovery of gold in Georgia was a major factor in the Trail of Tears, and subsequent discoveries in the West fed the movement in that direction. The expansion of territory, moreover, meant the expansion of markets. And if that involved taking land by force, so be it—especially since those whose land it was were of different skin color, different cultures, and different religious beliefs. The idolatries of wealth, power, and privilege thus combined with that of race to justify four hundred years of brutal war; and those same idolatries are at work today as American Indians still struggle for justice in a land that was once theirs.

46. Ibid., 444.
47. Ibid.
48. "Q & A: Winona LaDuke," 5.

We can also identify another idol that emerged in that long war—the country itself, as an object of unquestioned devotion, often understood as a divinely commissioned savior of the world. The seeds of such a sense of identity were sown as far back as 1630, when John Winthrop used the concept of "a city on a hill" in a sermon to the Puritans who would form the Massachusetts Bay Colony. His vision of a peaceful community that could serve as a moral example to the world was in some ways inspiring and challenging. It has been used, however, to support a version of American exceptionalism that self-righteously and ironically exempts this country from the judgments Americans so easily make against others. This becomes quite clear as we examine some other military actions in which this country has engaged.

# 15

# Conquest and Imperialism Continued

## The Path to Perpetual War

> In strictest confidence . . . I should welcome almost any war, for I think this country needs one.
>
> —THEODORE ROOSEVELT, 1897[1]

> Then Jesus said to him, "Put your sword back in in its place; for all who live by the sword will perish by the sword."
>
> —MATT 26:52

### "FIGHTING FOR OUR FREEDOM"?

IN ORDER TO PUT into context what I feel compelled to say about some of this nation's military actions, I quote from an editorial in the *Christian Century*. While acknowledging the nobility of the sacrifices made by

---

1. From a personal letter, quoted in Zinn, *History*, 290.

military personnel on behalf of their country, the editors go on to caution that *"sacrifice can be a form of idolatry, a gift offered to a false god. Therefore we can fully respect the sacrifices made by American soldiers in Iraq without feeling obliged to defend or retain the policies that provoked them."*[2]

I agree wholeheartedly with this statement but must emphasize that what I consider idolatrous is not the sacrifice made *by* those who give their lives in the war efforts. It is rather the sacrifice *of* these brave persons *by those who send them to war unnecessarily and without just cause,* as well as those who give uncritical support to our nation's use of violence no matter what the cause. Although well aware of the complexity of international politics and the moral ambiguities in virtually all disputes among nations, I find the military actions I discuss below to be glaring examples of imperial domination and evidence that our nation is addicted to the use of violence as well as to economic exploitation on a global basis. The most blatant idolatries or false gods I see at work in all this are a self-righteous Zealous Nationalism and a pervasive lust for wealth and power. I believe that those who actually fight our wars are generally motivated by genuine patriotism, as well as a sense of justice, and sincerely believe that they are indeed "fighting for our freedom." Our leaders, however, have far too often used this phrase as a call to arms when the threat to our country is grossly overstated, or when the real agenda is not national defense but either imperial expansion or economic domination of other nations.

I do not consider all the wars this country has fought to be unjust or unnecessary. If there is such a thing as a just war, in my opinion World War II heads the list, even though it turned out to serve the empire-building I reject—a point I will touch upon later. Nor do I condemn the use of arms in achieving this nation's independence, even though that war could be described as the splitting apart of an empire rather than the unequivocal rejection of imperial rule. My intention, moreover, is not to render judgment on all our military engagements. It is rather to show that the following examples, together with the four hundred years' war outlined in the last chapter, describe a thread of conquest, domination, and exploitation that runs throughout our history. And that thread has brought us from a rebellion against tyranny to a posture early in this century that some have described as "perpetual war."

---

2. Editors of the *Christian Century,* "Sacrificed for What?"; italics added.

## "FROM THE HALLS OF MONTEZUMA TO THE SHORES OF" . . . THE PHILIPPINES!

At the signing of the treaty that concluded the Mexican-America War, a Mexican participant remarked to Nicholas Trist, the American negotiator, "this must be a proud moment for you; no less proud for you than it is humiliating for us." Trist later said to this to his wife, however: "Could those Mexicans have seen into my heart at that moment, they would have known that my feeling of shame as an American was far stronger than theirs could be as Mexicans. For though it would not have done for me to say so there, that was a thing for every right minded American to be ashamed of, and I was ashamed of it, most cordially and intensely ashamed of it."[3]

What could have led an agent of the United States government to make such an astonishing statement about what many Americans saw as a glorious victory? Nothing, I suggest, other than *conscience*, which in fact had prompted others to oppose the war in the first place—among them Frederick Douglass, Horace Greeley, Henry David Thoreau, and Colonel Ethan Allen Hitchcock, who commanded a regiment in the conflict.[4] Such dissenters knew that this war was not about any injustice done to the United States by Mexico but about American expansionism and to some extent the preservation of slavery. Government officials and business leaders had long had their eyes on Texas, California, and the territory in between, and the slaveholding states saw Texas as potentially adding to their number and strengthening their hand.

Although Texas had originally been Indian territory, within the framework of European colonization it belonged to Spain, along with almost all of what is now the American southwest. When Mexico gained independence from Spain in 1821, it included "Texas and what are now New Mexico, Utah, Nevada, Arizona, California, and part of Colorado."[5] Because Texas was sparsely populated, the Spanish had opened it to Anglo American settlers in 1820, and Mexico continued the policy.[6] One motive, which proved ironical in the long run, was "to protect its northern territorial frontiers from further incursion by the United States."[7] The presupposition was that the immigrants would become Mexicans. Thus, "beginning in 1824, when

---

3. Virginia Randolph Trist to Tockerman, July 8, 1864, Nicholas Trist Papers, Box 10, Library of the University of North Carolina at Chapel Hill; cited by Velasco-Marquez, "Mexican Viewpoint."
4. Zinn, *History*, 147–58.
5. Ibid., 147.
6. Texas State Historical Association, "Anglo-American Colonization."
7. Schiller, "Brief History."

the Mexican republic adopted its constitution, each immigrant took an oath of loyalty to the new nation and professed to be a Christian."[8] Most of the settlers, however, "believed that the United States would buy eastern Texas from Mexico" and "expected annexation would stimulate immigration and provide buyers for their land."[9] And the influx of settlers, who quickly outnumbered the Mexicans, clearly served the purpose of American expansionists and proponents of slavery.

When Antonio Lopez de Santa Anna, elected president of Mexico in 1833, "proclaimed a unified central government that eliminated states' rights" and granted him dictatorial powers, the American- and mostly southern-born Texans rebelled. They "declared their independence on March 2, 1836, and adopted a constitution legalizing slavery." Human bondage was outlawed in Mexico but had been allowed on a limited basis in Texas, which was one reason "states' rights" mattered so much to the Texans.[10] With the rallying cry of "Remember the Alamo," in commemoration of the heroic but romanticized battle that took place in the old mission in San Antonio, the rebels gained strength from American volunteers and defeated and captured Santa Anna. In captivity, the president agreed to a treaty that granted independence to Texas "with the Rio Grande River as its southwestern boundary." After returning to Mexico, however, he repudiated the treaty. Mexico thus refused to recognize independence, warned the U.S. that annexation of Texas would lead to war, and declared the Nueces River, about 150 miles north of the Rio Grande, as the southwestern boundary of Texas.[11] The Nueces, in fact, had been the traditional border,[12] but the conflicting claims regarding this matter eventually provided a convenient pretext for war.

In 1845, under President James K. Polk, the United States granted statehood to Texas. Mexico then severed relations, contending that this act violated "the 1828 border treaty, which had recognized Mexico's sovereignty over that territory."[13] In order to settle this controversy and in an effort to buy California and New Mexico (which then included the present state of Arizona), President Polk sent John Slidell to Mexico to negotiate.[14] The Mexican government refused to accept Slidell, however, partly because it

8. Texas State Historical Association, "Anglo-American Colonization."
9. Ibid.
10. American Public University System, "Manifest Destiny."
11. Ibid.
12. Ibid., 148.
13. Velasco-Marquez, "Mexican Viewpoint."
14. American Public University System, "Manifest Destiny."

was in a fragile state and hampered by constitutional restrictions on the transfer of territory.[15] At that point, Polk ordered General Zachary Taylor "to move his troops across the Nueces to the Rio Grande."[16] Not surprisingly, the provocative move led to violence, as Mexican troops attacked an American patrol. As Zinn comments,

> The Mexicans had fired the first shot. But they had done what the American government wanted, according to Colonel Hitchcock, who wrote in his diary, even before these first incidents: "I have said from the first day that the United States are the aggressors . . . We have not one particle of right to be here . . . It looks as if the government sent a small force on purpose to bring on a war, so as to have a pretext for taking California and as much of this country as it chooses."[17]

Hitchcock's words proved prescient. The United States declared war, General Taylor's troops advanced all the way to Mexico City, and Mexico surrendered. The terms of the treaty set the border of Texas at the Rio Grande and ceded to the U.S. for $15 million over half of Mexico's land.[18] "From the halls of Montezuma," the opening line of the Marine Hymn, celebrates this victory in an apparent reference to a hill located in Mexico City. As a child, I loved that hymn and knew all the stanzas. Now that I know the origin of that line, however, it has lost its appeal.

American eyes were soon to look beyond the continent for commercial opportunities. The business establishment was generally satisfied with open international markets rather than colonization, and thus with peaceful free trade rather than military conquest and direct control of foreign governments. As Zinn comments, however, all this "was subject to change. If peaceful imperialism turned out to be impossible, military action might be needed."[19] Thus, when Cuban rebels began fighting for independence from Spain, the Republican president, William McKinley, and major American industrialists began to contemplate intervention on their side. Many Americans supported the independence movement out of sympathy for the rebels' cause, but the president and the industrialists—particularly those dealing in iron, munitions, and transportation—saw the opportunity for profit. A rebel victory in itself would not have ensured "American military and economic influence in Cuba," however. Only direct U.S. participation could

15. Ibid.
16. Ibid.
17. Zinn, *History*, 149.
18. Ibid., 166.
19. Ibid., 295.

do that; and the explosion of the U.S.S. Maine in Havana harbor, an event whose cause was never determined, provided a convenient pretext for war.[20]

At McKinley's urging, Congress authorized the use of force to secure Cuban independence. Spain then declared war, and the United States followed suit.[21] Within three months, the U.S. prevailed; but from the rebels' perspective, one master had been exchanged for another. The Americans excluded Cubans from the peace process, banned armed rebels from the capital city of Santiago, and "told the Cuban rebel leader, General Calixto Garcia, that not Cubans, but the old Spanish civil authorities, would remain in charge of the municipal offices in Santiago."[22] The U.S. Army remained as an occupying force, and American investors quickly took control of railroads, mines, the sugar and fruit industries, and minerals. The exploitative and undemocratic nature of the new arrangements is testified, moreover, by the series of workers' strikes and the U.S.-initiated arrests of strike leaders. Most tellingly, the U.S. made removal of its troops conditional upon the incorporation into the Cuban constitution a provision granting America the right of military intervention and the establishment of naval stations.[23]

The first battle in the conflict was in another Spanish possession, the Philippines, and one of the conditions of peace was the cession of these islands, along with Guam and Puerto Rico, for twenty million dollars.[24] U.S. forces also occupied and claimed Wake Island, and President McKinley "used the war as a pretext to annex the independent state of Hawaii," whose government had been installed by business leaders and planters who had overthrown the rule of Queen Liliuokalani.[25] The new Hawaiian government had been seeking annexation, but Filipinos had no desire to exchange Spanish rule for American. Thus, "while the American public and politicians debated the annexation question, Filipino revolutionaries under [Emilio] Aguinaldo seized control of most of the Philippines' main island" and declared independence. War ensued, and it was no minor conflict. It "lasted three years and resulted in the death of over 4,200 Americans and over 20,000 Filipino combatants," while "as many as 200,000 Filipino civilians died from violence, famine, and disease."[26] The United States, moreover,

---

20. Ibid., 296–97.

21. United States Department of State, Office of the Historian, "Milestones: 1866–1898."

22. Zinn, *History*, 302.

23. Ibid., 303.

24. Ibid., 305

25. U.S. Department of State, Office of the Historian, "Milestones: 1866–1898," 2.

26. Ibid., 1.

"burned villages, implemented reconcentration policies, and employed torture on suspected guerillas, while Filipino fighters also tortured captured soldiers and terrorized civilians who cooperated with American forces."[27] U.S. policies eventually moderated, and the Philippines were granted independence in 1946. The price the Filipino people paid in their failed attempt to gain what Americans had long before claimed for themselves was enormous, however.

## FROM PEARL HARBOR TO VIETNAM

If you want to hear me wax both sentimental and patriotic, tell me stories of heroism in World War II, not just of Americans in combat but also of a mostly unified populace that rallied to support the cause. And, indeed, not just of Americans but also of all the Allied troops as well as the people of London, who bore up magnificently under rocket attacks; the courageous French resistance; and Germans who rejected Zealous Nationalism and plotted to end the war by assassinating Hitler. Tell me the stories, sing me the war songs, show me the videos of aged veterans visiting Normandy, and you may bring tears to my eyes.

This is not to say that I am unaware of ambiguities in even the most justifiable uses of violence. We must, to begin with, be honest about the causes of World War II. Japan's belligerence was in part a reaction to Western imperialism, and the rise of the Nazis was rooted largely in the harsh penalties imposed on Germany after World War I—severe financial reparations and territorial loss. Nor should we, as we celebrate the victory of the Allies, overlook the cost in civilian lives that came not only with the atomic bombing of Japan but with the saturation bombing of German cities. In Dresden alone, more than one hundred thousand died.[28] That said, no one need doubt World War II veteran Howard Zinn's description of that conflict as a campaign "against an enemy of unspeakable evil" that was "extending totalitarianism, racism, militarism, and overt aggression."[29]

But then came the aftermath. What emerged from the war was not an era of genuine peace but a new contest between empires, the Soviet Union and the United States, facing each other with incompatible ideologies and agendas and backing them up with military presence outside their borders. There was much to despise about the Soviet regime; Stalin's government was totalitarian and repressive, even murderous, and had no intention of letting

---

27. Ibid., 2.
28. Zinn, *History*, 412–13.
29. Ibid, 398

go of what became its "satellite" nations. The United States, for its part, made several moves to achieve financial domination in the new world order. Already in July of 1944, it had convinced the United Nations Monetary and Financial Conference in Bretton Woods, New Hampshire to establish the International Monetary Fund and the World Bank, both of which came, in John Cobb's words, "to function as tools of American policy."[30] And that policy has often involved exploitation of foreign nations for profit in ways that increased poverty in some areas. I will elaborate on this point in the next section; what concerns us now are the consequences of U.S. fear of Soviet expansionism.

One of the first persons to call attention to the dangers of Soviet expansionism was George F. Kennan, who served in President Truman's Department of State. He was the major theorist behind the Truman Doctrine, the policy of "containment" of the Soviet Union that involved both financial and military support for the war-torn countries of Europe. The financial component, expressed in the Marshall Plan that helped rebuild these countries, was to some extent an expression of humanitarian concern; but part of the motive was political. Strengthening market economies, it was also meant to reduce the appeal of Communism; and by providing military assistance and the presence of U.S. weapons and troops, it was intended as a check on Soviet aggression. Kennan became disillusioned, however, as the military aspect of the doctrine began to crowd out efforts at negotiation. Resigning from the State Department in 1950, he became a major critic of U.S. foreign policy, arguing that Soviets' own strategy was focused on "political pressures, subversion, and propaganda" rather than military conquest.[31] This aspect of his thought was ignored, however, as the U.S. turned more and more toward the military buildup, which fed the outrageously expensive arms race and fostered public hysteria that eventually led to the notorious witch-hunting of the McCarthy era. While Cold War extremists focused on "the enemy within," imagining hordes of Soviet agents and sympathizers infecting every aspect of American life, these extremists themselves became the severest threat to democracy by attacking freedom of speech and association.

The international consequences were also severe. The doctrine divided the globe into nations belonging to the "free world" and those designated as totalitarian, with a few designated as neutral. As Jewett points out, however, the classification was "clearly ideological rather than empirical."[32] Greece, for example, was considered "free" because it was not in the Soviet camp, even

---

30. Cobb, "Imperialism," 26.
31. Jewett, *Captain America*, 52.
32. Ibid., 32.

though British and American forces had suppressed a left-wing movement and installed a right-wing dictatorship after the war.[33] This ideological agenda, which identified virtually all revolutionary movements as Communist, also led the U.S. to support brutal dictatorships in Latin America, which is another point I will pursue in the next section. It also led, in time, to one of the costliest decisions in America history—costly not merely financially, but also in life, in our nation's standing within the world, in domestic tranquility, and in ecological health.

I was late in opposing the Vietnam War. It was difficult for me to admit that leaders I admired were wrong on such a crucial issue, although the more I learned about the background of the conflict, the more uncomfortable I became. Torn by internal conflicts, I was stuck in the middle ground, while many of my friends expressed, and some acted upon, their conviction that our country's actions were both unwise and unjust. It had never occurred to me to question the Korean War. I was only thirteen when it began, and I had no idea that the government of South Korea was at that time a dictatorship. I had not begun to ponder the more complex questions about the limitations of my country's responsibility, or right, to intervene in the affairs of others even for a just cause. Nor did I perceive the ambiguities at work when we try to define what *is* just. Neither had I thought about how the differences between a civil war and a conflict between nations might play into the issue or about the long-range consequences of intervention. Questions such as these, however, were forced upon me as the war in Vietnam wore on, so that by 1968 I had concluded that what my country was doing there was terribly wrong.

Stanley Karnow describes U.S. involvement in the Vietnam War as a "crusade" motivated by the "domino theory," which he defines as "the naïve belief that Communism would engulf the entire region if America lost Vietnam." The U.S. did "lose" Vietnam, but only two neighboring countries went Communist in its wake—Cambodia and Laos; and much of Laos "had been a Vietnam province for years."[34] The post–Vietnam War experience, together with the dramatic split between the Soviet Union and China, thus proved the domino analogy false. This analogy was appealing in its simplicity, but as Karnow observes, it "disregarded the national diversity of Southeast Asia."[35] Indeed, it ignored the national consciousness of peoples throughout the world and their desire to chart their own courses in history. It thus exhibited a misperception I saw at work in the opponents of

---

33. Zinn, *History*, 417.
34. Karnow, *Vietnam*, 56.
35. Ibid., 50.

the civil rights movement: the tendency to view social upheavals as resulting from the activities of "outside agitators" rather than from the people's own dissatisfaction with the social and political arrangements under which they live. The domino analogy was also characterized by the inadequacy I discussed in chapter 8—a simplistic understanding of "isms" as precisely defined complexes of ideas not subject to variation. Those who thought in these terms viewed Communism as a monolithic system, unified in its goals and methods and headquartered in Moscow.

To assume that Vietnam would become a mere puppet of either the Soviet Union or China was a vast oversimplification. The Vietnamese possessed a centuries-old national identity and had by no means been a compliant pawn in the hands of foreign governments. Although dominated by China for long periods, they frequently resisted and were sometimes successful in gaining independence.[36] In more recent times, they directed their anger at France, which, after missionary activity over the course of two centuries, had become their colonial masters in the late nineteenth century. Even after securing their rule, the French frequently found it necessary to put down resistance and did so, in the words of a French governor, with "acts of incredible brutality."[37] Throughout the colonial period, Roger Barr observes, the French "ruled Vietnam harshly . . . Vietnamese people were prohibited from traveling outside their districts without identification papers. They were not allowed to attend public meetings, nor could they organize or publish newspapers. They were subject to forced labor and could be imprisoned by the order of any French magistrate."[38]

The people paid dearly in other ways also. The French lust for profits created intolerable conditions bordering on slavery. "Rubber," Karnow comments, "was produced by virtually indentured workers so blighted by malaria, dysentery and malnutrition that at one Michelin company plantation, twelve thousand out of forty-five thousand died between 1917 and 1944."[39]

Then came World War II, which disrupted French rule and brought in its wake two monumental decisions, one by France and one by the United States. France took steps to reestablish control of Vietnam, and the United States provided assistance. President Truman's decision was an outgrowth of the policy of containment, accompanied by an early version of the domino theory. It was insensitive, however, to the hopes of the Vietnamese people, which were being awakened by a number of left-wing groups

36. Ibid., 110–13.
37. Ibid., 100.
38. Barr, *Vietnam War*, 11.
39. Karnow, *Vietnam*, 129.

who cooperated with one another at some points but espoused different approaches to revolutionary change. One of these eventually gained control over the movement, by brutal means I will discuss below, under the leadership of a man who in his youth studied in Paris and later named himself Ho Chi Minh, "The Enlightened One."

First attracted to anticolonial French socialists such as Leon Blum, who later became prime minister, Ho "ultimately opted for the Communists, figuring that their Soviet patrons had the potential power to spark the global revolution that would liberate Vietnam." His intention was not to draw Vietnam into servitude to the Soviet Union, however, but to use Soviet power to gain Vietnamese independence. In 1940 he "aligned himself . . . with the Allies, expecting them to defeat Japan, oust the discredited French from Vietnam and reward his country with independence." He did this, moreover, despite the fact that the Soviet Union had earlier "signed a pact with Germany and forbade Communists everywhere to resist the Axis powers." As Karnow comments, "Ho's sole concern was Vietnam."[40] Nor did Ho's animosity toward France initially extend to the United States. During World War II, he "helped rescue American pilots who had been shot down by the Japanese."[41] After the war, when he was desperate to alleviate the people's starvation that resulted partly from the French policy of confiscating rice, he appealed to the U.S. for humanitarian aid, counting on our stated commitment to national self-determination. However, none of the eight letters he sent to President Truman over a four-month period in 1945–46 received an answer.[42]

As the French tried to reestablish their rule, Ho Chi Minh's independence movement, known as the Vietminh, resumed the resistance that had begun in the 1930s. They did so with such ferocity that the French finally granted a semblance of independence, a status of "associated statehood" in which they retained the right to appoint the country's leader; and of course the person they appointed was pro-French. The United States recognized the new government, but the Vietminh continued their fight. After a defeat at Dien Bien Phu in 1954, the French surrendered; and a peace conference in Geneva achieved a cease-fire that divided the country into North Vietnam and South Vietnam and set up two governments, but only *as a temporary measure*. It thus provided for national elections *for all of Vietnam as a whole country*, to be held in 1956. However, both the newly formed South Vietnamese government and the United States, under President

---

40. Ibid., 138
41. Barr, *Vietnam War*, 14.
42. Zinn, *History*, 461.

## CONQUEST AND IMPERIALISM CONTINUED

Eisenhower, rejected the agreement. They did so, Roger Barr explains, because they "knew that *if free elections were held, the Communist Vietminh would surely win and take control of South Vietnam*."[43] So much, it would appear, for the American commitment to national self-determination and democratic processes!

Changing its name to the Vietcong, the Communist revolutionary group now started a campaign to reunite the south with the north. They began to organize rural peasants against the government of South Vietnam, which was growing increasingly unpopular among the populace, and to engage in guerilla warfare. When it became clear that the South Vietnamese were losing, President Kennedy radically increased the number of military advisers and began to establish "strategic hamlets" to separate the peasants from the Vietcong.[44] Not only were these efforts largely unsuccessful, however, but with so many Americans "in country," the inevitable happened: a number of American advisers were killed. It was not until Lyndon Johnson took office, however, that the United States took a direct role in combat. When two U.S. ships were attacked in the Gulf of Tonkin, the president responded with air strikes against North Vietnam, and Congress passed a resolution giving him the power "to take all necessary measures to repel any armed attack against the forces of the United States and to prevent further aggression." Thus the man who had campaigned for the presidency as the peace candidate, an alternative to the more hawkish-sounding Barry Goldwater, used this incident and this ambiguous resolution to justify a full-scale entrance into the war. Years later, Richard Nixon, whose campaign included a claim to have "a secret plan to end the war," began withdrawing troops but continued the military effort for four years, until the Paris Peace Accords ended U.S. military involvement.[45]

The South Vietnamese fought on alone, but the effort was futile. In April 1975, the capital city of Saigon fell, and the Communist victory was complete. The scenes shown on television were heartbreaking—hordes desperate people, who had supported the South Vietnamese government and the Americans, clamoring to get on board the helicopters that evacuated the remaining officials from our embassy. It was a stark human tragedy, and one could certainly sympathize with those now abandoned by the country they thought was their savior. By my account, however, the mistake that led to this tragedy was not the pullout of U.S. troops but U.S. involvement itself, beginning with support of French recolonization.

43. Barr, *Vietnam War,* 16–18; quotation from 18; emphasis added.
44. Ibid., 21.
45. Ibid., 6.

This is not to deny the deep flaws in the North Vietnamese government or the brutality of the Vietcong. Nor is it to make a saint of Ho Chi Minh, as some war protestors did. By some accounts, he was responsible for the slaughter of two hundred thousand Vietnamese.[46] His rise to power, moreover, was marked by the murder of political opponents of various stripes. Among these were the Vietnamese Trotskyists, a party of "working class socialists" who opposed not only foreign imperialists but Ho and his Stalinists and were slaughtered en masse by the latter in their rise to power in 1945.[47] Ho did not shrink from undermining peasant revolts against French rule when they deviated from his own group's plan of action.[48] His sins, however, do not excuse America's. I believe that U.S. intervention was wrong for at least two reasons. First, it ignored the right of the Vietnamese people to free themselves from colonial rule and to make their own choice of the governmental system under which they wanted to live. Second, the cost in human carnage was simply too high. There were over fifty-eight thousand U.S. deaths[49] and, although estimates of Vietnamese deaths vary wildly, a recent study places the number at roughly one million, which is higher than some estimates but considerably lower than others.[50] If we judge the Vietcong tactics inhumane, it is hypocritical to write off the suffering of the victims of U.S. bombing and the use of napalm and Agent Orange as "collateral damage." Nor should we ignore the incidents in which U.S. soldiers murdered noncombatants or the repressive aspects of the South Vietnamese governments that the United States supported.

The Vietnam War was a terrible tragedy, both for the Vietnamese people as a whole and for the United States. I mourn the American combatants who in good faith fought and died in this conflict, even as I also mourn the Vietnamese losses, both military and civilian, on both sides. I can also honor those who fought in this war even as I respect those who refused to fight and those who protested against it.

American involvement did not create the conflict, but it intensified and prolonged it. That involvement was the product of many factors, including an overblown fear of Communism, insensitivity to a people's desire for independence and determination to achieve it, and what critics of the war have named "arrogance of power." That arrogance, I believe, stemmed largely from what Jewett calls the "Captain America complex"—the belief

46. Jones, "From Stalin to Hitler."
47. "Forgotten Massacre."
48. Sharpe, "Stalinism and Trotskyism."
49. CNN, "Vietnam War Fast Facts."
50. Hirschman et al., "Vietnamese Casualties," 807–9.

that the United States is the ordained savior of the world, innocent of the sins of other nations. It involves a dangerous tendency to attribute all evil to the enemy and all good to one's own country and is thus an idolatrous form of patriotism. It also reflects an uncritical dependence upon violence as a way of combatting evil, whether real or perceived, and a total confidence in one's own perceptions of what is good and what is evil. None of these attitudes is compatible with biblical faith.

## FROM VIETNAM TO NICARAGUA

I thought I understood very well the motivation behind U.S. interventions in Latin America in the 1970s and '80s: the same overblown fear of Communist expansion that was at work in the Vietnam War. I was only partly right, however; and it took Ulises Torres, a United Methodist minister who had fled from his native Chile during the murderous military dictatorship of Augusto Pinochet, to open my eyes to another factor. I begin with an account of how Pinochet came to power; it is a story of which no American should be proud.

When Salvador Allende became president of Chile in 1970, both unemployment and inflation were alarmingly high, and poverty was so severe that "it was estimated that half of the children under 15 suffered from malnutrition." Allende had been instrumental in founding the Chilean Socialist Party, which was philosophically Marxist but *opposed the Communist Party because the latter was under Soviet influence.*[51] He was elected, however, "as the candidate of Popular Unity, a bloc of Socialists, Communists, Radicals, and some dissident Christian Democrats."[52] The election was indisputably democratic, following the Chilean constitution. Because Allende, one of three candidates, received a plurality rather than a majority, the choice fell to the legislature. At this point, the United States made an all-out effort to influence the legislature and keep him out of office. When economic pressure failed, President Nixon secretly authorized the CIA to encourage a military coup. A CIA document dating from shortly after the election is explicit: "It is firm and continuing policy that Allende be overthrown by a coup . . . it is imperative that these actions be implemented clandestinely and securely so that the USG [U.S. government] and American hand be well hidden."[53]

---

51. Spartacus Educational, "Salvador Allende."
52. Editors of *Encyclopedia Britannica*, "Salvador Allende: President."
53. Article in the *Boston Globe,* December 12, 2006, excerpted in Spartacus Educational, "Salvador Allende," 5–6.

A coup was in fact attempted, shortly after the CIA had withdrawn its support for fear that things would get out of hand, but it failed.[54] Allende thus took office and began to deal with the country's economic plight by such steps as nationalizing the copper industry and banks, authorizing wage increases, and expropriating "large agricultural estates for use by peasants."[55] The U.S., however, secretly spent $7 million to fund an all-out propaganda campaign against him[56] and made every effort to bring his government down. They manipulated the International Monetary Fund, the World Bank, and other financial institutions to withhold loans in an attempt to undermine the economy;[57] and the CIA "continued to encourage a coup."[58] In 1973, a second coup attempt succeeded, and Allende was found dead at his desk, reportedly as a result of suicide. The military junta installed Pinochet as president, and he immediately outlawed various leftist parties and dismantled the Chilean congress.[59] He also began a reign of terror. Some human rights groups place the number of murders at more than three thousand, and many people were subjected to torture.[60] Among the latter was Ulises Torres.

The "domino theory" was clearly at work in the Nixon administration's thinking, as were the arrogance of power and an imperialist mindset. As Henry Kissinger, Nixon's national security adviser, famously commented, "I don't see why we need to stand by and watch a country go communist due to the irresponsibility of its own people."[61] The other factor, however, was economic. The largest copper companies, which Allende expropriated, were American owned. Chile accepted the international precedent that although *nationalization of foreign assets was allowed as a matter of national sovereignty*, just compensation must be paid; but Allende claimed that these companies' excessive profits over a long period of time was compensation enough. Thus, as Maryam Elahi comments, the Nixon administration regarded Allende's actions as an assault of U.S. business interests. "Not only

---

54. Turner, *Secrecy and Democracy*, excerpted in Spartacus Educational, "Salvador Allende," 3–4.

55. "Salvador Allende: President," *Encyclopedia Britannica*, 1.

56. Turner, *Secrecy and Democracy*, excerpted in Spartacus Educational, "Salvador Allende," 4.

57. Elahi, "Impact," esp. 154.

58. Article by Julian Borger, *The Guardian*, July 6, 2001; excerpted in Spartacus Educational, "Salvador Allende," 4–5.

59 U.S. Department of State, Office of the Historian. "Milestones: 1969–1976," 2.

60. Article by Jeremy McDermott in *The Scotsman*, December 12, 2006; excerpted in Spartacus Educational, "Salvador Allende," 6.

61. Elahi, "Impact," 153.

were the interests of United States private corporations at stake, but . . . Allende's victory in Chile would have created dangerous precedent by providing ideological fuel for similar acts of nationalization and expropriation of United States' business interests from other Third World Nations."[62]

From the perspective of the laissez-faire ideology so pervasive in the United States, expropriation might seem the equivalent of theft, and the notion of "excess profits" is an oxymoron. This ideology, however, is (as I hope I demonstrated earlier) by no means biblically based. Because all land and resources are from a biblical perspective gifts of God for the common good, no human ownership is absolute. I grant that companies that provide investment and technological skill in a foreign country are entitled to a good return on their investments. From a biblical perspective, however, a *country* also has the right to a good return on the use of its God-given natural resources. And when foreign companies use those resources to make enormous profits that they take out of the country but contribute comparatively little to the general welfare in that country, the term "excess profits" begins to make sense. In fact, the principle of excess profits, even if imposed retroactively, has a place in U.S. legal precedent, with the taxes added to U.S. Steel after World War I as a case in point.[63] We are also familiar with prosecutions for war profiteering as well as for price gouging in times of emergency. In Chile as the two major American-owned copper companies made increasingly high annual profit rates, they refused to make the kind of investments that Chile needed to bolster its economy. Between 1955 and 1960, Anaconda's profit rate increased from 9.1 percent in the previous five years to 13.4 percent, and Kennecott's rose from 25.5 percent to 37.9 percent. Astonishingly, however, tax revenues from American companies fell from $156 million to $68 million between 1955 and 1961, and the "returned value to Chile from total production fell from 78 percent in 1955 to 56 percent in 1959."[64] It is thus hardly surprising that Chilean politicians *across the political spectrum* were seeking ways to return control of the copper industry to their own country when Allende opted for nationalization.

The U.S. intervention in Chile was not a direct military action, but it involved the encouragement of a violent military coup on the part of others and was clearly imperialistic. And it is this point that Ulises helped me to understand: although fear of Communism played a role in U.S. interventions in Latin America in the 1970s and '80s, so did the ideologically driven commitment to protect the profits, however excessive, of U.S-owned or

---

62. Ibid.
63. Gedicks, "Nationalization," 18; rates figured as a percentage of book value.
64. Ibid., 10; rates figured as a percentage of book value.

multinational corporations. *The economic motive behind U.S. intervention is evident, moreover, in the numerous interventions that took place long before there was a Communist threat.* In 1823, President James Monroe outlined before Congress a policy that became known as the Monroe Doctrine. Its intention was both to warn European nations against further colonization in the Americas and to declare the neutrality of the United States with respect to conflicts in Europe. The isolationist tendency of the policy was eventually overshadowed, however, as politicians later invoked it as a pretext for U.S. actions in what they regarded as our "sphere of influence." This was especially the case after President Theodore Roosevelt added what became known as the Roosevelt Corollary, a declaration of the right and duty of the United States to exercise "international police power" to quell chronic unrest in the Western Hemisphere.[65] Nor was this by any means an empty promise (or threat, depending on one's perspective). As Zinn summarizes, the United States

> engineered a revolution against Colombia and created the "independent" state of Panama in order to build and control the canal. It sent five thousand marines to Nicaragua in 1926 to counter a revolution, and kept a force there for seven years. It intervened in the Dominican Republic for the fourth time in 1916 and kept troops there for eight years. It intervened for the second time in Haiti in 1915 and kept troops there for nineteen years. Between 1919 and 1933 the United States intervened in Cuba four times, in Nicaragua twice, in Panama six times, in Guatemala once, in Honduras seven times.[66]

I want to stress, moreover, that these interventions were usually defended as necessary to "protect U.S. interests," which meant, specifically, *economic* interests. The result was that, as Zinn adds, "by 1924 the finances of half of the twenty Latin American states were being directed to some extent by the United States."[67] We should not delude ourselves that U.S. control generally benefited the people of these countries. The elites typically profited from the arrangements, but in many cases the poor became poorer; and the unjust arrangements were often enforced by repressive local governments with which the United States cooperated. Joseph Collins and Frances Moore Lappé describe the pattern that was in effect in the 1970s, using Brazil as an example. In 1976, there were riots protesting the military government then

---

65. National Archives and Records Administration, "Theodore Roosevelt's Corollary."

66. Zinn, *History*, 399.

67. Ibid.

in power and the economic policies involving U.S.-based companies. Why? The staple crop of the traditional society was black beans, a major source of protein for the poorer classes. With government support, however, the U.S. companies progressively took over huge portions of the land formerly used by peasants to grow black beans in order to produce soybeans for export to Japan; and the result was significant increase in hunger. Throughout the continent, U.S. and European companies repeated this pattern, with similar results: although a middle class developed because of new jobs, there were never enough to go around, and many peasants were left homeless. They typically migrated to the cities, where they found no work and ended up in shanty towns, far worse off than they had been pursuing subsistence farming.[68] A person sensitive to biblical ethics, I should think, could almost hear Isaiah railing against those "who join house to house, who add field to field" (Isa 5:8) or Jesus denouncing the rich: "Woe to you who are full now, for you will be hungry" (Luke 6:23).

Central America provides the most blatant examples of unjust economic arrangements enforced by U.S. power. In the 1970s, Guatemala, which received the heaviest U.S. investments in agriculture and industry in the entire region, was notorious for its misdistribution of wealth: more than 78 percent of the farmland was in the hands of around 2 percent of the landowning families. According to the World Bank, moreover, half of the people were getting less than 50 percent of the calories necessary to sustain a human body, with the result that only half the children survived age five![69] And, sadly, U.S. intervention was a contributing factor to this situation. In 1954, the CIA overthrew the democratically elected president out of fear that his agrarian reforms would threaten the enormous profits of U.S. fruit companies. In subsequent years, successive governments murdered thousands of dissident people in order to keep the resources in the hands of the ruling elites. Because of this, the U.S., under President Carter, canceled military aid in 1977; but later President Reagan declared that Guatemala had gotten a "bum rap" on human rights and renewed the aid. A civilian government eventually came to power, but the military retained much influence and prevented any major economic reforms; and they failed to control the notorious death squads that murdered people who worked for fundamental changes in the system.[70] Can we now, perhaps, hear Jeremiah's indictment along with the words of Isaiah and Jesus? *"Also on your skirts is found the lifeblood of the innocent poor"* (Jer 2:34)?

68. Collins and Lappé, "Still Hungry," 30.
69. Food First, "Guatemala," 2; citing aWorld Bank report.
70. Ibid., 1.

It is important to keep in mind the exploitative profits of U.S.-based companies and multinational corporations, along with the desperate poverty that these profits helped create, when we consider the revolutionary movements that the United States opposed under the banner of anti-Communism. Victor Halle of the University of Peace in Costa Rica stresses that these movements were rooted in events *before the existence of the Soviet Union*. Consider the case of El Salvador. "The key period was the leadership of Rafael Zaldivar (president 1876–85) who enforced radical changes in land tenure which had the effect of *expropriating the lands of indigenous communities and peasants and transferring them to the new coffee planters*."[71] The changes brought El Salvador into the world economy but on terms highly unfavorable to the peasantry. Authoritarian rule developed as a means of economic control, and by 1932 the poverty was so severe that a peasant revolt erupted. It had the support of the Communist Party, but the main impetus was the deep dissatisfaction of the peasantry, which was composed largely of indigenous people. The government response was a massacre of perhaps as many as thirty thousand Salvadorans.[72] As the slaughter took place, two United States destroyers and a cruiser stood by to make sure the uprising did not succeed![73]

A half century later, the situation in El Salvador remained largely unchanged, as government-backed death squads roamed the country and murdered anyone they suspected of working for economic reform. Among the victims were four American churchwomen—three nuns and a layperson. The Carter administration, despite its stated commitment to human rights, continued to support that government even after Oscar Romero, a Salvadoran Roman Catholic archbishop, wrote President Carter and asked for an end to military aid. Soon afterward, the archbishop was assassinated while giving communion; and, although there was considerable evidence that a right-wing leader named Roberto D'Aubuisson had ordered the killing, the U.S. assistant secretary of state declared his innocence. When President Reagan took office, he increased the aid radically. By this time, Congress had become concerned about the murders and made disbursements contingent upon certification that the human rights situation was improving. Reagan quickly provided such certification, although many critics thought this absurd; and three days later "soldiers stormed the homes of poor people in San Salvador, dragged out twenty people, and killed them." In 1983, Congress tried to renew the requirement for certification, but

---

71. Halle, "El Salvador's Long Walk," 1; italics added.
72. Ibid.
73. Zinn, *History*, 577.

the president vetoed the bill.[74] The slaughter thus continued, and in 1989 government soldiers murdered four Jesuit priests who had worked for the rights of the poor, along with their housekeeper and her daughter.[75]

The Regan administration, moreover, seemed willing not only to overlook serious human rights violations among U.S. allies but to circumvent the laws of Congress. Shortly before Regan took office, a popular movement in Nicaragua, known as the Sandinistas, deposed the Somoza government, a corrupt dynasty "long supported by the United States."[76] The movement was composed of "Marxists, left-wing priests, and assorted nationalists." Upon taking office, Reagan authorized the CIA to organize a counterrevolutionary force, which came to be known as the "contras," to overthrow the Sandinista government. The "contras" had little support among the Nicaraguan people, and many of its leaders came from the upper echelons "of the hated National Guard under Somoza." Based in Honduras, "they moved across the border, raiding farms and villages, killing men, women and children, committing atrocities."[77] Support for the contras was weak in the United States, and Congress eventually passed a law prohibiting direct or indirect support for them. The Reagan administration, however, used surreptitious means to secure such support, partly by making use of third parties such as Saudi Arabia, Guatemala, and Israel. And in 1986 the story broke "that weapons had been sold by the United States to Iran (supposedly an enemy), that in return Iran had promised to release hostages being held by extremist Moslems in Lebanon, and that profits from the sale were being given to the contras to buy arms."[78] Despite administration denials, subsequent revelations proved the claims true, although it remained unclear for a long time just how much the president and vice president knew about incident. In 2011, however, Georgetown University's National Security Archives disclosed documents obtained under the Freedom of Information Act proving that Reagan had in fact been briefed ahead of time about each of the arms sales and that Vice President George H. W. Bush's knowledge was roughly the same.[79]

In a testimony before the World Court, a former colonel associated with the contras described their use of torture, robbery, rape, and murder. He stated, moreover, that CIA advisers had considered such tactics

---

74. Ibid., 577–78.
75. Center for Justice and Accountability, "Jesuits Massacre."
76. Zinn, *History*, 572.
77. Ibid., 573.
78. Ibid.
79. National Security Archives, "Iran Contra at 25."

necessary in counterrevolutionary warfare.[80] Nor is such a charge to be doubted. Among the numerous "dirty little secrets" in our history that have been disclosed partly through the Freedom of Information Act are two manuals on counterintelligence interrogation, composed in the 1960s and 1980s by the CIA.[81] Among the abusive tactics recommended are practices that "for long periods of time have been decried or banned by the United States"—for example, "starvation, keeping inmates in small, windowless cells with unchanging artificial light and forcing inmates to sit or stand in uncomfortable positions . . . for long periods of time." The absence of more physical forms of abuse is apparently due to the fact that CIA experiments in the 1950s found that psychological methods were actually more effective than the infliction of physical pain.[82] More recently, however, U.S. officials were for a time willing to sanction an interrogation technique that is very physical indeed—waterboarding. It has been justified as necessary to combat an enemy that is replacing Communism in the eyes of those who pander to our fears and insist that the only answer to violence is violence in return. What concerns me as much as the torture itself is the broader policy that has not only led this country to the use of such an inhumane tactic but has led to a state of "perpetual war." Before I pursue that theme, however, I must first take account of the standard way of documenting a "Communist threat" in Latin America.

## THE SCARE TACTIC SUPREME: CASTRO, CUBA, AND THE "COMMUNIST THREAT"

"Why the 'bloodbath'?" That was the essence of a test question I had to answer in an undergraduate sociology course titled Social Control. The reference was to the execution of hundreds of persons associated with the dictatorship of Fulgencio Batista in Cuba by the revolutionary government established in the wake of the revolution led by Fidel Castro in 1959. One of my early impressions of that government was thus quite negative. And, indeed, the new government, as it evolved over the next few years, was by no means an example of the democratic socialism I discussed in chapter 8. Despite the romanticizing of Castro and especially his comrade-in-arms Che Guevera by some on the Left, more thoughtful progressives have decried Castro's human rights abuses, censorship of the media, and curtailment of the rights of labor unions. Nor is there any doubt that Castro eventually

---

80. Zinn, *History,* 573.
81. National Security Archives, "Prisoner Abuse."
82. Clark, "Is There a Torture Manual?"

sided squarely with the Soviet Union in the Cold War. Not surprisingly, then, "Communist Cuba" provided a convenient example that U.S. government officials could use to justify suppression of other revolutions in Latin America. "We can't afford another Cuba" became the cover for supporting dictatorships that murdered peasants, priests, and nuns—that robbed the common people of their land and fed the coffers of the rich.

This use of Cuba as a scare tactic was effective, but it was also hypocritical. The United States, unclear about Castro's intentions and increasingly uncomfortable with the repressive Batista regime, initially welcomed the change. However, the U.S. had backed the notorious Batista government for years, until shortly before the revolution. On the economic front, moreover, "American companies controlled 80 to 100 percent of Cuba's utilities, mines, cattle ranches, and oil refineries, 40 percent of the sugar industry, and 50 percent of the public railways."[83] In other words, the same pattern of domination and exploitation described above prevailed in Cuba as well. And another of my early impressions of the revolutionary government was very positive. Castro had, after all, overthrown a brutal regime; and he was taking steps to alleviate the crushing poverty in the country. It was not immediately clear that he would ultimately join the Soviet camp; I well remember how he was hailed by huge crowds when he came to the United States and spoke at the United Nations. His initial government included a wide range of political perspectives, and early on he sought aid from the International Monetary Fund to help jump-start a new economy. The U.S.-dominated Fund refused to make the loans, however, "because Cuba would not accept its 'stabilization' conditions, which seemed to undermine the revolutionary program that had begun."[84] That program involved major attempts to improve education and housing as well as the distribution of land, confiscated from U.S. companies, to peasants. It was thus clearly socialist in nature, but at this point Cuba was still trying to maintain neutrality with respect to the U.S.-Soviet divide. When Castro concluded a trade agreement with the Soviet Union, however, U.S. oil companies in Cuba refused to refine Soviet crude oil. Castro retaliated by seizing the companies, the U.S. replied by reducing its purchase of Cuban sugar, and the Soviet Union immediately took up the slack.

The path to alienation was thus set, and President Eisenhower authorized the CIA to back Cuban exiles in an attempt to overthrow Castro. Carried out under President John F. Kennedy in 1961, the Bay of Pigs invasion, a clear violation of a prior treaty, was a colossal failure. And it was

---

83. Zinn, *History*, 431.
84. Ibid.

only after this blatant attempt to depose the Cuban government that Cuba struck a deal with Soviet First Secretary Khrushchev to place Soviet missiles on Cuban soil. The Cuban missile crisis was thus a problem largely of our government's own making. And so also was the threat—to the extent that it actually existed at all—that Soviet-style Communism would, under Cuba's influence, spread throughout Latin America.

## AND NOW, PERPETUAL WAR? AN IMPRESSIONISTIC ACCOUNT

The memories remain vivid:

- the phone call ("turn on the TV") and the scene that appeared on the screen—an airplane crashing into the World Trade Center;
- the disclosures, one by one, revealing the nature and scope of the attack;
- the student I could see and hear outside my office window—"they don't know where my father is";
- my colleague and friend, a Senagalese Muslim, his face distorted in agony, devastated that the deed was carried out in the name of his religion and fearful of the repercussions against his people;
- both pundits and people I knew predicting that things will never be the same;
- the memorial service on campus for alumni who died; the solemn faces of the students;
- story after story—some of terrible loss, others of astonishing heroism, all filled with human pathos;
- and the thread that ran through it all—the sense that our space, our place in the world, had been violated in a way that we had never before experienced.

We know it now simply as 9/11. It has changed things, of course—the way we travel, the degree of government surveillance we experience, but most of all *attitudes*: fear of "the other" brings violence against innocents; anger feeds Zealous Nationalism; and lust for retaliation trumps reason. I agonize as my country invades Afghanistan: it seems in many ways justified (the harboring of terrorists who attacked us), but what blowback, what long-range consequences, will it bring? I feel no ambiguity on the next move. Iraq? Really? A despotic regime, like many others, some of whom my country counts as friends. But the justification hangs on claims without merit. There is no credible link to 9/11; evidence of "weapons of mass destruction" is based on suspect intelligence eventually proven false; Saddam Hussein's atrocities against the Kurds occurred earlier, when he was something of an ally of my country. And, once again, what will the blowback be? President George W. Bush had promised to abandon nation building, but now my country has taken on two wars, each with just such a task involved.

The wars rage on, the second taking precedence over the first, and in neither case does a stable government emerge. The attacks on 9/11 had brought a sympathetic response from nations around the world, a lessening of that "anti-American" mood so many Americans found puzzling. But now the sympathy evaporates as our leaders seem to know no path to peace other than through war. And the president defines the mission of our troops as a war on terror in a way that some analysts term "perpetual war." Does he not know that even if in extreme circumstances violence may sometimes be necessary, it should always be the last resort and always accompanied by redoubled efforts to make peace? Or that genuine peacemaking involves examining our own motives, our own possible contributions to the situation that has led to violence?

A new president, Barack Obama, takes office, promising to end the wars. There are hopeful signs. He travels to several countries the Middle East in an effort to mend fences and restore good relations, admitting that the U.S. has made mistakes in the past. In another context, he admits that the war on terror "went off course."[85] He also begins withdrawing troops, as promised. But the wars continue, and the use of drones, which kill innocents along with combatants, increases, although new guidelines for their use are designed to limit civilian casualties. Critics on the Right deride him for "apologizing."[86] Those on the Left criticize him for continuing the wars. He disavows "perpetual war."[87] But then, the inevitable blowback from the intervention in Iraq: a new enemy, ISIS, appears in the U.S.-created power vacuum,[88] opposing the U.S.-instated government that has excluded Sunni Muslims. It is dangerous, more brutal and fanatical than al-Qaeda. The president vows to combat the threat, gathering a coalition and predicting an extended conflict. Where should persons of biblical faith stand now? It seems unthinkable to allow the violent creation of a new fanatically belligerent state. But where will the violence end? Andrew Bacevich of Columbia

85. Gardner and Roach, "Top 10 Apologies."
86. Ibid.
87. Editorial Board of the *New York Times*, "End of Perpetual War."
88. Marans, "What the Iraq War."

University makes the essential point. Although hoping for a victory over the fanatical group, he draws this grim conclusion: "No matter how long it lasts, America's war for the Greater Middle East will end in failure."[89] This is not because he believes the United States is weak but because he knows the region well enough to realize that no matter how much force the U.S. and its allies apply, they cannot beat the fanatical perversions of Islam into submission any more than either France or the United States could beat the Vietminh or Vietcong into submission. And this observation is rooted in a principle that applies far beyond the particular circumstance of the Middle East: violence begets violence.

## IDENTITY REVISITED: THE FUNDAMENTAL CHOICE

The choice seems clear: either continue on the path to perpetual war or re-think some basic principles of our foreign policy. But what might a new policy look like? President Obama took a preliminary step in admitting mistakes; but a fundamentally new policy would require acknowledgement of the specific nature of those mistakes, not by the United States alone but of the Western world—mistakes reaching back as far as the Crusades but continuing into very recent history:

- the Europeans' arrogant restructuring of the Middle East following World War I, as they carved up the remains of the Ottoman Empire;

- U.S. support for the corrupt regime of Mohammed Reza Shah Pahlevi in Iran as well as for a coup that deposed a democratically elected prime minister in order to bring back foreign oil companies after a period of nationalization;

- the invasion of Iraq ("one of the most colossal blunders of recent history," according to an Algerian diplomat and U.N. peace negotiator);[90] the subsequent dismantling of Iraq's Sunni army, which left an enormous force of disaffected people with clear incentives for joining a fight against the U.S.-instituted Shiite government that excluded their group from power;

- the largely uncritical support and enormous military aid the U.S. has given Israel in its disputes with the Palestinians, even in the face of the

---

89. Bacevich, "Even If We Defeat."

90. Lakdar Brahimi, former Algerian diplomat and UN peace negotiator, quoted in Crossette, "When Will American Foreign Policymakers."

continuing occupation of Palestinian territory, the endless expansion of settlements in that territory, and the wildly disproportionate use of force in the conflicts that have erupted.

The final point is difficult for me to report, given the role of Israel as a homeland for Jews following the Holocaust as well as the shameful history of Christian anti-Judaism. So I discuss the issue with Marc Ellis, a Jewish theologian and peace activist. "But you *must* speak," he says, arguing passionately that Israel's treatment of Palestinians is hurting Jews and Judaism deeply. In his writings,[91] he considers the question of Jewish identity in our time, a question parallel to that which our country faces; and he answers it in a way that is difficult for some of his people to hear.

But how will we, as Americans, answer our question? How will we define ourselves in the years to come? Will we insist on preserving a role as sole superpower in an attempt to remake the world in our own image, dominating world economics and politics, toppling governments at will and suppressing uprisings of the oppressed masses because they may not adhere to the ideologies we deem proper? Or can we find a way to engage the world by accepting our place as one nation among others? This will not be easy. It will mean an ongoing "peace offensive" with regard to the Middle East, even as we struggle to deal with terrorist violence, whether inspired by foreign groups such as ISIS or by homegrown forms of fanaticism. And it will mean finding a way to put an end to such violence without giving in to the politics of fear that would have us forfeit our most sacred principles. But the Middle East is not the only area in which U.S. policies need to change. My hope is that we can learn to be strong advocates of democracy throughout the world without insisting that the prevailing economic system is the only worthy partner of democracy; without trying to dictate other nations' paths to freedom, prosperity, and justice; and without constantly resorting to military action.

The choice we face in terms of our national identity is similar to that faced by persons of biblical faith. We have already seen that there are strains of biblical thought that sanction violence against those who do not share that faith, but also that the more central and pervasive motif is God's desire for peace and justice in the world. And that motif is complemented by strains that prohibit violence, suggesting that retaliation, even against injustice, has a tendency to increase unjust violence rather to reduce it. Which strains we choose will determine not only our national identity but our destiny. Every empire that has ever existed has been exploitative in nature and possessed by the illusion that it could last forever. If we continue along the path to

---

91. See, e.g., Ellis, *Toward a Jewish Theology*.

perpetual war—the path of empire, domination, and exploitation—we will surely lose both our power and our national soul. For that way, I am firmly convinced, stands in marked opposition to the commonwealth of God— that is, to the vision of a world marked by peace, justice, and a respect for the integrity of creation. I believe, however, that we can find another way; and I earnestly pray that we will. For this is the country that I claim as my own, the country that I love.

# 16

# Justice Untempered, Justice Denied
## Courtroom, Prison, Death Row

### WHAT "EVERYONE KNOWS," AND WHY IT ISN'T TRUE

IT WAS CHALLENGING, BUT highly rewarding—my brief experience teaching a college course at a maximum-security state prison in Massachusetts. I wanted to make the course part of my regular teaching load, but the entire program was discontinued after my first semester. Neither the college nor the prison was responsible for that decision, however. The United States Congress, under the influence of Senator Jesse Helms, Republican of North Carolina, cancelled the Pell Grants that had funded such ventures. This astonishingly shortsighted move was an ominous sign of the times, one component in a wave of "get tough on crime" measures that have had disastrous consequences. The widespread support for these measures is based largely upon serious misconceptions fostered by politicians, political pundits, and mean-spirited talk-show hosts. These misconceptions are appealing in their simplicity and reliance upon what seems like common sense and "what everyone knows" about our judicial system. "Everyone knows," for example, that the serious crime problem in the United States is largely the result of lenient sentences by liberal judges and the "coddling" of criminals in the prisons. What "everyone knows," however, is often quite false; and that is particularly so with regard to our courtrooms and prisons.

Consider the perception that lenient sentencing in the courts has allowed thousands of criminals back on the streets. Criminologist-sociologist Elliott Currie gives a vivid example of how politicians have manipulated figures to create this false impression. In 1993, Senator Phil Gramm, a Democrat-turned-Republican from Texas, referred to a study by Texas A&M professor Morgan Reynolds regarding the estimated time to be spent in prison for various offenses. The results were startling: murder—1.8 years, rape—60 days, robbery—23 days, car theft—1.5 days! Currie observes, however, that "anyone who has ever followed a serious criminal trial, or knows anyone who was actually sentenced to prison, knows that there is something very wrong indeed with these figures."[1] In actuality, as statistics from the Bureau of Justice clearly show, the numbers Reynolds gave were outrageously misleading. The expected penalty for murder, for example, was actually around ten years; and this included the lesser offense of non-negligent manslaughter. For rape, the estimate was over seven years, and for robbery more than four.[2] Reynolds's figures were not simply made up, but they might as well have been; for they have little to do with the issue of light or heavy sentencing. Here is the "trick," as Currie aptly describes it: "Reynolds's figure of 23 days for robbery is derived by dividing the average time served by the robbers who are arrested and convicted *by the total number of robberies committed, whether anyone is ever caught or not, much less convicted.*" Thus, Currie concludes, "it is pure sleight of hand to argue, as Gramm and others do, that weak sentencing practices account for the numbers, or that we treat the robbers we catch with shocking leniency."[3] According to data from the International Center for Prison Studies in Oxford, England, in the United States prison sentences are now much harsher than in those countries to which we are usually compared. In addition, in the United States nonviolent crimes are much more likely to result in imprisonment. In fact, among advanced countries, we are distinctive in imprisoning people for such minor offenses as passing bad checks.[4]

What we really need is more emphasis on crime prevention. Sadly, however, the "get tough on crime" campaign has resulted in the decimation of social programs to alleviate the poverty that remains one of the major factors in the generation of crime. And although the initial push for this

1. Currie, *Crime and Punishment,* 43–44; quotation from 44.
2. Ibid., 45.
3. Ibid., 47; italics original.
4. Liptak, "U.S. Prison Population."

approach came mostly from Republicans, Michelle Alexander lays much of the blame for the cuts in social programs at the feet of Democratic president Bill Clinton. The so-called welfare-reform bill, on which he and Congress cooperated, "imposed a five-year lifetime limit on welfare assistance, as well as a permanent, lifetime ban on eligibility for welfare and food stamps for anyone convicted of a felony drug offense—including simple possession of marijuana."[5] As we saw in chapter 5, the United States has in recent decades pursued a policy of mass incarceration; and the connection between this policy and the reduction of aid for the poor is indisputable. "Funding that had once been used for public housing was being reallocated to prison construction. During Clinton's tenure, Washington slashed funding for public housing by $17 billion (a reduction of 61 percent) and boosted corrections by $19 billion (an increase of 171 percent)."[6]

The outrageous rate of incarceration in this country, moreover, is itself a refutation of the charge of leniency. Some analysts defend mass incarceration by tracing a drop in crime to the high rate of imprisonment. Both Currie and Alexander acknowledge that this policy has resulted in some reduction in crime. Estimates on the actual amount of reduction vary widely, however, and there are indications that we have reached a "tipping point," beyond which the benefits drop radically.[7] In any case, the larger question is whether a different approach would actually have better effects; and the answer seems clear that it would. Currie is adamant on the point:

> If the question is whether marginal increases in incarceration of repeat nonviolent offenders "work" better than investment in high-quality prevention programs for at-risk adolescents, it is increasingly clear that the answer is "no." And if the question is whether an overall national strategy of sinking more and more resources into the prisons while slighting other crucial public investments can effectively protect us from violent crime, then history would seem to offer a particularly compelling negative.[8]

Alexander supports contentions such as this by contrasting the negative fallout of mass incarceration with the positive results of specific preventive programs. On the one hand, she cites scholars who argue that imprisonment "now creates far more crime than it prevents, by ripping apart social networks, destroying families, and creating a permanent class of unemployables." On the other, she points to "the success of pilot programs like

5. Alexander, *New Jim Crow*, 57.
6. Ibid.
7. Ibid., 236.
8. Currie, *Crime and Punishment*, 55.

Operation Ceasefire and Oakland's Lifeline program—which reach out to gang members and offer them jobs and opportunities rather than prison time if they cease their criminal activities."[9] As far back as 1979, moreover, a sociologist who had once concluded that efforts at rehabilitation do not affect recidivism conducted a study that forced him to reverse his position radically, concluding that the effect is in fact appreciable.[10]

The forces supporting mass incarceration are powerful enough, however, to drown out calls for a reversal of current policy. The "get tough" approach has produced a massive new industry that some have called the "prison-industrial complex." Construction of new prisons has ballooned, and states have even resorted to the use of private, *for-profit* prisons, effectively making prisoners into commodities. As Alexander observes, prisons are now "big business and have become deeply entrenched in America's economic and political system. Rich and powerful people, including former vice president Dick Cheney, have invested millions in private prisons."[11] Lest anyone doubt that the profit motive is consciously at work in the increases in prison capacity, moreover, she quotes this stunning statement in the 2005 report of the Corrections Corporation of America: *"The demand for our facilities and services could be adversely affected by the relaxation of enforcement efforts, leniency in conviction and sentencing practices or through the decriminalization of certain activities that are currently proscribed by our laws."*[12] It would be difficult to imagine a cruder reflection of the idolatry of financial gain or a worse motive for deciding public policy. The enormous increase in incarceration is largely the result of the war on drugs, which not only targets black communities disproportionately, but also sweeps up an inordinate number of persons involved in minor offenses.[13] How to deal with the drug problem is a complex issue, but the determining factor should not be protection of the interests of private investors who profit from the expansion of this "market." A nation that keeps people in prison less to protect society or to rehabilitate them than to profit from their misery is a nation in deep moral crisis.

Conventional wisdom regarding the coddling of prisoners is just as false as that concerning lenient sentencing. "In practice," Currie writes, "rehabilitation was never much more than a distant vision in America's justice system . . . Even at the height of the Great Society era, the commitment

9. Alexander, *New Jim Crow*, 237.
10. Benko, "Radical Humaneness," 11.
11. Alexander, *New Jim Crow*, 230.
12. Ibid., 231; italics added.
13. Ibid., 66–69, 104–109, 123–26.

to rehabilitation in the prisons was shallow at best; in many states, it was virtually nonexistent."[14] The president's crime commission reported in 1967 that "the most striking fact about the correctional apparatus today is that, although the rehabilitation of criminals is presumably its major purpose, the custody of criminals is actually its major task . . . What this emphasis on custody means in practice is that the enormous potential of the correctional apparatus for making creative decisions about its treatment of convicts is largely unfulfilled."[15]

Since 1967, moreover, the situation has become much worse. As we have crammed more and more offenders into prison,

> we have simultaneously retreated from the already minimal commitment to help them reenter productive society. *Indeed, many states have moved beyond their traditional indifference to rehabilitation and now embrace what some criminologists call "penal harm"—the self-conscious use of "tough" measures to inflict pain and deprivation on inmates in the name of retribution and deterrence.* The pragmatic (if mostly rhetorical) support for rehabilitation has been pushed aside by an angry reaction to anything that might seem to "coddle" criminals. One sign of this shift is the reemergence of chain gangs, punitive and degrading inmate labor, and prison stripes. Another is the increasing criticism of job training, education, and even drug treatment in prison as frills that make life too easy for inmates. And so we continue . . . to recycle offenders from unproductive confinement to unsupportive, chaotic communities and back again, but now with a certain self-righteous satisfaction that we are doing so in the name of justice and morality.[16]

Should anyone need documentation of the punitive attitude Currie criticizes, consider this statement by Charles H. Logan, a sociologist and passionate advocate for private prisons: "Doing justice is the mission of a prison, and the single most important thing we can do to aid this is to purge them of any official responsibility for rehabilitation." The name of the prison where I taught was the Massachusetts *Correctional* Institution–Cedar Junction. Logan, however, states baldly that *"prisons should not try to be correctional institutions."*[17] It is clear that his understanding of the role of imprisonment differs radically from that of the president's 1967 crime com-

---

14. Currie, *Crime and Punishment*, 164.
15. Quoted in ibid.
16. Ibid., 165; italics added.
17. Logan, "Criminal Justice System," 30; italics added.

mission, Elliott Currie, and whoever it was who named the Massachusetts prison system. So what, then, is the mission of our prisons? Legal scholars, judges, criminologists, legislators, and others who reflect on that question obviously have a wide range of opinions. Part of my task in the next section will be to bring biblical insights to bear upon that issue.

Conventional wisdom, what "everyone knows," is difficult to refute, no matter how false it might be. This is partly because it usually confirms our prejudices and preconceptions, and partly because it releases us from the obligation of either thinking deeply or having to plow through actual evidence. And all too often, I say with great regret, conventional wisdom makes use of religion to bolster that self-righteous satisfaction that cruel and counterproductive policies are in fact both just and moral. In the present case, that satisfaction is often based upon a particular reading of the Bible. What I hope to show now is that the current policy of "getting tough on crime," although it draws upon one strain of biblical thought, runs directly counter to the most basic biblical values.

## TEXTS OF TENDERNESS, TEXTS OF TERROR: THE BIBLE ON CRIME AND PUNISHMENT, JUDGMENT AND REDEMPTION

Why do we have a criminal justice system? Why do we apprehend suspected offenders, try them in court, and sentence those found guilty? Why do we require them to spend time in prison or on probation or to pay fines or render community service? And why do we condemn some to death? One answer to these questions, which is endorsed by many persons of biblical faith, is supplied by the retribution theory. It is based upon the concept of moral law, a particular understanding of the meaning of justice, and a strong doctrine of human free will and responsibility. Grounded in the law of nature, Scripture, or both, the retribution theory is concisely expressed in the concept of *lex talionis*, a Latin phrase meaning "law of retaliation." Behind it lies the notion that the law of nature or law of God demands that wrongs committed by an offender be punished in a way commensurate with the offense. It was at work in the ancient Babylonian Code of Hammurabi and the Bible, both of which explicitly endorsed the principle of "an eye for an eye." It also became a fundamental principle of Roman law and eventually of Western law in general.

Charles Logan's rejection of rehabilitation as a purpose of incarceration rests upon the notion of retribution, as does C. S. Lewis's criticism of what he calls the humanitarian theory of punishment. Lewis, an English lay theologian, argues that the humanitarian approach, with its emphasis upon rehabilitation and deterrence to the exclusion of retribution, ignores the fundamental issue of justice. Charging that this approach replaces the concept of guilt with that of disease, he claims that it demeans human beings by denying their responsibility for their actions. He also charges that to use prison as therapy is to violate prisoners' basic human rights. He thus advocates a return to the theory of retribution, claiming that it upholds the fundamental dignity of the human person by acknowledging personal responsibility.[18] Drawing partly upon Lewis's arguments, Charles W. Colson also invokes the retributive theory in his defense of the death penalty. Noting that it was only after his conversion to Christianity that he came to embrace this view, he cites specific biblical passages to make his point. Colson, a member of President Nixon's administration who served time for obstruction of justice in relation to the Watergate affair, became a strong advocate of prison reform and founded organizations that minister to incarcerated persons and their families. I therefore cannot imagine him endorsing the practice of "penal harm." He is, however, adamant in his support of retributive justice. He contends, for example, that "mercy extended to offenders whose guilt is certain but simply ignored creates a moral travesty which, over time, helps pave the way for the collapse of the entire social order."[19]

It is beyond dispute that retributive justice plays a major role in biblical thought. It is explicit in Lev 25:19-20: "Anyone who maims another *shall suffer the same injury in return*: fracture for fracture, eye for eye, tooth for tooth; the injury inflicted is to be the injury suffered." Deut 19:21, moreover, explicitly prohibits leniency: "*Show no pity*; life for life, eye for eye, tooth for tooth, hand for hand, foot for foot." The point is clearly that the punishment must be proportional to the crime. On the one hand, this means that it must be severe enough to express the degree of loss suffered. However, against the background of the ancient world in which a person might avenge the loss of an eye by killing the offender, or a murder by destroying an entire family, this had a limiting function: the punishment *must not be greater than* the crime.

In any case, retribution is by no means the only form of justice that the Bible endorses. When we turn from bodily injury to other crimes of one person against another the principle at work is better described as *restorative*, rather than *retributive*, justice. We thus find in Exod 21:33-34: "If someone leaves a pit open, or digs a pit and does not cover it, and an ox or a donkey falls into it, the owner of the pit shall make restitution, giving money

18. Lewis, "Humanitarian Theory."
19. Colson, "Death Penalty Is Morally Just," 62.

to its owner, but keeping the dead animal" (Exod 21:33–34). Likewise in Exod 22:5, "When someone causes a field or vineyard to be grazed over, or lets livestock loose to graze in someone else's field, restitution shall be made from the best in the owner's field or vineyard." There is a sense of proportionality in these cases, but the purpose of the penalties is less punishment than compensation for loss. And although there is a punitive element in cases such as Exod 22:1, where a thief must give four sheep for one stolen, we can understand the discrepancy as easily in terms of deterrence as in terms of retribution.

The emphasis on retribution on the human level is grounded partly in biblical views regarding the character of God as one who rewards good and punishes evil. This is particularly clear in the writings of the prophets. When Amos foresees the destruction of the Northern Kingdom of Israel, he interprets it as God's judgment against the rich and powerful who oppress the poor (Amos 5:10–13); and when Jeremiah holds out the possibility of Judah's security in the land he makes it contingent upon a rejection of idolatry as well as of oppression of the poor and the alien (Jer 7:5–8). Similarly, in the long historical account that runs from Deuteronomy through 2 Kings, the same principle is at work. It is stated explicitly in Deut 30:15–20: if the people are faithful to God, the nation will prosper; if they are not, God will bring disaster upon them.

As Bruce Birch comments, however, retribution is also "tempered by the activity of God in relation to Israel and the nations. *That activity can take the form of grace, mercy, and forgiveness . . . and thus, retributive consequences are never inevitable.*"[20] The prophets frequently foresee a restoration of the nation beyond the punishment that God brings, and Jeremiah envisions a new covenant between God and the people to be established after the devastation and exile. He can attribute to God these words of grace: "I will forgive their iniquity, and remember their sin no more" (Jer 31:34). Nor are grace and forgiveness necessarily delayed until after punishment. In Hos 11:8–9 we find God in an internal struggle, ultimately *choosing not to bring the judgment the people deserve*: "How can I give you up, Ephraim? How can I hand you over, O Israel? . . . *I will not execute my fierce anger . . . for I am God and no mortal.*" Interestingly, in Exod 34:6–7, we find retribution and forgiveness intertwined in this self-description of God as "slow to anger and abounding in steadfast love and faithfulness . . . forgiving iniquity and transgression and sin, yet by no means clearing the guilty, but visiting the iniquity of the parents upon their children and the children, to the third and fourth generations." In Rom 3:21–26, moreover, we read that God "passed

---

20. Birch, *Let Justice*, 338; italics added.

over sins previously committed" but honors the demand for justice by pronouncing righteous those who have faith in Jesus.

The retribution texts, which are often terrifying in their brutality, clearly signify a moral order that must not be violated. Restoration texts also imply a moral order but seek justice less through punishment than through compensation of those who have suffered loss. Mercy texts, on the other hand, recognize a moral order but temper God's enforcement of justice with compassion for the sinner and signify God's ultimate desire for human *redemption*. They deal with the divine-human relationship rather than with laws governing human relations, but the two realms are intertwined. From the biblical perspective, an offense against any member of the community is a violation of God's covenant with the people and hence an offense against God also. Conversely, a sin against God is a disruption of human community, a tearing of the fabric of society. God's way of dealing with human sin, moreover, serves as an example for humans to follow in their own relationships. A number of passages speak explicitly of the imitation of God. The Hebrew Bible commands the people to rest on the Sabbath because God did so (Exod 20:10-11), to love the stranger as God does (Deut 10:18-19), and to be holy as God is holy (Lev 19:2). In the Talmud, moreover, there is an explicit command to imitate God's mercy: "Just as [God] is called 'merciful,' so should you be merciful."[21]

Turning to the New Testament, Eph 5:1 commands believers to "be imitators of God." In Matt 5:48, moreover, Jesus counsels his followers to "be perfect . . . as your heavenly father is perfect," which in context means to love one's enemies because God causes the sun to "rise on the evil and the good." That is to say, God treats all persons alike, both the righteous and the unrighteous—a declaration that constitutes a blatant refutation of the notion of strict retribution on God's part!

Colson makes a partly valid point when he contrasts private relations to civil law, but when he uses this distinction to criticize the exercise of mercy in the latter realm, he undermines a major function of the biblical portrayal of the character of God.[22] If God's way of relating to the world is in fact to serve as a model for human beings, then it makes no sense to mark off the legal system as somehow exempt from the basic values that are supposed to govern interpersonal relationships. Justice and mercy should pertain in both cases. The crucial question for the legal system, though, is how to negotiate between the strict demand for retribution on the one hand and

---

21. Sifri, Devarim; also Shabbat 133b; cited in Ziegler, "Philosophy of Rav Soloveitchik."
22. Colson, "Death Penalty Is Morally Just," 61.

the tempering of justice with mercy on the other. Both Colson and Lewis clearly give retribution the upper hand. I would argue, however, that mercy is both logically prior and more in keeping with the Bible's most central proclamations regarding the character of God. Why, we might begin by asking, is God interested in justice in the human realm? The answer seems indisputable: God cares for human beings. Thus, when human actions disrupt the peace, when they harm other persons and destroy community, God's retributive justice is itself an act of mercy on behalf of those harmed. But the retribution is not an end in itself; it serves the *prior* values of love and mercy. And if this ordering of priorities is extended to the legal realm, the point of sentencing in the courts should not be retribution alone or even primarily. It should rather restore to victims what they have lost, insofar as this is possible; it should be designed to deter further infractions; it should protect the community; and it should seek to rehabilitate the offenders.

Is there *any* place for retribution, then? For a long time I thought not, but I have come to think that there is, depending upon whether we can distinguish it from mere revenge. Biblical scholar Matthew Schlimm's defense of the biblical emphasis on the anger of God can help to make my point. Schlimm begins with a potent illustration. A student of his, who worked with troubled youths, was finding it impossible to communicate the love of God to one particular boy who had an extremely difficult childhood. Understandably, the youth wanted to know why a loving God would have allowed terrible things to happen to him. So eventually Schlimm's student tried a different approach. "He told the teen that God was fiercely angry with the person who harmed him." At that point, everything changed: "the boy wanted to know more. For the first time, Christianity made sense."[23] Reflecting on this incident, Schlimm continues: "The biblical God refuses to do nothing. Our God opposes all who harm other human beings or creation. Our God grows angry when children suffer, when people live in mansions while others are homeless, when corporations pollute God's beautiful world . . . There's a reason God says to Pharaoh, 'Let my people go!' instead of 'I love you.'"[24] The point is that for God simply to look the other way when injustices occur would in fact be a monumental failure to care. If God is both loving and *just*, then God must name evil as evil and must hold those who do evil accountable.

The crucial question for a criminal justice system informed by the biblical understanding of God, however, is what form accountability should take. Untempered retribution leaves no room for mercy or the consideration

---

23. Schlimm, "God's Slow Anger," 20.
24. Ibid.

of mitigating circumstances. It allows no assessment of the effects of punishment on the wider society, and it tends to obscure the hope of redemption for the offender. A biblically based system of justice, however, would include all of these. It would acknowledge human responsibility, recognize extenuating circumstances, and take account of mental illness. It would not deny free will or human responsibility, but it would acknowledge that these are qualified by circumstance. It would also make rehabilitation more central than punishment, place a strong emphasis on nonmanipulative forms of therapy, and consider the good of society as a whole. The South African Truth and Reconciliation Commission did some of this when it held those who had committed heinous racially motivated crimes accountable not by automatically condemning them to imprisonment but by allowing them the possibility of amnesty *if they named their actions as criminal by publicly confessing them*. Such an approach will not be appropriate in all circumstances, but it should serve for all nations as an example of an alternative to *untempered* retribution.

Another way to approach the issue of retribution is to ask what we mean by "moral order," the term so important to persons such as Lewis and Colson. To say that there is a moral order means that right and wrong, good and evil, are not simply matters of human preference. Injustice is *objectively* unjust, *really* wrong whatever some individual or society might think. In biblical terms, it is a sin, a violation of the laws of God. Of course, our actual laws and customs do not perfectly reflect these objective values. True right and wrong are what we *strive* to express in our legislation and cultural traditions. But to make the effort to discern true right and wrong implies that there is a moral order to which we are responsible. The deeper question, however, has to do with the nature of this order. By some accounts, the moral order is abstract, having its reality apart from the concrete relationships in the actual world. When we think of it in this way, we tend to define right and wrong in rigid ways that ignore the complexities that are always at work in real life. Take, for example, the case of Inspector Javert in Victor Hugo's magnificent novel *Les Miserables*, set in nineteenth-century France.

Fully dedicated to the law, Javert spends much of his life in pursuit of Jean Valjean, a fugitive from justice. Originally imprisoned for five years for stealing a loaf of bread to feed starving family members, Valjean serves nineteen years because of attempted escapes. Finally paroled, but destitute, rejected by society, and hardened by his long imprisonment, he steals from a bishop who has offered him kindness. When Valjean is apprehended by the police, however, the bishop pretends that the stolen items were a gift, and Valjean goes free. Although he commits a minor robbery after this and becomes a wanted man, the bishop's kindness eventually works a dramatic change in him. He assumes a new identity, builds a new life, and grows into a saintly figure, selflessly caring for others in numerous ways. At one point, he even confesses his true identity to save a man falsely thought to be him. He escapes from custody, however, and creates yet another new life for himself. Through all of this, Javert, although knowing of Valjean's now saintly character and the hardships that brought him to prison in the first place, pursues him relentlessly and eventually finds him. But finally overwhelmed by the discrepancy between true justice and the strict demands of the law, as well as the fact that Valjean passed up an opportunity to kill him, Javert allows the fugitive to escape. Then, unable to reconcile his own act of compassion with his fanatical dedication to the law, he takes his own life. Because for Javert the law represents an inflexible moral order in which mercy can appear only as a disruption, and mitigating circumstances can play no role, there is no other course.

We need not think of the moral order in Javert's terms, however. Why do we define theft, murder, rape, and assault as crimes? We do so because we first value persons and, doing so, ascribe rights to those persons; and actions such as these harm persons and violate their rights. From these concrete valuations we project a system of values about right and wrong, justice and injustice, and hope that it can approximate a moral order instituted by God or inherent in nature. However, whether we think in terms of the laws or nature of the laws of God, we must remember that *the values affirmed in this order should always refer back to the actual world in which we live*, a world in which there are always ambiguities and mitigating circumstances. When we ignore those complexities in the name of an abstract and unbending moral order unrelated to the actual world, we subvert the very reason to speak of right and wrong or to have a system of justice in the first place. Our merciless enforcement of justice becomes injustice, and our attempts to enforce what is right becomes cruel and inhumane.

When we do this, moreover, we find ourselves bowing down before yet another object of idolatry—either the *humanly constructed* law itself or the *humanly defined* moral order in which we believe it to be grounded. We can find biblical support in those texts that promote retributive justice, but if we recognize the mercy texts as primary, we will view the matter differently. And there are mercy texts far more powerful than those already mentioned. They not only stand in tension with the retribution texts but also subvert the very notion of God as heavenly accountant keeping track of good and evil deeds in mechanical fashion. I think particularly of Jesus's parable of the Prodigal Son in Luke 15:11–32. In this story, a man's younger son demands his inheritance while the father still lives, in effect showing that he wishes his father were dead. But after leaving home and wasting the money in profligate living and violating numerous aspects of biblical law, he decides to come home and ask his father to take him in as a servant. When the father sees him approaching, he runs out to meet him, violating conventional standards of dignity. And rather than requiring any kind of trial period or work to demonstrate the authenticity of the son's repentance, he showers him with kindness. Telling the servants to clothe him in the best robe in the household and give him a ring and sandals, the father then orders them to kill the fatted calf and prepare a great feast in celebration of the son's return. Understandably, the older son, who has served his father faithfully all these years, objects, contrasting his brother's outrageous behavior with his own. The father answers, however: "Son, you are always with me, and all that is mine is yours. But we had to celebrate because this brother of yours was dead and has come to life; he was lost and has been found."

It would be hard to imagine a clearer subversion of a strict system of retributive justice. The son, although repentant, had done nothing to validate his remorse; and his offenses to the father were in fact outrageous. The father's *instantaneous and unconditional forgiveness* was thus itself outrageous by conventional standards. And although the story operates on the level of interpersonal relationships rather than civil law, its challenge to the value system at work in untempered retributive justice surely has implications for the legal sphere. The father could have required the son to prove himself by working as a servant for a period, but to what end? To satisfy an abstract moral order? Instead, the father chose mercy out of love for the son and a desire to restore the family, as we see in his reminder to the older son that the younger *was his brother*. We need not take this story as a literal prescription for dealing with either family or judicial issues in order to appreciate its relevance. There is a place for "tough love" in both spheres. What matters is the guiding principle that informs our decisions in either the interpersonal or the legal sphere. What do we want to accomplish when we deal with violations of relationships or the law? Is our goal to satisfy a "ledger" of offenses and punishments or, *once having held the offenders accountable*, to restore relationships and create an environment in which human life can flourish? If the latter, then our justice system, like our relationships, must operate with something other than mere retribution in mind. We will think less in terms of punishment than of the protection of society, rehabilitation of offenders, and restorative justice for those who have suffered loss.

If we are looking for a model for a different approach to crime and punishment, we should give close attention to Norway, whose Correctional Service focuses explicitly "on rehabilitating prisoners through education, job training, and therapy" as well as reintegration into society, with a special emphasis on helping inmates find housing and work with a steady income before they are even released."²⁵ In addition, numerous efforts are made to treat the prisoners humanely, which creates a stark contrast with the "penal harm" philosophy. A system of "dynamic security," which facilitates interpersonal relationships between prisoners and staff (!) replaces traditional approaches that seek "to control prisoners with as little interaction as possible, minimizing the risk of altercation."²⁶ Astonishingly, no one has ever tried to escape from Halden, the country's showpiece maximum security prison using this approach.²⁷ And although it is difficult to compare rates of recidivism internationally, since different countries count it differently, indications are that the Norwegian rates are lower than ours.²⁸ Perhaps more importantly, there are a small number of prisons in the U.S. that take a similar approach to security, and "data from those jails over the last 40 years has shown that they have lower levels of violence among inmates and against guards and reduced recidivism." In fact, some of these institutions, when directly compared to the institutions they replaced, saw a 90 percent drop in violent incidents.²⁹

Interestingly, when questioned about the effectiveness of the humane approach, an anthropologist who participates in the training of correctional officers in Norway puts less emphasis on the effects on the prisoners than on the officers themselves, as well as on the nation as a whole. As reported by journalist Jessica Benko, he "cited a line that is usually attributed to Dostoyevsky: 'The degree of civilization in a society can be judged by entering its prisons.'" I fear, however, that if judged by such a standard, my country does not do very well. Both the prodigal's older brother and inspector Javert might give high praise to our approach to crime and punishment, but it falls far short of the highest ideals of the biblical tradition. And there is no clearer instance of a Javert-like approach to crime and punishment in our system than the issue to which I now turn.

## RETRIBUTION UNTEMPERED: THE DEATH PENALTY IN BIBLICAL PERSPECTIVE

Both Charles Colson and C. S. Lewis base their support of the death penalty on a concept of a moral order, for which they claim biblical support. Their views are consistent with those of many persons of biblical faith as well as

25. Benko, "Radical Humaneness," 3.
26. Ibid., 4–5.
27. Ibid., 1.
28. Ibid., 12–16.
29. Ibid., 11–12.

with the positions of some biblically based religious bodies through the centuries. It is not difficult to support such views by proof-texting, since the Bible explicitly commands the death penalty for numerous offenses. Many other persons of biblical faith, however, have opposed capital punishment on biblical grounds. Once again, therefore, we find that what the Bible means concretely in human affairs depends largely upon how we choose to read it. So, then, how *should* we read it, when it comes to this matter of life and death?

## The Hebrew Bible and Jewish Tradition

Perhaps the passage most frequently cited in defense of the death penalty is Gen 9:6: "Whoever sheds the blood of a human, by a human shall that person's blood be shed; for in his own image God made humankind." The passage is particularly useful in this regard because it explicitly refers to murder, which proponents of the death penalty regularly wish to name a capital offense. We must be careful, however, in defining precisely what the text authorizes. As James M. Megivern notes, what it originally sanctioned was "the tribal practice of blood-vengeance, whereby the nearest relative of the victim had the duty to avenge the slaying of his kinsman. In that sense, the verse has nothing to do with authorizing a state to kill. To be consistent, if one treats the verse as divine law, the modern application would be, not the authorization of state-regulated executions, but the legitimation of blood-feuds, whereby a victim's relatives are invited to take their revenge on the killer."[30] In addition, it is striking that this text fails to distinguish intentional killing from that which is merely accidental.[31] Were we to try to enforce it in its literal sense, we would have to execute a parent who stumbles on a stone and drops an infant to its death!

We should also be cautioned by an examination of the Bible's specific applications of the death penalty. Those who cite the Bible in defense of capital punishment focus almost entirely on the case of murder, but what about the many other cases in which it is prescribed? Should we not apply it to "stubborn and rebellious" sons (Deut 21:18–21); anyone who strikes a parent (Exod 21:15); a man who has consensual sex with a betrothed virginal woman, as well as the woman herself (Deut 22:23–24); a man caught having sex with the wife of another man, as well as the woman herself (Deut 22:22)? Why not also to anyone who profanes the Sabbath (Exod 31:14), to men (not women!) who engage in same-sex relations (Lev 18:22), and to

30. Megivern, *Death Penalty*, 16.
31. Ibid., 15.

those who "blaspheme the name of the LORD" (Lev 24:10–16) or worship other gods (Deut 17:1–20)? Above all, why not include those who speak false words of prophecy in God's name (Deut 18:20), starting with those who have erroneously proclaimed the end of the world on a specific date?

It is important also to consider the ways in which language actually functions. As Megivern comments,

> Language has many uses. Law codes are not automatically to be understood literally as simple mirrors of practice. One function of the juridical death threat was to give solemn warning, to alert all to the extreme seriousness of certain misdeeds. This pedagogical function of the law is accomplished by the texts themselves. They articulate what the society's top values are and what is beyond the range of acceptable behavior in the ideal order. If they were ever implemented literally, however, the streets of the community would run red with blood.[32]

I do not imagine that the considerations I have raised make the case against using the Bible to support capital punishment. However, I hope I have made clear that it is an absolute dead end to approach the question through simplistic proof-texting. What we need to do, rather, is to try to discern the most central values that lie at the heart of the Bible and to evaluate the various pronouncements on the issue both in the biblical texts themselves and in the later traditions based upon them.

Although there are no biblical texts that clearly controvert the provisions for the death penalty, there are numerous passages that stand in marked tension with them. Gen 9:6 is in fact a subtle example of such tension. By alluding to Gen 1:26–27, according to which human beings are created in God's image, the verse invites critical reflection. For although the verse justifies the death penalty on the basis of the sacredness of human life, one could just as logically argue against this extreme penalty on the same basis. Also, it is striking that God does not apply the principle of Gen 9:6 in dealing with Cain, who murdered his brother Abel (Gen 4:8–16). In fact, God not only declines to kill Cain, sending him away instead, but places a protective mark on him. The murderer thus remains under God's care. Although having committed the ultimate offense against a fellow human being, he is still a child of God, still bearing God's own image. Some interpreters argue that since Gen 9:6 comes after the Cain-Abel incident as a part of the covenant with Noah, it would not have applied in earlier times. This contention, however, ignores the proverbial, as opposed to judicial,

---

32. Ibid., 11–12.

character of the verse. Because it states a principle, there is no reason it should not have applied earlier.

We can thus see that enforcement of the moral order can involve mercy as well as retribution, even in the case of premeditated murder. And this reminds us again of the Bible's sense of the ultimate purpose of God's actions in the world. That purpose is *redemption*, not the separation of the good from the bad, not the enforcement of an abstract moral order, not punishment of evil *as an end in itself*. God's desire is the reconciliation of humanity to God and among all the peoples of the world, the creation of what the Bible calls *shalom*. We translate this term as "peace," but it means more than the absence of violence. It is a state of total well-being, symbolized in such passages as Isa 11:6-9, not in which all wolves and poisonous snakes have been exterminated but rather in which "the wolf shall live with the lamb . . . and the weaned child shall put its hand on the adder's den." In an indirect but powerful way the Hebrew Bible thus becomes its own critic on the issue of the death penalty by creating a provocative tension between retribution on the one hand and mercy and redemption on the other. And that tension continues in later Jewish tradition, as the Talmud records the conflicting opinions of various rabbis regarding the death penalty, with two stating boldly that "if we were in the Sanhedrin, no [person] would ever have been executed."[33] Today, moreover,

> all of the major Jewish movements in the United States either advocate for the abolition of the death penalty or have called for at least a temporary moratorium on its use. The Conservative, Reform, and Reconstructionist movements in the United States oppose the death penalty in all instances. In 2001, Orthodox Jewish leaders called for a moratorium in light of perceived problems in the nation's justice system, and urged the creation of a commission to review death penalty procedures.[34]

## The New Testament and Christian Tradition

In the New Testament, Jesus directly controverts the "measure for measure" principle in Matt 5:38-42:

> "You have heard that it was said, 'An eye for an eye, and a tooth for a tooth.' But I say to you, Do not resist an evildoer. But if

---

33. Makkot I, 10, quoted by Erez, "Thou Shalt Not Execute," 37; cited by Megivern, *Death Penalty*, 11.

34. Pew Research Center, "Religious Groups' Official Positions," 3.

anyone strikes you on the right cheek, turn the other also; and if anyone wants to sue you and take your coat, give your cloak as well; and if anyone forces you to go one mile, go also the second mile."

Some interpreters question the relevance of this passage with respect to the death penalty, since it refers to personal relationships rather than public governmental action. It is true that here Jesus *applies* the principle of nonresistance to the personal level, but the fact remains that he states this principle as a direct rejection of the "eye for an eye" ideology on which the death penalty is based. Is it wrong to argue that, by extension, it should apply to the judicial sphere as well, insofar are persons of biblical faith have a say in that sphere?

Some interpreters also claim to find explicit support for the death penalty in the New Testament, but their arguments are weak. In Rom 13:4, Paul warns his readers that the governing authority "does not bear the sword in vain." To take this as an explicit endorsement of capital punishment, however, is to miss the metaphorical function of the term "sword" here, which clearly stands for "the punitive function of the state"[35]—that is, for the state's broad right to hold persons accountable for crime rather than for the death penalty specifically. And Matt 26:52, which proclaims that those who take the sword will perish by it, is a proverb indicating the inevitable result of an action. Its reference is clearly to the endless round of retribution that results from violence, not to the state's power over life and death. Nor is it convincing to cite Matt 5:18, which states that every letter of the Jewish law remains valid; for in the verses that follow Jesus himself opposes not only the "eye for an eye" principle but also overturns a scriptural provision regarding divorce (5:31–32)! Yet another passage that some have enlisted in the capital punishment cause is Matt 15:3–4, where Jesus quotes Lev 20:9, which prescribes death for those who "speak evil" of a parent. The context of the New Testament passage, however, has nothing to do with the death penalty. It combines the Levitical quotation with the commandment to honor one's parents (Exod 20:12; Deut 5:16) in order to give emphasis to an entirely different point. Here Jesus accuses his opponents of failing to honor their parents by using "the tradition of the elders" to justify failing to meet their financial obligations to them. Language, let us remember, has many functions; and the function of the quotation is not to endorse the death penalty but to indict Jesus's opponents for failing to honor their parents. I wonder whether those who cite this passage in defense of the death penalty

---

35. Megivern, *Death Penalty*, 17.

think it sanctions this punishment for those "speaking evil" of a parent and that we should apply it to such cases today!

In postbiblical times, Christians have testified on both sides of the issue. Our sources from the earlier centuries are sparse and largely ambiguous, but we do get a glimpse of the horror with which Christians viewed executions. In the late second century, for example, Athenagoras of Athens wrote that they "cannot endure even to see a [person] put to death, though justly" and that they consider watching "a [person] put to death is much the same as killing him [or her]."[36] As Megivern comments, the passage seems "to take for granted that the death penalty could be imposed 'justly,'" but also "judges the practice totally incompatible with Christian sensibilities."[37] Around the same time, Minucius Felix wrote that "for us it is not permissible either to see or to hear of human slaughter; we have such a shrinking from human blood that at our meals we avoid the blood of animals for food."[38]

This refusal to watch, much less participate in executions, however, eventually gave way after the emperor Constantine granted Christianity a favored position in the Roman Empire and Christians began to participate more fully in Roman society. From their new position of power, Christians now began to advocate for the extermination of pagans, and near the end of the fourth century the precedent was set for the execution of fellow Christians deemed to be heretics.[39] "Ironically," Megivern writes, "the lethal combination of the Bible and Roman law provided surprisingly cruel penal codes, invariably viewed as directly willed by God. The entire repressive system of Roman Law was brought to bear actively on the project of 'Christianizing' the Empire when it was under challenge from external 'barbarian' forces."[40] In later times, we find such luminaries among Christian theologians as Thomas Aquinas, Martin Luther, and John Calvin giving strong support to the death penalty.[41] Throughout Christian history, moreover, there has been significant support for capital punishment on the official level, and the churches themselves often played the role of executioner of those deemed heretics.

There is much more to the story than this, however, as there have been important dissenters on the issue, such as the Waldensians in the twelfth century, the Anabaptists in the sixteenth century, and the various "peace

---

36. Athenagoras, "Plea," 147; quoted in Megivern, *Death Penalty*, 20.
37. Megivern, *Death Penalty*, 21.
38. Minucius Felix, *Octavius* xxx, 6; quoted in Megivern, *Death Penalty*, 21.
39. Megivern, *Death Penalty*, 30.
40. Ibid., 27.
41. Ibid., 115–16, 141, 147.

churches" (notably the Church of the Brethren, the Religious Society of Friends, and the Mennonites) that continue today.[42] And on an official level, by the mid-twentieth century the tide began to turn in their direction. The Episcopal Church, the Presbyterian Church (U.S.A.), and the United Methodist Church have officially opposed the death penalty since the 1950s.[43] The United Church of Christ has taken the same stance since 1969,[44] the American Baptist Churches in the U.S.A. since 1982,[45] the Orthodox Church in America since 1989,[46] and the Disciples of Christ since 2003.[47] The National Council of Churches, "which represents 35 mainstream Protestant and Orthodox churches, has advocated for" abolition since 1968.[48] There has also been a sea change in the Catholic Church. "Although the Catechism of the Catholic Church sanctions the use of the death penalty as a last resort, the U.S. Conference of Catholic Bishops has repeatedly called for the abolition of the death penalty in the United States in all circumstances."[49] While recognizing the state's right to execute people, the bishops argue that it should forgo this right. Pope John Paul II, moreover, called for the abolition of the practice,[50] and Pope Francis has followed suit.[51]

The trend is not overwhelming. Some Christian groups in this country continue to support the death penalty, among them the Southern Baptist Convention, the Lutheran Church–Missouri Synod, and the National Association of Evangelicals.[52] In addition, the rank-and-file members of the denominations on record in opposition to capital punishment are often at odds with the official statements. The trend is nevertheless real, both in the churches and in society at large. As for the latter, consider this comment by Sister Helen Prejean, a tireless proponent of abolition:

> As public discourse on the death penalty heats up, Gallup polls show a drop in popular support for the death penalty from 80 percent in 1994 to 65 percent in 2000. Following the events of September 11, 2001, support for the death penalty rose during

42. Ibid., 99–107, 199–207
43. Pew Research Center, "Religious Groups' Official Positions."
44. General Synod 7 of the United Church of Christ, "Resolution to Abolish."
45. Pew Research Center, "Religious Groups' Official Positions."
46. Orthodox Church in America, "Minutes," 24.
47. General Assembly of the Disciples of Christ, "Resolution."
48. Pew Research Center, "Religious Groups' Official Positions."
49. Ibid.
50. Pew Research Center, "Religious Reflections," 3–4.
51. Francis I, Pope, "Death Penalty."
52. Pew Research Center, "Religious Groups' Official Positions."

2002 and early 2003 but then slipped back to the lowest recorded level in twenty-five years—64 percent. Yet even these numbers are misleading. When citizens are asked to choose between death and life imprisonment without parole, support for death falls to 50 percent or less.[53]

Among Christian groups, the change in the Catholic Church is particularly strong. Whereas polls in 2001 registered 68 percent in favor of capital punishment, a Zogby Poll in 2005 found only 48 percent in favor! According to a 2004 Gallup poll, 71 percent of Protestants support the death penalty. However, Gallup surveys from 2001 through 2004 also showed that those who attend church most frequently are slightly less likely to support it than those who attend less frequently, with those in the weekly or nearly weekly group registering at 65 percent in support and those in the seldom or never category registering at 71 percent.[54]

## Beyond an Anachronism: The Grounds for Abolition

As Sister Prejean observes, the world in which we live is radically different from that in which the law codes of the Hebrew Bible were formulated. Prescriptions such as "an eye for an eye," she notes, "were promulgated in a seminomadic culture in which the preservation of a fragile society—without benefit of prisons and other institutions—demanded quick, effective, harsh punishment of offenders."[55] I can accept, although reluctantly, that there are circumstances in the world today in which killing is justifiable, that is, in which it represents a lesser evil. Participation in wars of defense or liberation from oppression, along with protection of the innocent seem to me to qualify in this regard. As Pope Francis points out, however, "the death penalty is applied to people whose capacity to cause harm is not current, but has already been neutralized, and who are deprived of their freedom."[56] So why, then, do we still practice it in this country? Is it to satisfy an abstract sense of moral order, such as that which motivated Inspector Javert? Or do we use the notion of "justice for the victim" as a cover for the rawer desire for simple revenge? Either way, the most fundamental and enduring aspects of the biblical witness rise up against such arguments. If God's

---

53. Prejean, *Death of Innocents*, 233–34.
54. Death Penalty Information Center, "Religion."
55. Prejean, *Dead Man Walking*, 194.
56. Francis I, Pope, "Death Penalty."

deepest desire for human beings is in fact redemption and reconciliation rather than punishment of evil for its own sake, then we simply cannot justify executing anyone whose capacity to harm has been neutralized. As Pope Francis further observes, "With the application of capital punishment, the person sentenced is denied the possibility to make amends or to repent of the harm done; the possibility of confession, with which [human beings express their] inner conversion; and of contrition, the means of repentance and atonement, in order to reach the encounter with the merciful and healing love of God."[57]

There are those who say that the interval between conviction and execution offers adequate time for a person to repent, but I find this argument quite arrogant. Who are we to set a deadline on such a matter? To deny that human beings change is a blatant denial of the biblical faith, but fundamental changes in the human heart seldom come easily or quickly. And we know of remarkable life journeys of perpetrators of the most heinous crimes imaginable, who eventually became persons with a deep concern for their fellow human beings. Colson mentions some of these, to whom he ministered on death row. Despite his "heavy heart," however, he does not allow their radical turnarounds to shake his commitment to the death penalty.[58] For my part, I find it quite bizarre that we should work hard to rehabilitate a human being and then put that person to death.

Images haunt me. Some are my mental reconstructions of brutal actions about which I have read or seen reenacted. Among them are the murders committed by Patrick Sonnier, who raped a young woman, promised to let her go if she had sex with his younger brother, and then, after the bargain was fulfilled, killed her anyway, along with her boyfriend. Other images are those captured on camera: the human corpses uncovered at Auschwitz; innocent captives kneeling as a hooded murderer stands behind them with knife sharpened for beheading; scenes from the explosions at the World Trade Center, Oklahoma City, and the Boston Marathon; pictures of small children who died in such horrific acts against humanity and of victims missing arms and legs; charred black bodies hanging from trees in my native South. I am horrified by such images, which deeply offend my sense of justice and evoke an overwhelming sympathy for the victims and their loved ones. Nor am I immune to feelings of outright hatred and a lust for revenge. Something in me wants to make the perpetrators of such atrocities experience what their victims experienced, to suffer as the families of the

---

57. Ibid.
58. Colson, "Death Penalty Is Morally Just," 64.

murdered suffer. Something in me wants not only to kill them but to do so in the most painful, drawn-out way I can think of.

That is what I feel, and I feel it partly because of a biblically based sense of justice. When I examine my feelings more closely, however, I discover that what I want most of all is for the perpetrators of these horrible crimes to understand the evil nature of what they have done, to acknowledge the injustice and inhumanity of their deeds, and to undergo a fundamental change of heart. This desire comes from my understanding of the biblical values of redemption and reconciliation, and it calls forth a different set of images. One of these is in a prison setting: family members of murder victims sitting in a circle composed of murderers. There is nothing sentimental at work here. In these encounters the victims' families are able to pour out their feelings, holding nothing back. No, there is nothing sentimental or Pollyannaish about the process, but there is something deeply moving about it. For the scene I watched in a television report ends with the victims' loved ones tearfully embracing the perpetrators; it is a dramatic example of what we mean by redemption and reconciliation.

I am not naïve about the possibilities of such turnarounds. But even if the cases in which dramatic change takes place are relatively few, if we take seriously the value of human life—all human life—then efforts toward rehabilitation are always worth our while. The ultimate question we have to ask is whether we believe that those who have committed the most heinous of crimes against humanity have in fact forfeited their status as human beings, persons of worth, children of God. Even if we believe so, it would seem to me that it is God alone who is in a position to judge which persons to place in that category. But I cannot accept that there is anything a person could ever do that would remove him or her from God's love and care, and I say this not on the basis of sentiment but on what I consider sound theological grounds. To say that creation itself is good, which is a fundamental tenet of biblical faith, is to say that that existence itself is inherently good, so that nothing in the universe could ever be utterly devoid of positive value. Saint Augustine argued along these lines centuries ago, contending that evil cannot exist on its own, but only as a privation or corruption of the good. Since the fundamental nature of all things is good, "the good which is its 'nature' cannot be destroyed without the thing itself being destroyed . . . Where there is evil, there is a corresponding diminution of the good. As long, then, as a thing is being corrupted, there is good in it of which it is being deprived."[59] The good in a brutal murderer may be extremely difficult to find, but Sister Prejean has been able to find it even in such a person as Patrick Sonnier, to

---

59. Augustine, *Enchiridion*, chapter IV, 12.

whom she ministered on death row, and whose story she tells in *Dead Man Walking*. This is not to deny the genuine evil that such people exhibit, and Sister Prejean does not do so; but it is indeed to deny that those who exhibit such evil are no longer persons of sacred worth in the eyes of God.

After many decades of considering this issue, I hold essentially the same opinion as I did in my youth. I do not judge those who think differently, and I both understand and respect their point of view, especially in the case of the families of murder victims. I do not, however, believe that the execution of a murderer actually brings the closure that many of these families seek; and I simply cannot reconcile the death penalty with my biblical faith. My primary reason, moreover, has remained the same through all these years: even the most inhumane of criminals remains a child of God, capable of redemption. There are other reasons, however. To begin with, both race and social class play disturbingly large roles in determining to whom the penalty is applied. No study has ever shown that executions actually deter violent crime, and 88 percent of criminologists believe that it does not.[60] Above all, there is the inevitability of mistakes resulting in the execution of the innocent. We have learned in recent years just how fallible the justice system is, and I have been stunned by the number of false convictions that have been uncovered. Between 1973 and 2012, 140 persons on death row were found to have been wrongly convicted and thus were released. Nor has the trend reversed. As Sister Prejean reports, "stories of exonerated death row inmates, coming from twenty-five states, continue to find their way onto the nightly news."[61] According to a federal judge in New York, moreover, "the best available evidence indicates that, on the one hand, innocent people are sentenced to death with materially greater frequency than was previously supposed and that . . . convincing proof of their innocence often does not emerge until long after their convictions."[62] The judge, Jed Rakoff, made this statement in a decision declaring the federal death penalty unconstitutional, although his decision was eventually overturned by the U.S. Supreme Court.[63]

All the reasons I have listed so far are rooted in concern for those who, whether innocent are guilty, face the possibility of execution. There is another reason, however: my perception of what capital punishment does to the society that practices it, what it does *to us as a people*. Sister Prejean recalls statements by political commentator George Will to the effect that

60. Amnesty International, "Death Penalty Facts: Death Penalty and Deterrence."
61. Prejean, *Death of Innocents*, 230.
62. Quoted in ibid., 231.
63. Ibid., 289 n. 11.

putting a person to death out of vengeance is a noble act but that showing an execution on television would have a "very bad coarsening effect" on our country. In response, she remarks, "How, I wonder, does a noble act *coarsen* society?" Then she adds that

> it's not the presence of television cameras or the composition of the crowd or even whether the crowd acts politely or not that makes the execution of a human being ugly. An execution is ugly because the premeditated killing of a human being is ugly. Torture is ugly. Gassing, hanging, shooting, electrocuting, or lethally injecting a person whose hands and feet are tied is ugly. And hiding the ugliness from view and rationalizing it numbs our mind to the horror of what we are doing. This is what truly 'coarsens' us.[64]

The death penalty, contrary to its stated purposes, anaesthetizes us to the taking of life. It makes us comfortable with killing, thus adding to rather than curtailing the cycle of violence. We go to great lengths to disguise is true nature. We dress it up in judicial garb and sanctify it with biblical prooftexts and the presence of prison chaplains; we justify it as just retribution, deterrence, or closure for the families of victims. In doing so, we as a people lie to ourselves about what we are doing—coldly, systematically, and u*nnecessarily* extinguishing a human life. And to lie to oneself is to damage one's own soul. I therefore oppose the death penalty not only because of what it does to those upon whom it is practiced, along with their families, but because of the scars it leaves upon the souls of the people of my nation.

The God of biblical tradition, as I have stressed throughout this book, has an eye toward the future, toward dismantling the oppressive structures human beings have built and leading us beyond the inhumane practices of the past. In so many ways, the United States has also looked toward the future and has been a beacon light for other nations. In other ways, however, it has remained tied to shameful practices of bygone eras. My country, sad to say, was late in abolishing slavery; and even now it has much work to do to in combatting the lingering effects of that evil institution. It is also behind other industrialized nations in solving the problem of poverty and inequality and has done very little to come to terms with climate change—all because of the inability to let go of economic theories belonging to a bygone era. On the matter of the death penalty too it remains woefully behind the times. All the countries of western of Europe and most in eastern Europe have abandoned it. It has been abolished in Canada and a number of countries in Latin America. It is illegal in the Republic of South Africa,

---

64. Prejean, *Dead Man Walking*, 215–16.

as it is in several other countries on the African continent. And the list goes on—Australia, New Zealand, Iceland, Nepal, Turkmenistan, Greece. In all, ninety-eight countries have abandoned the death penalty for all crimes, seven retain it for exceptional crimes only, and thirty-five are abolitionist in practice. Among our companions in the list of countries that retain it, moreover, are some countries we constantly criticize for their violations of human rights—China, North Korea, Iran, and Cuba.[65] We should ponder carefully Pope Francis's reminder that the death penalty "is a frequent practice to which totalitarian regimes and fanatical groups resort, for the extermination of political dissidents, minorities, and every individual labelled as 'dangerous' or who might be perceived as a threat to their power or to the attainment of their objectives."[66]

Despite a disappointing record on the issue of the death penalty in the United States, there are some hopeful signs. Eighteen states have abandoned it, and the number of yearly executions is on the wane. I believe that the nation as a whole will eventually abolish the practice. I wonder, however, how many persons will be executed in the meantime—whether guilty or innocent, whether unrepentant or repentant. I wonder also how many of those we put to death will be of extremely low mental capacity, how many will be clearly deranged but do not fit the narrow definitions of insanity we use, and how many will be persons who committed their crimes as minors but have grown old enough to "qualify" for execution. For we have in fact executed persons in each of these categories. I cannot help but wonder, also, on which side of the debates the majority of persons of biblical faith will stand as the struggle between the past and the future goes on. Will Christians, specifically, take seriously Jesus's rejection of the "measure for measure" principle when he countered the demand, "an eye for an eye," with *But I say unto you . . .*"?

---

65. Death Penalty Information Center, "Abolitionist."
66. Pope Francis I, "Death Penalty."

# Conclusion
## Putting Away the Idols

> Then God spoke all these words: I am the LORD your God . . .
> You shall have no other Gods before me."
>
> —EXODUS 20:1–2

THERE IS A COMPELLING scene in Jos 23–24 that expresses a central aspect of biblical faith. It culminates in a call to abandon idolatries and follow the God who has led the people out of bondage in Egypt. With the Israelites now in partial possession of the promised land, Joshua invites them to participate in a ceremony of covenant renewal to reaffirm their loyalty to this gracious God. He begins by reminding them that their survival in the land will depend upon their obedience to God's commands. Then he recites the history of God's mighty actions on their behalf, from the call of Abraham to leave his homeland and become the ancestor of a great nation, through the exodus under Moses and Aaron, and finally to the gift of the land that is to be their own. At the climactic moment, he puts this challenge before them: "*choose this day whom you will serve*, whether the gods your ancestors served in the region beyond the River or the gods of the Amorites in whose land you are living; but *as for me and my household, we will serve the LORD*" (Josh 24:15). Without hesitation, the people answer: "*Far be it from us that we should forsake the LORD to serve other gods*; for it is the LORD our God who brought us and our ancestors up from the land of Egypt, out of the house of slavery, and who did those great signs in our sight" (Josh 25:16–17),

False gods—idols—are seductive. They tell us what we want to hear. They make us comfortable with our prejudices, our self-deceptions, and our injustices. They are easier to follow, harder to abandon, than a God who looks into the depths of our hearts, demanding honesty, faithfulness, and courage. The paths they lay out for us are often broader, seemingly safer, but also less challenging and rewarding, than the way of the One who calls us out of our present state to higher ground, who asks us to change and grow. Sometimes they can lead to an unthinking kind of devotion that ends in fanaticism, precisely because they oversimplify complex issues and give us easy answers to difficult questions. No wonder, then, that the Bible portrays God's chosen people as continually fleeing to the false gods. No wonder, too, that so many leaders and people of our own nation today are so easily seduced by the promises our contemporary idols make. Throughout this book I have tried to show how wealth, power, privilege, race, and Zealous Nationalism have worked together to lead this nation astray, breeding injustice at home and imperialism abroad. In the final chapter we have seen how adherence to a rigidly defined moral order, often claiming biblical support, can foster gross injustice. And perhaps its most deceptive trait is that it fosters a self-righteousness that discourages the self-examination we so desperately need. It convinces us that all is well when there is in fact much in our nation that is very wrong. Or, perhaps more often and more insidiously, this self-righteousness tells us that it is precisely the attempts to do justice and exercise mercy that are our problems.

The idols lie. They tell us, specifically,

- that punishment is more important than rehabilitation and that mercy is incompatible with justice;
- that it is natural and just for one class of people to rule over others;
- that our nation is innocent of conquest and imperialism, or that a righteous nation such as ours is divinely commissioned to pursue such policies;
- that the market should be our master rather than our servant and that it can solve all problems;
- that the resources of the earth are inexhaustible, that climate change is a hoax, and that human beings have the right to do with the land whatever they wish;
- that there is no poverty in our country, that the poor have created their own lot, or that the very policies that create poverty can somehow eradicate it if we just pursue them long enough;

- that extreme inequality does not exist or is inevitable, or even that God has ordained it;
- that the race problem in our country has been solved, or that it is the oppressed rather than the oppressors who are to blame for the current unrest;
- and, above all, that we can continue with our current practices in human relations, economics, consumption, and crime and punishment without courting disaster.

When Joshua asked the Israelites to choose between false gods and the God who led them out of slavery, he identified some of the idols as those their ancestors once worshiped. What he asked of the people, however, was not a rejection of their entire heritage. He asked them, first of all, to choose between two elements in their past—on the one hand, the idolatry of those who came before the call of Abraham; on the other, worship of the God who called Abraham and who gave them a land of their own. He also asked them to choose between that God and a new set of idols, the gods of the land where they now dwelled. Our choices are similar. There are elements in our American heritage that reflect what is best in the biblical tradition, but there are also destructive elements that run counter to the highest ideals we profess. And there are even more destructive possibilities that we have not as yet pursued but are in danger of embracing. The choice we make will determine our future. It will determine whether the United States will move toward a truly just society, will descend into totalitarianism, or will simply stagnate and fall apart. It will also determine whether this nation will play a positive role as example and peacemaker in the world at large or will be a hindrance to international cooperation in the creation of a just and sustainable world economy.

We can be justly proud, as Americans, of the grand experiment that the founding of our nation was. The rejection of monarchy and the proclamation of the equality of all persons were bold and admirable steps, as was the institution of a democratically governed republic. And although the initial vision was imperfect—not *fully* democratic, marred by slavery, granting only limited rights to women, and insensitive to the rights of American Indians—we can celebrate the movements that have sought to correct these imperfections. We must acknowledge, however, how hard-fought the progress we have made has been. We must also confess the ways progress once made has begun to slip away from us, as well as the lack of significant progress in other areas. We are in need, that is to say, of repentance for a multitude of sins, especially those idolatries that I have emphasized in this book. But the good news that lies at the heart of the biblical faith is that repentance is possible and can bring about dramatic change in both individuals and nations. If we can find the courage to acknowledge our failures and glean from our national heritage what is just and life-giving and lay the idols aside, we can in fact become what we have always professed to be. We can *become* "one nation, indivisible, with liberty and justice for all." And we can *become* "a city on a hill," a beacon of justice, democracy, and hope for all the world, "a light to the nations." We cannot do this, however, unless we are willing to admit our shortcomings and also acknowledge that we will not be alone on that that hill. Other nations have positive roles to play, too, and *we have much to learn from some of them* about freedom, justice, and democracy. Nor can we fulfill our best potential unless we learn to ask, in all humility, *for the healing of our nation.*

# Epilogue
## Jazz, Gumbo, the Bible, and God

> The pure conservative is fighting against the essence of the universe . . . [T]he very essence of actual reality—that is, of the completely real—is *process*."
> —Alfred North Whitehead, 1933[1]

> [A]ll lesser organisms are parts of one inclusive organism, the universe.
> —Charles Hartshorne, 1962.[2]

> God is no longer thought of as utterly unchangeable and empty of all temporal distinctions. Rather, [God], too, is understood to be continually in the process of self-creation . . . This implies, naturally, that God is . . . a living and even growing God . . . and is related to the universe of other beings somewhat as the human self is related to its body.
> —Schubert M. Ogden, 1963[3]

---

1. Whitehead, *Adventures*, 274; italics original.
2. Hartshorne, *Logic*, 194.
3. Ogden, *Reality*, 59.

THE PULL OF THE past is enormous. By basic inclination, I am a person who resists change and is fascinated with the past. I suppose one has to have this fascination to teach biblical studies with any integrity. My interest in the past, however, came long before I chose my profession. My father's tales of growing up on sugar plantations and my mother's accounts of life as a Methodist minister's daughter in small Louisiana towns were perhaps the roots of it. I often found myself overcome with a gentle nostalgia when I pondered the inherent sadness of the passage of time. But of course my parents' childhoods had to pass so that I could have my own, as all childhoods must pass for adulthood to develop. And as I have made my journey through life, I have come more and more to understand that change, or process, is what makes life meaningful, challenging, and exciting—indeed, what makes it *real*.

## ALL THINGS IN PROCESS

### Jazz, Gumbo, the Bible, and Plato

Process is in fact at work in all aspects of life, and three of my greatest loves can serve as metaphors for this dimension of our human experience and, indeed, for an important quality of the universe itself. In Wynton Marsalis's narration of Ken Burns's magnificent documentary on jazz, he frequently compares jazz to a staple dish in his (and my) native Louisiana—gumbo. Both are composite realities, made up of various elements from various sources. And it is crucial to understand that composite realities are by nature the products of process. The ingredients come together precisely because time moves on and new circumstances bring them together. Jazz did not simply pop into being one day as the result of one individual's genius. It developed slowly, as Africans in America brought their native rhythms into play with Western instruments, drawing upon their suffering as slaves and victims of Jim Crow but also their dogged refusal to give up hope. Nor did gumbo appear out of nowhere; it is a modulation of French bouillabaisse that makes use of ingredients native to south Louisiana.

It is equally important to note that neither jazz nor gumbo has ceased to develop, and we should celebrate that fact. It would be odd indeed to honor realities born of innovation and improvisation by stopping their evolutionary processes in their tracks. I tried for many years to replicate my mother's exquisite shrimp and okra gumbo, for which she had no recipe. I think I came fairly close, but in time I gave myself permission to experiment and create my own versions. I love the traditional jazz I heard on the

New Orleans Jazz Club and later at Preservation Hall in the 1960s; indeed, it remains my favorite style. I would count it tragic, however, had not the newer styles come along and added to the pantheon of jazz luminaries. And, as Preservation Hall's Ben Jafee comments, traditional jazz itself continues to evolve. He can therefore call what they play there now by several different names, including "contemporary traditional New Orleans jazz"![4] New occasions breed new expressions, even when the old remain vibrant! But not only that. The jazz I value most is in fact improvisational at its core, so that what is true of music in general in some degree is especially true of this music. Every performance becomes an exercise in the performing artist's creativity. As Preservation Hall musician Maynard Chatters says, "This was the thing with New Orleans jazz, or traditional jazz. It's freedom. It gives you that sense of freedom."[5] Such jazz, in other words, *is* process.

The lesson I learned from jazz and gumbo is also available in the study of the Bible. As I have stressed throughout this book, the Bible is complex, voicing many perspectives that are often in tension, even contradiction, with one another. It too is the product of process, of modulations on existing themes produced in part by changing circumstances and in part by individual genius. The Bible differs from jazz and gumbo in one important way, of course; it comes to an end. We do not, at least in the vast majority of biblically based faith communities, add new books to it. We do, however, continue to *reinterpret* the Bible, finding new insights and nuances based on new historical knowledge or changed perspectives. As we do this, moreover, we find ourselves sorting out the competing voices in the Bible in different ways as well as building on biblical themes with different tools. And one of the most important ways in which some religious thinkers are accomplishing these tasks today has to do with the ways in which we image God.

The biblical images of God were necessarily rooted in the cultures of the time. They were, however, diverse, growing also out of specific circumstances and individuals' creative insights and varying moods. Most of us have been conditioned to think first of those images that reflect the patriarchal cultures of biblical times, most especially the images of king and father. But there are others upon which contemporary thinkers are calling as we try to meet the challenges of changed times and circumstances. At some points, feminine images of the divine appear. In Isa 42:14, for example, God is compared to a woman crying out in labor, and Deut 32:18 describes God as giving birth to Israel. Nor are the images limited to the human realm; Ps 91:4 envisions God as an eagle protecting its young: "[God] will cover

4. Brinkman, *Preservation Hall*, 5.
5. Ibid., 52.

you with [God's] pinions, and under [God's] wings you will find refuge." Even inanimate objects are used to suggest specific divine qualities: God is frequently termed "rock" and "fortress."

*Image*s are one thing, finely honed *concepts* another. The biblical writings are generally content with the former and thus contain very little explicit *theology* in the sense of logically ordered *doctrines*. The biblical writers were more interested in proclaiming their faith through stories and poetry, or in issuing moral injunctions, than explaining or justifying their beliefs intellectually. In time, however, persons of biblical faith felt the need to give a more systematic account of those beliefs and to defend them in the marketplace of human ideas. When they did so, they naturally turned to philosophy; and, given their original geographical locations, that meant Greek philosophy specifically. Thus, as they went about the task of deriving concepts and doctrines from the biblical writings, they used categories of thought belonging to that philosophical tradition. The result, predictably, was that the biblical understanding of God, the world, and life in general took on characteristics of Greek thought. I suspect that if we were to ask persons of biblical faith about the source of their doctrines, most would say, simply, the Bible. Such an answer, however, would be only partially correct; for the classical statements of Christian belief owe a great deal to the Greek philosophical tradition as well.

That tradition served theology well for many generations. In more recent times, however, human experience has taken turns that have opened up some new perspectives on the biblical faith; and these perspectives have called into question two particular aspects of ancient Greek thought. One of these is the belief that what is most fundamental in the universe, most fully real, is that which does not change.

It was Plato who first developed this way of thinking, and he had good reason to do so. In a world in which the realities we know are continually passing away, it seemed important to believe in something stable, something beyond change. And in a world in which we know only imperfections, it seemed important to believe in something perfect. Plato was interested in justice, for example, but he knew that all human attempts at justice fall short of what it seemed to him *true* justice would be like. So he speculated that there must by an eternal, *ideal* justice by which to judge our human attempts.

Plato's insight was important, for it provided a way of saying that the most important values by which we live are not mere whims or human prejudices. Even though our attempts at justice or goodness or any other ideals always fall short, it seems important to believe that there are objective standards that we must seek to identify and live by. Unfortunately, however,

Plato made this point at the expense of the physical universe. For him, only the realm of unchanging ideas was fully real; objects in the physical world, where changes take place, were merely imperfect imitations of those ideas. He thus obscured the insights of Heraclitus, an earlier Greek philosopher. Observing that a person can never step into the same river twice, since the water is constantly flowing, Heraclitus argued that change is a fundamental aspect of the universe. And this is precisely the point that human experience in recent times, largely under the influence of modern science, has brought back into focus. We do not, as people thought for many centuries, live in a universe of endless repetition, of heavenly bodies that rotate forever in precise patterns. The universe is constantly expanding, and stars are continually being born and dying. On the earth itself, life-forms are ever evolving, as is evidenced not only by fossils that represent different stages on slow developmental paths but also by the way viruses are constantly and rapidly undergoing change. And when we examine the physical universe on the smallest scale, we find not only constant motion but also pulsations of energy, rather than the tiny, self-consistent particles that some of the ancient Greeks imagined. It would thus appear that process, far from a secondary characteristic of the universe, is in fact an essential trait of all reality.

## God, Love, Freedom, and Relatedness

Traditional Christian theology was ill equipped to incorporate this sense of a dynamic universe. Enamored of the Greek emphasis on changelessness, early theologians developed a concept of God as in all respects unchanging. And this sense of an unchanging God naturally reinforced one particular aspect of biblical thought—an emphasis on God as the keeper of order, a stabilizing force keeping chaos in check. In medieval times, theologians also adopted the hierarchical view of the universe developed by philosophers influenced by Plato, which was known as "the great chain of being," a matter I discussed in chapter 4.

Some of these emphases of traditional theology can find support in the Bible. God certainly appears as the ultimate spiritual being who rules the universe and is often imaged as king as well as a warrior who defeats the powers of chaos to establish order. In Jas 1:17 moreover, we find a description of God as the one "with whom there is no variation or shadow due to change"—a passage clearly influenced by Greek thought. We can also find elements of a hierarchical scheme at some points. There are, however, strong countercurrents to all these elements, although we tend to overlook them because traditional theology has obscured them. To say that in the Bible

God does not change at all is simply false. In some passages, God changes God's mind. To cite only a few examples, in Gen 16:22–33, Abraham bargains God down on the number of faithful necessary to save the cities of Sodom and Gomorrah; in Hos 11, we find God engaging in an internal debate that ends in a revised decision; and in Gen 6:6, God expresses sorrow over creating human beings! To think of God as utterly unchanging, moreover, runs counter to the pervasive biblical understanding of God as loving. To love another is to be changed by the other, deeply affected by the other's joys and sorrows as well as the other's response to the love offered. To think of God as interested *only* in order, moreover, is equally false. At many points God brings down empires and unjust social structures, destroying existing orders and establishing new ones. We can also find in the Bible a strong strain of antimonarchical sentiment and equally strong critiques of hierarchical governance, as in Mark 10:42–44:

> You know that among the Gentiles those whom they recognize as their rulers lord it over them, and their great ones are tyrants over them. But it is not so among you; but whoever wishes to become great among you must be your servant, and whoever wishes to be first among you must be slave of all.

With respect to the physical universe, biblical thought is worlds apart from the Greek tendency to play down its importance. The Greek perspective makes a limited appearance in Heb 8:5, which names the earthly sanctuary in Jerusalem a mere copy of the heavenly one. However, such notions as this are overwhelmed by passages praising creation as God's handiwork (e.g., Psalm 8) and pronouncing it "good" (Gen 1). Even those apocalyptic passages that envision an eventual destruction of the earth are balanced by the notion of a new creation that is clearly physical in nature (e.g., Isa 65:17; 2 Pet 3:8–13).

Traditional theology, with its emphasis on God as the unchanging monarch who stabilizes an unchanging hierarchical order is thus out of tune with much in the biblical tradition as well as with human experience in our time. Many theologians have therefore sought to replace some aspects of the Greek element in our understanding of God with philosophies more congenial to the biblical images of God—as more interactive with the world and more expressive of our growing sense of the universe as dynamic and ever changing. Some have therefore proposed models of God as constantly feeding new possibilities into the world, luring the evolutionary process toward greater degrees of consciousness and urging the human community towards peace, justice, and oneness with creation. One particular philosophical/theological perspective, known as "process" or "process-relational" thought, draws upon the twentieth-century philosophers Alfred North Whitehead and Charles Hartshorne.[6] I first encountered this way of thinking in a seminary course taught by Schubert M. Ogden.[7] It appealed to me immediately, fostering an aha moment in which it seemed to me that of course, "This is precisely the way things are in the world."

Process theologians play down those aspects of biblical tradition that present God as all controlling and stress human free will to respond or not respond to God's promptings. In this sense, they envision God's relationship to the world in more democratic than authoritarian, terms. That is, they understand God's action upon the world as more persuasive than coercive. These and other contemporary theologians, moreover, often propose new images of and names for God that in some ways contrast with those that predominated in traditional theology. Among them are Mother, Friend, Parent, Holy Wisdom, Eternal One, God of All Being, Redeemer of the Oppressed, Life of the Universe, Creator of All, each of which has advantages and disadvantages. One image I find particularly appealing is that proposed by process-feminist theologian Ann Pedersen—God as jazz bandleader. Here she combines it with that of playful dancer:

> God gives order and yet is the ground from which comes creativity and novelty. God is also the playful dancer, the Wisdom of the World. God's leadership, like the jazz bandleader's, will encourage each member to find his or her own musical voice. The music occurs within the nurturing atmosphere where each individual can perfect the art of hanging out. Community occurs over time through the rich interactions of relationships, particularly between Creator and creation. Improvisation is interdependence set to rhythm.[8]

To image God as a jazz bandleader is first of all to suggest that God, although playing the indispensable role of providing a framework for what happens in the world, does not exercise total control over it. All the beings

---

6. For more on process thought, visit the websites of the Center for Process Studies (http:www.ctr4process.org/) and Process and Faith (http:www.processandfaith.org/). See also below, note 7.

7. The writings of Charles Hartshorne were central to the seminary course: see his *The Logic of Perfection*, ch. 7, "A World of Organisms," for the insights that initially intrigued me. Another important element in the course was John B. Cobb Jr.'s *A Christian Natural Theology*. For Ogden's own use of process thought, see the lead essay in *The Reality of God*; and Ogden, *Understanding of Christian Faith*, 30–32. In Pregeant, *Mystery without Magic*, chapters 8 and 9, I have tried to summarize key aspects of process theology in nontechnical language.

8. Pedersen, *God, Creation*, 73.

in the world have roles to play also, and these roles involve more than following predetermined scripts. God provides possibilities, but the beings in the world are free to exercise their own creativity, for better or worse; and as they do so, they help to create new situations that affect what God is able to propose in the next moment. The relationship between God and the world is thus reciprocal. This means, of course, that the future remains indeterminate in terms of specifics. To believe in the biblical God at all is to believe that God can provide a future out of whatever decisions the beings in the world make, so that the universe can never reach a point of total chaos and meaninglessness. But to believe in a God who acts persuasively rather than coercively is also to accept that the future is open, yet to be determined by the leader and the ensemble in concert. This means that we cannot take literally the apocalyptic elements in the biblical tradition—those elements that predict an "end of the age" in specific detail. But it is actually impossible to do this anyway, since what those texts predicted was supposed to have happened centuries ago. The authors of Daniel and Revelation expected the end in their immediate futures. These books have other values for us; they are important proclamations that God does not ultimately abandon the world to injustice and oppression. But to use them as roadmaps for the future in our time is to deny human free will and to discourage our own efforts to conquer injustice and save the planet from destruction.

If the relationship between the jazz leader and the band is reciprocal, the relationships among the players are also reciprocal. Each individual is dependent on all the others; what one plays both limits what the others can do and opens up possibilities. We thus have a beautiful example of individuality-within-community. There is room for solos, but only within the framework of the integrity of the whole piece; and when several instruments play together, the individual contributions are parts of a greater whole. Individual identities remain but are transformed by their inclusion in the group's identity. The group is thus something like an organism, a composite entity in which all the parts work together. And the metaphor of organism suggests another God-image that is frequent in contemporary theology: God and the world united as mind and body. This might seem out of step with biblical thought, since one of the distinctive factors of the Israelite understanding of God was to distinguish God from the forces of nature. Only a God who is in some sense other than and sovereign over nature could exercise moral judgment and challenge the status quo in the name of justice. To reach this understanding was indeed an innovation and an advance, and any attempt to understand the universe itself as God, as in pantheism, would be a genuine loss. To understand God as the Mind of the Universe, however, is not to deny God's transcendence over the world. It is rather to balance the emphasis on transcendence with a strong sense of the divine immanence within the world.

This sense of divine immanence, moreover, has strong biblical support. Psalm 139 declares God's ubiquitous presence in dramatic fashion:

> Where can I go from your spirit?
> Or where flee from your presence?
> If I ascend to heaven, you are there;
> if I make my bed in Sheol, you are there.

In the book of Proverbs we find the female figure of Wisdom, named as the first of God's creative acts, who is present in human affairs and mediates between God and the world to impart wisdom to human beings (Prov 1:20–21; 3:19–20; 8:1–36, esp. 22–24). In the Wisdom of Solomon, a later work included in the Roman Catholic secondary canon and the Protestant Apocrypha, both her immanence in the world and her association with God are even more clearly stated. Here she "pervades and penetrates all things" as "a breath of the power of God, and a pure emanation of the Glory of the Almighty" (7:24–26). In the New Testament, the Gospel of John introduces a figure parallel to Wisdom, the divine Logos or Word. (John 1:1–4) Co-eternal with God, this Logos, who becomes incarnate in Jesus, is God's agent in creating the world, and "the light of all people." And in Col 1:15–20 the preexistent Christ appears not only as the agent of creation but as the one "in whom all things hold together."

To think of the world as pervaded by the divine presence, indeed as in some sense part of God's own divine being, is not to make the world itself an object of worship, that is, an idol. It is, however, to bring God and the physical universe much closer together than has generally been the case in Western thought. Having separated God and the world so severely, and often having deleted God from the equation altogether, the Western world has tended to treat nature as an object to be manipulated solely for human purposes, exploited for material gain with no sense of its value-in-itself. To think of the world as God's body, however, is to restore to it a sense of sacredness. It is also to add to the sense of the kinship of all beings in the world. If all entities in the world are parts of a larger whole, then they are more closely related to one another than we generally imagine. And if we grant that all entities are always in process, this sense of relatedness becomes even stronger. For the changes that entities undergo take place precisely by incorporating elements from their environments. We breathe in oxygen from outside our bodies and exhale carbon dioxide; we ingest food and emit waste. Our skins are thus porous boundaries between our bodies and our environments, which means that the distinction between ourselves and our environments is only relative. Although not drawing explicitly upon process-relational thought, Pope Francis's encyclical on the environment, *Laudato Si*, expresses a strong sense of the relatedness of all things that reveals a kinship with this perspective: "Everything is related, and we human beings are united as brothers and sisters on a wonderful pilgrimage, woven together by the love God has for each of [God's] creatures and which also unites us in fond affection with brother sun, sister moon, brother river and mother earth."[9]

Our separateness from one another is also relative. When a child is born, the genes of her parents become part of her. When one person encounters another, the other's words and deeds become part of his experience, which means part of his actual identity. The environments in which we live contribute to our personal identities. Had my parents moved to New England or the Midwest before I was born, I would not be the same person I am today. I would not have absorbed as much of the distinctive culture of south Louisiana as I have, probably not have listened to the New Orleans Jazz Club or become entranced by Spanish moss on live oak trees. I would be a different person, because I would have incorporated different elements into myself. And this means that our relationships to other persons and to other entities in the world are not merely external relationships. They are internal, because they affect who we are in our inmost selves. My parents' stories, and now also my wife's engaging and sometimes hilarious tales of her own childhood, are essential parts of who I am. The unity of humankind and humankind's unity with the environment, as well as the unity of all things in God, are essential traits of life in the world. To deny them is to distort our true identities.

In sum, human experience in recent times has given many persons of biblical faith a new perspective on the Bible, God, and our relationships with one another and with the world, as well as our own identities. All things in the universe are in process, and all things are related. Nothing is what it is in and of itself, because all things are ultimately parts of a greater whole. All things, moreover, are continuously incorporating elements from their environments. And this means that no identity remains stable but is constantly in process, ever changing, for better or worse. And therein lies an important lesson for all of life and for our country.

---

9. Francis I, Pope. *Laudato Si*, V.92 (pdf, 27).

# EPILOGUE

## A LESSON FOR AMERICA, A LESSON FOR LIFE

### Contingency, Choice, and the Action of God

I am often struck by the enormous role played by contingency in both our personal lives and human history. My very existence is the result of innumerable contingencies. If two young Englishmen, Archie White and Lewis Coon, had not been shanghaied and brought to America to fight for King George, they would never have fled after a battle in Tennessee and found their way to Mississippi, married American women, and become my mother's ancestors. Had Flora Hyde not married George Philip White, the Methodist minister who migrated from Mississippi, neither my mother nor I would have been born. Nor would I exist had not the British expelled my Cajun ancestors from Nova Scotia, or if Ida Long had not married Victor Eusebe Pregeant and given birth to my father. A more somber thought is that my parents would not have married had not my father's first wife died following childbirth. And my life would have been rather different had she not made the dying request that her infant daughter, my half-sister Odessa, be raised by my father's brother and his wife, who were otherwise childless. And had they not moved to Virginia, to be joined much later by my half brother Gene after World War II, my half siblings would have been much more a part of my life than they have been. How different also would my life have been had not Sammie Maxwell moved from Georgia to New Orleans and found her way to Rayne Memorial United Methodist Church, where we met and married. And who knows where life would have taken us had I not happened upon the catalog of Curry College on a shelf at the New Orleans Public Library as I was sending out one after another letter of inquiry in quest of a teaching position.

To say that life is filled with contingencies, however, is not to say that mere randomness rules. Events in the world grow, in part, out of prior events that influence them. Both the Bible and process thought, moreover, have a strong sense of the role of human decision. The choices we make in life thus matter, and some of them matter greatly. But prior events and human choices are not the only counterforce to randomness. To believe that God is always at work luring the world toward the good is also to believe that we are not alone in our attempts at making peace, doing justice, and saving the planet from destruction. *The question thus becomes whether our choices conform to the vision that God has for our world, that is, whether we in our actions cooperate with God in serving the common good.*

## Making the Choices for Creative Transformation

On the wall in our living room hangs a picture by an artist in the area, titled *The Grand Era*. It depicts a small hotel named the Glenbrook, which once stood in Tallulah Falls, Sammie's hometown, twelve miles south of where we now live. The town is the site of beautiful Tallulah Gorge, along whose bed are seven magnificent waterfalls, although the dams built by the Georgia Power Company have largely silenced their tumultuous roar. The Glenbrook was one of seventeen hotels and boarding houses that the small town once boasted. Until 1946 excursion trains on the Tallulah Falls Railway brought tourists by the hundreds to view the awesome sight and enjoy elegant leisure in the hotels. Today, the Interpretive Center that overlooks the gorge displays a model of the town during its heyday as a resort. It was a charming place in a charming time; and our picture of the Glenbrook captures some of the flavor of the period—women in long dresses, men wearing white suits and bow ties, children playing croquet in sailor suits. That time, however, is long past. Most of the hotels perished in a fire in 1921, and the others fell into decay. The last survivor was the Glenbrook, which continued into my wife's childhood but is today a complete ruin. Nor was it the fire alone that spelled the end of an era for the town. Times changed. The dams reduced the attractiveness of the gorge, and the coming of the automobile reduced the appeal of excursion trains and made farther destinations accessible. And, of course, not just for Tallulah Falls but for the whole country, "the grand era" simply passed into history.

It is an easy feat of the imagination for me to transport myself into the world of that time gone by. To do so, however, is more than a little deceptive. I am entranced by the seeming romance of the period, but I know in my heart that its formalism would have produced in me a very different consciousness, one of which today I might disapprove. Despite the undeniable elements of charm, it was a world marred by injustices of many sorts—racial segregation, class snobbery, squalid conditions for the working class, limited rights for women, and intolerance of lesbians and gays. And so it is with all our longings for a glorious period in the past. People who want to return to some supposed golden age of America are constructing a fantasy in their imaginations, a world that never existed. The truth is that there have been many Americas, defined by a variety of times and places. Each has had its glories, but each its shortcomings. We have been many things, each of which was constructed out of influences from prior times and places. One of our most distinctive traits is the diversity of cultures and geographical settings that have defined these many Americas. My beloved Louisiana was originally the territory of seven American Indian tribes—the Atakapa, the Caddo, the Chitimacha, the Choctaw, the Tunica, the Houma, and the Natchez.[10] Everything changed, however, with the coming of the French and Spanish explorers, the importation of African slaves, and the arrival of the displaced Acadians ("Cajuns"). Over time, many others were added to the mix, among them English, Germans, Italians, Irish, and, in recent times, Vietnamese and Mexicans. This resulted in a creative blending, a kind of cultural gumbo whose recipe is ever changing and constantly enriched, an ongoing jam session with new instruments constantly added. So it has been in other regions of this great land, and so it is with the whole. The massive immigrations of the nineteenth and early twentieth centuries not only changed our ethnic makeup radically but provided the energy for industrialization and the building of our great cities. And the earlier movement westward fostered the development of different regional cultures with varying lifestyles, speech patterns, and to some extent values.

We have been many things indeed, changed by much more than geography and cultural infusion. The Civil War ended an evil institution that had belied our professed belief in equality. World War I changed the world and the United States along with it; some historians see it as the true turning point from the outlook of the nineteenth century to that of the twentieth. World War II propelled the United States into a role on the international scene we had not played before, stemming the tide of imperial expansion and of fascism with a racist face. Subsequent military involvements and developments in other parts of the world, however, have now called aspects of that role into question. On another front, popular movements have broken down barriers that denied many people full participation in the society they called their own. Political philosophies, economic policies, and social arrangements have all undergone changes, as one or another point of view gains popularity, then fades, and perhaps reemerges in another form. Through all of this, there have been threads of continuity, holding us together in a sometimes fragile unity. But that unity has never been total conformity, however much some have tried to force it upon us. There have been many Americas and many definitions of American identity. If we are to continue to thrive as a people, we must be willing to accept dissent as a possible source of creative transformation, as well as to engage the future with a determination to shape what it means to be America in ever new ways to meet ever new situations. We cannot be again what we once were, and we should not be.

Such a view of American identity is something that persons of biblical faith should not only accept but also celebrate. We should celebrate it, that

---

10. Native Languages of the Americas, "American Indians."

is, if we believe that the God of biblical faith is in fact ever luring the world toward peace among nations, reconciliation among all peoples, justice and equality for all, and loving care for the creation itself. We should celebrate it also because that God is the one who in the book of Isaiah declares, "Do not remember the former things, or consider the things of old. I am about to do a new thing" (Isa 43:18–19a). And we should celebrate it because it is that same God whose risen Son, in the book of Revelation declares, "See, I am making all things new" (Rev 21:5b).

This is not to suggest that all change is good. Nor does it mean that human progress is inevitable; surely the past century should have debunked this fantasy once and for all. It does mean, however, that God is always focused on the future, seeking to transform our imperfect systems and institutions in order to refashion human society as increasingly just and humane. As I have stated, theologians who stress that all things are in process also insist that the future is open, *dependent in part upon on human choice*—the decisions we human beings make in our individual and collective lives. Americans of the present generation will, for better or worse, determine American identity for the years ahead and with it the meaning of America on the stage of world history. What we decide, moreover, will wield great influence on the fate of the planet. People of biblical faith should therefore pray that we choose wisely, with the good of all life on this fragile earth in mind.

As we do so, we can take inspiration from a biblical theme too often overlooked—the faith community as a "pilgrim people," always on the move, struggling to follow the lead of a God who promises to be with them on their journey. Long before the Israelites possessed the promised land, Abraham and Sarah and their progeny "tented" in that land as strangers; and on the final journey there, the band led by Moses wandered forty years in the desert. Even after the next generation had at last claimed the land, moreover, it remained more a promise than a secure possession, as corruption on the inside and threats from the outside threatened their stability. The people were on a journey toward reception of a promise that was never fully realized. In the New Testament, the book of Hebrews proclaims fulfillment of the promises made to the Israelite ancestors and blends it with a new version of "pilgrim theology." It thus recognizes an ongoing struggle, a race still to be run with perseverance in the knowledge that there is on this earth "no lasting city" (11:39; 13:14). What we should therefore pray for, and struggle to achieve, is not a static social system that would inevitably decay, but a continuing process of creative transformation, a perpetual revolution in search of peace, justice, and harmony with nature.

# OF TIME AND PLACE AND STORY
# (IF THE LAND COULD SPEAK)

If the Land could speak,
What stories would it choose to tell?
What epics grand played out upon its face
That turned the tide of history in its course?
What smaller tales, of common folk,
Who simple lives pursued
With tragedies and triumphs
No less poignant than the larger tale,
And sometimes when in concert acting bold
Became a Force far greater than the might of kings?
And would the Land a drama of its own recount
Of eons long before the human race appeared
And what its coming meant for Mother Earth?

If the Land could speak,
Would it speak thus?—

Of a boiling planet fresh from the Creator's hand
That over many a millennium cooled down
To host the birth of life in myriads of forms,
Of glaciers huge that came and went
To carve the wonders of the West
Upon this continent so vast.
Of plants and mammals long extinct,
Of dinosaurs and saber-toothed,
Of life abundant, free and wild,
Of landscapes changing through the march of time,
As the mills of God ground slow but fine
And purple mountain majesties came forth
Along with plains and forests vast and green,
Upon a soil full rich with life,
From sea to shining sea spread out.

Of then the human trek across the Strait
To form new cultures and new tribes
Who close to Nature's bosom dwelt,
In harmony with all of life
Nor wasted aught of what they took

And honored well the spirits
That they sensed in all that is.

Of time still moving, now at faster pace,
That brought new peoples to the shores,
Who came at first as Empire's reach,
For gold, for power, or for trade,
Or religious persecution to avoid,
Transforming place with each new settlement they made.
And then, within this newly forming world
Bold thoughts, ideas from ancient times transformed,
Began to shake the powers of the world.
Sweet freedom's song rang out,
And democratic spirit filled the air
As "We, the People" claimed the place
That Privilege and Empire once held fast!

Of Liberty and Justice meant for all
Now claiming both the heart and mind—
*Although, alas, to some they were denied.*
For as the growing Nation made its march
It took the land of those
Who crossed the Strait so long ago,
Took it even with a genocidal thrust
Nor learned from them the sacred path
Of living lightly on the earth
But ravaged Nature as they went.
Nor did some shrink from yet another sin,
Enslavement of a people brought by ship
To labor in their fields and homes,
Enriching self by labor of another's hand
And even with the cost of freedom paid in blood
Conspired anew, creating bondage of another type.

Of industry and wealth created, cities built,
Of open doors to the wretched refuse of the earth
To come and build and breathe free air
Upon the surface of a broad and fertile earth.
And so they came, with hopeful hearts and willing hands,
To make a newborn nation strong.

And yet, within this young and vibrant and emerging world
Two souls were struggling to emerge victorious in a strife,
Both Liberty proclaiming loud and clear
But holding different takes on what it means.
The one, Community, gave birth to rights
For all the people and the Land itself,
Considered all the entities on earth
As parts of one great whole
And so made sacrifices great
In Freedom's cause throughout the world.
The other, though, Autonomy its name,
Made wealth and power, privilege and race its gods
And thought that freedom was a license to exploit.

Of voices bold, raised in Dissent
When crass injustice rules the land.
Of workers in our factories and mines,
With bodies broken but with courage still intact,
Who ask a decent wage and workplace safe.
Of women marching for the vote and equal rights
And pay that's equal to a man's.
Of descendants of the slaves of long ago
Continuing the struggle still today
As New Jim Crow reveals his ugly face.
Of Natives seeking justice still
And ancient heritage to keep
As others, newest to our shores,
Whose toil contributes to us all,
Ask nothing more than decency demands.
Of anguished faces mourning all the dead and maimed
While standing fast against an unjust war;
And anguished faces too at prisons' gates,
Who cry that "eye for eye" will make the whole world blind.

Of those, also, because the Land in fact can have no voice
Give voice themselves on its behalf:
> "Have I not nurtured you through all these years?
> Have I not given place for all your strivings and your hopes?
> Has not my bounty been enough that all could share?
> Could you not receive in gratitude with care for times to come
> Instead of frenzied ravaging of all the gifts I gave,

> While poisoning the wells of life from which all creatures drink
> And bringing all the earth to boiling point again?"

If the Land could speak,
What heroes would it name,
What values now enshrine?
What stories choose to tell of time and place?
And which of those competing souls
(Identifies that different deities would serve)
Choose for its people to embrace?
What vision might it then put forth
To reconcile our differences,
When the common good's our common aim,
To bind our wounds and heal our hearts,
To make a broken nation whole
And peace and justice spread abroad,
Around a thriving globe?

# Bibliography

Abdul-Jabbar, Kareem. "Kareem Abdul-Jabbar: Baltimore Is Just the Beginning." *Time* (May 6, 2015). http://time.com/3848474/kareem-abdul-jabbar-baltimore-is-just-the-beginning/.
Adams, Edward. "Retrieving the Earth from the Conflagration." In *Ecological Hermeneutics: Biblical, Historical, and Theological Perspectives*, edited by David G. Horrell et al., 108–20. London: T. & T. Clark, 2010.
Albright, William Foxwell. *From the Stone Age to Christianity: Monotheism and the Historical Process*. 2nd ed. Baltimore: Johns Hopkins Press, 1946.
Alexander, Michelle. "Criminal Injustice: Michelle Alexander on Racism and Incarceration." Interview by Amy Fryckholm. *Christian Century* 29 (May 16, 2012).
———. *The New Jim Crow: Mass Incarceration in the Age of Colorblindness*. Rev. ed. with a new Foreword by Cornel West. New York: New Press, 2012.
Ali, Mazher et al. "Austerity for Whom?" State of the Dream 2011. Boston: United for a Fair Economy, 2011. http://d3n8a8pro7vhmx.cloudfront.net/ufe/legacy_url/483/State_of_the_Dream_2011.pdf?1448060271/.
Allegretto, Sylvia. "The State of Working America's Wealth, 2011." Economic Policy Institute (March 24, 2011). http://www.epi.org/files/page/-/BriefingPaper292.pdf/.
American Public University System. "Manifest Destiny." AP U.S. History Notes. http://www.apstudynotes.org/us-history/topics/manifest-destiny/.
Amnesty International. Death Penalty Facts (May, 2012), www.amnestyusa.org/ pdfs/DeathPenaltyFactsMay2012.pdf/.
Arsenault, Raymond. *Freedom Riders: 1961 and the Struggle for Racial Justice*. Oxford: Oxford University Press, 2006.
Athenagoras. "A Plea for the Christians." In *The Ante-Nicene Fathers*, vol. 2. *Fathers of the Second Century*, edited by A. Roberts and J. Donaldson. 10 vols. Grand Rapids: Eerdmans, 1967.
Augustine, Saint. *Enchiridion on Faith, Hope, and Love*. Newly translated and edited by Albert C. Outler, 1955. http://www.tertullian.org/augustine_ench_02.trans.htm#C4/.
Bacevich, Andrew. "Even if We Defeat the Islamic State, We'll Still Lose the Bigger War." *Washington Post* (October 3, 2014). https://www.washingtonpost.com/opinions/even-if-we-defeat-the-islamic-state-well-still-lose-the-bigger-war/2014/10/03/e8c0585e-4353-11e4-b47c-f5889e061e5f_story.html/.

Bailey, Randall C. "Beyond Identification: The Use of Africans in Old Testament Poetry and Narratives." In *Stony the Road We Trod: African American Biblical Interpretation*, edited by Cain Hope Felder, 165–84. Minneapolis: Fortress, 1991.

Bainton, Roland. *Christian Attitudes toward War and Peace: A Historical Survey and Critical Re-evaluation*. Nashville: Abingdon, 1960.

Baker, Dean. "Romney's Success at Bain Capital: The Scam as Business Model." *Truthout* (September 4, 2012). www.truth-out.org/news/item/11316-romneys-success-at-bain-the-scam-as-business-model#.

Baldwin, James. "Autobiographical Notes." In *James Baldwin: Collected Essays*, edited by Toni Morrison, 5–9. New York: Library of America, 1998. From Baldwin, *Notes of a Native Son*. Boston: Beacon, 1955.

Barr, Roger. *The Vietnam War*. America's Wars. San Diego: Lucent, 1991.

Benko, Jessica. "The Radical Humaneness of Norway's Halden Prison." *New York Times Magazine* (March 26, 2015). http://www.nytimes.com/2015/03/29/magazine/the-radical-humaneness-of-norways-halden-prison.html/.

Berger, Peter L., and Thomas Luckmann. *The Social Construction of Reality: A Treatise on the Sociology of Knowledge*. Anchor Books. New York: Doubleday, 1967.

Berman, Ari. "The GOP's New Southern Strategy." *The Nation* (February 20, 2012). http://www.theinvestigativefund.org/investigations/politicsandgovernment/1603/the_gop's_new_southern_strategy/.

Birch, Bruce C. *Let Justice Roll Down: The Old Testament, Ethics, and the Christian Life* Louisville: Westminster John Knox, 1991.

BlackPast.org. "Selma, Alabama (Bloody Sunday, March 7, 1965)." http://www.blackpast.org/aah/bloody-sunday-selma-alabama-march-7-1965/.

Boer, Roland. *The Sacred Economy of Ancient Israel*. Library of Ancient Israel. Louisville: Westminster John Knox, 2015.

Boring, M. Eugene. *Revelation*. Interpretation. Louisville: John Knox, 1989.

Braziel, Jana Evans. "History of Lynching in the United States." ACLAnet. https://www.umass.edu/complit/aclanet/USLynch.html/.

Brinkman, Shannon, photographer. *Preservation Hall: Photographs by Shannon Brinkman; Interviews with Preservation Hall Band Members by Eve Abrams*. Baton Rouge: Louisiana State University Press, 2011.

Brown, Dee. *Bury My Heart at Wounded Knee: An Indian History of the American West*. New York: Holt, Rinehart & Winston, 1970.

Brueggemann, Walter. *The Book of Exodus: Introduction, Commentary, and Reflections*. In *The New Interpreter's Bible*, edited by Leander E. Keck, 1:675–981. Nashville: Abingdon, 1994.

———. *The Land*. Overtures to Biblical Theology 1. Philadelphia: Fortress, 1977. 2nd ed. Minneapolis: Fortress, 2002.

Buchanan, Pat. *Suicide of a Superpower: Will America Survive to 2025?* New York: Dunne, 2011.

Callahan, Allen Dwight. *A Love Supreme: A History of the Johannine Tradition*. Minneapolis: Fortress, 2005.

Cash, W. J. *The Mind of the South*. New York: Knopf, 1941.

Catholic World News. "Archbishop: Alabama law threatens religious liberty" (August 3, 2011). https://www.catholicculture.org/news/headlines/index.cfm?storyid=1152.

Center for Justice and Accountability. "The Jesuits Massacre Case: El Salvador: Justice for the Murders of November 16, 1989." http://cja.org/article.php?list=type&type=84/.

Chomsky, Aviva. *They Take Our Jobs! and 20 Other Myths about Immigration.* Boston: Beacon, 2007.
"Civil Rights Act of 1964." *Wikipedia: The Free Encyclopedia* (modified Oct. 20, 2015). http://en.wikipedia.org /wiki/Civil_Rights_Act_of_1964.
Civil Rights Cold Case Project. "Henry Dee and Charles Moore Case." http://coldcases.org/cases/henry-dee-and-charles-moore-case.
———. "Silver Dollar Group." http://coldcases.org/silver-dollar-group.
———. "Wharlest Jackson Case." http://cold.cases.org/wharlest-jackson-case.
Civil Rights Movement Veterans. "Civil Rights Bill Battle in the Senate (March-June)." http://crmvet.org/timhis64.htm1964cra64#.
Clark, Josh. "Is There a Torture Manual? KUBARK Manual: A User's Guide to Torture?" HowStuffWorks. http://science.howstuffworks.com/torture-manual1.htm.
CNN. "Vietnam War Fast Facts." http://www.cnn.com/2013/07/01.
Cobb, James C. *Away Down South.* New York: Oxford University Press, 2005.
Cobb, John B., Jr. *A Christian Natural Theology Based on the Thought of Alfred North Whitehead.* Philadelphia: Westminster, 1965.
———. "Imperialism in American Economic Policy." In David Ray Griffin, et al., *The American Empire and the Commonwealth of God: A Political, Economic, Religious Statement*, 23–43. Louisville: Westminster John Knox, 2006.
———. *Spiritual Bankruptcy: A Prophetic Call to Action.* Nashville: Abingdon, 2010.
Collins, Joseph, and Frances Moore Lappé. "Still Hungry after All These Years: The Not-So-Grand Opening of the Global Supermarket." *Mother Jones* 2 (August, 1977) 27–38.
Colson, Charles W. "The Death Penalty Is Morally Just." In *The Death Penalty: Opposing Viewpoints*, edited by Paul A. Winters, 60–65. San Diego: Greenhaven, 1997.
Cone, James H. *Black Theology and Black Power.* New York: Seabury, 1969.
———. *Martin and Malcolm and America: A Dream or a Nightmare?* Maryknoll, NY: Orbis, 1991.
———. *My Soul Looks Back.* Maryknoll, NY: Orbis, 1986.
Congress on Racial Equality. "Freedom Summer." http://www.core-online.org/History/freedom_summer.htm/.
Copher, Charles B. "The Black Presence in the Old Testament." In *Stony the Road We Trod: African American Biblical Interpretation*, edited by Cain Hope Felder, 146–64. Minneapolis: Fortress, 1991.
Crossan, John Dominic. *The Historical Jesus: The Life of a Mediterranean Peasant.* New York: HarperCollins, 1991.
———. *In Parables: The Challenge of the Historical Jesus.* 1973. Reprinted, Sonoma, CA: Polebridge, 1992.
Crossette, Barbara. "When Will American Foreign Policymakers Learn from Their Mistakes in the Middle East?" *The Nation* (September 24, 2015). http://thenation.com/article/when-will-american-foreign-policymakers-learn-their-mistakes-middle-east/.
Currie, Elliott. *Crime and Punishment in America: Why the Solutions to America's Most Serious Social Crisis Have Not Worked—and What Will.* New York: Henry Holt, 1998.
Daly, Herman E. *Beyond Growth: The Economics of Sustainable Development.* Boston: Beacon, 1996.

———. "Full Employment versus Jobless Growth." *Daly News*, July 15, 2013. http://steadystate.org/full-employment-versus-jobless-growth/.

———. "A Medical Missionary's Environmental Epiphany." *Daly News*, March 4, 2014. http://steadystate.org/a-medical-missionarys-environmental-epiphany/.

———. "Top 10 Policies for a Steady-State Economy." *Daly News*, October 28, 2013. http://steadystate.org/top-10-policies-for-a-steady-state-economy/.

Daly, Herman E., and John B. Cobb Jr., with Clifford W. Cobb. *For the Common Good: Redirecting the Economy toward Community, the Environment, and a Sustainable Future.* Boston: Beacon, 1989.

Darling-Hammond, Linda. "Redlining Our Schools: Why Is Congress Writing Off Poor Children?" *The Nation* 297 (January 30, 2012).

Death Penalty Information Center. "Abolitionist and Retentionist Countries." http://www.deathpenaltyinfo.org/abolitionist-and-retentionist-countries.

———. "Religion and the Death Penalty." http://deathpenaltyinfo.org/article.php%3Fdid%3D2249.

Dell, Katharine J. "The Significance of the Wisdom Tradition in the Ecological Debate." In *Ecological Hermeneutics: Biblical, Historical, and Theological Perspectives*, edited by David G. Horrell et al., 56–69. London: T. & T. Clark, 2010.

Deloria, Philip J. "Part Five: The Twentieth Century and Beyond." In *The Native American: An Illustrated History*, edited by Betty Ballantine and Ian Ballantine, 384–462. North Dighton, MA: World, 2001.

Dietz, Rob. "Approaching a Steady State Economy, Part 1—Getting Around." *Daly News* (September 9, 2013). http://steadystate.org/approaching-a-steady-state-economy-part-1-getting-around/.

Douthwaite, Richard. *The Growth Illusion*. Totnes, UK: Green Books, 1999.

Du Bois, W. E. Burghardt. *The Souls of Black Folk*. Centennial Edition. Introduction by David Levering Lewis. New York: Modern Library, 2003. First published in 1903 by McClurg.

Dugan, Andrew. "Fewer Americans Identify as Economic Conservatives in 2013." Gallup (May 2, 2013). www.gallup.com/poll/162746/fewer-americans-identify-conservatives-2013.aspx.

Dunigan, Brian. "Citizens United v. Federal Election Commission." *Encyclopedia Brittanica*. http:///www.britannica.com/event/Cirizens-United-v-Federal-election-Commission/.

Ebersole, Ryan C. "Mississippi Is Still Burning, Vicious Murder Shows." *People's World* (August 10, 2011). http://peoplesworld.org/mississippi-is-still-burning-vicious-murder-shows/.

Editorial Board of the *New York Times*. "The End of the Perpetual War." *New York Times*, The Opinion Pages (May 24, 2013). http://www.nytimes.com/2013/05/24/opinion/obama-vows-to-end-of-the-perpetual-war.html/.

Editors of *Christian Century*. "Sacrificed for What? The Dark Side of Sacrificial Action." *Christian Century* (July 9, 2014) 7.

Editors of *Encyclopedia Britannica*. "Salvador Allende: President of Chile." In *Encyclopedia Britannica*. http://www.britannica.com/biography/Salvador-Allende.

Egerton, John. *Speak Now against the Day: The Generation before the Civil Rights Movement in the South.* New York: Knopf, 1994.

Elahi, Maryam. "The Impact of Financial Institutions on the Realization of Human Rights: Case Study of the International Monetary Fund in Chile." *Boston College*

*Third World Law Journal* 6 (June 1, 1986), 142–60. http://lawdigitalcommons.bc.edu/cgi/viewcontent.cgi?article=1431&context=twlj/.

Elliott, Neil. *Liberating Paul: The Justice of God and the Politics of the Apostle.* 1994. Reprinted with a new Preface, Minneapolis: Fortress, 2005.

Ellis, Marc H. *Toward a Jewish Theology of Liberation.* Maryknoll, NY: Orbis, 1987.

Erez, Edna. "Thou Shalt Not Execute: Hebrew Law Perspective on Capital Punishment." *Criminology* 19 (May 1981) 25–43.

Fang, Lee. "The Shadow Lobbying Complex." *The Nation* 299 (March 10/17, 2014), 12–22.

Faulkner, William. *The Sound and the Fury.* 1929. Reprinted, New York: Vintage, 1964.

Felder, Cain Hope. "Race, Racism, and the Biblical Narratives." In *Stony the Road We Trod: African American Biblical Interpretation*, edited by Cain Hope Felder, 127–45. Minneapolis: Fortress, 1991.

———, ed. *Stony the Road We Trod: African American Biblical Interpretation.* Minneapolis: Fortress, 1991.

———. *Troubling Biblical Waters: Race, Class, and Family.* Maryknoll, NY: Orbis, 1989.

Firestone, Reuven. "Judaism as a Force for Reconciliation: An Examination of Key Sources." In *Beyond Violence: Religious Sources of Social Transformation in Judaism, Christianity, and Islam*, edited by James L. Heft, S.M., 74–87. New York: Fordham University Press, 2004.

Food First. "Guatemala: Hungry for Change." *Food First Action Alert* (March, 1983).

"The Forgotten Massacre of the Vietnamese Trotskyists." *Workers' Liberty* (September 12, 2005). http://www.workersliberty/org/story/2005/09/12/forgotten-massacre-vietnamese-trotskyists.

Fox, Nili S. "Numbers: Introduction and Annotations." In *The Jewish Study Bible*. New York: Oxford University Press, 1999.

Francis I, Pope. *Encyclical Letter Laudato Si of the Holy Father Francis on Care for Our Common Home.* The Holy See, 2015. http://laudatosi.com/.

———. "Letter of His Holiness Pope Francis to the President of the International Commission against the Death Penalty." http://w2vatican.va/content/francesco/en/letters/2015/documents/papa-francesco_20150320_lettera-pena-morte.html/.

Fretheim, Terence E. *The Book of Genesis: Introduction, Commentary, and Reflections.* In *The New Interpreter's Bible*, edited by Leander E. Keck, 1:319–674. Nashville: Abingdon, 1994.

Fry, Richard, and Paul Taylor. "A Rise in Wealth for the Wealthy; Declines for the Lower 93%: An Uneven Recovery, 2009–2011." Pew Research Center (April 23, 2013). http://www.pewsocialtrends.org/files/2013/04/wealth_recovery_final.pdf.

Furnish, Victor Paul. "Uncommon Love and the Common Good: Christians as Citizens and the Common Good." In *In Search of the Common Good*, edited by Dennis P. McCann and Patrick D. Miller, 58–87. Theology for the Twenty-first Century. London: T. & T. Clark, 2005.

Gallagher, Charles A. *Rethinking the Color Line: Readings in Race and Ethnicity.* 5th ed. New York: McGraw-Hill, 2012.

Gardner, Nile, and Morgan Lorraine Roach. "Barack Obama's Top 10 Apologies: How the President Has Humiliated a Superpower." Web Memo #2466 on Europe. (June 2, 2009). The Heritage Foundation. http://www.heritage.org/research/reports/2009/06/barack-obamas-top-10-apologies-how-the-president-has-humiliated-a-superpower/.

Gedicks, Al. "The Nationalization of Copper in Chile: Antecedents and Consequences." *Review of Radical Economics* 5 (1973). http://rrp.sagepub.com/content/5/3/1. citation.

General Assembly of the Disciples of Christ. "Resolution on the Death Penalty." www. http://disciples.org/Portals/0/PDF/ga/pastassemblies/2003/resolutions/0324. pdf/.

General Conference of the United Methodist Church. "Book of Resolutions: Call for Comprehensive Immigration Reform." http://www.umc.org/what-we-believe/call-for-comprehensive-immigration-reform.

General Synod 7 of the United Church of Christ, 1969. "Resolution to Abolish Capital Punishment." www.uccfiles.com/pdf/Resolution-to-Abolish-Capital-Punishment.pdf/.

George, Susan, and Fabrizio Sabelli. *Faith and Credit: The World Bank's Secular Empire*. Boulder, CO: Westview, 1994.

Germany, Kent B. "Lyndon B. Johnson and Civil Rights: Introduction to the Digital Edition." Presidential Recordings of Lyndon B. Johnson, Digital Edition. http://presidentialrecordings.rotunda.upress.virginia.edu/essays?=CivilRights/.

Gerson, Jack. "Obama, Austerity, and Change We Can Really Believe In." *New Politics* 52 (Winter, 2012) 23–29.

Gever, John et al. *Beyond Oil: The Threat to Food and Fuel in the Coming Decades*. Cambridge, MA: Ballinger, 1987.

Gibson, C. Robert. "Austerity: Planned Poverty." *HuffPost* (July 10, 2015). www.huffingtonpost.com/carl-gibson/austerity-planned-poverty_b_3165136.html.

———. "National Debt? No Such Thing." *HuffPost* (July 30, 2012). http://www.huffingtonpost.com/carl-gibson/national-debt-no-such-thing_b_ 1717698html.

Gilbert, Daniel. *Stumbling on Happiness*. New York: Vintage. 2006.

"Glass-Steagall Act (1933)." Adapted from an article in the Law Library. *New York Times*. http://topics.nytimes.com/top/reference/timestopics/subjects/g/glass_steagall_act_1933/index.html.

Global Footprint Network. "August 13th Is Earth Overshoot Day This Year." (August 12, 2015). www.footprintnetwork.org/en/index.php/GHN/page/contact_us/.

———"Earth Overshoot Day 2014." (Sept. 4, 2014). http://www. footprintnetwork.org/ en/index. php/GEN/page/earth_overshoot_day/.

———. *The Living Planet Report 2012*. http://www.panda.org/about_our_earth/ all_publications/living_planet_report/2012_lpr/.

Gongloff, Mark. "U.S. Companies Lobbying Furiously to Save Corporate Tax Loopholes: Study." *HuffPost* (June 18, 2013). http://www.huffpost.com/2013/06/18/companies-lobbying-corporate-tax-loopholes-study_n_3461044. html.

Gore, Al. "The Turning Point: New Hope for Climate Change." *Rolling Stone* (June 18, 2014). http://www.rollingstone.com/politics/news/the-turning-point-new-hope-for-the-climate-20140618/.

Gottwald, Norman K. *The Hebrew Bible: A Socio-Literary Introduction*. Philadelphia: Fortress, 1985.

Goudzwaard, Bob. *Capitalism and Progress: A Diagnosis of Western Society*. Grand Rapids: Eerdmans, 1979.

Gould, Elise. "U.S. Lags behind Peer Countries in Mobility." Economic Policy Institute (October 10, 2012). http://www.epi.org/publication/usa-lags-peer-countries-mobility/.

Gould, Elise, and Hilary Wething. "U.S. Poverty Rates Higher, Safety Net Weaker, Than in Peer Countries." Economic Policy Institute (July 24, 2012). http://www.epi.org/publications/ib339-us-poverty-higher-safety-net-weaker/.

Greenberg, Irving. "Religion as a Source for Reconciliation and Peace: A Jewish Analysis." In *Beyond Violence: Religious Sources of Social Transformation in Judaism, Christianity, and Islam,* edited by James L. Heft, SM, 88–112. New York: Fordham University Press, 2004.

Griffin, David Ray. "America's Non-Accidental, Non-Benign Empire." In David Ray Griffin, et al., *The American Empire and the Commonwealth of God: A Political, Economic, Religious Statement,* 3–22. Louisville: Westminster John Knox, 2006.

Griffin, David Ray et al. *The American Empire and the Commonwealth of God: A Political, Economic, Religious Statement.* Louisville: Westminster John Knox, 2006.

Gross, Terry. "Get on the Bus: The Freedom Riders of 1961: Interview with Raymond Arsenault." *Fresh Air* (Originally published on January 12, 2006. Updated October 23, 2012). http://www.npr.org/2006/01/12/5149667/get-on-the-bus-the-freedom-riders-of-1961/.

Hagner, Donald A. *Matthew 1–13.* Word Biblical Commentary 33A. Dallas: Word, 1993.

Hall, Anthony L. "Stimulus vs. Austerity: The Verdict." *iPINIONS Journal* (May 22, 2013). http://www. theipinionsjournal.com/2013/5.

Halle, Victor. "El Salvador's Long Walk to Democracy." open Democracy (May 26, 2006). http://www.opendemocracy.net/democracy-protest/salvador_democracy_3592.jsp.

Harper, Douglas. "Slavery in New Jersey." Slavery in the North. http://www.slavenorth.com/newjersey.htm/.

Harrington, Michael. *Socialism: Past and Future.* New York: Arcade, 1989.

Hartshorne, Charles. *The Logic of Perfection and Other Essays in Neoclassical Metaphysics.* LaSalle, IL: Open Court, 1962.

Hays, Richard B. *The Moral Vision of the New Testament: Community, Cross, New Creation; A Contemporary Introduction to New Testament Ethics.* New York: HarperSanFrancisco, 1996.

HBO. "The Loving Story." HBO Documentary. Synopsis. http://www.hbo.com/documentaries/the-loving-story/synopsis.html/.

Heft, James L., SM, ed. *Beyond Violence: Religious Sources of Social Transformation in Judaism, Christianity, and Islam.* New York: Fordham University Press, 2004.

Heilbroner, Robert L. *The Worldly Philosophers: The Lives, Times, and Ideas of the Great Economic Thinkers.* 3rd ed. New York: Simon & Schuster, 1967.

Herzog, William R., II. *Prophet and Teacher: An Introduction to the Historical Jesus.* Louisville: Westminster John Knox, 2005.

Hill, John E. *Adam Smith's Equality and the Pursuit of Happiness,* forthcoming.

———. *Democracy, Equality, and Justice: John Adams, Adam Smith, and Political Economy.* Lanham, MD: Rowman, 2007.

Hill, Michael. "Qualla Boundary." *NCpedia.* http://ncpedia.org.

Hirschman, Charles et al. "Vietnamese Casualties during the American War: A New Estimate." *Population and Development Review* 21 (December, 1995) 783–812. http://links.jstor.org/sici?sici=0098-7921% 28199512%2921%3A4% 3C783%3AVCDTAW%3E2.0.CO%3B2-Q/.

Honey, Michael K. *Going Down Jericho Road: The Memphis Strike, Martin Luther King's Last Campaign*. New York: Norton, 2007.
Hoppe, Leslie J. *There Shall Be no Poor among You: Poverty in the Bible*. Nashville: Abingdon, 2004.
Horrell, David G. et al., eds. *Ecological Hermeneutics: Biblical, Historical and Theological Perspectives*. London: T. & T. Clark, 2010.
Horsley, Richard A. *Covenant Economics: A Biblical Vision of Justice for All*. Louisville: Westminster John Knox, 2009.
Hughes, Langston, and Arna Bontemps, eds. *The Poetry of the Negro 1746–1970*. Rev. and updated edition. Garden City NY: Anchor, 1970.
Hunter-Gault, Charlayne. *In My Place*. New York: Random House, 1992.
Jefferson, Thomas. *Notes on the State of Virginia*, first published in 1784; available in Digireads.com edition, 2009. http://digireads.com/.
Jewett, Robert. *The Captain America Complex*. 2nd ed. Santa Fe, NM: Bear, 1984.
Jobling, David. "Wealth." In *The New Interpreter's Dictionary of the Bible*, edited by Katharine Doob Sakenfeld, 5:825–28. Nashville: Abingdon, 2009.
John Lewis for Congress. "John Lewis Getting into Good Trouble since 1960." http://johnlewisforcongress.com/content/john-lewis-geting-good-trouble-1960/.
Johnson, Luke Timothy. *Reading Romans: A Literary and Theological Commentary*. New York: Crossroad, 1997.
Johnston, Carol A. "A Whiteheadian Perspective on Global Economics." In *Handbook of Process Theology*, edited by Jay B. McDaniel and Donna Bowman, 188–200. St. Louis: Chalice, 2006.
Jones, Nigel. "From Stalin to Hitler, the most murderous regimes in the world." *MailOnline* (Updated October 7, 2014). http://dailymail.co.uk/moslive/article/Hitler-Stalin-The-murderous-regimes-world.html.
Kahn, Natasha, and Corbin Carson. "Comprehensive Database of U.S. Voter Uncovers No Evidence that Photo ID Is Needed." *News21* (August 12, 2012). http://votingrights.news21.com/article/election-fraud/.
Kaminsky, Joel. "Chosen." In *The New Interpreter's Dictionary of the Bible*, edited by Katharine Doob Sakenfeld, 1:594–601. Nashville: Abingdon, 2006.
Karnow, Stanley. *Vietnam: A History*. 2nd ed. New York: Viking Penguin, 1991.
Keim, Brandon. "One-Third of U.S. Honeybee Colonies Died Last Winter, Threatening Food Supply." *Wired* (May 8, 2013). http://www.wired.com/2013/05/winter-honeybee-losses/.
Kindig, Jesse. "Selma, Alabama (Bloody Sunday, March 7, 1965)." BlackPast.Org. http://www.blackpast.org/aah/bloody-sunday-selma-alabama-march-7-1965.
King, Martin Luther, Jr. *Why We Can't Wait*. New York: New American Library, 1963.
Knight, Douglas A. *Law, Power, and Justice in Ancient Israel*. Library of Ancient Israel. Louisville: Westminster John Knox, 2012.
Koester, Helmut. "Imperial Ideology and Paul's Eschatology in 1 Thessalonians." In *Paul and Empire: Religion and Power in Roman Imperial Society*, edited by Richard A. Horsley, 158–66. Harrisburg, PA: Trinity, 1997.
Kozol, Jonathan. *Amazing Grace: The Lives of Children and the Conscience of a Nation*. New York: Crown, 1995.
Krugman, Paul. "The Big Fail." *New York Times* (January 6, 2013). http://www.nytimes.com/2013/01/07/opinion/krugman-the-big-fail.html?_r=0.
———. *The Conscience of a Liberal*. New York: Norton, 2007.

———. "Profits without Production." *New York Times* (June 20, 2013). http://www.nytimes.com/2013/06/21/opinion-krugman-profits-without-production.html.

———. *The Return of Depression Economics and the Crisis of 2008*. New York: Norton, 2009.

Lantigua, John. "How the GOP Gamed the System in Florida." *The Nation* (April 30, 2001). http://www.thenation.com/article/how-the-gop-gamed-system-florida/.

Lewis, C. S. "The Humanitarian Theory of Punishment." In C. S. Lewis, *God in the Dock*, edited by Walter Hooper, 287–94. Grand Rapids: Eerdmans, 1970.

Lewis, John, with Michael D'Orso. *Walking with the Wind: A Memoir of the Movement*. San Diego: Harcourt, 1999. Originally published by Simon and Schuster, 1998.

Liptak, Adam. "U.S. Prison Population Dwarfs That of Other Nations." *New York Times* (April 23, 2008). http://www.nytimes.com/2008/04/23/world/americas/23iht-23prison.12253738.html?pagewanted=all&r=0/.

Logan, Charles H. "The Criminal Justice System Should Focus on Punishment." In *Criminal Justice: Opposing Viewpoints*, edited by David M. Haugen. San Diego: Greenhaven, 1998.

Lowell, James Russell. "The Present Crisis." Read Book Online. http://www.readbookonline.net/readOnLine/7194/. First published in 1844.

Löwy, Michael. "Ecosocialism: Putting the Brakes on Before Going Over the Cliff." *New Politics* (Winter 2014), 24–29.

Lyubomirsky, Sonja, *The How of Happiness: A Scientific Approach to Getting the Life You Want*. New York: Penguin, 2008.

Magdoff, Fred. "Global Resource Depletion: Is Population the Problem?" *Monthly Review* (August 19, 2013). http://monthlyreview.org/2013/01/01/global-resource-depletion. Originally published in *Monthly Review* 64/8 (January, 2013).

Malcolm X. "God's Angry Men." *Los Angeles Herald Dispatch*, October 3, 1957.

Mandell, Betty Reid. "The Crime of Poverty." (Review of Loïc Waquant, *Punishing the Poor: Neoliberal Government of Social Insecurity*) *New Politics* 50 (Winter 2011) 141–55.

Marans, Daniel. "What the Iraq War Can Teach Us about Fighting Isis." *The World Post*, November 21, 2014. http://www.huffingtonpost.com/entry/iraq-war-fighting-isis_5650db14e4b0879a5b0b4918/.

Martin, Clarice J. "A Chamberlain's Journey and the Challenge of Interpretation for Liberation." *Semeia* 47 (1989) 105–35.

Marx, Karl, and Friedrich Engels. *The Manifesto of the Communist Party*. Marxists Internet Archive. http://www. marxists.org/archive/marx/works/1848/communist-manifesto/ch.02.htm.

Matera, Frank J. *New Testament Ethics: The Legacies of Jesus and Paul*. Louisville: Westminster John Knox, 1996.

McElwee, Joshua J. "Sainthood Process Open for Hélder Câmara." *National Catholic Reporter* (March 31, 2015). http://ncronline.org/people/report-sainthood-process-opened-h-ldeer-c-mara.

McKibben, Bill. *Eaarth: Making a Life on a Tough New Planet*. New York: St. Martin's Griffin, 2011.

Meeks, M. Douglas. *God the Economist: The Doctrine of God and the Political Economy*. Minneapolis: Fortress, 1989.

Megivern, James M. *The Death Penalty: An Historical and Theological Survey*. New York: Paulist, 1974.

Miller, Brandon. "2015 Is Warmest Year on Record, NOAA and NASA Say." http://www.cnn.com/2016/01/20/us/noaa-2015-is-warmest-year/.

Miller, Stephen P. "From Politics to Reconciliation: *Katallagete*, Biblicism, and Southern Liberalism." *Journal of Southern Religion* 7 (November, 2004). http://jsr.fsu/edu/Volume 7/Millerarticle.htm/.

Minucius Felix. *Octavius*. Translated by G. H. Randall. Loeb Classical Library 250. Cambridge: Harvard University Press, 1931.

Mishel, Lawrence. "The Wedges between Productivity and Median Compensation Growth." Economic Policy Institute: Report/Wages Incomes and Wealth (April 26, 2012). www.epi.org/publication/ib330-productivity-vs-compensation/.

Mishel, Lawrence, and Josh Bivens. "Occupy Wall Streeters Are Right about Skewed Economic Rewards in the United States." Economic Policy Institute: Report/Inequality and Poverty (October 26, 2011). http://www.epi.org/publication/bp331-occupy-wall-street/.

Mooney, Chris. "It's Official: 2014 Was the Hottest Year in Recorded History." *The Washington Post* (January 16, 2015). http://www.washingtonpost.com/news/wonkblog/wp/2015/01/16/its-official-2014-was-the-hottest-year-in-recorded-history/.

Morgan, Edmund S. *American Slavery, American Freedom: The Ordeal of Colonial Virginia*. New York: Norton, 1975.

Mott, Stephen Charles. *A Christian Perspective on Political Thought*. New York: Oxford University Press, 1993.

Moyers, Bill. "Bernie Sanders on Why Big Media Shouldn't Get Bigger." Moyers & Company (December 7, 2012). http://billmoyers.com/segment/bernie-sanders-on-why-big-media-shouldnt-get-bigger/.

———. *Moyers on Democracy*. New York: Doubleday, 2008.

———. "Second Thoughts: Reflections on the Great Society." *New Perspectives Quarterly* 4 (Winter, 1987).

Muray, Leslie A. *Liberal Protestantism and Science*. Westport, CT: Greenwood, 2008.

Myrdal, Gunnar, with the assistance of Richard Sterner and Arnold Rose. *An American Dilemma: The Negro Problem and Modern Democracy*. New York: Harper & Brothers, 1944.

Nabokov, Peter. "Part Four: The Long Thread." In *The Native Americans: An Illustrated History*, edited by Betty Ballantine and Ian Ballantine, 301–83. North Dighton, MA: World, 2001.

Nader, Ralph. "Suddenly Baltimore—Wonder Why?" *The Nader Page* (May 8, 2015). https://blog.nader./org/2015/05/08/suddenly-baltimore-wonder-why.

National Archives and Records Administration. "Theodore Roosevelt's Corollary to the Monroe Doctrine (1905)." OurDocuments.gov. www.ourdocuments.gov/doc.php?flash=true&doc=56.

National Climatic Data Center. "Global Analysis-Annual 2013" (January, 2014). http://www.ncdc.noaa.gov/sotc/global/2013/13/.

National Organization for Women. "Violence against Women in the United States." http://www.now.org/issues/violence/stats.html.

National Security Archives. "Iran Contra at 25: Reagan and Bush 'Criminal Liability' Evaluations." http://www2gwu.edu/~nsarchive/NSAEBB/NSAEBB365/.

———. "Prisoner Abuse: Patterns from the Past." http://ww2.gwu.edu/~nsarchiv/NSAEBB/NSAEBB122/.

Native Languages of the Americas. "American Indians in Louisiana." http://www.native-languages.org/louisiana.htm/.
Nichols, John, and Robert W. McChesney. "The Assault of the Super PACS." *The Nation* 294 (February 6, 2012) 11–18.
———. "Dollarocracy." *The Nation* 297 (September 30, 2013) 22–26.
Niebuhr, Reinhold. *The Children of Light and the Children of Darkness: A Vindication of Democracy and a Critique of Its Traditional Defense*. New York: Scribner, 1972.
"Nobel Laureate Paul Krugman: Too Little Stimulus in Stimulus Plan." Knowledge@Wharton (February 19, 2009). http://knowledge.wharton.upenn.edu/article/nobel-laureate-paul-krugman-too-little-stimulus-in-stimulus-plan/.
Ogden, Schubert M. *The Reality of God and Other Essays*. New York: Harper & Row, 1966.
———. *The Understanding of Christian Faith*. Eugene, OR: Cascade Books, 2010.
Oliver, Pamela. "Racial Disparities in Criminal Justice." http://www.wisc.edu/~oliver/RACIAL/RacialDisparities.htm/.
Orthodox Church in America. "Minutes of the Ninth Plenary Session" (1989). www.deathpenaltyinfo.org/ortho.pdf.
Palmer, Parker J. *The Courage to Teach: Exploring the Inner Landscape of a Teacher's Life*. San Francisco: Jossey-Bass, 1998.
Parenti, Christian. "Rethinking the State: Shadow Socialism in the Age of Environmental Crisis." *New Politics* (Winter 2014) 11–17.
Pedersen, Ann. *God, Creation, and All That Jazz: A Process of Composition and Improvisation*. St. Louis: Chalice, 2001.
Petersen, Norman. *Rediscovering Paul: Philemon and the Sociology of Paul's Narrative World*. 1985. Reprinted, Eugene, OR: Wipf & Stock, 2008.
Pew Research Center. "Religious Groups' Official Positions on Capital Punishment." www.pewforum.org/2009/11/04/religious-groups-official-positions-on-capital-punishment/.
———. "Religious Reflections on the Death Penalty." http://pewforum.org/2001/06/religious-reflections-on-the-death-penalty/.
Pilkey, Orrin H., and Keith C. Pilkey. *Global Climate Change: A Primer*. Durham, NC: Duke University Press, 2011.
Powell, Mark Allan. *God with Us: A Pastoral Theology of Matthew's Gospel*. Minneapolis: Fortress, 1995.
Pregeant, Russell. *Christology beyond Dogma: Matthew's Christ in Process Hermeneutic*. Philadelphia: Fortress, 1988.
———. *Knowing Truth, Doing Good: Engaging New Testament Ethics*. Minneapolis: Fortress, 2008.
———. *Mystery without Magic*. Oak Park, IL: Meyer-Stone, 1978.
———. *Reading the Bible for All the Wrong Reasons*. Minneapolis: Fortress, 2011.
Prejean, Sr. Helen. *Dead Man Walking*. New York: Vintage, 1994.
———. *The Death of Innocents: An Eyewitness Account of Wrongful Executions*. New York: Vintage, 2006.
———. "The Death Penalty is Morally Unjust." In *The Death Penalty: Opposing Viewpoints*, edited by Paul A. Winters, 55–59. San Diego: Greenhaven, 1997.
"Q & A: Winona LaDuke." *The Nation* 299 (July 7, 2014).
Reich, Robert. "Why Democrats Can't Be Trusted to Control Wall Street." *Robert Reich*. http:// robertreich.org/post51226404952/.

Roman Catholic Archdiocese of Atlanta. "Pastoral Statement on Immigration by the Catholic Bishops of Georgia." http://www.archatl.com/archbishops/declarations/2011-immigration-eng.html.

Ross, Janell. "Welfare Reform Leaving More in Poverty." *HuffPost Business* (August 23, 2011). www.huffingtonpost.com/2011/08/23/welfare-reform-poverty_n_9324990.html/.

Rossing, Barbara. "Alas for Earth! Lament and Resistance in Revelation 12." In *The Earth Story in the New Testament*, edited by Norman C. Habel and Vicky Balabanski, 180–92. London: Sheffield Academic, 2002.

Rusin, David. "Hate Crimes: FBI Stats on Muslims, Jews, Gays, Hispanics." *Dearborn Free Press* (June 12, 2012). http://www.dearbornfreepress.com/2012/01/27/hate-crimes-fbi-stats-on-muslims-jews-gays-hispanics/.

Sabine, George H., and Thomas L. Thorson. *A History of Political Theory*. 4th ed. Hinsdale, IL: Dryden, 1973.

"Sacrificed for What? The Dark Side of Sacrificial Action." *The Christian Century* 131 (July 9, 2014) 7.

Sanders, Bernie. "What Can We Learn from Denmark?" *HuffPost* (May 26, 2013). http://www.huffingtonpost.com/rep-bernie-sanders/what-can-we-learn-from-de_b_333973.html.

Santmire, H. Paul. *The Travail of Nature: The Ambiguous Ecological Promise of Christian Theology*. Philadelphia: Fortress, 1985.

Schiller, Mark. "A Brief History of American Imperialism." *La Jicarita: An Online Magazine of Enviromental Politics in New Mexico* (October 9, 2012; reprinted from October, 2009). http://lajicarita.wordpress.com/2012/10/09/a-brief-history-of-american-imperialism/.

Schlimm, Matthew. "God's Slow Anger." Living by the Word: Reflections on the Lectionary. *Christian Century* 131 (Nov. 26, 2014) 20–21. http://www.christiancentury.org/blogs/archive/2014-11/gods-slow-anger/.

Schoen, Doug. "Super PACs' Super Influence and Their Destruction of Our Political System." *Forbes* (February 17, 2012). http://www.forbes.com/sites/dougschoen/2012/17/super-pacs-super-influence-and-their-destruction-of-our-political-system/.

Seligman, Martin E. P. *Flourish: A Visionary New Understanding of Happiness and Well-being*. New York: Free Press, 2011.

Sharpe, John. "Stalinism and Trotskyism in Vietnam." Transcribed by John Heckman. MarxistInternetArchive.https://www.marxists.org/etol/document/icl-spartacists/vietnam/trotskyism.html.

Silver, James W. *Mississippi: The Closed Society*. New York: Harcourt, 1963.

Solomon, Norman. "Judaism and the Ethics of War." *International Review of the Red Cross* 87 (June, 2005) 295–309. https://www.icrc.org/eng/assets/files/other/irrc_858_solomon.pdf/.

Smedley, Audrey, and Brian D. Smedley. *Race in North America: Origin and Evolution of a Worldview*. 4th ed. Boulder, CO: Westview, 2012.

Smith, Adam. *An Inquiry into the Nature and Causes of the Wealth of Nations*, edited by R. H. Campbell and A.S. Skinner. Oxford: Oxford University Press, 1976.

Smith, Lillian. *Killers of the Dream*. Rev. ed. New York: Norton, 1961.

Southern Poverty Law Center. "Report: FBI Hate Crime Statistics Vastly Understate Problem." (Winter, 2005). http://www.splcenter.org/get-informed/intelligence-report/browse-all-issues/2005/winter/hate-crime.
Spartacus Educational. "Salvador Allende." http://spartacus-educational.com/COLDallende.htm.
Stein, Jill. "Economic and Ecological Transformation: There Is no Alternative." *New Politics* 56 (Winter 2014) 6–10.
Stiglitz, Joseph E. *Freefall: America, Free Markets, and the Sinking of the World Economy*. New York: Norton, 2010.
———. "A Tax System Stacked against the 99 Percent." *New York Times* (April 14, 2013). http://opinionator.blogs.nytimes.com/2013/04/14/a-tax-system-stacked-aginst-the-99-percent/.
———. "Globalisation Isn't Just about Profits: It's about Taxes Too." *The Guardian* (May 27, 2013). http://www.guaradian.co.uk/commentisfree/2013/may/27/globalisation-is-about-taxes-too/.
"Stimulus v austerity: Sovereign Doubts." *The Economist* (September 28, 2013). http://www.economist.com/news/schools-brief/21586802-fourth-our-series-articles-financial-crisis-looks-surge-public/.
Taibbi, Matt. "Greed and Debt: The True Story of Mitt Romney and Bain Capital." *Rolling Stone* (August 29, 2012). http://www.rollingstone.com/politics/ newsgreed-and-debt-the-true-story-of-mitt-romney-and-bain-capital-20120829/.
———. "The Last Mystery of the Financial Crisis." *Rolling Stone* (June 19, 2013). http://www.rollingstone.com/politics/news/the-last-mystery-of-the-financial-crisis-20130619.
———. "While Wronged Homeowners Got $300 Apiece in Foreclosure Settlement, Consultants Who Helped Protect Banks Got $2 Billion." *Rolling Stone* (April 26, 2013). http://www.rollingstone.com/politics/news/while-wronged-homeowners-got-300-apiece-in-foreclosure-settlement-consultants-who-helped-protect-banks-got-2-billion-20130426.
———. "Why Baltimore Blew Up." *Rolling Stone* (May 26, 2015). http://rollingstone.com/politics/news/why-baltimore-blew-up-20150526.
Tamez, Elsa. *The Scandalous Message of James: Faith without Works Is Dead*. Translated by John Eagleson. New York: Crossroad, 1990.
Tebbel, John. *A Compact History of the Indian Wars*. New York: Tower, 1966.
Texas State Historical Association: A Digital Gateway to Texas History. "Anglo-American Colonization." https://tshaonline.org/handbook/online/articles/umao1.
Thompson, A. C. "Katrina's Hidden Race War." *The Nation* 288 (January 5, 2009) 11–18.
Tidwell, Mike. *Bayou Farewell: The Rich Life and Tragic Death of Louisiana's Cajun Coast with a New Afterword on the Impact of Hurricanes Katrina and Rita*. New York: Vintage, 2004.
Tilson, Everett. *Segregation and the Bible: A Searching Analysis of the Scriptural Evidence*. Nashville: Abingdon, 1958.
Tindall, George Brown. *The Ethnic Southerners*. Baton Rouge: Louisiana State University Press, 1976.
Toedtman, Jim. "Obstacles and Obligations." *AARP Bulletin* (May, 2012).
Tolnay, Stewart E., and E. M. Beck. *A Festival of Violence: An Analysis of Southern Lynchings, 1882–1930*. Urbana: University of Illinois Press, 1992.

Tonry, Michael. *Thinking about Crime: Sense and Sensibility in American Culture.* New York: Oxford University Press, 2004.
Tucker, Gene M. "The Book of Isaiah 1–39: Introduction, Commentary, and Reflections." In *The New Interpreter's Bible*, edited by Leander E. Keck, 6:27–395. Nashville: Abingdon, 2001.
Turner, Graham. "A Comparison of the Limits to Growth with Thirty Years of Reality." *Global Environmental Change* 18 (2008) 397–411.
Turner, Stansfield. *Secrecy and Democracy.* Boston: Houghton Mifflin, 1985. Excerpted in "Salvador Allende." Spartacus Educational. http://spartacus-educational.com/COLDallende.htm/, 3–4.
Tutu, Desmond. *God Has a Dream: A Vision of Hope for Our Time.* New York: Doubleday, 2004.
United States Commission on Civil Rights. "Voting Irregularities in Florida During the 2000 Presidential Election, Chapter 9: Findings and Recommendations; Chapter 1: Voting System Controls and Failures; *Voter Disenfranchisement:* Findings" (June, 2001). http://www.usccr.gov/pubs/vote2000/report/ch9.htm.
United States Department of Health and Human Services. "Information on Poverty and Income Statistics: A Summary of 2014 Current Population Survey Data" (September 16, 2014). http://aspe.hhs.gov/report/information-poverty-and-income-statistics-summary-2014-current-population-survey-data.
United States Department of Justice, Civil Rights Division (March 4, 2015). "Investigation of the Ferguson Police Department." http://www.justice.gov/sites/ default/files/opa/press-release-/attachments/2015/03/04/ferguson-police-department-report/pdf.
United States Department of State, Office of the Historian. "Milestones: 1969–1976, The Allende Years and the Pinochet Coup, 1969–1973." https://history.state.gov/milestones/1969–76/allende.
———. "Milestones: 1866–1898: The Spanish-American War, 1898." https://history.state.gov/milestones/1866–1898/spanish-american-war.
United Press International. "Six Dead after Church Bombing." *Washington Post* (September 16, 1963). http://www. washingtonpost.com/wp-srv/national/longterm/churches/archives1.htm/.
United Synagogue of Conservative Judaism, Commission on Public Policy and Social Action. "Immigrants and Immigration" (December 2007). http://www.uscj.org/images/Immigrants_and_Immigration.pdf.
Velasco-Marquez, Jesus. "A Mexican Viewpoint on the War with the United States." PBS. http://ww.pbs.org/kera/usmexicanwar/prelude/md_a_mexican_viewpoint.html.
Wallis, Jim. *God's Politics: Why the Right Gets It Wrong and the Left Doesn't Get It.* New York: HarperCollins, 2005.
Weems, Renita J. "Reading Her Way through the Struggle: African American Women and the Bible." In Felder, ed. *Stony the Road,* 57–77.
West, Cornel. *Prophesy Deliverance: An Afro-American Revolutionary Christianity.* Philadelphia: Westminster, 1982.
———. *Prophetic Fragments.* Grand Rapids: Eerdmans, 1988.
———. *Race Matters.* Boston: Beacon, 1993.
Whitehead, Alfred North. *Adventures of Ideas.* 1933. Reprinted, New York: Free Press, 1967.

Wilkinson, Richard, and Kate Pickett. *The Spirit Level: Why Greater Equality Makes Societies Stronger*. New York: Bloomsbury, 2009.

Willis, Timothy M. "Clan." In *The New Interpreter's Dictionary of the Bible*, edited by Katharine Doob Sakenfeld, 1:679. Nashville: Abingdon, 2006.

Wogaman, J. Philip. *The Great Economic Debate: An Ethical Analysis*. Philadelphia: Westminster, 1977.

Wright, Jacob. "War, Ideas of." In *The New Interpreter's Dictionary of the Bible*, edited by Katharine Doob Sakenfeld, 5:800–805. Nashville: Abingdon, 2009.

Yeoman, Barry. "Saving Louisiana: What Can We Do?" on earth (January 7, 2011). http://ww.onearth.org/article/saving-louisiana-what-can-we-do.

Ziegler, Rav Ronnie. "Introduction to the Philsophy of Rav Soloveitchik." The Israel Koschitzky Virtual Beit Midrash. http://etzion.org.il/vbm/english/archive/ ravo5. htm.

Zinn, Howard. *A People's History of the United States 1492–Present*. Rev. ed. New York: HarperCollins, 1995.

www.ingramcontent.com/pod-product-compliance
Lightning Source LLC
Chambersburg PA
CBHW020109010526
44115CB00008B/761